KANT'S IMPURE ETHICS

KANT'S IMPURE ETHICS

From Rational Beings to Human Beings

Robert B. Louden

New York   Oxford

Oxford University Press

2000

Oxford University Press

Oxford   New York
Athens   Auckland   Bangkok   Bogotá   Buenos Aires   Calcutta
Cape Town   Chennai   Dar es Salaam   Delhi   Florence   Hong Kong   Istanbul
Karachi   Kuala Lumpur   Madrid   Melbourne   Mexico City   Mumbai
Nairobi   Paris   São Paulo   Singapore   Taipei   Tokyo   Toronto   Warsaw

and associated companies in
Berlin   Ibadan

Copyright © 2000 by Robert B. Louden

Published by Oxford University Press, Inc.
198 Madison Avenue, New York, New York 10016

Oxford is a registered trademark of Oxford University Press

Library of Congress Cataloging-in-Publication Data
Louden, Robert B., 1953–
    Kant's impure ethics : from rational beings to
human beings / Robert B. Louden.
        p.   cm.
    Includes bibliographical references and index.
    ISBN 0-19-513041-3
    1. Kant, Immanuel, 1724–1804—Ethics.
2. Applied ethics—History—18th century.   I. Title.
B2799.E8L68   1999
170′.92—dc21   99-13606

9 8 7 6 5 4 3 2 1

Printed in the United States of America
on acid-free paper

TO TAMA

PREFACE

This is a book about the *second* part of Kant's ethics, a part that—nearly two hundred years after his death and who knows how many books and articles about his ethics—unfortunately remains a well-kept secret, even among Kant scholars. Kant referred to this second part variously as "moral anthropology," "practical anthropology," "applied moral philosophy," and sometimes simply "anthropology," but the important point is that it deals with the empirical (or what I call "impure") study of human nature rather than with pure (non-empirical) principles. Although Kant was adamant that the first or pure part of ethics was foundational and thus fundamentally more important than the second part, he was equally insistent that the second part was absolutely necessary whenever one wished to apply the results of the first part to human beings.

In the past, moral philosophers sympathetic to (what they thought were) Kant's ideas have tended to view empirical research about human beings as being irrelevant to ethical theory, claiming that since we cannot get moral oughts from is-es, empirical facts about human beings are not important for moral theory. At the same time, many of those critical of (what they thought were) Kant's ideas have dismissed his ethical theory as a quasi-rationalist relic, on the ground that his alleged purist approach fails to acknowledge the contribution that empirical studies of human beings can bring to our understanding of morality. On my view, both positions are fundamentally wrong. They are certainly wrong in their readings of Kant: if I have succeeded in showing anything in the following study, it is that he placed a much higher premium on the value of empirical study for moral theory than most of his foes as well as friends have given him credit for. But I believe they are also wrong philosophically: both pure and impure studies play necessary and complementary roles in understanding ethics (not to mention other areas of inquiry). To reject either one is to forfeit the possibility of comprehension.

The book has two aims: first, to draw readers' attention to an important and severely neglected dimension of Kant's ethics; second, to reassess the philosophical strengths and weaknesses of his ethics once the second part is readmitted into its rightful place within his practical philosophy. Much more space has been devoted to the first aim than to the second; in part because it seems necessary first to secure agreement concerning what Kant said before we are in a position to evaluate its philosophical significance, but also because (given the ongoing contentiousness of moral philosophy) the chances of achieving success with regard to the first aim seem higher and more readily obtainable. Given the towering influence that the image of Kant continues to exert on modern ethical thought, it is also my hope that correcting interpretive errors concerning his ethics can begin to effect changes in the ways that philosophers think about the relationship between ethical theory and empirical studies.

The overall structure of the book is as follows. Chapter 1 ("What is Impure Ethics?") introduces the major themes of the study, drawing readers' attention to Kant's under-explored applied and popular works, examining the multiple causes behind the continued popularity of the purist reading of his ethics, assessing the numerous pitfalls associated with the very concept of "empirical ethics" within Kantian philosophy, all with the aim of clarifying the meaning, role, and status of "impure ethics." Additionally, a detailed defense of the importance and necessity of moral anthropology for Kant's overall system of practical philosophy is presented.

Chapters 2–5 together comprise the major "fields of impurity"—that is, those subject areas within Kant's writings that are most directly relevant to his impure ethics. One major obstacle confronting anyone who sets out to examine the second part of Kant's ethics is that it remained in an unfinished and not entirely systematic state at his death: to track it accurately, one needs to look not only at his published writings and lectures on ethics, but also his lectures on education, anthropology, and physical geography, his essays on history, and relevant aspects of his writings in aesthetics and religion. These middle chapters are often quite textual and exegetical. Here I present the data to support my own interpretation of Kant's ethics, and often more seemed better than less. Throughout this examination of fields of impurity, new intertextual alliances in Kant's corpus are established and underscored in order to demonstrate his serious and ongoing commitment to the importance of empirical studies of human nature for ethical theory.

Chapter 2 ("Education") assesses Kant's major writings in education from the standpoint of his empirical ethics. These include his *Lectures on Pedagogy* and two essays on the Philanthropinum Academy, the *Methodenlehre* sections of both the second *Critique* and *The Metaphysics of Morals*, and occasional informal discussions of pedagogy in other lectures and essays. Critical issues treated at length in this chapter include a reassessment of Kant's moral education strategies for teaching practical judgment skills to students, and a qualified defense of his strong "species perfectionism"—his conviction that education must have as its primary goal not national or parental purposes but rather cosmopolitan ones.

Chapter 3 ("Anthropology"), the longest chapter, deals primarily with the moral dimensions of lecture course materials from Kant's annual course in anthropology. These materials include not only his own published version, *Anthropology from a Pragmatic Point of View* (1798), but also different student and auditor versions, many of which have only recently appeared in the German Academy Edition of his works (vol. 25—1997), related lectures from his annual course on physical geography, relevant sections of his early proto-anthropological work *Observations on the Feeling of the Beautiful and the Sublime* (1764), and his essays on race. Chapter 3 opens with a detailed discussion of the precise nature of Kant's own conception of the new science of anthropology and an articulation of the different ways in which it bears on the second part of his ethics. In addition to evaluating the material on individual character that one finds in his anthropological works, the normative aspects of his analyses of the major subgroups within the human species as presented in the anthropology writings are also evaluated—the sexes, peoples, and races. This chapter presents and defends a new, gradualist reading of the meaning and importance of universality in Kant's applied ethics, a reading that differs significantly both from traditional interpretations of Kant's moral philosophy and from recent criticisms made by feminists, critical race theorists, and others.

Chapter 4 ("Art and Religion") reassesses, from the standpoint of the second part of his ethics, two central areas of Kant's philosophy that address surprisingly similar issues in empirical ethics. The major texts here are the *Critique of Judgment* (1790) and *Religion within the Boundaries of Mere Reason* (1793). Major issues examined in the first part, on art, include Kant's arguments that art and aesthetic appreciation serve as a preparation for morality, that beauty serves as a (humanly graspable) symbol of morality, and the connection between morality and the sublime. The second part, on religion, evaluates Kant's views on the church as a necessary institutional vehicle for the development of a global moral community and the anthropological underpinnings of his doctrine of radical evil.

Chapter 5 ("History") examines Kant's writings on history from the standpoint of impure ethics. Here we encounter a distinct body of work lying in between the popular, edited versions of classroom lectures and large, systematic works published by himself. For the most part, his views on the philosophy of history are presented in a series of short essays published between the mid-1780s and mid-1790s, most of which first appeared in scholarly journals. (Sections 83–84 of the *Critique of Judgment* also count as being among Kant's most important discussions of the philosophy of history.) Major themes addressed in chapter 5 include the different ways in which historical progress in Kant's view both is and is not about internal, moral progress; the gradualist cosmopolitanism in Kant's view of history; and the various ways in which empirical assumptions about human nature affect his particular understanding of the classical conception of the *summum bonum*.

Finally, chapter 6 ("Saved by Impurity?") reassesses Kant's overall project in ethical theory from the more inclusive standpoint of his empirical ethics. What are the chief strengths and weaknesses of Kant's ethics, once "the other member of the division of practical philosophy as a whole" is readmitted into its rightful place? Major strengths that emerge include an empirically informed ethical theory that is much less formalistic than the standard caricature of Kantian ethics, a more useful ethical theory that possesses much greater applicability to human subjects, an outlook that explicitly endorses claims (claims made by some of Kant's severest critics) regarding human dependence and the need for institutional and communitarian supports in moral development, and a more contiguous history of practical philosophy. The common assertion that Kant initiated an unwelcome sharp separation between ethics and the empirical study of human nature, a separation that cuts him off from more naturalistic currents in ethics that both precede as well as follow him, is shown to be false. Central weaknesses include the incompleteness of Kant's project, its lack of empirical detail, its racial, ethnic, religious, and sexist prejudices, and its lack of internal coherence. Nevertheless, I argue that the broader, two-tiered approach to ethics that Kant himself practiced (but that subsequent philosophers, in their desire to keep philosophy pure, have systematically ignored) is a worthy model of inspiration (if not always precise imitation or emulation) for those who are concerned to construct humanly useful moral theories.

This book has taken me longer to write than intended, but the upside is that I now have a chance to thank more people for their help and advice. The bulk of the manuscript was written during 1996–97, while I was a guest of the Philosophical Seminar at the University of Münster in Germany. I would like above all to thank my host, Ludwig Siep, for his generous assistance with all aspects of my visit. Additional thanks are due to Michael Anderheiden, Kurt Bayertz, Christoph Halbig, Norbert Herold, Michael Quante, Peter Rohs, Marcus Willaschek, and Axel Wüstehube for philosophical conversation and support; Edith Diehl and Norbert Mertens for library help; Dieter Janssen for computer assistance; and Stephanie v. Beverfoerde for multiple kinds of aid and encouragement.

The basic idea for the manuscript began to take shape during my first trip to Germany, in 1991–92, when I was a guest of the Philosophical Seminar at the University of Göttingen and working on a translation of Kant's writings on education. Here my host was Günther Patzig, whose sponsorship was crucial in fulfilling a longstanding dream of going to Germany in order to learn more about Kant. While in Göttingen I also benefited from conversations with Wolfgang Carl, Conrad Cramer, the late Lorenz Krüger, Bettina Schöne-Seifert, Jürgen Sprute, and Jens Timmermann.

I remain grateful to the late Mary J. Gregor, for first encouraging me to pursue my interests in translating Kant's writings on education, which were the initial stimulus for this project. Allen Wood and Barbara Herman also provided crucial help at the beginning stages of my work.

Thanks are extended to the language instructors at the SPEAK + write Gesellschaft für Sprachunterricht in Marburg, Germany, where I was a student for four months in the summer of 1991. In Marburg I also had the good fortune of meeting and working with Reinhard Brandt and Werner Stark, who were busy editing Kant's anthropology lectures for the Academy Edition. At the time I could only understand (at most) every other word that they were saying, but this proved sufficient to convince me that a book on the empirical side of Kant's ethics was worth trying. Further language instruction was undertaken with the Deutsch als Fremdsprache Program at the University of Münster in 1996–97.

Mara Uban's German courses at the University of Southern Maine, which I sat in on in 1991 and again in 1996, were also very helpful.

Participation in Thomas E. Hill Jr.'s 1993 National Endowment for the Humanities (NEH) Summer Seminar on Kant's Moral Philosophy, held at the University of North Carolina, Chapel Hill, enabled me to clarify my project on several key points.

The opportunity to work with students in a variety of settings on some of the texts and ideas discussed in this book has also been a big help. A Hauptseminar called "Moralische Skepsis und ethische Theorie" that I was invited to teach at the University of Göttingen in spring 1992 presented me with the humbling (and occasionally humorous) opportunity to teach parts of Kant's ethics to German university students. A graduate seminar on "Kant's Practical Philosophy" at Emory University, where I was visiting professor in spring 1995, gave me a chance to articulate some of the book's themes in my native language. An invitation to serve as external examiner for honors graduates in moral philosophy at Swarthmore College came as I working on the last chapter, and conversations with students there about Kant helped me to finally pull a few loose threads together. Over the years, I have also benefited from many discussions about Kant with my own students in a variety of undergraduate courses at the University of Southern Maine.

Earlier versions of different chapters were presented at the Maine Philosophical Institute and as invited lectures to audiences at the University of South Carolina, Western Michigan University (special thanks here to host Michael S. Pritchard), and the University of Konstanz, Germany (thanks to host Neil Roughley). An earlier, shorter version of chapter 2 was published in the *Journal of Education* 179 (1997): 77–98, as an invited contribution for a special issue, "Cultural Foundations & Educational Heritage." I am indebted to guest editor Steven S. Tigner for advice on several points.

Research on this project was supported by an NEH Fellowship for College Teachers (1996), an Alexander von Humboldt Foundation Research Fellowship (1991–92, 1996–97), and a sabbatical leave from the University of Southern Maine (1996–97). I am very grateful to all three organizations for providing me with an extended period of free time to devote to the work.

Keith Witherell, software support specialist at the University of Southern Maine, helped straighten out my unruly computer disks when it was at last time to print the results. The staff at Oxford University Press, particularly Catharine Carlin, Peter Ohlin, and Robert Milks, assisted in many ways, big and small.

Last but not least, my thanks to the individuals who read and commented on the manuscript in its various stages. The two anonymous readers for Oxford University Press offered a variety of insightful comments and suggestions. Karl Ameriks, Richard Eldridge, Patrick Frierson, Pauline Kleingeld, Eric Nelson, Philip Rossi, Walter Schaller, Claudia Schmidt, Ludwig Siep, and Marcus Willaschek all gave expert advice on different parts of the work. But I am responsible for the errors that undoubtedly remain.

CONTENTS

ABBREVIATIONS

Kant's writings are cited in the body of the text according to volume and page number in *Kants gesammelte Schriften*, edited by the Königliche Preußische [now Deutsche] Akademie der Wissenschaften (Berlin: Georg Reimer [now De Gruyter], 1902– ; traditonally referred to as the Academy Edition. The Academy pagination is reproduced in nearly all recent English translations of Kant's writings. Translations are my own, though I have benefited and learned a great deal from a variety of earlier English translations of Kant's works.

The following abbreviations are used to refer to specific works of Kant's:

Anfang	*Mutmaßlicher Anfang der Menschengeschichte* (*Conjectural Beginning of Human History*), 8:107–23.
Anth	*Anthropologie in pragmatischer Hinsicht* (*Anthropology from a Pragmatic Point of View*), 7:117–333.
Beob	*Beobachtungen über das Gefühl des Schönen und Erhabenen* (*Observations on the Feeling of the Beautiful and the Sublime*), 2:205–56.
Beweisgrund	*Der einzig mögliche Beweisgrund zu einer Demonstration des Daseins Gottes* (*The Only Possible Argument for the Existence of God*), 2:63–163.
De mundi	*De mundi sensibilis atque intelligibilis forma et principiis* (*On the Form and Principles of the Sensible and Intelligible World*, 2:385–419.
Ende	*Das Ende aller Dinge* (*The End of All Things*), 8:325–39.
Frieden	*Zum ewigen Frieden* (*Perpetual Peace*), 8:1–116.
Gebrauch	*Über den Gebrauch teleologischer Principien in der Philosophie* (*On the Use of Teleological Principles in Philosophy*), 8:157–84.

Gemeinspruch	*Über den Gemeinspruch: Das mag in der Theorie richtig sein, taugt aber nicht für die Praxis (On the Common Saying: That May be Correct in Theory, But It Is of No Use in Practice)*, 8:273–313.
Geo	*Physische Geographie (Lectures on Physical Geography)*, edited by Friedrich Theodor Rink, 9:151–436.
Gr	*Grundlegung der Metaphysik der Sitten (Groundwork of the Metaphysics of Morals)*, 4:385–463.
Idee	*Idee zu einer allgemeinen Geschichte in weltbürgerlicher Absicht (Idea for a Universal History from a Cosmopolitan Point of View)*, 8:15–31.
KrV	*Kritik der reinen Vernunft (Critique of Pure Reason)*—references here are to the standard A and B pagination of the first and second editions.
KpV	*Kritik der praktischen Vernunft (Critique of Practical Reason)*, 5:1–163.
KU	*Kritik der Urteilskraft (Critique of Judgment)*, 5:165–485.
MAN	*Metaphysische Anfangsgründe der Naturwissenschaft (Metaphysical Foundations of Natural Science)*, 4: 465–565.
MdS	*Metaphysik der Sitten (Metaphysics of Morals)*, 6:203–493.
Menschenrace	*Bestimmung des Begriffs einer Menschenrace (Determination of the Concept of a Human Race)*, 8:89–106.
Nachricht	*Nachricht von der Einrichtung seiner Vorlesungen in dem Winterhalbenjahre von 1765–1766 (Announcement of the Program of his Lectures in the Winter Semester of 1765–66)*, 2:303–13.
Naturgeschichte	*Allgemeine Naturgeschichte und Theorie des Himmels (Universal Natural History and Theory of the Heavens)*, 1: 215–368.
Päd	*Pädagogik (Lectures on Pedagogy,* edited by Friedrich Theodor Rink), 9:437–499.
Pro	*Prolegomena zu einer jeden künftigen Metaphysik die als Wissenschaft wird auftreten können (Prolegomena to Any Future Metaphysics)*, 4:253–383.
Racen	*Von den verschiedenen Racen der Menschen (Of the Different Races of Human Beings)*, 2:427–443.
Refl	*Reflexionen (Notes and Fragments)*, 14–23—references here are first to the Academy *Reflexion* number, followed by the Academy volume and page number.
Rel	*Die Religion innerhalb der Grenzen der bloßen Vernunft (Religion within the Boundaries of Mere Reason)*, 6:1–202.
Streit	*Der Streit der Fakultäten (The Conflict of the Faculties)*, 7:1–116.
Träume	*Träume eines Geistersehers, erläutert durch Träume der Metaphysik (Dreams of a Spirit-Seer, Explained through Dreams of Metaphysics)*, 2:315–73.

Other texts cited from the Academy Edition—particularly lecture transcriptions—are referred to by shortened (or, in many cases, full) titles that are easy to identify.

The following two lecture transcriptions, not included in the Academy Edition, are cited in the body of the text by page number:

Dohna   *Die philosophischen Hauptvorlesungen Immanuel Kants. Nach den neu aufgefundenen Kollegheften des Grafen Heinrich zu Dohna-Wundlacken.* Edited by Arnold Kowalewski. (Munich and Leipzig: Rösl and Cie: 1924.)

Starke II   *Immanuel Kant's Anweisung zur Menschen- und Weltkenntniß. Nach dessen Vorlesungen im Winterhalbjahre von 1790–1791.* Edited by Friedrich Christian Starke (Leipzig: Die Expedition des europäischen Aufsehers, 1831.)

I

Introduction

In order for the wheel to turn, for life to be lived, impurities are needed.

Primo Levi, The Periodic Table

1

WHAT IS IMPURE ETHICS?

Pure and Applied Philosophy

> [O]nly that part of metaphysics that deals with form has re-
> mained undisputed, whereas quarrels and hypotheses have
> arisen when material knowledge is at issue.
>
> J. H. Lambert to Kant,
> February 3, 1766

Throughout his mature writings[1] Kant makes a strong distinction between that part of a science which is allegedly "pure" or "absolutely independent of all experience" (*KrV* B 3) and that part which admits in empirical data and assumptions in its application to a particular body of experience. Natural and moral philosophy and (sometimes[2]) even logic are all held by Kant to require both pure and empirical parts (*Gr* 4:387–88, 410 n; *KrV* A 53–55). Like many scientists, philosophers, and intellectuals before and since, he holds the pure part in higher esteem than the applied part. Pure philosophy "must lead the way [*muß . . . vorangehen*]" (*Gr* 4:390) if our knowledge is to achieve a sufficiently secure footing. Indeed, sometimes Kant's love of the pure is so intense that it leads him to exclude the empirical entirely from the scope of philosophy and to assert that all forms of knowledge that are solely or even partially empirical have only instrumental and subsidiary roles to play in human life. Metaphysics, which he defines as "nothing but the *inventory* of all of our possessions through *pure* reason" (*KrV* A xx),

> alone properly constitutes what we may call philosophy, in the strict sense of the term. . . . Mathematics, natural science, even our empirical knowledge,

have a high value as a means, for the most part, to contingent ends, but also, in the ultimate outcome, to ends that are necessary and essential to humanity. This latter service, however, they can discharge only as they are aided by a knowledge through reason from [pure] concepts alone [*aus bloßen Begriffen*], which however we may choose to entitle it, is really nothing but metaphysics. (*KrV* A 850/B 878)

This obsession with "keeping philosophy pure," along with the concomitant vision of a successfully purified form of philosophy as the savior and protector of all that is essential to humanity, has been dear to the hearts of many philosophers both before and after Kant.[3] And contemporary critics of Kant such as Johann Georg Hamann were quick to jump on the "*gnostic* hatred of matter" and "*mystical* love of form"[4] that allegedly lay behind it. But in Kant's less missionary moments he adheres to a more traditional conception of the scope of philosophy. A few pages earlier in the first *Critique* he asserts: "All philosophy is either knowledge from pure reason, or knowledge obtained by reason from empirical principles. The first is called pure, the second empirical philosophy" (*KrV* A 840/B 868). A parallel passage occurs in the preface of the *Groundwork*: "One can call all philosophy insofar as it rests on the grounds of experience *empirical*, while that which sets forth its doctrines as depending entirely on *a priori* principles can be called *pure*" (4:388).

Kant's broader conception of philosophy as including both pure and empirical (or what I call "impure") parts is in part a reflection of the curricular obligations of university philosophy programs in his time. German universities in the eighteenth century (in keeping with a tradition going back to the Middle Ages) were divided into four different faculties, which were then arranged in two broad groups. The three so-called higher faculties consisted of theology, law, and medicine; the fourth and only "lower" faculty was philosophy. Essentially, all of the liberal arts came under the purview of the philosophy faculty. In his late essay "The Conflict of the Faculties" (1798), Kant makes the following remarks concerning the concept and division of the lower faculty:

> Now the philosophy faculty consists of two departments: a department of *historical knowledge* (to which history, geography, philology, and the humanities all belong, along with all the empirical knowledge contained in the natural sciences), and a department of pure rational knowledge (pure mathematics and pure philosophy, metaphysics of nature and of morals). And it also studies the reciprocal relation of these two divisions of learning to one another. It therefore extends to all parts of human knowledge (including, from a historical point of view, the teachings of the higher faculties). (7:28)

So Kant's own considered view, as well as the institutional reality of the time, was that philosophy consists of both a pure as well as an empirical part. Particularly when we examine his teaching record at the University of Königsberg, we see that the author of the *Critique of Pure Reason* devoted a considerable portion of his teaching life to a wide variety of decidedly impure disciplines. In addition to the expected lecture courses on logic, metaphysics, and moral philosophy, Kant also gave lecture courses on natural law (twelve times between 1767 and 1788), the encyclopedia and history of philosophy (eleven times between 1767 and 1787), natural theology (once in 1785–86), pedagogy (four times between 1776 and 1787), anthropology (twenty-four times between 1772 and 1796), physical geography (forty-six times between 1756 and 1796), theoretical physics (twenty times between 1755 and 1788), mechanics (twice between 1759 and 1761), and mineralogy (once in 1770–71).[5] His physical geography course, which was quite innovative and well received,[6] was given more often than every lecture course he taught except for logic (offered fifty-four times between 1755 and 1796) and metaphysics (forty-nine times between 1756 and 1796). However, logic, metaphysics, and moral philosophy (offered twenty-eight times between 1756 and 1789) were all required courses; geography was an elective. Although accurate judgments concerning the precise amount of attention given by Kant to pure versus empirical elements in these courses are impossible to arrive at from course titles alone, and the amount may have varied from year to year (see, e.g., his inconsistent remarks concerning "applied logic" in n. 2) this tally does show us, contrary to what is often assumed, that a considerable portion of Kant's teaching life was devoted to the empirical sciences.[7]

Although Kant occasionally seems to equate the pure part of moral philosophy with the form of knowledge and the empirical part with the matter of knowledge obtained by the senses (e.g., *Gr* 4:400, *KpV* 5:26–27), it is a mistake to view the pure part as totally empty of content or "merely formal." The pure part of ethics, on Kant's view, is not "completely separated from reality," and practical reason on his view does not involve "the complete abstraction from all content."[8] However, any information or content gleaned from the pure part of moral philosophy will always concern universal and necessary aspects (aspects which on Kant's view are more than merely human) of moral reality rather than particular and contingent ones. As Barbara Herman notes: "Purely formal principles . . . are said to give reasons that are necessary and universally valid, reasons that hold in virtue of features that are constitutive of our rational natures. Purely formal principles do not have *no* content; they have *noncontingent* content."[9] Still, the pure part of moral philosophy never gives us anything close to sufficient content to know precisely what to do in any particular situation. A priori moral laws always "require . . . a power of judgment sharpened by experience" (*Gr* 4:389) for their application in real life.

Practical or moral knowledge, on Kant's view, is also purer than theoretical knowledge, insofar as knowledge of moral principles is totally independent of "the special nature of human reason" (*Gr* 4:411–12). Practical reason, as William A. Galston remarks, "includes no admixture of human particularity. . . . It is therefore impossible to even imagine modes of moral judgment that differ from human moral judgment."[10] Theoretical reason, on the other hand, "permits and even at times finds [it] necessary" to make its principles "depend upon the special nature of human reason" (*Gr* 4:411–12).

Tracking Kant's Impure Ethics

> The metaphysics of morals or *metaphysica pura* is only the first part of morals—the second part is *philosophia moralis applicata*

[applied moral philosophy], moral anthropology, to which the empirical principles belong.

Moral Mrongovius II

Just as there is metaphysics and physics, so the same applies here . . . Moral anthropology is morals applied to human beings. *Moralia pura* is based on necessary laws; therefore it cannot be grounded on the particular constitution [*besondere Beschaffenheit*] of a rational being, [such as] the human being.

Praktische Philosophie Powalski

The particular constitution of the human being, and the laws which are grounded on it, are found in moral anthropology, under the name of ethics.

Moralphilosophie Collins

Again, this is a book about the empirical or impure side of Kant's project in ethics, a side which, even today, has yet to be investigated by Kant scholars. Before proceeding, it is important to ask why, given the massive amounts of attention so many other areas of Kant's philosophy have received from nearly every ideological perspective imaginable, virtually nothing has been written on this topic before. J. H. W. Stuckenberg, Kant's first English-language biographer, makes the following observation in summarizing Kant's lectures as a professor:

> [Kant] was not content with giving theoretical knowledge, but wanted also to give it a practical application; accordingly, he prepared lectures on fortification, applying to this subject his knowledge of mathematics. From the very beginning of his connexion with the university he aimed to connect the practical with the theoretical, a tendency which characterized his whole life afterwards, but which is largely ignored, because his eminence in speculation has obscured his practical efforts.[11]

While it is certainly true that Kant's "eminence in speculation has obscured his practical efforts," this is not the whole story.

An additional fundamental reason for the continued popularity of the purist reading of Kant's ethics and the subsequent neglect of his empirical ethics is that Kant himself did not finish (or even develop systematically) the second part of his ethics. In saying that he did not finish it, I do not at all mean to endorse the anything-goes interpretive strategies of arguing (as J. N. Findlay did in the case of Plato) that we need to turn aside Kant's written works and speculate instead about his *agrapha dogmata* (unwritten doctrines)[12] or of claiming (as Hannah Arendt did in the case of Kant's political philosophy) that he simply "did not write" his empirical ethics and that it must therefore be squeezed out of seemingly unrelated texts.[13] Rather, I mean simply that though he wrote bits and pieces about this crucial dimension of his ethics in a variety of works, it unfortunately remained in an unfinished and not entirely systematic state at this death. To track Kant's empirical ethics accurately, one must look not only at his published works in ethics, but also at his lectures on education and anthropology, the various student and auditor versions of his lectures on moral philosophy,[14] and his writings on history, as well as selected aspects of his work in aesthetics and religion. The relevant portions of these texts need to be re-examined from the perspective of Kant's own self-declared division of practical philosophy, and then brought together (if possible) into a coherent doctrine. (For further discussion, see "Fields of Impurity" later in this chapter.)

Kant's failure to pursue systematically the empirical side of his ethics may also reflect deeper philosophical doubts on his own part concerning the coherence of this project with other important aspects of his official philosophical system. One such doubt is his lingering rationalist conviction that "*what is empirical* cannot be divided completely" (*MdS* 6:205). The contingency and particularity of the empirical prevent theorists from ever capturing it completely in the nets of their theories. In this respect, there is a sense in which Kant agrees with Kierkegaard: "an existential system is impossible."[15] However, the proper Kantian (if not quite Kierkegaardian) reply to the objection that complete systematicity at the empirical level is an impossible ideal would seem to be that a partial completion is preferable to none at all. Agreed, moral choices are necessarily made at specific times and in specific places by agents with unique life histories. But if moral theory is to make good on its claim to be action-guiding, it must be able to inform choice at this level of radical contingency, however imperfectly.

A deeper doubt is whether the idea of a moral anthropology "to which empirical principles belong" is itself consistent with Kant's own dualistic views concerning transcendental freedom and nature. The very idea of "empirical ethics" would seem to occupy an extremely awkward position within his official philosophical system. How could there even be such a thing as empirical ethics or moral anthropology for a stern anti-naturalist such as Kant, who writes, at least in one of his personas, that "morals . . . can never contain anything but pure a priori principles (since freedom can under no circumstances be an object of experience)" (*Erste Einleitung, KU* 20:195)? Given Kant's explicit acknowledgment that the precepts of moral anthropology are based on experience (*MdS* 6: 217, 385, 406), how can he include them as part of ethics?

As is well known, Kant often claims that freedom and nature constitute two separate worlds, each with its own unique set of laws, between which an "inestimable gulf" (*eine unübersehbare Kluft*—literally, "an abyss that one cannot see across") exists, and over which "no crossing [*kein Übergang*]" is possible (*KU* 5: 176). Even sympathetic readers of Kant often give up on him at this point, resorting to tired jokes about timeless actions and the causal efficacy of noumenal agents. But we need also to remember that Kant also states explicitly that freedom "is *meant* [*soll*] to influence" nature, that is, "the concept of freedom is meant to actualize in the sensible world the end proposed by its laws" (*KU* 5: 176). He definitely assumes here that interrelationship between the two realms is possible; and indeed, much of his work in education, anthropology, aesthetics, religion, and history focuses primarily on this gargantuan task. While the details of how this crossing from one realm to the other is to be effected remain a matter of much controversy,[16] it is clear that Kant holds both that human beings are supposed to use their knowledge of nature and the world around them in order to create a moral realm (*Frieden* 8:366–67, cf. *MdS* 6:218) and that they therefore must presuppose that nature can "play into their hands" if they are to pursue this project of creating a moral world (cf. *KU* 5:455). Kant's applied moral philosophy is concerned chiefly with this project of creating a moral world out of nature. (For further discussion, see "Nature and Freedom" later in this chapter.)

Kant's alluring remarks about an eventual *Übergang* from nature to freedom in many of his writings suggest that his assumed anti-naturalism in ethics may not be quite as thoroughgoing as he sometimes leads readers to believe it is. Indeed, many of his specific statements in defense of the necessity of moral anthropology do suggest a much different picture. For instance, in the *Collins* lectures from the winter semester of 1784–85 (written immediately before the publication of the *Groundwork*), we are told that "ethics cannot exist without anthropology [*Die Moral kann ohne die Anthropologie nicht bestehen*],[17] for one must first know of the subject whether he is also capable of doing what is demanded of him. . . . People are always preaching about what ought to be done, and nobody thinks about whether it can be done" (27:244; see also *Moral Mrongovius* 27:1398).

This remark from *Collins*, which Kant echoes at the beginning of the *Groundwork* and elsewhere (moral philosophy requires an empirical part in order to formulate successfully laws "for the will of the human being insofar as it is affected by nature" [4:387]), suggests strongly that he in fact is committed to a form of weak naturalism in his ethics. By "weak naturalism" I mean the view that empirical facts about human nature, though they cannot in themselves establish or justify normative moral principles, also cannot contradict such principles. We do not (and cannot) have moral duties to do things that are physically impossible for us, and this knowledge of what is physically impossible is empirical, that is, comes from the second part of Kant's ethics. "Ought" presupposes "can"—we cannot be obligated to do the impossible, though figuring out what we are truly capable of is no easy matter.[18] As Kant himself remarks in his essay "Theory and Practice:" "[I]t would not be a duty to pursue a certain effect of our will, if this effect were not also possible in our experience (whether it be thought of as completed or as always approaching completion), and this is the only kind of theory that is at issue in the present essay" (8:277).

Granted, one needs to be careful when attributing such a view to Kant. As is well known, in other places he hardly sounds like a friend of naturalism. For instance, in the first *Critique* we are told that "nothing is more reprehensible than to get laws concerning what I *ought to do* from what *is done*" (A 319). And in the *Moralphilosophie Collins* lectures he asserts:

> Ethics can propound laws of morality that are lenient, and adjusted to the weakness of human nature. It can make itself comfortable to the human being, so that it demands of people only so much as they can perform. But on the other hand ethics can also be rigorous and demand the highest moral perfection. The moral law . . . must not be lenient and accommodate itself to human weakness; for it contains the norm of moral perfection. But the norm must be exact and rigorous—geometry, for example, lays down rules that are strict; it pays no heed to whether a human being can observe them in practice or not; the center point of a circle, for example, is too thick to be a mathematical point. Now since ethics also propounds rules, which are meant to be the guideline for our actions, they must not be adjusted to human capacity, but have

to show what is morally necessary. An indulgent ethics is the ruin of moral perfection in the human being. The moral law must be pure. (27:301)

But these latter passages do not contradict the former, once the traditional distinction between perfect and imperfect obligation (cf. *Gr* 4:421 n. 2; *MdS* 6: 390–91) is brought into play. Ethics is "indulgent" when its principles of imperfect obligation are pitched too low—when they are constrained by moral agents' past performance and assume falsely that they can do no better. A regulative ideal of perfection needs to be built into such principles. We (or our distant descendants) gradually approach and even "realize asymptotically"[19] this ideal; indeed, we have a duty to do so. The duty is not to be perfect but rather to strive for perfection. And this is an "imperfect" duty (a duty to promote a general ideal or end); not a "perfect" duty (a duty to perform a specific act, such as keeping one's promise). In formulating perfect duties theorists obviously need to keep much closer tabs on what moral agents are actually physically capable of than is the case with imperfect duties. A perfect duty requiring human beings to jump one hundred feet in the air makes no sense; an imperfect duty requiring them to perfect their natural powers does (cf. *MdS* 6:444).

A second related way in which Kant's ethics is more naturalistic than most people realize is revealed in his strong concern to make moral principles efficacious in human life. Again and again in his impure ethics he asks: What are human beings like, such that following pure moral principles will be relatively difficult or easy for them, compared to the life situations of other possible rational beings (cf. *MdS* 6:217; *Gr* 4:387)? When difficulties are discovered, the next step is not to revise the principles and declare them unrealistic[20] (drag them down, so to speak, to an easy level of human mediocrity). Rather, one needs to think much more carefully about when, where, and how to introduce the principles to human beings; and the subsequent advice will often entail extensive institutional and social reform.

Surprisingly then, Kant actually agrees with John Dewey that "everything that can be known of the human mind and body in physiology, medicine, anthropology, and psychology is pertinent to moral inquiry."[21] "Pertinent," however, at least for Kant, does not mean "determines." We don't derive moral norms from empirical facts; but when these norms are applied to human beings they must be consistent with the facts of human life.

In addition to these textual and philosophical problems surrounding Kant's empirical ethics, there has also been a strong disciplinary or cultural obstacle to appreciating his moral anthropology. As noted earlier, professional philosophers since Kant's time have been increasingly obsessed with keeping philosophy pure, that is, with differentiating their discipline from all others on account of its supposed detachment from empirical matters. The subsequent shrinking of the curricular scope of philosophy since Kant's time and its new self-image as a discipline set off from all others as a special kind of a priori science has also made it more difficult for subsequent generations to appreciate fully the empirical side of his project in ethics. Admittedly, Kant's own personal role in putting philosophy on the path of "a knowledge through reason from pure concepts alone" adds an ironic dimension to this problem, which further complicates matters. (He himself is partly responsible for the subsequent neglect of the second part of his ethics.) However, there are numerous signs at present that philosophy's self-image is (once again) beginning to open up a bit. The time is ripe finally to look at Kant's ethics in the way that he wanted it to be looked at.

I believe the lack of previous attention given to Kant's empirical ethics is largely a function of the issues just presented. Each of them also carries its own appropriate warning concerning the pitfalls awaiting those who try to understand this under-appreciated aspect of Kant's practical philosophy. To focus on the empirical side of Kant's ethics is to examine under-explored and occasionally strange territory that has been (and to a large extent, still is) left out of the standard accounts of Kantian views about moral terrain. But since it is a central conviction of Kant's that ethics "cannot exist without anthropology" (27:244), it behooves us to look closely at this second part of his practical philosophy.

Degrees and Kinds of Impurity

A totally pure ethics would contain no empirical content whatsoever. The greater the amount of empirical content brought into the system, the more impure it becomes.[22] However, when empirical content is brought in, it is not to be "mixed" with the a priori principles. In constructing scientific as well as ethical theories, there exists an "indispensable duty" to expound the pure part "separately and entirely unmixed [ganz unbemengt] with the empirical part," in order that the "apodeictic certainty sought by reason" can be achieved (MAN 4:469; cf. Gr 4:389).

The kind of impurity to be investigated in the present study is also not one in which the pure and empirical parts of the theory are co-present at the beginning of theory construction—such an enterprise

> does not even deserve the name of philosophy (for what distinguishes philosophy from common rational cognition is just that it puts forward in separate sciences what the latter comprehends only mixed together); much less does it deserve the name of a moral philosophy, since by this very mixture it even damages the purity of morals themselves and proceeds contrary to its own end. (Gr 4:390)

It is only in the later application[23] of pure principles to empirical circumstances that non-pure elements are to be brought in, and in every such application the pure aspects of the theory are to be "in charge of" the empirical aspects. In Kant's ethics, for instance, a pure (that is, non-empirical) motive must be the determining ground of the will for an action to have moral worth. The principle of action must be "free from all influence by contingent grounds, the only kind that experience can supply" (Gr 4:426). On Kant's view, human moral agents are not "hopelessly 'impure' . . . agents of, rather than outside, the world of space, time and causality, agents whose histories and actions belong to it."[24] Rather, they are mixed creatures in which a pure component interacts with an impure component. And the goal in ethics is that this interaction be one in which the pure component exerts control over the empirical.

Similarly, contrary to popular belief, Kant's approach to ethics is also not an example of a "purist view of morality" which rejects any "biological . . . [or] historical and psychological understanding" of human morality.[25] Nor did Kant mistakenly hold "that an abstract idea of practical reason applicable to rational beings as such could take us all the way to anything like our own moral code."[26] Rather, his project is simply one that explicitly seeks both to construct the foundational principles of theory from non-empirical sources and then to bring in empirical content for purposes of application to human life. And in explicitly asserting the need to bring in empirical data in order to apply pure moral principles to the human situation, Kant certainly does not see himself as giving in to an "imperfect morality which is therefore impure [unrein], or is immorality."[27] "Impure," in the sense used in the present discussion, is not at all a term of disapprobation. Rather, Kant's view is merely that pure ethics, although it must come first, does not take us as far as we need to go. It can show us what the foundational principles of moral thought and action are for rational beings in general, but it can never show us (or any other specific kind of finite rational being) what to do in a concrete situation. Principles of pure ethics, precisely because they are pure, have no special connection to human life. Such a connection can only be established by bringing empirical knowledge of human nature into the picture.

Several key points exist along this continuum from pure to impure which merit special comment, as follows.

Pure Ethics

In the first *Critique*, Kant writes that "pure ethics [reine Moral] . . . contains only the necessary moral laws of a free will in general" (*KrV* A 55). At this highly abstract level, no information concerning the peculiar nature of human beings or of any other specific type of rational being is allowed in. Most of Kant's *Groundwork* does not even qualify as "pure ethics" in this austere sense. For the concept of duty, with which much of the text is concerned, involves "subjective limitations and obstacles" (4:397) which are not part of the psychology of all rational beings, and the moral law does not confront all rational beings as an imperative. Indeed, it is debatable whether pure ethics in this highly rarefied sense should even count as ethics. Does it still make sense to talk of morality when the concepts of duty and constraint are not applicable? But regardless of where one stands on the conceptual issue concerning the limits of the moral, it is clear that the intentional lack of material content at this level of investigation severely limits the applicability of such a pure ethics.

Morality for Finite Rational Beings

This is the level of analysis at which Kant operates during most of the *Groundwork*. The categorical imperative, as Nancy Sherman notes, "addresses the problem of moral law for a finitely rational agent who can be aware of that moral law and yet oppose it because of inclination."[28] Even here though, none of the principles enunciated are supposed to depend on specific information about human nature or culture. Granted, Kant employs such information in *illustrating* the principles—assumptions about all-too-human shopkeepers, money, debtors, and so on appear prominently in his attempt to derive four basic types of obligation from the categorical imperative. But unless the illustrations are to be entirely hypothetical and fictional, his only recourse is to employ data concerning human nature and culture. This is the only species of rational being we know— "experience does not present us with a second species of rational being" (*Anth* 7:321; cf. *Menschenkunde* 25:859).

Determination of Moral Duties for "Human Beings As Such"

This is Kant's project in the *Metaphysics of Morals*. It does presuppose a certain minimal amount of empirical information concerning the actual nature of human beings: "the special determination of duties as human duties . . . is possible only after the subject of this determination (the human being) is known as he is really constituted, though only to the extent necessary with reference to duty generally" (*KpV* 5:8; cf. *MdS* 6:217). The idea, though, is still to let in only a very minimal amount of empirical information: the concept of a human being *in general*, as opposed to one situated in a specific culture, class, gender, or race. Consideration of the duties of the latter "cannot properly constitute a *part* of the *metaphysical* first principles of a doctrine of virtue" (6:468). What instincts, inclinations, capacities, and powers that are common to all members of the human species need to be considered in applying the moral law to this particular type of rational being? Similarly, in moving from a metaphysics of nature to natural science, philosophy "makes use of no particular experiences [*keine besonderden Erfahrungen*]" but rather only the concept of matter in general (*MAN* 4:472).

However, this derivation-of-duties-for-humans project of the *Metaphysics of Morals*, which has already been studied fairly extensively by philosophers[29] (in keeping with their desire to "keep philosophy pure"?), is still metaphysics. Kant's metaphysics of morals is explicitly intended to be "a system derived from reason" in which empirical principles are *not* "brought into the system as integral parts of it" (*MdS* 6:205). In contrast, the project of the second part of ethics, moral anthropology, which is the focus of this study, explicitly involves "teachings and precepts based on experience" at its core (6:217).

But before descending to a greater level of specificity, two different kinds of application projects should also be noted.

Species-Specific Applications

Species-specific empirical knowledge will be needed whenever a priori moral principles are applied to non-human types of rational being as well. In other words, there will be an analogue of the project of the *Metaphysics of Morals* for each distinct species of rational being. While the mature Kant was much less willing to speculate about the lifestyles and intellectual capacities of non-human rational beings than was his younger self, throughout his career he took it as obvious that there are other forms of rational life in the universe and that the details of morality will be different for them than for us.[30] And although he often tags the empirical part of ethics as "practical anthropology" (*Gr* 4:388) or "moral anthropology" (*MdS* 6:217; *Moral Mrongovius* II 29:599), the study of what specific problems and advantages non-human rational beings experience in dealing with a priori moral principles is also in principle part of Kant's project. If experience ever does present us with a second species of rational beings (cf. *Anth* 7:321; *KU* 5:467), other species-specific application projects will become feasible.

Aids and Obstacles to Morality

Suppose one analyzes human nature and culture, not with the intent of simply deriving (with the help of a very minimal amount of empirical information) a list of duties that will hold across the species, but rather with the aim of locating factors that will help or hinder the development and spread of morality within human life. This application task does not represent a greater level of specificity than the determination of duties project, insofar as both are still concerned with "human beings as such" rather than with subgroups of human beings. However, this task does require much more empirical information than does the determination of duties project, for there the aim is simply to arrive at a complete classification of the moral duties which hold for human beings as such by applying the categorical imperative to a very limited amount of empirical knowledge concerning human nature. But after the list of duties is arrived at and assumed to be complete, a host of new questions arises concerning the effective application of these principles to the human situation: How should moral principles be taught to human beings? Given what we know about human development, at what stages in human life should people learn about morality, and how should they learn about it? What specific passions and inclinations are human beings subject to that will tend to make their adherence to moral principles difficult (or easy)? Are there specific cultural aspects of the modern era that make the establishment of the "rule of right" (see *Frieden* 8:366–67) more or less likely than in previous eras? What stage of moral development is the human race itself in at present? How should political, cultural, educational, and religious institutions be organized to best further moral aims? The possibility of an answer to any of these questions will require a much greater amount of empirical information than is allowed into the "determination of duties" project of the *Metaphysics of Morals*.

In all of Kant's references to "empirical ethics" or "the second part" of ethics or "moral anthropology" or "practical anthropology" or "applied moral philosophy" (as used by Kant, these are all synonymous expressions), it is precisely these sorts of questions which are being addressed. In other words, the second part of ethics is not about deriving duties from the categorical imperative, but rather about making morality efficacious in human life. In the *Groundwork*, for instance, the empirical part of ethics is charged with formulating moral laws "for the will of the human being in so far as it is affected by nature" (4:387) and with "finding access to the human will for them [namely, moral a priori laws] and influence over practice" (4:389). And while the principles enunciated in the *Groundwork* allegedly "have to hold for every rational being as such," Kant also emphasizes that ethics "needs [*bedarf*] anthropology for its *application* to human beings" (4:412). A fuller description of moral anthropology is offered in the *Metaphysics of Morals*:

> The counterpart [*das Gegenstück*] of a metaphysics of morals, the other member of the division of practical philosophy as a whole, would be moral anthropology, which, however, would deal only with the subjective conditions in human nature that hinder human beings or help them in *the carrying out* [*die Ausführung*] of the laws of the first part [namely, the metaphysics of morals]. It would deal with the development, spreading, and strengthening of moral principles (in education in schools and in popular instruction), and with similar teachings and precepts based on experience [*auf Erfahrung gründende Lehren und Vorschriften*]. (6:217)

Similar descriptions occur throughout his various lectures on ethics. In the *Praktische Philosophie Powalski* lectures, for instance, Kant argues:

> One must not merely study the object (that is, moral conduct), but also the subject (that is, the human being). This is necessary because one must see what sorts of hindrances to virtue are present in the human being. The first part of ethics contains the criteria of discrimination of that which is practically good and evil. . . . The second [part of ethics] contains the rules and means of execution—the means by which it is possible for a will to act according to rules. This second part is the most difficult, because one must study the human being. (27:97–98)[31]

And in the *Moralphilosophie Collins* lectures we are told that consideration of rules "is useless [*unnütz*] if one cannot make human beings willing to follow them" (27:244). If one chooses unwisely to pursue practical philosophy "without anthropology, or without knowledge of the subject, then it is merely speculative, or an idea; the human being must therefore at least be studied later on [*hernach*]" (27:244; cf. *Moral Mrongovius* 27:1398).

Subgroups within a Species

The next level of specificity would concern identifiable subgroups within a given species of rational beings that share morally relevant features with one another, features that entail special moral obligations, character traits, rights, and so on. As Kant asks toward the end of *The Metaphysics of Morals* (6:469): "How should people be treated in accordance with their differences in rank, age, sex, health, prosperity or poverty, and so forth?" Here we confront yet another puzzling feature of Kant's applied ethics. Although this level of application "belongs to the complete presentation of the system" (6:469), it belongs, on Kant's view, only as an "appendix" to it rather than as a "division" of it. And in fact the appendix was never written. Why? Supposedly, at this level of specificity, the amount and kinds of empirical data required exceed the theorist's abilities to classify them thoroughly and systematically: the sheer contingency and openness of the empirical data means that "they do not admit of a classification that could be guaranteed to be complete" (6:468; cf. 205).[32]

However, in classroom lectures as well as elsewhere, Kant does not always allow this concern for classificatory completeness to stand in the way. Toward the end of the *Collins* lectures, for instance, he criticizes Alexander Gottlieb Baumgarten's *Philosophical Ethics* (one of two approved textbooks for Kant's lecture course on moral philosophy) for having an incomplete enumeration of special duties:

> The author has not hit on a good ordering at all; he could have divided these duties with respect to differences of standing, of sex, and of age. The difference of sex is not as minor as one perhaps thinks. The incentives [*Triebfedern*] of the male sex are very different from the incentives of the female sex. In regard to the distinction of sex one can check in the Anthropology, from which the duties can then be drawn. (27:466)[33]

And when we do turn to Kant's *Anthropology from a Pragmatic Point of View*, we are informed that woman cannot "engage in civil affairs for herself, but only through a representative" (*Anth* 7:209). Or, as he bluntly states elsewhere, she lacks "civil personality" (*MdS* 6:314). However, in *Collins* the audience is spared further endorsement by the critical philosopher of the prejudices of the day by the assertion a few lines later that a complete classification of types of duty based on human differences is impossible: "Morality in general is an inexhaustible field" (27:466).

As is well known, Kant makes frequent (and even more prejudicial) remarks about subgroups of human beings in other contexts. "Humanity has its highest perfection in the white race. The yellow Indians have a somewhat lesser talent. The Negroes are much lower, and lowest of all is part of the American races" (*Geo* 9:316). And woman's philosophy

> is not to argue [*vernünfteln*], but to feel [*empfinden*]. In the opportunity that one wants to give to women to cultivate their beautiful nature, one must always keep this relation before his eyes. One will seek to broaden their total moral feeling and not their memory, and that of course not by universal rules but by some judgment upon the conduct that they see about them. (*Beob* 2: 230)

While Kant does not try to arrive at a systematic classification of moral duties owed to and by the various subgroups of humanity, he cannot resist making normative judgments about many of these subgroups. As I show later, an unresolved tension exists between the core message of universality in his ethics and his frequent assertions that many different groups of people (who when taken together constitute a large majority of the human race) are in a pre-moral state of development.[34]

Judging What to Do in a Specific Situation

This is the most specific level of application, but here too—for reasons given earlier (n15)—there is a sense in which we are now "out of the system" in Kant's view. We are out of the system in the sense that no complete classification of the requisite empirical information is possible at this level. Because the precise data will be somewhat different for each individual and for each choice situation in each individual's life, no systematic theory is possible at this level. But (again) action and choice occur at precisely this level of contingency, and if moral theory is to be truly action-guiding it must be able to inform deliberation at this level too. Kant addresses issues concerning judgment in situations of radical contingency in a variety of ways, and I examine them in detail in chapter 2 when I turn to his writings on moral education. Two essential distinctions should be noted here, as follows.

Moral Catechism   For children, the "first and most essential" form of moral education recommended by Kant is a "moral catechism" in which the instructor presents casuistic questions to students and writes out their answers "in definite words that cannot easily be altered" (*MdS* 6:478–79; cf. *Logik Pölitz* 24:599–600) so that they will then commit them to memory.[35] Carrying out the catechism "through all the articles of virtue and vice" (which Kant himself does not undertake for us), the teacher helps students "feel the progress of their power of judgment" (*KpV* 5:154) by challenging them to reflect on the increasingly difficult problems he puts to them (*MdS* 6:482–83). The cases may be drawn either from "ordinary life" (*Päd* 9:490) or from "biographies of ancient and modern times" (*KpV* 5:154). In his *Lectures on Pedagogy*, Kant deplores the lack of suitable moral catechism texts and recommends that teachers "set aside an hour daily" to discuss cases with students if and when such books become available (*Päd* 9:490).

Casuistry   In the *Metaphysics of Morals*, Kant asserts that casuistry is "neither a science nor a part of a science." It is "not so much a doctrine [*Lehre*] about how *to find* something as rather a practice [*Übung*] in how *to seek* truth," and is "*woven* into ethics in a *fragmentary* way, not systematically" (6:411). Here again we see him alluding to the unattainable ideal of systematicity within human experience. In the *Tugendlehre*, this fragmentary weaving is achieved by appending specific casuistic questions concerning (e.g.) suicide, sexual morality, alcohol and drug use, and deception to several of the discussions of imperfect duties. Unlike the cases presented to students in the moral catechism, these casuistic questions are intended for adults only and are much more open-ended. But in both cases, the aim is to provide training in the practice of moral judgment. So although no complete theory of practical judging is possible (there will always be new and unforeseeable situations for judgment to consider), and while the art of judgment cannot be formally imparted to students by means of rules (rules are never self-deploying: there are no rules which tell us how to apply rules [*Anth* 7:199; *KrV* A 133/B 172]), much can and should be done by theorists and educators to help judgment be sharpened correctly by experience.

Nature and Freedom

As noted earlier in this chapter ("Tracking Kant's Impure Ethics"), perhaps the most difficult issue confronting anyone who sets out to investigate Kant's empirical ethics concerns its awkward status within his own philosophical system.

How can a body of knowledge based on empirical precepts constitute a legitimate part of ethics in any sense for Kant? In this section I examine a bit more closely some relevant issues concerning nature and freedom and their relationship to the second half of Kant's ethics.

Commentators have often ridiculed Kant's empirical ethics as a conceptual confusion. According to H. J. Paton:

> 'applied ethics' is used [by Kant] for a special kind of moral or practical psychology (or anthropology as he calls it) concerned with the conditions which favour or hinder the moral life. . . . There is, however, no reason why we should regard such a psychology as practical: it is a theoretical examination of the causes of certain morally desirable effects. Still less is there a reason why we should regard it with Kant as a kind of applied or empirical ethics.[36]

Similarly, his student Mary Gregor writes in *Laws of Freedom*:

> Moral anthropology is . . . not ethics but rather a sort of psychology, a study of the natural causes which can be made to contribute toward the development of moral dispositions and toward making our actions in fulfillment of duty easier and more effective. Why should Kant regard this science as a division of moral philosophy?[37]

This issue of whether to place empirical ethics under practical or theoretical philosophy is part of the larger problem of freedom and nature in Kant's philosophy, particularly as concerns the interpretation of human thought and action. On the one hand, insofar as human beings are a part of nature, they will have empirical characters, "the causality of which must stand under empirical laws" (*KrV* A 546/B 574). And in respect to this empirical character there is "no freedom" (A 550/B 578). On the other hand, as rational beings who have the power to determine their own actions through efforts of will, human beings also follow "a rule and order altogether different from the order of nature" (A 550/B 578). And in respect to this intelligible character the acting subject "stands under no conditions of time, for time is only the condition of appearances, not of things in themselves" (A 539/B 567). Our moral character itself, as a product of free choice, also stands entirely outside the conditions of time on Kant's view:

> To look for the temporal origin of free acts as such (as though they were natural effects) is . . . a contradiction; hence it is also a contradiction to seek the temporal origin of the human being's moral character . . . since this character signifies the ground of the *exercise* of freedom; which (like the determining ground of the free will generally) must be sought in representations of reason alone. (*Rel* 6:40)

Similarly, his remarks in the first *Critique* concerning the kind of "ought [*sollen*]" found in practical imperatives imply a totally non-natural quality: " '*Ought*' expresses a kind of necessity and connection with grounds which is found nowhere else in the whole of nature. . . . When one has the course of nature alone before one's eyes, 'ought' has no meaning whatsoever [*ganz und gar keine Bedeutung*]" (A 547/B 576).

In his sterner moments, Kant insists that practical philosophy properly consists only of principles "which are founded entirely [*gänzlich*] on the concept of freedom, to the complete exclusion of grounds taken from nature for the determination of the will" (*KU* 5:173). His remark in the *Groundwork* that the pure or "rational part" of ethics "might properly be called *morals* [*eigentlich Moral*]" (4:388) seems also intended in this spirit. According to this narrower conception of practical philosophy, it thus appears that the precepts of moral anthropology would fall under the domain of theoretical rather than practical philosophy, since they contain empirical principles and are founded on nature rather than freedom.

But this narrower conception of the practical does contradict Kant's repeated assertions, in the *Groundwork* and elsewhere, that ethics, like physics, "will have its empirical part" (4:388; cf. *Moral Mrongovius II* 29:599). Part of the problem is that he occasionally uses the term "practical" inconsistently. In the stricter, narrower sense, "practical" is interchangeable with "moral," where both refer to the possibility of categorical imperatives based on freedom. In the looser, broader sense, practical principles "are simply general rules that regulate action. Some practical rules are moral, namely categorical imperatives, and some are nonmoral, e.g., subjective maxims and hypothetical imperatives."[38]

One way out of this difficulty would be to say simply that empirical ethics is practical in the broader but not in the narrower sense, and leave it at that. But since the narrower sense of "practical" is Kant's official one (and the one that critics such as Paton and Gregor latch onto), it is important also to see whether and in what sense empirical ethics can qualify as practical even in the narrower sense. On my view (and here I agree with Paton and Gregor), Kant's empirical ethics is theoretical insofar as it consists of the study of natural phenomena that hinder or contribute to the development of morality in human life. But it is also practical (and here I disagree with them) in the sense that the use which human beings make of these precepts is free (grounded on practical reason) rather than unfree (determined by the interplay of natural causes) (cf. *MdS* 6:456–57). We have a moral duty to learn how nature works in order to put into effect "what reason prescribes to us" (6:218; cf. *Frieden* 8:366–67). In other words, a moral purpose lies behind the acquisition of this theoretical knowledge; and since we are regulating our actions by a moral motive, this regulation counts as "practical" even in Kant's narrower, official sense. We are to learn about human nature and the world we live in precisely in order to construct a moral world. Part of the necessary work of freedom and of practical reason involves using our knowledge of nature in order to create a moral realm. Again, the concept of freedom "is meant [*soll*] to actualize in the sensible world the end proposed by its laws" (*KU* 5:176), and this can only happen if moral agents use their knowledge of nature and culture to promote moral goals. In this second, practical, sense, Kant's empirical ethics contributes to the larger task of effecting a bridge between nature and freedom *via* judgment (cf. *KU* 5:195–96). The precepts of practical anthropology help strengthen moral agents' power of judgment by giving them detailed information concerning how the natural and social worlds in which they live actually work.

But from where precisely is this empirical information supposed to come? A further problem concerns the essential contestability of much empirical knowledge concerning human beings. As Lambert remarks in his letter to Kant of February 3, 1766, "quarrels and hypotheses have arisen when material knowledge is at issue" (10:61; see the epigraph of this chapter). When one decides to seek help from the empirical, where precisely should one go? To biology? Sociology? Psychology? Cultural anthropology? Whose version of which empirical science is to provide moral agents with the requisite data to make informed moral decisions? Once the commitment to gaining help from the empirical (however the latter is to be construed) is made, the possibility of getting one's facts wrong always looms large. In Kant's case, disastrous practical advice could easily follow from his false assertion, in the *Lectures on Pedagogy*, that the "temperature of children's blood is 110 degrees Fahrenheit and the blood of adults only 96 degrees" (9:458). It is not known how many parents in cold climates put their children to bed in the winter with this advice in mind. Unfortunately, in the case of Kant's (and others') false assertions concerning (e.g.) intelligence, race, and gender, we can readily trace the moral fallout.

Finally, if moral character does indeed stem from a timeless free choice that is outside the chain of natural causality, what real impact can the various empirical percepts of practical anthropology and moral education have? Won't they affect only our empirical character, and not our intelligible character? How can two such qualitatively different realms interact with one another? As Johann Friedrich Herbart wrote, in one of the first reviews of Kant's *Lectures on Pedagogy*:

> How did Kant imagine moral education? As an effect of transcendental freedom? Impossible, for the concept of the latter comes to an end, as soon as one thinks it is not entirely free from every causal nexus. Transcendental freedom does what it does by itself; one cannot hinder it through anything, one cannot help it through anything. *It* discovers maxims; what the teacher says to it is immaterial.[39]

But in fact, Herbart's objections apply not just to moral education but rather to *all* aspects of human life (art, science, culture, politics, etc.) that on Kant's view lead people to the threshold of a truly moral existence. As Pierre Hassner notes, if we insist on too strict a union between these preparatory steps and the moral life itself, we

> import a determinism or mechanism into the conditions of morality that would jeopardize the essential freedom of morality itself. [On the other hand, too] stark a disjunction of them, too radical a transition from nature to freedom or from the phenomenal to the noumenal world, renders idle the entire project ... which was precisely to attempt to bridge that gap.[40]

Kant did not satisfactorily address these issues, and in order for me to do so it will be necessary to offer conjectures that occasionally go beyond his texts. But before we gloat too much at the breakdown of the critical philosopher's system, we should remind ourselves that these problems are by no means peculiar to Kant. Versions of them will be present in every account of human action that rejects determinism, and even deterministic theories cannot escape the problem of the deep-rooted contestability of empirical knowledge claims concerning human nature and culture.

Why Impure Ethics?

> True philosophy . . . has to follow the diversity and manifoldness
> of matter through all time.
>
> *Physische Georgraphie*

> High towers and metaphysically great men resembling them,
> around both of which there is commonly much wind, are not for
> me. My place is the fruitful *bathos* of experience.
>
> *Prolegomena zu einer jeden künftigen Metaphysik*

Every student of Kant is familiar with his defense of pure ethics. The absolute necessity and strict universality that are characteristic features of moral judgment cannot be derived from experience and must therefore "have their source completely a priori in pure, but practical, reason" (*Gr* 4:408; see also 4:389, 425; *KrV* B 4, B 124, A 112, A 547/B 575). "Only that whose certainty is apodictic can be called real science [*eigentliche Wissenschaft*]" (*MAN* 4:468). The apodictic certainty required by true science cannot be achieved via empirical principles. Ethics and physics pass the litmus test of apodicity; chemistry and psychology (not to mention the biological sciences) all fail (*Gr* 4:388–89; *MAN* 4:468, 471; cf. *KrV* B 152, A 343, A 848/B 876).[41] Ethics requires a normative standard or touchstone, by means of which "one must test the moral content of every action" (*KpV* 5:155). Appeals to nature or cultural traditions may constitute an accurate causal explanation of how standards find their way into society, but such accounts are unable to address satisfactorily the normative status of these standards (cf. *MdS* 6:229–30; *Gr* 4:308; *KrV* B 373, *Collins* 27:333). Finally, the sense of freedom on which the possibility of ethics is based "is no concept of experience [*kein Erfahrungsbegriff*], and also cannot be one" (*Gr* 4:455). Freedom is "the condition of the moral law" (*KpV* 5:4), but it remains "the stumbling block for all *empiricists*" (5:7). For the sense of freedom necessary for ethics is transcendental—"independent of empirical conditions (i.e., those belonging to the world of sense)" (5:29).

But what is the rationale for the second part of Kant's ethics? Why is impure ethics necessary and important? There has been very little discussion of this latter issue. However, on Kant's view there are compelling claims to be made on behalf of empirical ethics, as follows.

A Propaedeutic to the Moral Life

Human beings, to a much greater degree than other animals, require enormous expenditures of care, nurture, training, enculturation, and education in order to develop their capacities. As Kant announces (with perhaps an excusable amount of excited professorial overstatement) in the opening sentence of his *Lectures on Pedagogy*: "The human being is the only creature that must be educated" (9:441). He stretches the point even further when he proclaims a few pages later that the human being "can only become human through education. He is nothing except what education makes of him" (9:443). Similarly, human morality itself is held to grow out of political, cultural, religious, and educational institutions: "by nature man is not a moral being at all" (9:492). Rather, "the idea of morality belongs to [gehört . . . zur] culture" (Idee 8:26). Cultural formation (or what the Germans call Bildung) cannot guarantee morality on Kant's view, for morality is not simply a causal product of nature and/or society. "We live in a time of disciplinary training, culture, and civilization, but not by any means in a time of moralization [Moralisierung]" (Päd 9:451; cf. Refl 1460, 15:641). A person can be highly cultured but still immoral. But human morality does presuppose a sufficiently developed, inter-connected web of cultural institutions as a necessary condition for its own presence: "The human being is destined by his reason to be in a society with human beings and in it to cultivate himself, to civilize himself, and to moralize himself through [durch] the arts and sciences" (Anth 7:324). The most difficult step in this journey, one which humanity has yet to take, is "the crossing-over [Übergang] from civilization to moralization" (Starke II, 124; cf. 125). Human beings cannot instantly pick up a priori moral principles and make moral judgments and decisions by means of them. They need first to learn what counts as a moral problem, what sorts of situations in human life are most liable to raise moral issues, which features of human action require moral attention and which do not, and so on.

One reason why practical anthropology is important is that it serves as a necessary propaedeutic or introduction to the moral life. In an early summary of his physical geography and anthropology lecture courses, Kant characterizes them both as constituting "the preliminary exercise in the knowledge of the world" (Racen 2:443 n; cf. Anth 7:119–20, Geo 9:158–59). This knowledge of the world (Weltkenntis) has two parts, "namely nature and the human being," and both parts must be treated "cosmologically," that is, not as narrow, self-contained sciences of physics and psychology, but rather synthetically and inter-disciplinarily in terms of "what their relationship is in the whole in which they stand and in which each has its own position." Such knowledge is also to be viewed pragmatically—"useful not only for school but for life"; so that the student will be "introduced to the stage of his destiny, namely the world" (2:443 n; cf. Menschenkunde 25:853–54).

In Kant's anthropology lectures, the human component of Weltkenntnis is understandably stressed. For instance, in the preface to his Anthropology from a Pragmatic Point of View (the manual for his course that Kant himself published in 1798), he states that knowledge of the world "is not properly called pragmatic when it is an extensive knowledge of things in the world—for example, the animals, plants and minerals of various lands and climates—but only when it is knowledge of man as a citizen of the world" (7:120). In other versions of these lectures, he is even more blunt: "The human being knows the world, that is, he knows human beings in all status groups [Stände]. Knowledge of the world in the usual sense means knowledge of the human being" (Menschenkunde 25:854). Surprisingly, even in his Geography lectures, this emphasis on knowledge of human beings rather than mere nature is declared to be essential: "[W]hen it is said of this or that person that he knows the world, it is understood that he knows both the human being and nature" (9:158). "There is no greater or more important investigation for the human being than knowledge of the human being" (Pillau 25:733).

Within the world-knowledge that human beings need to learn will be specific kinds of moral knowledge concerning human beings and their social environments. Human beings cannot simply jump unaided into pure ethics; background knowledge of their own empirical situation is a necessary prerequisite. This necessary empirical background for moral judgment has been well described by Barbara Herman in her discussion of "rules of moral salience." Such rules, she writes, are acquired

> as elements in a moral education, [and] they structure an agent's perception of his situation so that what he perceives is a world with moral features. They enable him to pick out those elements of his circumstances or of his proposed actions that require moral attention. . . . Typically they are acquired in childhood as part of socialization; they provide a practical framework within which people act. . . . The rules of moral salience constitute the structure of moral sensitivity.[42]

Obviously, not all world-knowledge will constitute empirical moral knowledge (just as not all socialization is moral socialization). But many examples of world-knowledge that appear to be non-moral can suddenly acquire moral significance when placed in the right circumstances. If "morality is *pervasive,* in the sense that no voluntary human action is in principle resistant to moral assessment,"[43] then human moral agents cannot always confidently determine in advance which aspects of their *Weltkenntnis* might turn out to be relevant to a moral issue.

A Propaedeutic to Moral Science

Closely related to the previous argument is the claim that the conceptual tools of pure ethics are of little use unless and until agents possess empirical knowledge of situations and contexts to which they are to be applied. Conceptually and logically speaking, ethics on Kant's view is grounded in the a priori principles provided by the pure part of ethical theory. But when viewed temporally, from the perspective of human cognitive development, it is actually empirical ethics that must come first. In this sense, practical anthropology also serves as a necessary background to the science of pure ethics. Moral agents (including philosophers) must first have a solid sense of the empirical situations and circumstances of human beings before they are in a position to apply effectively a priori moral theory. This is merely an acknowledgment of the facts of human cognitive development, or what Kant calls "the natural progress of human knowledge":

> first of all, the understanding develops by using experience to arrive at intuitive judgments, and by this means arrives at concepts. After that, these concepts come to be known in relation to their grounds and consequences through reason. Finally, by means of science, these concepts come to be known as parts of a well-ordered whole. This being the case, teaching must follow exactly the same path. (*Nachricht* 2:305)

Similarly, Herman, in her discussion of rules of moral salience, also points out that "unless agents have some moral understanding of their actions *before* [my emphasis] they use" the categorical imperative procedure, the categorical imperative itself "cannot be an effective practical principle of judgment."[44]

Material Content

Empirical ethics provides the bulk of the content or material for the form of pure ethics. Just as "thoughts without content are empty" (*KrV* A 51/B 75), so pure ethics without practical anthropology is severely deficient. Not entirely empty, for, as noted earlier, we do get important noncontingent content from pure moral principles concerning (e.g.) the dignity of rational agency; and this content does have numerous implications for how moral agents are to treat one another. But contrary to received opinion, it is definitely not Kant's view that a priori truths alone give us sufficient content for the details of human ethics. Again, as he declares at the beginning of his *Collins* lectures, the study of "practical philosophy without anthropology, or without knowledge of the subject . . . is merely speculative, or an idea [*eine Idee*]; the human being must therefore at least be studied later on" (27:244).

Completion of the System

The pure part of ethics gives us noncontingent foundations, but in order to complete the system of ethical knowledge we need to bring in the material content provided by practical anthropology. At the same time, the material content must be brought in under the guidance of "the idea" (cf. the preceding quotation from *Collins*) provided by pure ethics: otherwise we have a mere aggregate rather than a coherent system. As Kant states in the introduction to his *Geography* lectures:

> we have to know the objects of our experience as a whole so that our knowledge does not form an aggregate but rather a system; in a system it is the whole that comes before the parts, whereas in an aggregate the parts are first. . . . The idea [*Die Idee*] is architectonic; it creates the sciences. For example, he who wants to build a house first creates for himself an idea of the whole, from which all the parts will be derived. So our present preparation is an idea of the knowledge of the world. Here we make for ourselves in a similar way an architectonic concept, which is a concept wherein the manifold is derived from the whole. (9:158; cf. *KrV* A 832/B 860)

In each of his three best-known ethical works, Kant cautions readers that he is presenting only a small part of the system of ethics. At the conclusion of the preface to the *Groundwork*, for instance, he sharply delimits his project by stating that it is intended as "nothing more than the seeking out and establishing of *the supreme principle of morality*" and that "the application of the principle to the whole system" must be reserved for another occasion (4:392). In the *Critique of Practical Reason*, he reminds readers that the limited task of a *critique* of practical reason is to give "an account of the principles of the possibility of duty, of its extent and limits, without particular reference to human nature" (*KpV* 5:8). To offer a classification of the moral duties of human beings is possible only if the human being "is known in his actual nature," a task which belongs "to the system of science, not to the system of criticism" (5:8). As noted earlier in this chapter ("Determination of moral duties for 'human beings as such'"), this goal of providing a complete classification of the moral duties of human beings "as such" is pursued in the *Metaphysics of Morals*. However, due to the limited amount of empirical information allowed into that work, Kant notes at several points that his system of ethics still remains incomplete in this later work as well. In the preface he cautions readers that "the system itself cannot be expected, but only an approximation" when the metaphysical first principles (*Anfangsgründe*) are applied to specific cases (*MdS* 6:205). And toward the end, when he briefly raises (alas, without pursuing) the more specific empirical questions of how people "should be treated in accordance with differences in rank, age, sex, health, prosperity or poverty, and so forth," he states that the answers to these questions "cannot be presented as sections of ethics and members of the *division* of a system (which must proceed *a priori* from a rational concept), but can only be appended to the system. Yet even this application belongs to the completeness of the presentation of the system" (6:469).

While there exists an unresolved tension here between "the demand of reason for complete systematic unity" (*KrV* A 840/B 868) on the one hand and the recognition of the ultimately unsystematic character of experience once one reaches its more radically contingent and particular aspects on the other ("*what is empirical* cannot be divided completely"—*MdS* 6:205), the point with which we began still holds: in order to complete the system of ethics, practical anthropology must be brought in. Realistically speaking, only a partial rather than complete unity is feasible. But anthropology is necessary for this more modest and attainable unity as well.[45]

The Second Part

As noted at the beginning of this discussion, the major division within theory that Kant makes is that between its pure and empirical parts (cf. *KrV* A 840/B 868; *Gr* 4:388; *MAN* 4:469–70; *Geo* 9:156). Although this division between pure and empirical does not originate with Kant, he certainly has no wish to alter or demolish it. Ethics, like physics, "will have its empirical part" (*Gr* 4:388). And while subsequent philosophers (particularly those who count themselves as his followers) have not always followed Kant in this respect, he regards empirical studies as having an important and necessary place in his work as a moral philosopher. Obviously, Kant urges us to start with the pure, but it is wrong to infer from this that the subsequent move to the impure is not important or necessary. His own conception of the structure or major division of theory already implies a commitment to empirical ethics. All sciences have pure as well as empirical components, ethics included.

The Progress of the Power of Judgment

Agents need moral anthropology throughout the course of their lives in order to continually sharpen and refine their powers of judgment. In the preface to the *Groundwork*, Kant remarks that a priori moral laws always require "a power of judgment sharpened by experience" for their application (4:389). Though one searches in vain throughout his writings for a detailed account of practical judgment, it is clear that one of the primary tasks of moral anthropology is to strengthen agents' powers of judgment. It does this by organizing and presenting relevant aspects of human experience to agents to reflect on under controlled circumstances. For instance, in its educative role practical anthropology provides a moral catechism to students so that they may begin to exercise their moral judgment "by comparing similar actions under various circumstances and marking the greater or lesser moral significance of them" (*KpV* 5:154). When carried out properly, such a catechism enables students to "feel the progress of their power of judgment," thus laying "a good foundation for uprightness in the future course of life" (5:154–55). Here as elsewhere, an informed theory of empirical cognitive development lies behind Kant's theory of moral education:

> [T]he understanding must be brought to maturity and its growth expedited by exercising it in experiential judgments [*Erfahrungsurtheilen*] and focusing its attention on what it can learn by comparing the impressions which are furnished by the senses. It ought not to venture any bold leap from these judgments or concepts to higher and more remote ones. (*Nachricht* 2:306)

But the progress of the power of judgment is not something that ends with the emergence of adulthood. On the contrary, we call judgment "the understanding that comes only with age, that is based on one's own long experience" (*Anth* 7:199; cf. *KrV* A 133–34/B 172–73). Even after agents have ventured on to "higher and more remote" moral concepts, they must still continually apply them to concrete situations. And since principles cannot be self-deploying but always require judgment for their application, ethics itself "falls into a casuistry" (*MdS* 6:411), that is, methods for improving one's judgment of particular cases are always needed.[46]

Bridging the Gap between Nature and Freedom

For adults, moral anthropology also contributes to the progress of their powers of judgment in a more comprehensive way. The *Weltkenntnis* provided by pragmatic anthropology and geography gives agents relevant empirical knowledge of the field in which their future moral endeavors are to take place—"the stage of [our] destination, namely the world" (*Racen* 2:443n.) In this broader role, the precepts of moral anthropology contribute to the larger project of effecting a bridge or crossing (*Übergang*) from nature to freedom via judgment (*KU* 5:195) and of helping to insure that the concept of freedom is successful in "actualizing in the sensible world the end given by its laws" (*KU* 5:176).

Empirical ethics seeks to contribute to this ambitious bridging effort between nature and freedom by giving us accurate, empirical knowledge of who and what we are.[47] It helps promote this bridging effort in four distinct ways. First, empirical ethics provides human beings with an accurate empirical framework of the field or horizon in which their moral endeavors are to take place, primarily by developing biological and psychological knowledge concerning human nature that highlights species-specific obstacles and advantages to acting on moral principle (in Kant's words, "the subjective conditions in human nature that hinder human beings or help them in the *carrying out* of the laws of a metaphysics of morals" [*MdS* 6:217]). Second, on the wider cultural front, moral anthropology helps "to prepare human beings for a sovereignty in which reason alone shall have authority" (*KU* 5:433) through exposure to the arts and sciences, which themselves are instrumental to the establishment of morality. And third, in its educative role, empirical ethics enables agents to "feel the progress of their power of judgment" by presenting controlled opportunities for moral reflection which are framed by an accurate understanding of human development. Finally, in its connection to Kant's philosophy of history, empirical ethics helps provide a long-term orientation for human action by highlighting the path to moral progress and by showing us what specific steps need to be taken in order to reshape the natural world to fit moral demands.

Fields of Impurity

As noted earlier in this chapter ("Tracking Kant's Impure Ethics") a serious *textual* problem confronts anyone who sets out to understand his empirical ethics. Despite Kant's frequent references to and justifications of the necessity and importance of moral anthropology, he never brings to completion or even systematically develops the second part of his ethics. There exists no one central text to which we can turn in order to find out his views about it. Furthermore, those Kantian texts that intelligent readers might think would contain detailed discussions of moral anthropology or empirical ethics often do not.

The interpretive strategy I adopt in this work is therefore multi-textual. The idea is to look at the major fields or regions within the Kantian corpus that are relevant to empirical ethics, examining them specifically from the perspective of impure ethics and Kant's own self-declared division of practical philosophy. Because this side of Kant's ethics has not been previously studied in detail and occasionally involves texts that have not been yet been translated into English, the investigation often involves extensive citations from his texts. This is necessary both to allow Kant speak for himself and to offer readers sufficient data to form their own views concerning the contours and content of Kant's impure ethics. The hoped-for result is a much fuller and more systematic portrait of empirical ethics than Kant himself offered in any one text, but one that nevertheless is constrained by his own writings as well as those of students and auditors of his classroom lectures.

In the second part of this study, I critically examine the following central fields of Kant's impure ethics. While these fields do not exhaust the content of impure ethics, they do represent the major areas or subdivisions within it about which Kant himself wrote in some detail.

Education

In the *Metaphysics of Morals*, Kant briefly sketches the "counterpart of a metaphysics of morals, the other member of the division of practical philosophy as a whole" (6:217) before proceeding on his metaphysical way. This other member, "moral anthropology,"

> would deal only with the subjective conditions in human nature that hinder human beings or help them in *carrying out* [*die Ausführung*] the laws of a metaphysics of morals. It would deal with the development, spreading, and strengthening of moral principles (in education in schools and in popular instruction), and with other similar teachings and precepts based on experience. (6:217)

Although Kant briefly mentions anthropology on three other occasions in this work (6:385, 406, 477), this passage is unfortunately his most detailed comment on moral anthropology within this particular text. But as this passage indicates, his actual description of the kinds of questions addressed by moral anthropology suggests strongly that a more likely place to look for further details about it would be in his educational writings. These consist chiefly of the *Lectures on Pedagogy* (9:437–99—edited by his former student Friedrich Theodor Rink and published in 1803, the year before Kant died); two short essays on the Philanthropinum Academy (2:445–52); the "Announcement of the Program of his Lectures in the Winter Semester 1765–66" (2:303–13); the "Methodenlehre" sections of the second *Critique* (5:149–163) as well as the *Metaphysics of Morals* (6:475–85); and occasional informal discussions of pedagogy in other lectures (e.g., *Logik Pölitz* 24:599–602; *Friedländer* 25:722–28).

In addition to linking up with certain aspects of the anthropology lectures, Kant's educational writings, as Lewis White Beck has convincingly argued, often overlap with his essays on the philosophy of history.[48] This particular example of intertextual connection is one of many that exist within Kant's impure ethics, and constitutes an additional reason for approaching the topic from a variety of texts. These intertextual relationships are also exploited in the following discussion.

Anthropology

The term "anthropology" occurs in the vast majority of Kant's references to the empirical part of his project in ethics. Sometimes his preferred phrase is "moral anthropology" (*MdS* 6:217; *Moral Mrongovius II* 29:599); sometimes "practical anthropology" (*Gr* 4:388); sometimes simply "anthropology" (*Gr* 4:412; *MdS* 6:385, 406; *Moralphilosophie Collins* 27:244; *Moral Mrongovius I* 27:1398). This frequent use of term "anthropology" in Kant's discussions of the second part of his ethics suggests that the most obvious source of information concerning it should be his anthropology writings. These consist chiefly of the manual for his anthropology course that Kant himself published himself in 1798, *Anthropologie in pragmatischer Hinsicht* (7:119–333); numerous student and auditor versions of his anthropology lectures dating from the early 1770s to the mid 1790s;[49] the abundant *Reflexionen zur Anthropologie* (vol. 15 of the Academy edition); portions of his early work *Observations on the Feeling of the Beautiful and the Sublime* (2:207–56); the essays on race (2:427–43; 8: 89–106, 159–84); and those portions of the *Lectures on Physical Geography* dealing with human beings (9:153–436; esp. 9:311–20).

However, one central weakness of the material on anthropology (when viewed from the perspective of empirical ethics) is that one finds very little detailed discussion of *moral* anthropology in it. In the version that Kant himself published in 1798, he says that anthropology "can adopt either a *physiological* or a *pragmatic* point of view. Physiological knowledge of the human being concerns the investigation of what *nature* makes of him; pragmatic of what *the human being* as a free-acting being makes, or can and should [*soll*] make of himself" (*Anth* 7:119). This pragmatic "*soll*," while clearly a normative notion, is nevertheless not quite a categorical moral "ought." In versions of Kant's anthropology lectures published by other writers, this same emphasis on pragmatic rather than specifically moral anthropology pervades. For instance, in Starke's edition from the winter semester of 1790–91, Kant begins by stating that anthropology "can be treated scholastically and pragmatically. Scholastic anthropology concerns what the human being is; pragmatic anthropology, on the other hand, concerns how one can use human beings according to our intentions" (Starke II, 1; see also *Pillau* 25:733). And in the first set of lectures edited by Starke, entitled *Immanuel Kant's Menschenkunde oder philosophische Anthropologie* Kant states that

> knowledge of the human being is twofold: speculative knowledge of the human being makes us skillful [*geschickt*], and is treated in psychology and physiology. But practical knowledge of the human being makes us prudent [*klug*]; it is the kind of knowledge where one human being has influence on another, and can lead him according to his purpose. (25:855; for similar definitions of "pragmatic" and "prudence," see *Gr* 4:416 n, 417 n)

Ironically, some of the most specific statements concerning *moral* anthropology within a Kantian context are to be found not in Kant's own texts but in works written by contemporaries who seek to explain Kantian anthropology to the general reader. For instance, A. F. M. Willich, in *Elements of the Critical Philosophy*, one of the first English-language accounts of Kant's philosophy and based in part on the author's own experience as an auditor of Kant's lectures "between the years 1778 and 1781 . . . and . . . again in summer 1792," subdivides Kant's anthropology into theoretical and practical branches. "Anthropology," Willich writes,

> signifies in general the experimental doctrine of the nature of man; and is divided by Kant, into 1) *theoretical* or empirical doctrine of the mind, which is a branch of Natural Philosophy; 2) *practical* applied, and empirical Philosophy of Morals; Ethics—the consideration of the moral law in relation to the human will, its inclinations, motives, and to the obstacles in practicing that law.[50]

Similarly, both Georg Samuel Albert Mellin and Carl Christian Erhard Schmid, authors of two early German Kant dictionaries designed to make the critical philosophy accessible to a wider audience, subdivide Kant's anthropology into theoretical and practical, and describe the practical component in strongly moral terms. (For citations and discussion, see the subsection "Anthropology and Ethics" in "Which Anthropology?" chapter 3.) Accordingly, a key task in this part of my study is to extricate the specifically *moral* dimension of Kantian anthropology from its looser pragmatic neighbor. Because the concept of anthropology appears so frequently in Kant's descriptions of the second part of his ethics, and also because an abundance of Kantian texts on anthropology are now available, I will also explore this particular field of impurity at greater length than the others.

Art and Religion

Kant's educational and anthropological writings, though relatively neglected by Kant scholars, form the two most direct sources for the second part of his ethics. His writings on art and religion (chiefly *KV* 5:167–485 and *Rel* (6:3–202) together constitute a third important source for his impure ethics. These writings are treated together in this study because in each of them we find strongly analogous arguments concerning human beings' need both for graspable symbols of morality and for institutional and cultural preparatory steps for moral community. Philosophers have paid increased attention to these two important areas of Kant's work in recent years, often in ways that shed much light on their moral dimensions. My aim is not to duplicate this scholarship but rather to examine only selected aspects of his writings on art and religion from the standpoint of "the other member of the division of practical philosophy." How do the writings on art and religion add further content to the second part of ethics? What specific moral themes are addressed in these writings which involve empirical assumptions concerning human nature? To what extent are there relevant materials in the aesthetic and religious works which add further coherence and vindication to the project of Kantian moral anthropology?

History

Finally, a fourth important source exists within his writings on history. For the most part, these writings consist of informal essays written between the mid-1780s and mid-1790s, and are contained in volume 8 of the Academy Edition.[51] In recent years Kant's work in the philosophy of history has also received increased scholarly attention. However, it remains the case that the specifically moral dimension of this side of his work is still contested and not well understood. My aim here is to examine Kant's writings on history from the perspective of his empirical ethics. What precepts based on experience concerning human cultures and political societies do we find in these writings that bear directly on empirical ethics? In what ways do these precepts add further content to the second half of his project in ethics? In particular, how do the writings on history shed further light on the ambitious project of establishing an *Übergang* between nature and freedom?

This division of impure ethics into four fields of inquiry, though by no means artificial or ad hoc, should not be construed too rigidly. Again, these regions are interconnected in numerous ways. Also, they should be construed not as exhausting the content of empirical ethics, but simply as representing the major areas within Kant's works where he pursues in some detail questions and themes relating to impure ethics.

Saved by Impurity?

The third and final part of this study reassesses briefly Kant's ethical theory from the more inclusionary standpoint of his empirical ethics. What are the chief strengths and weakness of Kant's ethics, once the two divisions of his practical philosophy project are considered together? Where does the addition of this second part of his ethics leave us in terms of his own system? What does a fully developed Kantian moral system actually look like, and what fundamental assumptions and implications concerning the nature and goals of moral theory are embedded in it? In particular, what are Kant's considered views on the kinds of help that a fully developed moral theory can and should offer to moral deliberators? To what extent is Kant's ethics (and to what extent are we) saved by impurity?

II

Fields of Impurity

2

EDUCATION

Education as Impure Ethics

Pedagogy is the systematic guidance of the individual toward virtue; that is, its aim is to make him capable of the fulfillment of his ethical tasks.

Leonard Nelson, *System der philosophischen Ethik und Pädagogik* (1932)

As noted earlier, in *The Metaphysics of Morals* Kant describes the second part of practical philosophy, "moral anthropology," as dealing with "the development, spreading, and strengthening of moral principles (in education in schools and in popular instruction), and with similar teachings and precepts based on experience" (6:217). This description of the sorts of questions moral anthropology is to address gives the second part of ethics a pronounced pedagogical flavor, and suggests also that a likely place to look for details concerning Kant's impure ethics is in his writings on education.[1]

Kant's major work on education is a set of lectures entitled *Über Pädagogik* (*On Pedagogy*), edited by a former student named Friedrich Theodor Rink and first published in 1803, the year before Kant died. Before I examine the importance of this text for Kant's impure ethics, a few brief remarks concerning a longstanding controversy regarding its origins are in order.

Rink notes in his preface that the text's origins stem from a lecture course on pedagogy that the philosophy department at the University of Königsberg, "according to an old decree," was required to offer as well as to rotate among its faculty (9:439). According to Emil Arnoldt, Kant taught this particular course four times in his career (winter 1776–77, summer 1780, winter 1783–84, and winter 1786–87).[2] However, the text itself has struck many readers over the years as being extremely untypical and almost un-Kantian in its lax organization, occasionally conflicting classifications and definitions, and overall rough feel.[3] This in turn has led to numerous scholarly suspicions concerning the origins and authenticity of the text. The most detailed study of the problem is Traugott Weisskopf's *Immanuel Kant und die Pädagogik* (1970). Weisskopf's book runs 704 pages, which, when one considers the fact that Kant's pedagogy lectures themselves only fill up 58 pages in the Academy Edition, is quite an achievement. Nevertheless, he develops several important hypotheses that are intended to account for the book's unsystematic appearance, in addition to painstakingly surveying nearly all previous scholarly work on the text since the publication of the first edition in 1803.

Weisskopf believes that Rink's edition is in fact a compilation culled from three different Kantian sources originally written at different times and for different purposes: (1) fragments from a set of Kant's lectures on ethics, (2) sketches for his anthropology lecture course, and (3) personal notes on (and in some cases excerpts from) Rousseau's *Emile*.[4] Additionally, Weisskopf is quite critical of Rink's editing work, surmising that Rink "stylistically reworked almost every section of the text," acting on his own discretion to make the different parts fit together into a whole.[5]

However, as Weisskopf himself admits, all such conjectures are unfortunately doomed to remain "*immer hypothetisch.*"[6] No one has yet come up with the original manuscript(s?) from Kant's own hand on which Rink's text was based, and at this late date it seems a safe bet to assert that no one ever will. Furthermore, unlike the situation that exists with, say, Kant's much more frequently taught ethics and anthropology lecture courses, we lack even copies of student or auditor notebooks that profess to record his lectures and that could serve as a valuable control on overly imaginative interpretive hypotheses. As noted earlier, Kant taught the pedagogy course only four times. On the other hand, Arnoldt estimates that Kant taught ethics twenty-nine times,[7] and Kant himself writes in the preface to his *Anthropology* that he gave a lecture course on anthropology "for some thirty years" each winter semester (7:122 n). Because so many more people heard his ethics and anthropology lectures than did his pedagogy lectures, the paper trail is understandably much longer in the former cases.

Weisskopf's scholarship is impressive, and the careful and detailed documentation he provides in his work is an invaluable resource for all readers with serious interests in Kant's *Lectures on Pedagogy*. However, I do not think that the existence of allegedly parallel passages or positions (*Parallelstellen*) between *Über Pädagogik* and Kant's lectures on ethics and anthropology in itself constitutes a good reason for doubting the authenticity of the *Pädagogik*. There is a much simpler and more plausible hypothesis for explaining such similarities in his writings.

It is highly likely that Kant, like other busy professors before and since, occasionally used some of the same lecture note materials for more than one course when he thought it was appropriate to do so. Kant's normal teaching load was an astounding fourteen hours a week, with his first lectures often beginning at seven o'clock in the morning. Very few contemporary American (or German) philosophy professors have such heavy teaching loads. Given his work schedule alone, it would be quite understandable if he did not always present entirely new material for each class.[8]

Also, since the publication of Weisskopf's study in 1970, many new and significant versions of Kant's ethics and anthropology lectures have been published in the Academy Edition.[9] These materials, which were not available to Weisskopf, present even more textual grist for the scholarly mill. His long-winded attempts to establish *Parallelstellen* between Kant's lectures on education and those on ethics and anthropology (cf. n .4) are superseded by these newer materials.

Finally, and most importantly, even if one were to accept Weisskopf's creative conjecture concerning the trinitarian sources of the *Pädagogik*, this does not at all mean that the work is inauthentic in the sense of not coming from Kant himself. For each alleged source tracks back to Kant's own hand. As Lewis White Beck writes, in "Kant on Education:"

> It seems to me, however, that Weisskopf has proved too much for his own purpose. In fact, he has shown very good reason to take *Über die Pädagogik* [sic] seriously as a compendium of *echt-kantische* views on education, even if we cannot be confident that we are reading Kant's words and can be generally confident that we are not reading them in an order and context established by Kant himself.[10]

Although everyone wishes that Rink had exercised more care and precision in editing Kant's notes,[11] there is nothing that can be done about it now. Since the appearance of Rink's edition in 1803, editors of subsequent editions of the *Pädagogik* have occasionally tried to second-guess him, rearranging the text according to their own lights in order to produce something that is allegedly closer to what Kant would have "really" wanted.[12] But at this point each alteration in the text is likely to take us only further from Kant's original intentions.[13] While no informed reader regards Rink's editing work as faultless, the most prudent approach to Kant's *Lectures on Pedagogy* is still via Rink's original 1803 edition.[14]

Let me end this brief discussion of the background of Kant's *Pedagogy* on a more positive note. The text (literally) does not stand entirely on its own. Many important points raised in it link up directly with doctrines examined not only in Kant's anthropology and ethics lectures, but also in his writings on history and elsewhere. This basic fact, which is well supported by Weisskopf's extensive *Parallelstellen* argument, fits very well with my own approach to Kant's writings on education, for it is simply a different way of stating that Kant's education is part of a larger inter-connected web of anthropological, moral, and historical concerns. These intertextual links should definitely be exploited in interpreting Kant's philosophy of education. Also, it is important to keep in mind that *Über Pädagogik* is not Kant's only text on education. Also relevant are the *Methodenlehre* sections of the second *Critique* and the *Metaphysics of Morals*, the two short essays on the Philanthropinum academy, and the early *Nachricht* from 1765.[15] Occasional reference to these and other authentic texts of Kant's (where critics have not dragged questions of authorship into the debate) can serve as insurance against Rink's possible distortions. And since, as noted earlier, Kant at one point in effect declares pedagogy to be "the counterpart of a metaphysics of morals" (*MdS* 6:217), ultimately his education writings need to understood within the larger context of his ethical theory. Kant's educational theory is best read as a chapter within his larger applied ethics project, where "applied" means studying human nature and culture empirically in order to find out which aids and obstacles exist for the species as a whole[16] to the carrying out of a priori moral principles. At the same time, *Über Pädagogik* is a compact (albeit not always thoroughly consistent), authentic, and eminently graspable compendium of Kant's view on education. For readers who know Kant only as the author of the *Critique of Pure Reason* and other easy-reading classics and who wish to examine firsthand some of his views about education, the *Pedagogy* is a breath of fresh air. And it is still today a central but under-explored entrée into Kant's impure ethics, its textual and editing warts notwithstanding.

Rousseauian Roots

Philosophers and intellectuals in late eighteenth century Europe, unlike their late twentieth century American counterparts, were very serious about the philosophy of education. Many of the most influential thinkers of the day put forward original and well-received theories concerning the nature and aims of education and the need for fundamental reform[17] within existing educational institutions. Rousseau's *Emile* (1762) is the most celebrated example here, and because Kant's *Pädagogik* does owe serious debts to it, a brief summary of its leading themes is in order.

A large part of the appeal of *Emile* lay in its proto-Romantic glorification of nature. At the beginning of book 1 Rousseau announces: "Everything is good as it leaves the hands of the Author of things; everything degenerates in the hand of man. . . . [Man] disfigures everything; he loves deformity, monsters. He wants nothing as nature made it; not even man; for him, man must be trained like a school horse."[18]

A second major theme is what has come to be known as a "child-centered" approach to education. In the preface he writes:

> Childhood is unknown. Starting from the false idea one has of it, the farther one goes, the more one loses one's way. The wisest men concentrate on what it is important for men to know without considering what children are in a condition to learn. They are always seeking the man in the child without thinking of what he is before being a man. This is the study to which I have most applied myself.[19]

And once childhood is known, adults are admonished not only to respect it but also to love it: "Respect childhood, and do not hurry to judge it, either for good or for ill. . . . Love childhood; promote its games, its pleasures, its amiable instinct."[20]

Third, there is a sustained plea for freedom and "negative education" throughout the book: "All our practices are only subjection, impediment, and constraint. Civil man is born, lives, and dies in slavery. At his birth he is sewed in swaddling clothes; at his death he is nailed in a coffin. So long as he keeps his human shape, he is enchained by our institutions."[21] The resultant advice concerning negative education is a qualified "hands off" appeal: Let the child develop naturally; intervene only in cases where he[22] may harm himself. "The first education," Rousseau recommends, "ought to be purely negative. It consists not at all in teaching virtue or truth but in securing the heart from vice and mind from error. . . . Exercise his body, his organs, his senses, his strength, but keep his soul idle for as long as possible. . . . Let childhood ripen in children."[23]

While it is admittedly difficult to imagine Kant the stern Prussian agreeing with some of this advice, the fact is that on several points he is surprisingly close. Let me summarize the points of agreement in reverse order. Concerning negative education, Kant states: "In general it should be observed that the first stage of education must be merely negative, that is, one should not add some new provision to that of nature, but merely leave nature undisturbed" (9:459).[24] And of the freedom that provides the rationale for negative education, he notes: "From earliest childhood the child must be allowed to be free in all matters (except in those where it might injure itself)" (9:454).

At the same time, Kant's perspective is less child-centered than Rousseau's, at least in the sense that his endorsement of the allegedly nonstop pleasures of childhood is more restrained. The following more Teutonic-sounding passage brings this out clearly: "The child should play, it should have its hours of recreation, but it must also learn to work" (9:470). Still, the more developmental let-kids-be-kids approach that follows from the effort to take seriously the cognitive differences between children and adults is clearly present in Kant's *Pedagogy*: "Children must be taught only those things that are suitable to their age" (9:485).

Finally, as concerns the glorification of nature, Kant here is also a bit more restrained than Rousseau, though a hint of the same Weltanschauung is clearly detectable: "All artificial devices . . . are so much the more detrimental in that they run contrary to the end of nature in an organized, rational being, according to which it must retain the freedom to learn to use its powers. Education should only prevent children from becoming soft" (9:463).

Rousseau's new thoughts on education strongly influenced not only Kant but also other celebrated German educational theorists of the day such as J. B. Basedow (1723–90)[25] and his fellow Philanthropinists J. H. Campe (1746–1818) and G. H. Wolke (1741–1825), as well as later writers such as J. H. Pestalozzi (1746–1827) and F. Froebel (1782–1852). However, all these educational reformers (with the important exception of Basedow and the Philanthropinists)[26] focused primarily on developing individuality in the student. What is most distinctive about Kant's own philosophy of education is what may be termed its *species perfectionism*, that is, its claim that the ultimate objective of education is to advance not the welfare of the individual student but rather the moral perfection of the human species as a whole.[27]

To be sure, a robust sense of confidence in human moral progress is a defining feature of Enlightenment thought—one finds abundant examples of it in the writings of (e.g.) Condorcet (1743–94), Priestley (1733–1804), and Franklin (1706–90).[28] And closer to Kant (that is, on German soil) there is an important work of Lessing (1729–81), *The Education of the Human Race* (1780). While it is more directly theological than Kant's educational writings, there are obvious parallels. Toward the end Lessing proclaims:

> No, it will come, it will definitely come, the time of perfection, when the human being, the more convinced his understanding feels about an ever better future, will nevertheless not need to borrow motives [*Bewegungsgründe*] for his actions from this future; for he will do the good [*das Gute*] because it is good, not because arbitrary rewards are set upon it.[29]

As an *Aufklärer* Kant is definitely a part of this overly optimistic spirit. Nevertheless, as I show later, the critical role of education in the moral perfection of the human species is more deeply etched in his philosophy of education than in any other work of the eighteenth century.

The Stages of Education

Keeping this Rousseauian background in mind, and with an eye toward ethics, let us now look briefly at the main components and tasks of education as presented by Kant in the *Pädagogik*.

First, two general observations: (1) Kant's remarks about education are often framed in an intra-species context—one that enables him to emphasize both allegedly species-specific aspects of human nature and the species-wide scope of education. For instance, he is extremely fond of asserting that other creatures on earth do not require any education whatsoever. The opening sentence in *Über Pädagogik* reads: "The human being is the only creature that must be educated" (9:441). In the Starke anthropology lectures from 1790–91 he softens this exaggeration only slightly by stating: "The human being is, apart from songbirds, who must learn songs from their parents, the only animal that must be educated" (Starke II, 120; cf. *Anth* 7:323, *Päd* 9:443). And he occasionally speculates that other rational beings elsewhere may not need any education at all. In a footnote to the "Idea for a Universal History" we read: "How it may be with the inhabitants of other planets and their nature, we do not know. . . . It may perhaps be that among them every individual completely fulfills his destiny during his lifetime. But it is otherwise with us; only the species can hope for this" (8:23 n). So Kant's educational theory is directed at one particular species of rational animal, the members of which, due to certain root biological facts concerning their makeup, need to be educated. And the natural facts of human growth and development themselves partially determine what sort of education is appropriate for members of this species. Although Kant clearly has many of his facts about both human and non-human animals wrong, he is nevertheless attempting to produce an empirically informed theory of education.

(2) Human beings, due to their nature, need to be educated into (among other things) morality. Morality for human beings is, on Kant's view, the intended outcome of an extensive educational process. ("Behind education there lies the great secret of the perfection of the human race," 9:444.) Morality itself, at least as concerns human beings, thus presupposes education. Morality on

Kant's view cannot simply be a causal product of education, but it does presuppose education as a necessary precondition. "By nature the human being is not a moral being at all" (9:492). "[T]he idea of morality belongs to [gehört . . . zur] culture" (Idee 8:26). "Belongs" is perhaps too strong here, for (again) morality on Kant's view cannot simply be the causal outcome of any combination of natural processes such as education or culture. Morality "belongs" to culture in the sense that it necessarily presupposes cultural development and can only grow out of it; but morality does not "belong" to culture in the sense that at a certain level of culture one necessarily sees morality.

Kant describes the stages and divisions of education in a variety of different and occasionally inconsistent ways in the Pädagogik. Over the years many attempts have been made to iron out his (and/or Rink's) remarks into a coherent whole, attempts which when placed alongside one another themselves reveal a bewildering variety. In my view, one of the central weaknesses of Über Pädagogik is its unsteady terminology. Nevertheless, a brief look at the central divisions and stages of education presented in the lectures and supporting texts can serve as a useful orientation to Kant's educational theory, particularly if it is done charitably (i.e., without insisting on absolute consistency).

First of all, Kant uses several different words to refer to this area of inquiry. His favored term by far is "education" (Erziehung). Occasionally, however, "pedagogy" (Pädagogik), "doctrine of education" (Erziehungslehre) (9:455), and "art of education" (Erziehungskunst) (9:446–47) are all used as stand-ins. All four terms are used interchangeably, though the last three occasionally refer more to the theory of education and the first to the process itself.

The first stage or aspect of education is care (Wartung) (9:441). Here too, a variety of interchangeable terms are employed to refer to what is basically the same process: "maintenance" (Verpflegung) (9:441, 456), "support" (Unterhaltung) (9:441), "provision" (Versorgung) (9:452). Care deals with the child purely as a part of nature, and concerns the first stage of human life, when one is an infant (Säugling) (9:441). Care thus falls outside of the parameters of education as the latter term is commonly understood at present. Kant means by it "the precaution of the parents that children not make any harmful use of their powers" (9:441). Care is a part of "physical" as opposed to "practical" education, and forms that part of education "which the human being has in common with animals" (9:455). Since, as noted earlier, Kant opens the lectures by announcing that the human being "is the only creature that must be educated" (9:441), there is even a sense in which care also falls outside the parameters of education as he himself (at least sometimes) construes it.

The second stage of education is discipline (Disziplin) or training (Zucht). Like care, discipline too is best understood as a preliminary stage of education proper. "Discipline or training changes animality into humanity" (9:441). But "changes" does not mean "demolishes" or "eradicates." Rather, to discipline "means to seek to prevent animality from doing damage to humanity. . . . Discipline is therefore merely the taming of savageness" (9:449). Those animal impulses which are contrary to the ends of humanity are to be controlled by means of discipline: "Discipline prevents the human being from deviating by means of his animal impulses from his destiny: humanity" (9:442). In a broader sense, this disciplinary task of education is shared by what Kant elsewhere calls "negative culture"—"the freeing of the will from the despotism of desires" (*KU* 5:432; see also "The Means of Progress," chap. 5). Discipline forms merely the "negative" part of education and enculturation in the sense that its primary job is to "prevent bad habits [*Unarten*]" from developing as opposed to forming a way of thinking (*Denkungsart*) (9:480). Training too is "merely negative, that is to say, it is the action by means of which the human being's tendency to savageness is taken away" (9:442).

Discipline in turn prepares the way for the positive part of education, formation (*Bildung*) or culture (*Kultur*). This negative/positive way of referring to the discipline/culture distinction occurs elsewhere in Kant's writings as well. For instance, in the *Critique of Pure Reason* he asserts:

> The compulsion by which the constant tendency to disobey certain rules is restrained and finally extirpated is called *discipline*. It is distinguished from *culture*, which should give merely a certain kind of skill, without canceling any other skill already present. To the formation [*Bildung*] of a talent, which has already in itself an impulse to manifest itself, discipline will therefore offer a negative contribution; culture and doctrine [*Doktrin*] a positive contribution. (*KrV* A 709/B 737–A 710/B 738)

The two broad terms "*Bildung*" and "*Kultur*" are also used synonymously by Kant, and include within themselves a variety of more specific processes such as instruction (*Unterweisung*) (9:441), teaching (*Belehrung*) (9:449), and guidance (*Anführung*) (9:452). It is also important to keep in mind that "culture," like the other stages of education, is often used in a double sense by Kant: sometimes it refers to the general formation of humanity out of animality in the human race as a whole; sometimes it refers to more specific educational processes directed at particular groups as well as individuals.[30]

Culture "is the procurement of skillfulness [*Geschicklichkeit*]" (9:449). People are skillful when they can attain successfully all their chosen ends (whatever they may be)—that is, simply when they are good instrumental reasoners (cf. 9:455). Skillfulness "is the possession of a faculty which is sufficient for whatever purpose. Thus skillfulness determines no ends at all" (9:450). Or, as Kant puts it in the third *Critique*: "The production in a rational being of an aptitude for any ends in general of his own choosing (consequently of his freedom) is *culture*" (*KU* 5:431). In order to procure skillfulness, culture forms (*bildet*) both nature (9:469) and mind (9:464) within human beings so that they are no longer "raw" (*roh*) (9:444). "He who is uncultured is raw" (9:444; cf. *Refl* 1497, 15:766).

Kant often makes a further distinction between general culture and "a certain kind of [*gewisse Art von*] culture, which is called *civilization*" (9:450). This latter form of culture aims not just at skillfulness but at prudence (*Klugheit*), and thus represents a higher stage of development. "[A]ll prudence presupposes skillfulness. Prudence is the faculty of using one's skills in a socially effective manner [*gut an den Mann zu bringen*]" (9:455). The skillful person too is of course effective in reaching his goals, but he lacks the special kinds of human interaction skills that are the prudent person's forte. Virtually the same wording and corresponding emphasis on human relations skills is repeated later in the lectures: "As concerns *worldly prudence* [*Weltklugheit*],[31] it consists in the art of using our skillfulness in a socially effective manner [*an den Mann zu bringen*], that is, of how human beings can be used for one's purposes" (9:486). This blunt emphasis on using other human beings to achieve one's goals in turn hooks up prudence with (at least one of) Kant's definitions of "pragmatic" (for discussion, see "Pragmatic Anthropology" in "Which Anthropology?" in chap. 3). One of the three tasks of "practical education," he informs us in *Über Pädagogik*, is "*pragmatic* formation with regard to prudence" (9:455). And toward the end of *Anthropology from a Pragmatic Point of View* Kant states that one feature that distinguishes the human being from other inhabitants of the earth is his possession of the capacity to be "*pragmatic* (to use other human beings skillfully for his own purposes)" (7:322). The prudent, civilized person thus possesses certain social graces (graces that clearly have their manipulative side) that the merely skillful person lacks. The prerequisites of a civilized person "are manners, good behavior [*Artigkeit*], and a certain prudence in virtue of which one is able to use all human beings for one's own final purposes" (9:450).

Kant frequently uses "civilization" as part of a trio (and sometimes a quartet, when discipline is added) of necessary stages in human development. Toward the end of *Anthropology from a Pragmatic Point of View* he states:

> The sum of pragmatic anthropology with reference to the destiny of the human being and the characteristics of his education [*Ausbildung*] is the following. The human being is destined through his reason to be in a society with human beings and to *cultivate, civilize,* and *moralize* himself in it through [*durch*] the arts and sciences. (7:324)

Parallel passages occur in other versions of the anthropology lectures, for example, the Starke manuscript from 1790–91: "The human being who is formed [*gebildet*] is cultivated through school knowledge, civilized through dealing with others, and moralized though the unification [*durch Vereinigung . . . moralisiert*] of both of the previously mentioned parts" (Starke II, 2; cf. *Mrongovius* 25:1429). (The tail end of this passage understates the transition-to-morality problem somewhat. Kantian moralization cannot be a simple adding together of culture and civilization—it involves rather some sort of qualitative leap into the realm of freedom, one that nevertheless necessarily presupposes the preparatory steps of culture and civilization.) The trio of culture, civilization, and morality is invoked again toward the end of the second Starke lectures: "The natural capacities are formed [*ausgebildet*] through culture, through civilization, and through moralization" (122; cf. *Refl* 1496, 15:763).

However, Kant is not usually so sanguine about the crucial last step of moralization. His considered view is that humanity is still a long way off from the final stage of moralization (*Moralisierung*). In the *Pädagogik* he writes: "We live in a time of disciplinary training, culture, and civilization, but not by any means in a time of moralization" (9:451). Similarly, in the essay "Idea for a Universal History with a Cosmopolitan Intent": "We are, to a high degree, *cultivated* through art and science. We are *civilized* to the point of being overloaded with all sorts of social grace and decorum. But for us to maintain that we are *moral-ized*—for that much is still missing" (8:26). And in one of the *Reflexionen zur Anthropologie*:

> [We] human beings are . . . in the second grade of progress to perfection, namely cultivated and civilized, but not moralized. We have the highest grade of culture that we can possess without morality; civilization also has [reached] its maximum. The need [*Bedürfnis*] in both will eventually force moralization [*wird endlich die Moralisierung erzwingen*], namely through education, a political constitution, and religion. At present religion is nothing other than a civilizing through a discipline. (*Refl* 1460, 15:641; cf. *Menschenkunde* 25:1198)

Here the contributing roles of education, law, and religion in bringing about moralization are all stressed. But how exactly are the former to "eventually force" the latter? On this crucial question, Kant is surprisingly silent.

Finally, in the Starke manuscript from 1790–91:

> The most difficult condition of the human race is the crossing-over [*Übergang*] from civilization to moralization. . . . [O]ne must try to enlighten human beings and to better establish international law [*Völkerrecht*]. . . . We are now, those of us who are working on the unity of religion, on the step of this crossing-over from civilization to moralization. Inner religion stands in now for the position of legal constraint. In order to reach the great end, one can either go from the parts to the whole, that is to say, through education, or from the whole to the parts. (Starke II, 124–25)

What then is this great end (*großer Zweck*) of moralization? In what does it consist? How are we supposed to reach it? Why is humanity "*noch nicht morali-siert?*" In summarizing this fourth and final stage of human development in the *Pädagogik*, Kant writes: "One must also pay attention to *moralization*. The human being should not merely be skilled for all sorts of ends, but should also acquire the disposition to choose nothing but good ends. Good ends are those which are necessarily approved by everyone and which can be the simultaneous ends of everyone"(9:450).

This brief description contains three crucial ideas: 1. One needs to acquire a certain disposition (*Gesinnung*) in order to be moralized. A disposition in Kant's sense is not a habit, for a habit "is a mechanism of the way of sense [*Sinnesart*] rather than of the way of thinking [*Denkungsart*]" (*MdS* 6:479). Elsewhere we are informed that it is precisely the absence of a correct *Denkungsart* that has thus far prevented contemporary civilization from taking the step to moralization: "As far as moralization is concerned, certainly we have refined manners, but not a true, real *Denkungsart*" (*Menschenkunde* 25:1198). As for habits in Kant's sense of the term, "the more habits [*Angewohnheiten*] someone has, the less he is free and independent" (9:463). Small wonder, then, that he dismisses them in the *Anthropology*: "As a rule all habits are reprehensible [*verwerflich*]" (7:149; cf. Starke II, 81). Still, a Kantian moral *Gesinnung* is part of the deep structure of an agent's moral personality and as such must contain his or her basic orientation towards life. A disposition is distinguished from a habit primarily in the sense that it must involve conscious, rational deliberation concerning one's maxims and not be merely unconscious, reflex behavior. At the same time, other moral theorists who advocate a more positive role for habits within an agent's moral personality (e.g., Aristotle) also defend precisely this sort of internalized "thinking habit."[32] Given his own position, Kant is thus wrong to criticize them.

2. The disposition required is one that chooses "nothing but good ends." The emphasis on ends (*Zwecke*) here connotes more the later rather than the earlier formulations of the categorical imperative, for example, the kingdom of ends (*Reich der Zwecke*) and the end in itself (*Zweck an sich selbst*) (*Gr* 4:433–35, 427–29). Kant's description of the content of these ends ("only good ends") is exasperatingly brief, but it does serve to indicate that moralization necessarily involves not merely the formal structure of one's maxims but the content of one's willing as well.

3. Good ends are defined further as "those that are necessarily approved by everyone and which can be the simultaneous ends of everyone." Here the famous Kantian requirement of universalizability is invoked (cf. *Gr* 4:420–21). However, it is crucial to note that at the stage of moralization the various formulas of the categorical imperative are themselves part of the internalized disposition of the truly moralized agent. The moralized agent has acquired a deep-seated disposition to choose only good ends, ends which are characterized, at least in part, as being approved by everyone. In other words, the sorts of exotic calculations involving the application of the categorical imperative to problem cases that feature prominently in so many philosophical discussions of Kant's categorical imperative are not part of this person's mind-set. He or she has been educated to choose only ends that can be the simultaneous ends of everyone, but this choosing does not normally involve difficult excogitations. It must become an engrained way of thinking (*Denkungsart*) rather than a complicated decision procedure to be pulled out in times of doubt. Moral culture "must be based on maxims, not on discipline. The latter prevents bad habits, the former forms the *Denkungsart*. One must see to it that the child accustoms himself [*sich gewöhne*][33] to act according to maxims and not according to certain incentives" (9:480). Moral education "is based not on discipline but on maxims. Everything is spoiled if one tries to ground it on examples, threats, punishments, etc. One must see to it that the pupil acts from his own maxims, not from habit [*Gewohnheit*], that he does not only do the good, but that he does it because it is good" (9:475).

As noted earlier, when "moralization" is used by Kant to refer not to individual development but rather to humanity's development as a whole, he is clear in stating that we are "not by any means in a time of moralization [*Zeitpunkte der Moralisierung*]" (9:451).[34] Much more is required on a variety of cultural fronts before humanity is ready to take this critical step. For instance, nation-states (in Kant's day as well as in our own) expend far too much energy on "vain and violent expansion plans" that "continually inhibit the slow efforts toward the inner formation of the way of thinking [*innere Bildung der Denkungsart*] of their citizens" (*Idee* 8:26; cf. "Citizens of the World?" in chap. 5). And education systems are chronically underfunded: "[A]t present it is not conceivable that the great end of nature will be reached through education, for parents and princes do not want to contribute anything to education" (Starke II, 125).

At the same time, the hoped-for *Übergang* from civilization to moralization is not simply a matter of throwing money at a problem but involves a qualitative shift of perspective. Changes in material cultural conditions alone can never guarantee a moral change. As Kant stresses,

> physical formation of the mind [*Geist*] is distinguished from the moral formation of the mind in that the latter aims solely at freedom and the former solely at nature. A human being can be highly cultivated in physical terms, he can have a well-formed mind, but can still be poorly cultivated in moral terms, and thus be an evil creature (9:469–70).

In the broad sense, practical education as Kant conceives it thus has three parts: "1) *scholastic-mechanical* formation with regard to skillfulness . . . 2) *pragmatic* formation with regard to prudence . . . 3) *moral* formation with regard to ethics" (9:455). These three parts of practical education in turn map on both to the three stages of culture, civilization, and moralization within human history (cf. *Anth* 7:324) as well as to the three types of imperative (technical, pragmatic, moral) analyzed in the *Groundwork* and elsewhere (cf. *Gr* 4:416–17; *KU* 5:172–73). But the inner teleology of these three inter-linked parts injects a strong normative dimension into each one. As Hans Ebeling remarks in his essay "The Ethics in Kant's Anthropology," for Kant "*having* the world and *knowing* the world stand under the goal of making the world *better*."[35] All parts of education ultimately aim at moralization, even though individual participants acting at the proto-moral levels of culture and civilization are often unaware of this larger aim. Nature's plan is "the perfection of the human being through progressive culture" (*Anth* 7:322), and as I show later ("The Means of Progress," chap. 5), much of the time we are unwitting participants in this plan.

Experimentation and Revolution

Two rather unexpected features of Kant's theory of education deserve special comment: its advocacy of experimentalism and of revolution in education. Both these commitments tie in directly with Kant's strong endorsement of Basedow's Philanthropinum project.

Experimentalism

Like most theorists in the classical German tradition, Kant normally advocates an extremely top-heavy relationship between theory and practice. According to this top-heavy view, reason and theory always guide experience; not vice versa. Reason "has insight only into that which it itself produces according to its plan"—"chance [*zufällige*] observations" (i.e., those not made in obedience to this previously thought-out plan) carry no weight and cannot force us to modify our theory, and the only experiments to be tolerated are those "worked out in conformity with" reason and its principles (*KrV* B xiii). In short, Kant's conviction that "the worth of practice rests entirely on its appropriateness to its underlying theory" (*Gemeinspruch* 8:277) implies that practice must always follow the lead of theory.

But one surprise in the *Lectures on Pedagogy* is Kant's strong endorsement of experiments in education—experiments that are not themselves merely the handmaidens of preordained theory. In defending Basedow's poorly administered Philanthropinum Institute in Dessau, Kant writes:

> It is even commonly imagined that experiments in education are not necessary, and that one can already judge by reason alone whether something will be good or bad. But this is very mistaken, and experience teaches that our experiments often show quite different effects from the ones expected. One sees therefore that since experiments matter, no one generation can present a complete plan of education [*völliger Erziehungsplan*]. (9:451)

This conviction that "experiments matter," along with the connected claim that one cannot always judge by a priori reason alone "whether something will be good or bad," does suggest a much less top-heavy theory-practice relationship— one that appears to contradict the more familiar rationalist tone of the previously cited passages from *KrV* and *Gemeinspruch*. Indeed, it almost sounds as though Kant is here criticizing well-known positions he himself takes elsewhere. But "good or bad" in what sense(s)? Not in a moral sense, if he is to hold onto his core conviction that all fundamental concepts of morality "must rest only on pure reason, independently of all experience" (*Gr* 4:409). However, if we interpret him here to mean only good or bad in an instrumental sense, there is no necessary inconsistency. On this view, something is "good" in an instrumental sense if it efficiently promotes an end; "bad" if it does not. The end itself, however, must be established on a priori grounds. In the field of education, the end will be the full development of humanity's predispositions. Those means that efficiently promote this end are thus good in the relevant sense, while those that impede it are bad.

Viewed in this manner, Kant's endorsement of experimentalism in education makes good sense, for in most cases[36] we cannot know ahead of time how far our predispositions might be developed by which educational method. This can only be ascertained by actually trying out and assessing different educational methods. Kant is convinced that state-regulated schools are systematically unable to engage seriously in this necessary experimentation: "[R]ulers for the most part care only for themselves and take no part in the important experiment of education in such a manner that nature may take a step closer to perfection" (9:444). "Until now," he proclaims at the end of the *Moralphilosophie Collins* lectures, "not a single prince has ever contributed to the perfection of humanity, to inner happiness, or to the worth of humanity; rather they have merely looked always to the flourishing of their states, which for them is the main thing. . . . The Basedow institutes of education constitute a small, warm hope in this regard" (27:471). In the important concluding section of the *Friedländer* anthropology lecture ("On Education"), Kant expounds on his short-lived hope for Basedow's program as follows:

> There already exist many suggestions and writings on education by philosophers; one should have made the effort to inquire wherein the central concept of education consists. The present Basedowian institutes are the first which have come to pass according to the perfect plan [of education]. This is the

greatest phenomenon that has appeared in this century for the improvement of the perfection of humanity, through it all schools in the world will receive another form. (25:722–23)

Although Kant unfortunately does not go into details, his enthusiastic support for Basedow is clearly based on his own belief that Basedow's schools "are the first which have come to pass according to the perfect plan" of education. And this perfect plan is of course the full development of the predispositions of the human race in its entirety. All previous educational models are faulted for being narrowly provincial and nationalistic; Basedow's schools are declared to be the first to aim explicitly at educating students to be "citizens of our world" (cf. n. 26).

Revolution

A second unexpected feature of the educational writings is Kant's claim that a radical revolution in education is needed. As noted earlier (n. 17), in his second fundraising appeal on behalf of the Philanthropin Institute in Dessau, originally published in 1777, Kant proclaims:

> It is futile to expect this salvation [Heil] of the human species from a gradual improvement of the schools. They must be transformed [umgeschaffen] if something good is to come out of them because they are defective in their original organization, and even the teachers must acquire a new culture [Bildung]. Not a slow reform but a quick revolution [eine schnelle Revolution] can bring this about. (2:449; cf. Päd 9:444)

There is an odd parallel to this advocacy of revolution over reform in *Religion within the Boundaries of Mere Reason*. In part 1 Kant claims that the achievement of human virtue

> cannot be brought about through gradual reform so long as the basis of the maxims remains impure [unlauter], but rather must be brought about through a revolution in the disposition of the human being [Revolution in der Gesinnung] (a crossing-over [Übergang] to the maxim of holiness of the disposition). And he can become a new human being only through a kind of rebirth, as if through a new creation. (Rel 6:47)

The same contrast between reform and revolution occurs in each passage, and in each text revolution gets the nod over reform.[37] But the *Religion* passage raises an additional problem, for it is often interpreted as implying the impossibility of moral education. Supposedly, education effects only our empirical character; not our intelligible character. Lewis White Beck, for instance, writes: "Strictly speaking, moral education is perhaps impossible, since morality is a product of a sudden inward revolution in the manner of willing and each act must be regarded as if it were an entirely fresh beginning."[38] On the following page of the *Religion* Kant goes on to state that "the moral formation [moralische Bildung] of the human being must begin not in the improvement of customs [Sitten], but rather in the transformation of the Denkungsart and the grounding of a character" (6:48). Groothoff, in a note on this passage, writes: "although

Kant speaks here of moral formation, he makes it immediately clear—at any rate according to the general understanding of formation—that here one only can only speak of formation in a metaphorical sense."[39] However, Kant does explicitly refer to "*moralische Kultur*" in the *Pädagogik* and, as noted earlier, the German terms *Bildung* and *Kultur* are used synonymously by him in this text. In describing moral culture, Kant notes: "Moral culture must be based on maxims, not on discipline. The latter prevents bad habits, the former forms [*bildet*] the *Denkungsart*" (9:480). He also states on the following page that the "first effort in moral education [*moralische Erziehung*] is the grounding of a character" (9:481).

This same double emphasis on transforming the manner of thinking and grounding one's character is present in both the *Religion* and *Pedagogy* passages. So his employment of the concept of "moral formation" is not "metaphorical" but straightforward and clear: Kant believes that there is a kind of education that can (somehow) cut through natural causes and temporal circumstances and "get to the bottom"—that is, to the agent's manner of thinking and moral character. Moral education is successful only insofar as it achieves this goal, and Basedow's school (or so held Kant, albeit briefly) can reach it.

Kant is groping for an educational method that can cut through business as usual, and he thinks he has found it in the Philanthropium Institute. What is needed is a method of practical education that will produce a "genuine moral effect on the heart" (*KpV* 5:157). In his two short essays on the Philanthropinum Institute Kant signals his endorsement of a bold experiment in education, one which, he believes, "is established in a radically new way according to the genuine method [*nach der echten Methode von Grunde aus neu angeordent*]" (2:449). Such a method must not (as Kant believes is the case with all other existing educational institutions) "work against nature;" rather it should be "wisely extracted from nature itself [*weislich aus der Natur selbst gezogen*] and not slavishly copied from old habit and inexperienced ages" (2:449). (Here again we encounter a surprisingly naturalistic strand in Kant. See my discussion of "weak naturalism" in chap. 1.) Then the "good to which nature has given the predisposition [*Anlage*]" can be "drawn out of the human being," and "we animal creatures" will be "made into human beings" through the proper education (2:449; cf. 9:443). If this revolutionary educational method is adopted, "in a short time we would see very different human beings around us" (2:449).

Didactics, Ascetics, Casuistry, Judgment

> Perhaps one would come notably closer to one's goal of encouraging the improvement of the human race if one drew up a catechism, from which children from an early age would learn that virtue is essential to their happiness.
> Frederick the Great, *Die Eigenliebe als Moralprinzip* (1770)

Although the *Lectures on Pedagogy* and the related two "Essays Regarding the Philanthropinum" both reverberate frequently with strong moral overtones, surprisingly little space is devoted in them to some of the more mundane questions of moral education. How should children and adolescents learn about ethics? What methods should parents and teachers employ in trying to teach ethics? What are the proper aims of moral education? To be sure, these issues *are* broached in Kant's educational writings, but they are treated episodically, and tend to be sandwiched in between more ambitious *Aufklärung* hopes concerning the gradual perfection of the human species through culture and education (presented with Kant's own special concern for an eventual *Übergang* from nature to the new realm of morality) and discussions of the merely preparatory educational stages of nurture, discipline, and so on.

A good Kantian source of information concerning these questions of moral education, one that adds substantially to his overall educational theory, can be found in the *Methodenlehre* sections of the *Critique of Practical Reason* and *The Metaphysics of Morals*. Architectonic considerations as well as academic practice of the time lead Kant to divide all three critiques into an *Elementarlehre* (Doctrine of Elements) and *Methodenlehre* (Doctrine of Method), and the second half of the *Metaphysics of Morals* (the *Tugendlehre*, or *Doctrine of Virtue*) is similarly divided.[40] Several of the logic lectures are also divided into a "General Doctrine of Elements" and "General Doctrine of Method."

Essentially, a doctrine of elements is concerned with estimating and determining the "building materials" (*Bauzeug*) of thought, and with figuring out "what sort of building, of what height and strength" they are best suited for (*KrV* A 707/B 735). A doctrine of method, on the other hand, is more concerned with the practical application of the materials rather than with the materials themselves. Or, as Volker Gerhardt puts it, a *Methodenlehre* concerns "how reason gains effectiveness in human life. It contains the description of the *path* (Greek: *methodos*) reason takes (and should take), in order to arrive at its insights."[41]

However, this particular appearance of symmetry in Kant's works is misleading, for the various *Methodenlehre* sections of his writings differ substantially from one another. The *Methodenlehre* of the *Critique of Judgment*, for instance, can barely be said to exist at all: it consists of a two-page section added as an appendix to the "Dialectic of Aesthetic Judgment." Because "no *method of teaching* [*Lehrart*] (*methodus*)" exists for art, no doctrine of method professing to tell us how to teach it is possible on Kant's view (*KU* 5:355). The *Methodenlehre* of the first *Critique* is a much more substantial affair, being concerned with "the determination of the formal conditions of a complete system of pure reason," and is subdivided into a "discipline," a "canon," an "architectonic," and a "history" of pure reason (*KrV* A 708/B 736). However, it is understandably aimed more at readers who wish to study philosophy rather than those who are interested in moral education. It is the *Methodenlehre* sections of the second *Critique* and of the *Doctrine of Virtue* that are our primary concern here. When interpreted together simply as texts of moral education rather than as uncomfortable contributors to the architectonic, they add an important dimension to Kant's theory of education.

In the *Critique of Practical Reason* Kant writes that by "*Methodenlehre* is understood the way in which one can secure *entrance* into the human mind of the laws of pure practical reason, *influence* on the maxims of the same; that is, how one can also make objectively practical reason *subjectively* practical" (5:151). This emphasis on finding an entrance into the human mind for the laws of pure practical reason and on making objectively practical reason subjectively practical (subjectively practical, that is, for human beings) echoes the fundamental project of Kant's impure ethics: How can we make morality efficacious in human life? One specific way in which objectively practical reason is to be made subjectively practical for human beings (particularly human beings whose cognitive capacities are not yet fully developed) is by searching through "biographies of ancient and modern times with the purpose of having examples at hand of the duties they lay down" (*KpV* 5:154). Part of the goal here is to find a tangible representation of pure ethics, something that can be seen and felt. As I show in chapter 4, the same strategy is pursued at length in Kant's writings on aesthetics and religion.

Similarly, in the first section of the "Doctrine of Method" in the *Metaphysics of Morals*, he writes:

> The *experimental* (technical) means for the formation of virtue is the *good* example of the teacher himself (his exemplary conduct) and the *cautionary* example of other people, because imitation, for the still unformed human being, is the first determination of the will to accept maxims which he subsequently makes for himself. (*MdS* 6:479)

The still unformed or uneducated (*ungebildete*) human being needs a physical manifestation of virtue with which he can identify and from which he can learn. Eventually, of course, the student needs to let go of this "leading string" (*Gängelband*) (*KpV* 5:152; cf. *Päd* 9:461). The long-term goal, Kant advises the student, is to grasp that "the rule and instruction lies in your *reason* alone. This amounts to saying that you need not learn this rule for your conduct from experience or be taught it by other human beings. Your own reason teaches you what you have to do and directly commands you to do it" (*MdS* 6:481). But for young people this is not yet possible.[42]

Several of Kant's remarks in the Introduction to the *Doctrine of Virtue* shed further light on what he is aiming at. The doctrine of method of morally practical reason "deals not so much with judgment as with reason and its *exercise* in both the *theory* and the *practice* of its duties" (*MdS* 6:411). At the same time, a Methodenlehre in ethics must aim at "general directions (a method) as to how to proceed in judging" (6:411); even while recognizing (and here we encounter another tension) that strictly speaking there can be no science of judging and thus no method of judging. For by "method" is meant "systematic knowledge drawn up in accordance with reflected-upon rules [*nach überlegten Regeln*]" (*Jäsche Logik* 9:139). Only by means of rules of reason can a method be formulated. Exercises for strengthening and improving practical judgment can and should be offered, but one needs also to recognize that such exercises do not quite add up to a *wissenschaftliche Lehre* in the strict sense of the term (cf. *MdS* 6:478). However, since "judgment cannot be instructed (in accordance with rules) [*nach Regeln*], but rather only exercised" (*Refl* 423, 15:170–71), and because ethics "inevitably leads to questions that call upon judgment" (*MdS* 6:411), the sense in which a true Kantian *Methodenlehre* can be said to exist in ethics remains problematic. Exercises for developing, strengthening, and applying practical judgment can be given, but these do not quite constitute a full "doctrine of method."

Divisions of the Methodenlehre

Kant's subdivisions of the methods for teaching ethics are neither entirely original nor entirely consistent. Also, he appears to recommend one and the same *Lehrart* (method of teaching) for both ethics and logic. (On his view, there is and can be only one formal doctrine of method, but one may apply it to different subject matters.) Still, many of the specific remarks he makes about these subdivisions in their ethical setting are instructive.

If the doctrine of virtue is to be presented as a *Wissenschaft* it must also be systematic (*MdS* 6:478), and for this to occur one needs to choose between the following two broad teaching options: "The presentation can either be *acromatic*, where all but the teacher are mere listeners, or else *erotematic*, where the teacher asks his pupils what he wants to teach them" (6:478).[43] The same two teaching options are trotted out in some of the logic lectures. For instance, in a section called "On the Manner of Teaching" in the *Logik Pölitz* lectures, Kant writes: "The manner of teaching knowledge in a system is either acromatic, when I alone teach; or erotematic, when I ask questions" (24:599; cf. *Logik Dohna-Wundlacken* 24:780–81, *Logik Busolt* 24:684). But in moral education the question-and-answer or erotematic approach is clearly preferable, since here the central goal is to get the pupil to see "that he himself is capable of thinking" (*MdS* 6:478).

The erotematic method is in turn further subdivided into the "*dialogic* manner of teaching," if the teacher queries the student's reason; and the "*catechistic* manner of teaching," if the teacher merely queries the student's memory (*MdS* 6:478). The catechistic and dialogic methods are also discussed frequently in the various logic lectures and related *Reflexionen* (e.g., *Logik Pölitz* 24:599–600, *Logik Dohna-Wundlacken* 24:780, *Refl* 3381–85, 16:806–8), but they have a special employment within ethics. The catechistic method involves mere "memory work" in which the student recites thoughts that are not yet his own (*Refl* 3382, 16:807), but with the dialogic or Socratic manner of teaching the teacher and student alternate asking questions and giving answers to each other (*Logik Pölitz* 24:600). Alternatively, with the Socratic method "the student questions the teacher (who actually still is the student)" (*Refl* 3382, 16:807).

Because the dialogic method presupposes more maturity on the part of the student, the teacher necessarily employs it after rather than before the catechistic method. Nevertheless, in ethics it can be used fairly early, and in the *Methodenlehre* of the second *Critique* Kant describes a case that is put before "a ten-year-old boy" in order to see whether he arrives at the proper judgments without being instructed by his teacher (*KpV* 5:155). Still, the "first and most essential *doctrinal* instrument of the *Tugendlehre* for the still raw pupil is a moral *catechism*" (*MdS* 6:478). The initial job of moral education proper is to lay the foundations with "a purely moral catechism" (*KpV* 5:154)—that is, a catechism untainted by religious teaching (*MdS* 6:478, cf. *Päd* 9:495). In the *Pädagogik* lectures, Kant bemoans the fact that in our schools "something is almost universally lacking, something that would nevertheless greatly promote the formation of uprightness in children, namely a catechism of right [*Recht*]" (9:490). The teacher alone does the questioning at this stage of instruction, and the questions are supposed to be addressed only to the student's memory rather than his reason.[44] The moral catechism "should contain cases that would be popular, that occur in ordinary life, and that would always naturally raise the question whether something is right or not" (*Päd* 9:490). It is also supposed to "be carried out through all the articles of virtue and vice" and to "raise some casuistical questions in the analysis of every duty" (*MdS* 6:483). Taken together, these latter two requirements imply that a full-fledged moral catechism (which Kant himself does not provide) would itself constitute an extensive moral education.

"Ethical didactics" is Kant's umbrella term for the acroamatic, erotematic, catechistic, and dialogic methods of teaching.[45] These are all exercises in theory, that is, methods that teachers can employ in teaching ethics to students. The "practical counterpart" of these exercises in theory is *ascetics*, "in which is taught not only the concept of virtue but also how to put into practice and cultivate the *capacity for* as well as the will to virtue" (*MdS* 6:412). Moral ascetics is thus more a kind of "training (discipline) that the human being practices on himself [*an sich selbst verübt*]" rather than a theory that teachers use to educate students (*MdS* 6:485). As the second half of the doctrine of method it too consists of *rules* for the practice or exercise of virtue (*Regeln der Übung*) (*MdS* 6:484), but the rules in question are ones which one must practice on oneself rather than on others. As a self-practice it also necessarily comes later in moral education, after the student has reached the requisite stage of maturity and motivation. But teachers and parents can and should drop hints about it along the way.

"Ascetics" (*Asketik*), in modern English as well as German, carries a variety of negative connotations for most people—abstinence from creature comforts, a rigorous practice of self-denial, renunciation of the flesh, exercises in repentance, and so on. And of course Schiller, Nietzsche, and many others since have interpreted Kant's views on the place of human inclinations and emotions in ethics in precisely this "ascetic" manner. But it is important to note that Kant himself, in his brief remarks concerning moral ascetics, clearly tries hard to put a different spin on the concept.

To be sure, there is a necessary "negative" or renunciatory aspect to Kantian moral ascetics. Virtue needs to "muster all its forces to overcome the obstacles it must contend with," and it must also "sacrifice many of the joys of life, the loss of which can sometimes make one's mind gloomy and sullen" (*MdS* 6:484). But Kant goes on to state that this stoical side of moral ascetics is "merely a kind of *dietetics* for keeping a human being healthy." And health, he adds in the next sentence, "is only a negative kind of well-being" (*MdS* 6:485). To this negative side of moral ascetics something more positive must be added, a contribution that Kant attributes to "the virtuous *Epicurus*." Though "only moral," this positive side of ascetics "affords an agreeable enjoyment to life [*angenehmener Lebensgenuß*]" and consists chiefly in "the ever-cheerful heart" (*MdS* 6:485). "Cheerful (*fröhlich*)" and "cheerfulness (*Frohsinn*)" are by far Kant's favorite words in describing the positive side of moral ascetics: together, they occur six times on two pages of *The Metaphysics of Morals* (6:484–85). And in his famous reply to Schiller in an early footnote in the *Religion*, Kant also states that the proper "*aesthetic* constitution" of virtue consists in "a *cheerful* frame of mind" [*fröhliche Gemüthssstimmung*] (6:23–24 n; cf. *Friedländer 25:725*).[46] The specific sense of cheerfulness invoked is a strong one, and it is clearly more than emotional window-dressing: "[W]hat one does not do with pleasure [*mit Lust*] but merely as compulsory service has no inner worth for one who so attends to his duty" (*MdS* 6:484). At the same time, there is a Kantian (i.e., transcendental) side to this cheerfulness. It arises at least in part from a "consciousness of one's restored freedom" after one has succeeded in "combating natural impulses sufficiently to be able to master them in cases where they threaten morality with danger" (*MdS* 6:458; cf. *KpV* 5:160–61).

At any rate, "monkish ascetics" (*Mönchasketik*) is clearly not what Kant's moral ascetics is all about. The former "does not aim at virtue;" the latter does (*MdS* 6:485). And it is perhaps also worth noting that Greek words such as *askēsis*, *askētikos*, and *askētēs*, (from which the English "ascetics" and German *Asketik* are derived) also do not only carry negative connotations of abstention and renunciation. For instance, additional central definitions of the noun *askēsis* include "exercise, practice," and "mode of life, profession."[47]

Casuistry

Didactics and ascetics, the two main parts of the ethical *Methodenlehre*, are (again) both supposedly part of a *Wissenschaft*—a systematic body of knowledge that can be taught (and cultivated by oneself) by means of rules. Casuistry, on the other hand, in Kant's special sense, "is neither a *Wissenschaft* nor a part thereof . . . and it is not so much a method [Lehre] concerning how something is to be *found* as an exercise concerning how truth is to be *sought*. Therefore it is only *woven into ethics* fragmentarily, not systematically . . . as scholia are added to the system" (*MdS* 6:411). At the same time, toward the end of one of his discussions of the moral catechism Kant advises that "it would be of great value to the pupil's ethical formation to raise some casuistical questions in the analysis of every duty" concerning what is to be done in "tricky" (*verfänglich*) situations (*MdS* 6:483). So while he construes casuistry as falling under the Doctrine of Elements rather than the Doctrine of Method (*MdS* 6:413), in the actual practice of teaching ethics casuistry works hand in hand with aspects of didactics such as the catechistic and dialogic methods. And this makes sense, for the primary aim of all of these techniques is to help provide "general instruction (a method) as to how to proceed in judging" (*MdS* 6:411). The hope is that in working through these exercises students will gradually "feel the progress of their power of judgment" (cf. *KpV* 5:154), thereby acquiring a keener interest in moral issues (*KpV* 5:153).

So although no complete theory of practical judging is possible (there will always be new and unforeseeable situations for judgment to consider), and although the art of judgment cannot be formally imparted to students by means of rules (in part because rules are never self-deploying: there are no rules which can tell us how to apply rules; cf. *Anth* 7:199, *KrV* A 133/B 172), there is nevertheless a great deal that teachers can and should do to sharpen their students' power of judgment. Only if we construe teaching extremely narrowly—as something that takes places solely through the communication of rules (a fallacy that Kant unfortunately occasionally endorses: *Anth* 7:199)—need we conclude that judgment cannot be taught.

The Education of Humanity

> The final destiny of the human race is moral perfection. . . . But now how is this perfection to be sought, and from whence is it to be hoped for? From nowhere else except through education.
> *Moralphilosophie Collins*

> The Perfectibility of Man! Ah heaven, what a dreary theme!
> D. H. Lawrence, *Studies in Classic American Literature*

Education, on Kant's view, has a variety of interconnected aims: it must *nurture, discipline, cultivate, civilize* (particularly in the sense of fostering worldly wisdom or prudence—*Klugheit*) and *moralize* human beings (*Päd* 9:441, 449–50). But throughout his writings on education it this fifth and final aim of moralization which is clearly the most important to him, and on which this final section focuses. How exactly is education supposed to moralize us, and why such a strong emphasis on "us" as a species?

First of all, as I have shown, morality as Kant understands it is not present in human beings by nature, but grows out of a long and difficult process of enculturation and education: "[B]y nature the human being is not a moral being at all" (9:492). Rather, "the idea of morality belongs to [*gehört . . . zur*] culture" (*Idee* 8:26). Morality does not belong completely to culture or education, nor is it simply a causal product of them. All of us are familiar with people who have plenty of culture and education but little or no morality. Kant's society was much the same in this respect: "We live in a time of disciplinary training, culture, and civilization, but not by any means in a time of moralization [*Moralisierung*]" (9:451, cf. *Menschenkunde* 25:1198). Still, "the human being is destined by his reason to be in a society with human beings and in it to *cultivate* himself, to *civilize* himself, and to *moralize* himself through [*durch*] the arts and sciences" (*Anth* 7:324). Culture (in particular the arts and sciences) and education are, along with law, politics, and religion, all necessary but not sufficient conditions for human moralization. There is no guarantee that people who have been exposed to these preparatory steps will be morally good, but human beings who lack all contact with them cannot possibly be morally good.

Second, education aims not just to moralize the human individual or even a specific class or nation of individuals but rather the entire human species. It is "completely impossible for the individual to reach the destiny [*Bestimmung*] [of humanity]. . . . Not individual human beings, but rather the human species [*die Menschengattung*], shall get there" (*Päd* 9:445). With non-human animals, Kant holds, the situation is radically different. As he asserts toward the end of *Anthropology from a Pragmatic Point of View*:

> First one must note that when any other animal is left to its own devices, each individual attains its complete destiny; but in the human being's case only the *species* [*nur die Gattung*] achieves it, at most. So the human race can work its way up to its destiny only by *progress* through a series of innumerable generations (7:324).

Kant repeats this central conviction that "the human destiny is reached only by the *species*" (Dohna, 368) in many different versions of his anthropology lectures (e.g., *Menschenkunde* 25:1196, *Mrongovius* 25:1417, Starke II, 120–21, *Refl* 1499, 15:781–85) as well as in his essays on history (e.g., *Idee* 8:18–19). The destiny of, say, snailhood or foxhood has changed little over the centuries. The cultural life of these animals in the late twentieth century differs relatively little from that experienced by their ancient ancestors. Each individual within such species can single-handedly realize the maximum potential of the species, for that potential itself is very limited. An individual snail does not depend on its fellow species members in order to develop its maximum potential. But with human beings the situation is different. "The individual depends on the species and cannot leap like the ancient sage to rational perfection by himself."[48] Rather, education

> is an art [*Kunst*], the practice of which must be perfected over the course of many generations. Each generation, provided with the knowledge of the preceding ones, is ever more able to bring about an education which develops all of the human being's natural predispositions proportionally and purposively, thus leading the whole human species toward its destiny. (*Päd* 9:446)

In later chapters I will examine related formulations of this same perfectionistic species-orientation. It is definitely a dominant motif in all areas of Kant's impure ethics, and several large empirical assumptions about human nature and its level of development clearly lie behind it. "How it may be with the inhabitants of other planets and their nature, we do not know. . . . Maybe among them each individual can perfectly attain his destiny in his own life. Among us, it is different; only the species can hope to attain this" (*Idee* 8:23 n). Kant appears to hold that this aspect of species-dependence is unique to the human species. The human being is a *particular sort of* rational creature who needs to be educated into morality and who requires the aid of fellow species members to fully develop his capacities.

Unlike many of his more impatient followers as well as critics, Kant remains comfortably vague on the issue of how long all of this will take. At the conclusion of the *Moralphilosophie Collins* lectures, he states merely that humanity's highest moral perfection "is to be hoped for after the course of many centuries [*nach dem Verlaufe vieler Jahrhunderte zu hoffen*]" (27:471; cf. *Powalski* 27:235, *Friedländer* 25:696). The *Übergang* from civilization to moralization represents the most crucial and difficult step in humanity's destiny, but at present "we have done almost nothing at all [*beynahe gar nichts*]" to get there (*Menschenkunde* 25:1198; cf. Starke II, 124–25; *Refl* 1460, 15:641).

But what is most distinctive about this educational vision is not its perfection-ism but rather its "cosmopolitanism"; its stern conviction that education in all times and places must have as its primary goal not national or parental but rather species-wide purposes. As William Frankena notes, Kant

> does not even raise the possibility that education should promote the excel-lences of the good citizen as defined by the constitution and laws of one's country, thus varying from country to country in the dispositions it fosters. He simply takes it for granted as obvious that education in all countries is to promote human perfection . . . and not simply whatever dispositions their constitutions call for. Education must not serve simply parental or national purposes.[49]

What is wrong with educational schemes that do serve simply parental or national purposes? They are morally objectionable because they violate the in-junction to treat humanity as an end in itself: they treat students as instruments rather than as ends in themselves. As Kant argues in the *Pedagogy* lectures:

> Parents usually care only that their children get on well in the world, and princes regard their subjects merely as instruments [*nur wie Instrumente*] for their own designs. Parents care for the home, princes for the state. Neither have as their final end the highest good in the world [*das Weltbeste*] and the perfection to which humanity is destined, and for which it also has the dispo-sition. But the design for a plan of education must be made in a cosmopolitan manner. (9:448; cf. *Menschenkunde* 25:1202, Starke II, 125, 126–27; *Gr* 4: 427–29)

"In a cosmopolitan manner": that is, students must be taught to recognize the moral standing of all people around the world, so that "a violation of rights in *one* part of the world is felt *everywhere*" (*Frieden* 8:360). Universalizability, in Kant's impure ethics, is primarily about re-structuring educational and cultural institutions so that children and students will learn to respect and care for all moral agents, particularly all human beings.

What are we today to make of this ambitious *Aufklärung* doctrine? Should it still merit our attention? Among the many scholarly objections that have been made raised against it over the years, the following may be briefly noted.

1. Progress versus Dignity   Some have argued that the cosmopolitan strand of Kant's philosophy of education and history contradicts the individualist strand of his ethical theory which holds that each moral agent has absolute moral worth. Hannah Arendt, for instance, writes: "In Kant himself there is this con-tradiction: Infinite progress is the law of the human species; at the same time, man's dignity demands that he be seen (every single one of us) in his particular-ity. . . . [T]he very idea of progress . . . contradicts Kant's notion of man's dig-nity."[50]

2. Born Too Early   Closely related to the first objection is a charge of moral unfairness; a sense that on Kant's view earlier generations are merely doing the preparatory grunt work for later ones. Emil Fackenheim, in his important essay "Kant's Concept of History," claims that Kant makes "the free achievements of some the means to the freer achievements of others."[51] Similarly, Susan Shell remarks that Kant's "progressive history . . . condemns those who are born earlier (through no fault of their own) to busy themselves for the advantage of their distant progeny."[52]

3. Perfecting Others   According to other critics, Kant's vision of cosmopolitan education and its role in achieving humanity's destiny entails a duty on the part of teachers to work toward the moral perfection of their students. But in the *Metaphysics of Morals* he states explicitly that "it is a contradiction for me to make another's *perfection* my end and consider myself under obligation to promote this. . . . [I]t is self-contradictory to require that I do (make it my duty to do) something that no one but the other himself can do" (6:386). A teacher cannot make students morally good; only they themselves can do so.[53]

4. Education versus Transcendental Freedom   Another doubt concerns the alleged conceptual gap between educators' focus on developing students' natural abilities and powers, and the radical moral transformation that Kant sees education as bringing about. How exactly is the crossing-over from nature to freedom to be achieved, and how can two such qualitatively different realms interact with one another? As noted earlier (see "Nature and Freedom" in chap. 1), this objection was first articulated by the educational theorist Johann Friedrich Herbart (1776–1841), in his 1804 review of Rink's edition of Kant's *Pedagogy* lectures. It is "impossible," Herbart claimed, to view Kantian moral education as "an effect of transcendental freedom"—the latter is "entirely free from every causal nexus." Education affects only one's empirical character.[54] However, the moral realm as Kant understands it is not just a continuation of business as usual but a radical transformation into "the kingdom of God on earth" (*Collins* 27:471; cf. *Rel* 6:122). As Beck rightly notes, it is this religious, "super-natural, superhistorical" dimension of Kant's ethics that sets it off from its secularist neighbors:

> Kant teaches that there is a super-natural, superhistorical dimension to morality and the transition to it. In such an eschatology the social institutions of civilization, including that of education, play only a preliminary role; and it is this movement of his thought which principally distinguishes him from other enlightenment philosophers.[55]

5. Pre-modern, Pre-moral   The strong emphasis on progress (progress not just in a technological or material sense but also in a *moral* sense) seems to imply that those human beings currently living are morally better than their ancestors who lived in the past. Kant himself appears to embrace this particular implication of moral progress in his essay "The End of all Things" when he refers to "the empirical proofs [*Erfahrungsbeweise*] for the superiority of morality in our age over all former ages" (8:332). Similarly, in "Theory and Practice," he claims that "one can give many proofs [*manche Beweise*] showing that the human race in its entirety [*das menschliche Geschlecht im Ganzen*] really has in our age, by comparison with all earlier ones, bettered itself morally and to a considerable degree" (8:310). Particularly for those of us living at the end of the twentieth century, this assumption that present generations are morally superior to previous ones is very hard to swallow.

6. *The Lucky Ones* Finally, according to some critics, Kant's theory of history (which I examine in more detail in chapter 5) implies that later generations are eventually forced into a moral condition for which they themselves deserve no credit and from which they can derive no esteem. William Galston writes:

> At the end of history, man surveys the nearly unrelieved panorama of war, crime, vice, and vanity and realizes retrospectively that it all contributed to his present good fortune. But it is difficult to see why this "last man" should esteem either himself or his forebears. He is lucky, they were unlucky.[56]

In my view, none of these criticisms is quite as devastating as its proponents assert. Indeed, Kant himself explicitly accepts several of the criticisms, while denying that they constitute fatal defects in his theory. Briefly, a Kantian rejoinder can be formulated to each objection as follows.

Progress versus Dignity

Herder first raised a version of this objection in his *Ideas for a Philosophy of the History of Humanity* (1784–85), when he argued that Kant's philosophy of history sacrifices the happiness of individuals to the collective development of the human species. Kant, in his review of part 2 of Herder's work, replies as follows:

> [W]hat if the true end of providence were not this shadowy image of happiness which each individual forms for himself, but the ever continuing and growing activity and culture that are thereby brought into play, the highest degree of which can only be the product of a political constitution ordered according to concepts of human right, and consequently an achievement of human beings themselves? (8:64)

Kant's position is that the cultural and political development of the species is itself a condition for the species to develop its true worth. This dignity is thus an achievement, not a given. If nature had left people in the happy (pre-modern, pre-civilized) condition of shepherds, their existence would have no more value than that of the happy sheep they tend. For similar reasons, we sense that the romantic "wish for a return to the past age of simplicity and innocence" (*Anfang* 8:122) is vacuous. Such a life would not satisfy us; we know our destiny lies elsewhere.

Granted, there does at first appear to be a tension between Kant's strongly anti-consequentialist position concerning the dignity of individuals and his teleological view concerning the true worth of the species. As is well known, he denies that the dignity of persons is in any sense dependent on the consequences or results of their acts. "A good will is not good because of what it effects or accomplishes"—even if a morally good will were not able to accomplish *anything* it set out to do (so long as it summoned all means in its control), "then, like a jewel, it would still shine by itself, as something that has its full worth in itself" (*Gr* 4:394). However, insofar as the cultural and political development of the species is itself a precondition for human moralization, this tension is only apparent. The dignity of human individuals presupposes the development of the species. Without the latter, the former does not yet fully exist.[57]

Born Too Early

Kant himself acknowledges this particular difficulty when he remarks that

> it will always remain strange [*Befremdend bleibt es immer*] that earlier generations appear to carry through their toilsome labor only for the sake of later ones, and that only the most recent of the generations should have the luck [*Glück*] to live in the building on which a long line of their ancestors had labored (admittedly without any intention of their own), without being permitted to partake in the luck they had prepared (*Idee* 8:20).

"It will always remain strange"—that is, this is the way human history works. There is reason for regret here, but the situation cannot be changed. On Kant's view, this particular understanding of history necessarily follows once one accepts the following assumptions: 1) human beings are rational creatures, 2) as individuals they all die but the species is immortal,[58] and 3) the species should develop its predispositions to perfection (8:20). Kant does accept assumptions 1–3, but he admits that the result is still "puzzling" (*rätselhaft*) (8:20). However, once individual mortality is brought into the equation, and once we recognize that complete perfection is an unattainable ideal, it becomes clear that no individual or group participates fully in this destiny: we can only approximate it. And even though earlier generations cannot live in the house that they have helped build, by helping to build it they do participate in promoting an ideal. Ultimately, their own unhappiness can be justified in the manner of a theodicy: it makes possible the progress of the species. Each generation struggles so that future generations will have a better life. This participation in the promotion of an ideal is all that any human individual or group at any time can experience. But it does connect everyone directly to the final end of the species.

Perfecting Others

This alleged dilemma disappears, once one grants simple distinctions between (1) autonomous, adult moral agents versus children and (2) perfecting others versus developing the predispositions of others. Kant's remark at *MdS* 6:386 (quoted earlier) should be interpreted as applying to adults only. Adult moral agents are not obligated to perfect each other's characters. The remark is also clearly about the perfection of others (others who in this case are adults) rather than the development of the predispositions of others. In other words, Kant's stricture against "making another's *perfection* my end" has nothing to do with the moral education of those who are not yet adult moral agents.

The primary job of moral education, Kant asserts repeatedly in the *Lectures on Pedagogy*, is the grounding of character in students (9:481, cf. 469, 475, 480, 486–87). Character consists "in the aptitude of acting according to maxims" (9:481); maxims (intentions) which are acted on because the agent sees that they are grounded in and derived from concepts of duty (cf. 9:475). In order to develop and strengthen this aptitude, teachers are advised to help students gain control over their passions and inclinations (9:486–87); to draw their attention to "certain laws [*Gesetze*], known to them, that they must follow exactly" (9:481);[59] to inculcate primary virtues such as obedience (9:481–82), truthfulness, sociability (*Geselligkeit*), and cheerfulness (9:484–85); and to teach them their duties via specific examples and catechistic case studies (9:488, 490). We can see from this list that the grounding of character in students is indeed a tall order for even the most gifted teacher, but that it fortunately does not entail making students perfect. Teachers are obligated to morally educate their students (the chief task of which is to help students strengthen their native powers of judgment), but teachers do not have a duty to make their students perfect.

Education versus Transcendental Freedom

Education does primarily concern empirical character, not intelligible character. The same is true of all of the other preparatory steps for morality examined by Kant in other fields of impure ethics. Culture, art, science, politics, law—each of these areas of human life helps set the stage for moral life by shaping empirical character in ways that are analogous to that required by a virtuous moral disposition (e.g., by enlarging our sympathies, or by habituating us to principled behavior). At the same time, as I showed earlier in this chapter (see "Revolution") Kant does believe that efficacious moral education is education that somehow cuts through the surface causal network in order to effect the grounding of character. How this process works is something human beings cannot fully understand; we cannot know intelligible character, nor can we ever know with certainty that our attempts to shape and influence it are effective. But we can assume that such efforts may succeed, and, indeed, this assumption is a necessary presupposition of any program of moral education. We can think the possibility that we can form moral character without ever knowing for sure that we have done so.

Pre-modern, Pre-moral

Common wisdom has it that the moral horrors of the twentieth century have abolished any empirical plausibility that the strong Enlightenment assumption of moral progress may have once possessed. As noted earlier, Kant does assert that empirical proofs exist to support the claim that human beings in his age have made moral progress over their ancestors. The primary phenomenon to which he is alluding is the French Revolution (or more precisely, the "universal yet disinterested sympathy" expressed by spectators of the revolution, *Streit* 7:85), a transformation in human relations that in his view signaled the expansion of human rights and the enlargement of the moral community. Since Kant's day many other political and legal changes have occurred in numerous countries (e.g., in the United States, the Nineteenth Amendment to the Constitution (1920), which gave women the right to vote, and the Civil Rights Act of 1964, which prohibited discrimination for reason of color, race, religion, or national origin in places of public accommodation) that are further signs of this expansion process. It is most fundamentally this phenomenon of expansion or enlarge-ment (a wider sense of who counts morally, backed up by legal sanctions) to which Kant is referring with his thesis of moral progress. Obviously, he is paint-ing with a very large brush here. But thus construed, the moral progress thesis does not at all deny the possibility of a Hitler or Stalin in the twentieth century, or a Confucius or Jesus in previous eras. Neither individual moral heroes nor villains of the strongest degree possible are ruled out by his thesis. The reality of radical evil in human nature, and the possibility that at any moment human beings will once again freely choose to commit horrendous acts of moral evil, is in no way denied by Kant's claim that the modern era has witnessed moral progress. (For related discussion, see "'On the Radical Evil in Human Nature'" in chapter 4.)

The Lucky Ones

Finally, Kant certainly does not deny that luck plays a major role in many areas of human life. Indeed, since getting a good education is at least partly a matter of luck, and since the human being "is nothing except what education makes of him" (9:443), the role of luck in the shaping of (empirical) human temperament itself is considerable on Kant's view.[60] Obviously, whether one is born in 551 BC or 1724 AD is also a matter of luck. We don't deserve moral credit or blame for our dates of birth. Progress on Kant's view is achieved largely through the invisi-ble hand of our unsocial sociability; nature forces us to progress whether we want to or not (cf. *Idee* 8:24). Those who are born in a time or place of moral progress are indeed lucky; the rest are not so fortunate. (Though again, the suffering of previous generations can ultimately be justified by placing it in the larger context of nature's plan for the species and the progress that earlier efforts have made possible). Kant himself explicitly acknowledges all of this when he refers to the latest generation's *Glück* (luck, good fortune) in living in the build-ing that their ancestors have built (*Idee* 8:20).

But while Kant does not deny that luck looms large in many areas of human life, he does deny that what we ourselves make of our own moral characters is a matter of luck. The normative status of a person's moral character is a func-tion of how well this person "has tied himself to certain practical principles that he has unalterably prescribed for himself through his own reason" (*Anth* 7:292). Here the question is what we do to ourselves; not what nature and the environ-ment have done to us. As Kant remarks in *Anthropology from a Pragmatic Point of View*: "In this case it does not depend on what nature makes of the human being, but what the human being makes of himself; for the first belongs to tem-perament (in which the subject is largely passive), and only the latter allows him to recognize that he has a character" (*Anth* 7:292).

In short, human beings past, present, and future should not esteem either themselves or their forebears for being born into morally good or bad times. Judgments of moral esteem or scorn are warranted only in cases where we are talking about what people have done to their own moral characters. Such cases abound in human life, but here we also need to remind ourselves of Kant's own special brand of moral skepticism. The real morality of our conduct "remains entirely hidden [*gänzlich verborgen*] from us" (*KrV* A 551/B 579 n). Human beings cannot see into their own (much less each other's) moral characters. Smug judgments concerning the quality of anyone's moral character thus have no place in Kantian ethics.

It is easy to conclude in late twentieth century hindsight that Kant and his fellow *Aufklärer* went way over the top in their hopes for the moral progress of the human species. And this conclusion is correct. But Kant can acknowledge this criticism too, adding only the proviso that in ethics one needs to go over the top. Unattainable ideals are necessary and important in ethics, not only because of "their capacity to guide thought in beneficial directions,"[61] but also because they can help bring out the best in us—a best that cannot be known or measured beforehand. The full limits of our moral capacities are only successfully challenged when we are striving against a transcendental standard that we know we can never reach. Machiavelli—no naive optimist—once wisely echoed Aristotle in counseling that

> the prudent man . . . should proceed like those prudent archers who, aware of the strength of their bow when the target they are aiming at seems too distant, set their sights much higher than the designated target, not in order to reach to such a height with their arrow but rather to be able, with the aid of such a high aim, to strike the target.[62]

3

ANTHROPOLOGY

Origins

Kant first offered his anthropology course in the winter semester of 1772–73 and taught it annually thereafter twenty-four times until his retirement in 1796.[1] In a frequently cited letter to Marcus Herz written toward the end of 1773 he describes the aim of the course as follows:

> This winter for the second time I am giving a lecture course on anthropology, which I now intend to make into a proper academic discipline. But my plan is quite different.[2] The intention that I have is to disclose through it the sources of all sciences [*die Quellen aller Wissenschaften*],[3] of ethics, of skill, of human relations, of the method of educating and governing human beings, and therefore of everything that pertains to the practical. I seek then more phenomena and their laws rather than the first grounds of the possibility of modifying human nature in general. Hence the subtle and in my eyes eternally futile investigation concerning how bodily organs stand in connection with thoughts is left out entirely. I include so many observations of ordinary life that my listeners have constant occasion to compare their ordinary experience with my remarks and thus, from beginning to end, find the lectures always entertaining and never dry. In my spare time I am working on a preliminary exercise for students from this (in my opinion) very pleasant empirical study [*Beobachtungslehre*] of skill, prudence, and even wisdom [*Weisheit*][4] that, along with physical geography and distinct from all other instruction, can be called knowledge of the world [*Kenntnis der Welt*]. (10:138)

Over the years there has been much speculation concerning the origins of Kant's novel interest in anthropology. Benno Erdmann, in his book *Reflexionen Kants zur Anthropologie* (1882), argued that the anthropology course was itself developed out of parts of Kant's earlier physical geography course; specifically, out of "the disciplines of moral and political geography."[5] Emil Arnoldt, in his 1894 work, argues at length against Erdmann's hypothesis, labeling it "the product of arbitrary fabrication and rash conclusions."[6] However, in his early "Sketch and Announcement of a Physical Geography Lecture Course" from 1757, Kant does state that his course will include a discussion "of the inclinations [*Neigungen*] of human beings which flow from the climate in which they live, the variety of their prejudices and ways of thinking, in so far as this can all serve to make the human being more known to himself, [as well as] a short sketch of their arts, business, and science" (2:9).[7]

Norbert Hinske, in his essay "Kants Idee der Anthropologie" (1966), suggests plausibly that the anthropology lectures grew out of the empirical psychology portions of Kant's metaphysics lectures.[8] In the section of the 1765–66 *Nachricht* which concerns his metaphysics course, Kant announces: "Accordingly, after a brief introduction I shall begin with empirical psychology, which actually is the metaphysical science of the human being based on experience [*metaphysische Erfahrungswissenschaft vom Menschen*]" (2:309). And toward the end of this same section, Kant suggests that an additional reason for starting with empirical psychology is that the listener "will have heard something which he can enjoy, because it is easy to understand, and will have heard something which he can use, because of the frequency with which it can be given an application in life [*Anwendung im Leben*]" (2:309–10). Kant repeatedly stresses each of these three points (the experiential roots of anthropology, the inherent popularity of the subject matter, and its applicability to real life) in later versions of his anthropology lectures.

It seems therefore that Kant's anthropology lectures in fact grew out of both his physical geography and metaphysics lectures. As Frederick van de Pitte notes, in his sketch of the genesis of Kant's anthropology:

> Apparently Kant had planned to publish a manual on anthropology, and had already begun to segregate the material from that of his other lectures. The lectures on metaphysics, which he began with a discussion of empirical psychology, and those on empirical geography were sifted for materials which were more appropriate to anthropology. The process seems to have been completed by the summer of 1772.[9]

But regardless of whether or not one can point definitively to a pre-existing portion (or portions) of Kant's work out of which his anthropology lectures grew, it is also important to note that his growing interest in the new discipline of anthropology was part of a much larger cultural phenomenon. Throughout the seventeenth and eighteenth centuries scores of European authors issued tracts on "the doctrine of human nature." By means of the term "anthropology" they sought to emancipate the study of human nature from theologically oriented metaphysical traditions of inquiry and to situate it in a context which was not (yet) that of mathematical-experimental natural science. This burgeoning interest in anthropology, in which Kant himself played a key role, was part of a larger "turn toward nature" as well as a "turn toward the life-world [*Lebenswelt*]".[10] At the same time, Kant's own approach to anthropology, while broadly empirical, is a far cry from more strenuous, positivistic versions that were to have their day later.

In comparison with the *Lectures on Pedagogy*, Kant's anthropology lectures suffer from an embarrassment of textual riches. In addition to the version that he himself published in 1798 under the title *Anthropology from a Pragmatic Point of View*, many different student and auditor transcriptions (*Nachschriften*) of them have surfaced over the years. Also, nearly a thousand pages of relevant material is contained in volume 15 of the Academy Edition (subdivided into two separate books, due to length), edited by Erich Adikes and first published in 1913. Slightly over two-thirds of this material consists of Kant's "Reflexionen zur Anthropologie" (essentially, his unpublished notes on anthropology); about one-third consists of selections from different drafts of his anthropology lectures (*Collegentwürfe*) from the 1770s and 1780s. The anthropology Nachschriften present the usual dating and authentication problems, and their contents do sometimes differ substantially from Kant's own version. (Since he taught the course twenty-four times from 1772 to 1796, some variation is to be expected.) Volume 25 in the German *Akademie Ausgabe* contains seven different anthropology *Nachschriften*, along with short additions (*Zusätze*) from others.[11] However, despite (and to some extent also because of) this wealth of material, the relationship between Kant's anthropology lectures and his ethics remains a point of contention.

Which Anthropology?

> Our anthropology can be read by everyone, even by women getting dressed, because it contains a great deal that is entertaining.
> *Menschenkunde*

For various reasons, Kantian anthropology is an eclectic venture—one that reveals different origins, competing concerns and aims, and multiple application possibilities. In the present section I characterize briefly some of the more salient features of this particular body of Kant's work, concluding with some remarks about the relationship between his writings in ethics and anthropology.

Popularity

The various lectures on anthropology and physical geography which derive from Kant's annual courses were always intended for a popular audience (cf. *Anth* 7:122 n; *Refl* 1482, 15:658; *Mrongovius* 25:1213). His aim was not to contribute another tome toward "science for school" (*Wissenschaft für die Schule*) but rather to promote "enlightenment for common life" (*Aufklärung fürs gemeine Leben*) (*Menschenkunde* 25:853). If this kind of *Aufklärung* project is to succeed, its message needs to be conveyed in a way that will be of interest to both non-academics as well as academics; "here one must always understand how to apply one's knowledge simply in a popular way so that others understand us, not merely professional scholars" (*Menschenkunde* 25:853).

Although the suspicion that Kant was occasionally talking down to his audience is hard to shake off (for example, the comment in the epigraph concerning women),[12] his early biographers are all in agreement concerning his success in engaging a popular audience. For instance, Reinhold Bernard Jachmann, writes in his 1804 biography *Immanuel Kant geschildert in Briefen an einen Freund*:

His lectures on anthropology and physical geography afforded a lighter but extremely engaging instruction, which were also attended most frequently. Here one saw the lofty thinker strolling about in the material world, and the human being and nature illuminated with the torch of original reason. His astute remarks, which carried the stamp of a deep knowledge of human beings and nature, were fitted out in lectures filled with wit and genius, which charmed every single listener.[13]

The anthropology and physical geography lectures are thus not primarily intended as further contributions to Kant's critical, transcendental philosophy program. In other words, it is clear that the latter program (on which philosophers and scholars since Kant have tended to focus exclusively) was not his only concern. A major portion of Kant's teaching activity was devoted to trying to enlighten his students more about the people and world around them in order that they might live (pragmatically as well as morally) better lives.

Weltkenntnis

Related to the popular aim of these lectures is the *kind* of knowledge that they were intended to convey. Kant was trying to construct a "theory of the practice of life" (*Theorie der Lebenspraxis*),[14] one that would "be useful not merely for *school*, but for *life*, and through which the accomplished student is introduced to the stage of his destiny, namely, the *world*" (*Racen*, 2:443 n; cf. *Friedländer* 25:469). Kantian anthropology is thus "viewed as *knowledge of the world* [*Weltkenntnis*] which must follow school" (*Anth* 7:120)—that is, it must prepare students for life in the real world, after their formal education is over. In constructing anthropology as a Weltkenntnis, Kant also indicates that knowledge of the world as he construes it rightfully has an anthropocentric tilt. "The human being knows the world, that is to say, he knows human beings of all status groups [*alle Stände*].[15] Knowledge of the world (*Weltkenntnis*) according to common understanding means knowledge of the human being" (*Menschenkunde* 25:854; cf. *Collins* 25:9). Or, as he remarks tersely in a *Reflexion*: "*Weltkenntnis ist Menschenkenntnis*" (*Refl* 1482, 15:659).

Knowledge of the human being (*Menschenkenntnis*) in turn is subdivided into "1) knowledge of the human being as a thing of nature [*Naturding*]; [and] 2) as an ethical being" (*Refl* 1482, 15:660). (Here we see another hint of the not always carefully delineated moral dimension of Kant's anthropology. See n. 4 on the term *Weisheit*.) And it is the whole human being we are interested in understanding—not merely the noteworthy details concerning the soul with which empirical psychology concerns itself. As he remarks in a late version of the lectures: "Anthropology is not psychology, as Baumgarten believes. Psychology looks only at the soul, but anthropology is when I consider the human being as I see him ensouled [*beseelt*] before me."[16] Finally, the human being must also "be viewed not physiologically but cosmologically" (*Geo* 9:157; cf. *Racen* 2:443 n, *Pillau* 25:734). Kantian anthropology aims to teach us about human beings in "their relation to the whole of life [*ihr Verhältnis im Ganzen*] in which they stand and in which each person assumes his own position" (2:443 n).

So the aim was to produce a "course of studies for the world" (*Studium für die Welt*) (*Menschenkunde* 25:853); a common life road map for people to orient themselves by after their formal education is over. This striving for a body of knowledge that is intended to have real life applications is also described later by Kant in his own published version of the *Anthropology* as a "science for the common welfare [*gemeinnützige Wissenschaft*]" (*Anth* 7:122).

Empirical Science

As the last quotation indicates, although Kantian anthropology is a popular discipline intended to help orient students in the world outside the lecture hall, it is also supposed to be a science (*Wissenschaft*). Kant hopes that his anthropology will be not a mere "fragmentary groping around" but a proper *Wissenschaft* that is "systematically designed" (*Anth* 7:120, 121; cf. *Geo* 9:158). As we saw earlier in his letter to Herz toward the end of 1773, he wants "to make [anthropology] into a proper academic discipline" (10:145).

It would seem that these scientific, systematic yearnings which Kant pins on his anthropology stand at least occasionally in uneasy tension with the popular, *Weltkenntnis* aims outlined earlier. (Can a systematic *Wissenschaft* still be entertaining to women "getting dressed [*bei der Toilette*]"?)[17] But there is also the question of just what *kind* of science Kant wants his anthropology to be. An easy (and correct) answer is that Kantian anthropology is to be an *empirical* science. However, this answer raises problems of its own, both for philosophers (who often approach Kant's anthropology with a more transcendental agenda in mind) and for social scientists (who often assume a narrower conception of "empirical science" than Kant is willing to settle for).

As is well known, it is true that Kant in several different places speaks of anthropology as a *Grunddisziplin* of philosophy. In Jäsche's version of the *Logic* lectures, for instance, we are told that the questions of metaphysics, ethics, and religion "could at bottom all be reckoned to be anthropology," because their questions all relate back to anthropology's (9:25; cf. letter to Carl Friedrich Stäudlin of May 4, 1793, 11:414; *Metaphysik-Pölitz* 28:534). And in one of the *Reflexionen zur Anthropologie* (which itself appears to have generated at least two philosophy dissertations in Germany) Kant says also that it is "not enough to know many different sciences; one needs the self-knowledge of understanding and reason. *Anthropologia transcendentalis*" (*Refl* 903, 15:395).[18] Here philosophy itself becomes, as Volker Gerhardt remarks, "a *conceptual self-interpretation of the human being*," a discipline "turned back to its Socratic starting point that becomes not more and not less than *human self-knowledge*."[19]

However, while this concern for a transcendental anthropology that tracks all questions back to the nature of the knowing subject is definitely a concern of Kant's, and while there also is a rich tradition of philosophical anthropology, particularly strong in early to mid–twentieth century German thought but also detectable elsewhere (e.g., French existentialism) that has its roots in this Kantian concern, the various versions of Kant's own *Anthropology* lectures are for the most part not "philosophical" in this particular sense. Instead, they are chiefly concerned with the more empirical (but nevertheless vitally important) task of providing people with a road map of common life.

But this is not at all to say that the anthropology of Kant's lectures satisfies the more restrictive conditions of what is to count as empirical science that were popular in mainstream Anglo-American circles until recently. It clearly does not. Because of the dual emphases on self-consciousness and freedom that Kant places on his approach to the study of human nature, the goal of an observation-based science of behavior is not one he embraces. Among other things, he draws a firm, qualitative line between human beings and all other animals who live on earth: "The fact that the human being can form a conception of the I [*das Ich*] raises him infinitely above all other beings living on earth. Because of this he is a *person* . . . an entirely different being, because of his rank [*Rang*] and dignity, from *things*, such as irrational animals, to whom one can do as one pleases." (*Anth* 7:127; cf. Starke II, 9, 207–8; *Gr* 4:434–35). Or, as he remarks in the *Menschenkunde:* "The I contains that which distinguishes the human being from all other animals. If a horse could grasp the thought of I, then I would climb down and it would have to be viewed as a member of my society [*als meine Gesellschaft*]" (25:859).

Human beings' self-awareness also means that they make for extremely poor (indeed, impossible) subjects of scientific investigation; "still less does another thinking subject submit to our investigations in such a way as to be conformable to our purposes, and even the observation itself alters and distorts the state of the object observed" (*MAN* 4:471; cf. *Anth* 7:121; *Refl* 1482, 15:660, *Mrongovius* 25:1212). "One can indeed make experiments with animals and things, but not with human beings" (*Busolt* 25:1437). The alleged impossibility of an observation-based science of anthropology in turn requires that the anthropologist be somewhat resourceful in gathering source materials (see "Sources" later in this chapter).

Kant's strong focus on freedom further distinguishes his own anthropology from more strait-laced versions. Anthropology "from a physiological point of view" looks merely at what nature makes of the human being, but what Kant wants is an anthropology "from a pragmatic point of view," which concerns what the human being "as a free-acting being makes, or can and should make, of himself" (*Anth* 7:119; see also "Pragmatic Anthropology" later is this chapter). Throughout his lectures, he maintains that "the human being is the only free-acting being on earth" (*Pillau* 25:733).

In sum, what Kant aspires to in his *Anthropology* lectures is an empirical science; albeit a much more informal, less rigorous one than was (and to some extent still is) popular in more positivistic and behavioristic circles. As Brandt remarks: "Anthropology with Kant is not as it was in the Renaissance and with certain authors in the 18th and 19th centuries a combat discipline [*Kampfdisziplin*] that turns against metaphysics; rather it completes [*ergänzt*] metaphysics, that is to say transcendental philosophy."[20] Or, as Kant himself remarks in his reply to Carl Leonhard Reinhold's critique of his review of Herder's *Ideas for a Philosophy of the History of Humanity*, the proper materials for anthropology "are to be found neither in metaphysics nor in a museum of natural history in which the skeleton of the human being can be compared with that of other animals . . . rather these materials can be found only in human *actions*, in which human character is revealed [*offenbart*]" (8:56).

Sources

As noted earlier, Kant's conviction that accurate experiments and observations of human beings are not possible means that would-be empirical anthropologists need to be creative in their source materials. In his own 1798 *Anthropology* Kant says that "there are no real sources [*Quellen*] for anthropology, but nevertheless there exist aids [*Hilfsmittel*]" (7:121). And what are anthropology's aids? "World history, biographies, yes, even [*ja*] plays and novels"[21] (*Anth* 7:121). Travel also "belongs to the means [*Mitteln*] of enlarging anthropology, even if it is only the reading of travel books. But one must have first acquired one's knowledge of human beings at home through contact with one's city or country comrades, if one wants to know what to look for abroad" (7:120; cf. *Friedländer* 25:471).[22]

In the *Menschenkunde* lecture the stronger term *Quellen* is used, but the actual list is quite similar. Here we are informed that "contact with many status groups [*Stände*] and with educated persons is a very fruitful *Quelle* of anthropology" (25:857). "Another *Quelle* of anthropology is history" (25:857). In addition, "novels, comedies, plays, tragedies, for instance Shakespeare's, can give anthropological knowledge," but we must of course first judge all types of fiction carefully to see whether or not they have exaggerated or otherwise distorted human nature (25:857–58; cf. *Refl* 1482, 15:659; *Pillau* 25:734, *Mrongovius* 25:1213).

In our own time more and more social scientists have finally come around to the view that fiction also has truths to teach us about human nature. Moral philosophers who are skeptical of the abstractions of theory also frequently turn to fiction in hopes of finding a clearer illumination of the moral life. Kant's sense that social science can and should enlist the help of history, drama, fiction, travel books, and everyday conversation does not sound as strange as it once did. At the same time, as we shall see later, he does not always heed his own advice that social scientists must use such materials carefully if they are to successfully weed out fact from fiction. Particularly in his discussions of race, he accepts uncritically the gossipy and sensationalistic (that is to say false) reports of European explorers and travelers concerning *die Wilden* (savages, literally "the wild ones") and others.

Pragmatic Anthropology

As is well known, Kant advocates anthropology "from a pragmatic point of view." Surprisingly, this advocacy of a pragmatic point of view actually has a certain retrograde tone to it. Rudolf Eisler, for instance, in the entry for the German term *pragmatisch* in his *Wörterbuch der philosophischen Begriffe*, states that "the concept of the pragmatic in the philosophy of Christian Wolff is of great importance." He then cites a passage from Wolff's 1720 work *Vernünfftige Gedancken von Gott, der Welt und der Seele des Menschen, auch allen Dingen überhaupt*, where Wolff writes that his own philosophy "is completely pragmatic, that is to say, furnished with everything in such a way that it has let itself be employed in the sciences and in the so-called higher faculties as well as in human life."[23] Kant was certainly not the first German philosopher who sought to develop a style of theory that could illuminate everyday life.

It should also be noted that Kant himself uses the term "pragmatic" itself in at least four different ways. Sometimes "pragmatic" refers to the talent of "being skillful [*geschickt*] in the use of other human beings for one's purposes" (*Anth* 7:322, cf. Dohna, 72). When used in this particular manner, "pragmatic" always refers to how one handles others. A second use of "pragmatic" links it up with prudence (*Klugheit*) and refers to the ability to find efficient means to one's happiness. In his discussion of imperatives in the *Groundwork*, for instance, Kant mentions briefly "*counsels* of prudence," labeling them "*pragmatic* imperatives" (*Gr* 4:416–17). With the second usage one clearly can be pragmatic with regard to oneself. However, Kant also seems to link at least part of this second sense of "pragmatic" with the first when he distinguishes between two kinds of *Klugheit*: "The word *Klugheit* is used in two senses: in one sense it can go by the name *Weltklugheit*; in the second *Privatklugheit*. The first is the skill of a human being in having influence over others, in order to use them for his own purposes. The second is insight in uniting all of these purposes to one's lasting advantage" (*Gr* 4:416 n). Since relations with other people normally are necessary for our own happiness, one who lacks skill in dealing with others is unlikely to be happy. This second sense of "pragmatic" is also occasionally invoked in the *Anthropology* lectures. However, when it is invoked it is the "using others" aspect of *Klugheit* that is stressed. In the *Menschenkunde* manuscript, for example, we read that a "doctrine is pragmatic insofar as it makes us prudent and useful in public matters [*öffentliche Dinge*], where we necessarily have not merely theory but also practice [*Praxis*]" (25:856; see also *Mrongovius* 25:1210). Earlier in the same paragraph the author states that practical as opposed to speculative *Menschenkenntnis* "makes us prudent; it is a knowledge of the art of how a human being has influence on others and can direct [*leiten*] them according to his intention" (25:855).

However, in the foreword to *Anthropology from a Pragmatic Point of View* Kant invokes a third sense of "pragmatic" which is clearly distinct from the above two meanings. Here we are told that a doctrine of *Menschenkenntnis* can be approached from either a physiological or a pragmatic point of view. The former refers to "what nature makes of the human being"; the latter to "what the human being makes, or can and should [*soll*] make, of himself as a free-acting being [*als freihandlendes Wesen*]" (7:119). In this third sense, "pragmatic" refers to the capacity of human beings to set ends for themselves and to act in accordance with these ends. Although the pragmatic "should (*soll*)" in the definition is not unequivocally a categorical moral ought, it does indicate that we are now not merely talking about a manipulative *Klugheitslehre* that concerns our skill in handling others.

Finally, as noted earlier (n. 4), Kant does occasionally use "pragmatic" in a still wider sense that explicitly embraces moral concerns. In one of the *Reflexionen zur Logik*, for instance, we read: "The historical manner of teaching is pragmatic when it has another intention than the scholastic, [one which] is not merely for the school but for the world or morality [*oder die Sittlichkeit*]" (*Refl* 3376, 16:804).

In a short section entitled "Uses of Anthropology" in the *Pillau* manuscript, Kant summarizes four benefits of anthropology that map on fairly well to the above senses of "pragmatic:"

> The better we know human beings, the better we know how to regulate our actions so that they harmonize with those of others. Anthropology teaches how one is to win over people. It teaches self-satisfaction, when one finds that one also has in oneself the good that one finds in others. It gives us the subjective principles of all sciences. And these subjective principles have a great influence 1) in morals, 2) in religion, 3) and in education. (25:734–35; cf. *Busolt* 25:1437)

Unfortunately, the specifically moral sense of "pragmatic" (and more generally, the issue of the relationship between pragmatic anthropology and ethics) that is most relevant to the present study is not always carefully delineated by Kant. (For further discussion, see "Anthropology and Ethics" later in this chapter)

Divisions of Anthropology

Over the years Kant experimented with various ways of conceptualizing and bringing together the different parts of his anthropology. In his 1798 version, anthropology is said to consist of two parts: "Anthropological *Didaktik*. On the Art of How to Recognize the Interior as well as the Exterior of the Human Being" (7:125), and "Anthropological *Charakteristik*. On the Art of How to Recognize the Interior of the Human Being from the Exterior" (7:283). The "Didactics" is considerably longer than the "Characteristics," and is itself subdivided into three books: "On the Cognitive Faculty" (7:127–229), "On the Feeling of Pleasure and Displeasure" (7:230–50), and "On the Faculty of Desire" (7:251–82).

In the Dohna version, anthropology is also divided into two parts, but here they are called "The Doctrine of Elements [*Elementarlehre*]" and "The Doctrine of Method [*Methodenlehre*] or Characteristics." The latter is said to be the application (*Anwendung*) of the former (290), which is consistent with the *Elementarlehre/Methodenlehre* distinction employed in *KrV*, but the author also states that "The Doctrine of Method" can "actually more generally" be called "Characteristics"—which brings it into line with the terminology of the 1798 version (Dohna, 289–90; cf. 70). And according to Oswald Külpe, editor of the Academy Edition version of the 1798 lectures, Kant also wrote into the margin of the so-called Rostock manuscript (the only existing manuscript of the *Anthropology* written by Kant himself, held by the Rostock University Library): "Anthropology. First Part. Anthropological *Didactics*. What is the human being? Second part. *Characteristics*. How the peculiarity of each human being is to be known. The first part is at the same time the *Elementarlehre*, the second the *Methodenlehre* of knowledge of human beings [*Menschenkunde*]" (*Anth* 7:410).

In general then, a "theory/application" division is employed in most versions of the lectures. The first part probably derives more from the empirical psychology portions of Kant's lectures on Baumgarten's *Metaphysics*; the second from his *Physical Geography* lectures as well as his proto-anthropological 1764 work, *Observations on the Feeling of the Beautiful and the Sublime*. Other versions of the lectures adopt a similar division. For instance, part 2 of the *Friedländer* manuscript opens with the following remark: "Seeing as we have learned in the general part about the human being according to his powers of soul and faculties, so we must now in the special part try to apply [*anwenden*] the knowledge of the human being, and to make use of it" (25:624). Similarly, in *Mrongovius*, part 2 is entitled "Second or practical Part of Anthropology, which concerns the Characteristics of the Human Being" (25:1208), and begins with the following description: "While the first part contains the physiology of the human being and therefore at the same time the elements out of which he is composed, so the practical part of anthropology is that which teaches us how human beings in their voluntary actions are constituted" (25:1367; cf. *Busolt* 25:1437, 1530).[24]

It is clearly the second, applied (or "practical": here we see yet another hint of the moral dimension) part of anthropology that is most relevant to my purposes in this study. Accordingly, its major themes of individual and group character and the destiny of the human species will be examined in some detail later. At the same time, *all* parts of Kant's anthropology and physical geography lectures, insofar as they provide us with *Menschenkenntnis* and *Weltkenntnis*, are intended to be at least indirectly relevant to the second part of ethics. For the aim is to learn more about human beings and the world they live in, in order to determine what particular aids and obstacles to the realization of a priori moral principles exist within the natural life situation of this particular species of rational being. And while the *Kenntnis* of human beings and of the world that these sciences seek to provide must be objective, empirically accurate knowledge if it is serve the purpose for which it was intended, it is evident that this search for empirically accurate knowledge itself also stands under a moral imperative: we seek to understand the world so that we can make it morally better.

Anthropology and Ethics

Perhaps the most exasperating issue confronting anyone who sets out to write about Kant's anthropology is its awkward "neither here nor there" status. How can something that professes to be an empirical science also claim to be *moral* anthropology—normatively as opposed to merely descriptively "moral"? Arnoldt, for instance, in his 1894 study, describes the tension as follows:

> [A]s a part of practical philosophy it [Kant's anthropology] stands under the legislation of reason according to laws of freedom, which prescribe what ought to be; on the other hand, even if it is morally-practical, it is part of a comprehensive [empirical] anthropology which stands under the legislation of reason

according to the concept of nature, which indicates what is. Kant did not determine this relationship more closely.[25]

Closely related (and equally exasperating) to this much-debated conceptual problem of figuring out how something which is empirical can also be (in Kant's sense) practical or moral is the textual problem of determining what exactly the relationship is between the various versions of Kant's *Anthropology* lectures and his writings in practical philosophy. Again, in his writings on ethics Kant repeatedly invokes the term "anthropology" when describing the second, empirical part of ethics. Sometimes this second part is tagged as "moral anthropology" (*MdS* 6:217; *Moral Mrongovius II* 29:599); sometimes as "practical anthropology" (*Gr* 4:388); and sometimes simply as "anthropology" (*Gr* 4:412; *Moralphilosophie Collins* 27:244; *Moral Mrongovius I* 27:1398). This frequent employment of the term "anthropology" in Kant's statements about the second part of ethics in his writings and lectures on practical philosophy gives readers who turn to his *Anthropology* a thoroughly legitimate expectation that in the latter writings the myriad mysteries of Kantian empirical ethics will finally be addressed in detail. However, this expectation is not met.

It will not do to gloss over this odd lacuna by speculating that

in the *Groundwork* the question of how such an application [of ethics] is to be conceived and carried out does not interest Kant, because there he is primarily concerned with grounding the priority of moral philosophy as a pure science [*reine Wissenschaft*]. And in his lectures on *Anthropology from a Pragmatic Point of View* as well as in his history of philosophy and politics essays this problem plays no role, that is to say, it plays no role *any longer* [*spielt keine Rolle mehr*], because these writings already are the carried-out application [*bereits die durchgeführte Anwendung sind*].[26]

Although I believe it is true in a qualified sense[27] that the *Anthropology* and the essays on history and politics "already are the carried-out application," to simply assert this is to beg a very fundamental question. What we need to determine more precisely is how and in what respects these writings (as well as others that bear on his impure ethics project) can be said to be the carried-out application of pure ethics.

Remarkably, in Kant's own *Anthropology from a Pragmatic Point of View* the terms "moral anthropology" and "practical anthropology" do not even occur,[28] and in all of the versions of the *Anthropology* lectures that I have examined he is surprisingly quiet about the second part of ethics. As Brandt remarks:

It is difficult to determine the relation of the anthropology lectures to this practical or moral anthropology, as it is called in the actual [writings on] ethics. . . . [T]hey appear not to be identical, because Kant avoids speaking of pragmatic anthropology in the moral philosophy writings, which he speaks of as a new discipline in his lectures. The latter also does not correspond with the thematic determinations that *The Metaphysics of Morals* lays down.[29]

At the same time, as Brandt himself acknowledges, there are several explicit points of contact for moral anthropology within Kant's anthropology lectures, even though the former is not presented as the main theme of the latter and even though Kant does not address systematically the larger issue of how anthropology relates to ethics in his *Anthropology*. These points of contact, which I examine in greater detail later, include Kant's discussions of "The Character of a Person" (*Anth* 7:285–302) and the "Highest Physical" and "Highest Moral-Physical" goods (7:276–82). These latter two discussions in turn hook up directly with culminating section of *Anthropology from a Pragmatic Point of View*, "On the Character of the Species" (7:321–33), in which we encounter one of the dominant themes in all of Kant's writings under discussion here—the moral destiny of the human species.

Also, it is important to note that the fundamental claim that the second part of ethics is moral anthropology, which Kant asserts repeatedly in his moral philosophy writings, is by no means denied in the anthropology lectures. The problem rather is that the issue does not receive much explicit attention. As Wolfgang Becker notes: "[A] 'practical anthropology' must, in its conception, in its systematic method, and in its carrying-out, be tied much more tightly [*viel enger . . . gebunden*] to moral philosophy than is the case with the [1798] *Anthropology*."[30]

In addition to the several strong thematic points of contact between anthropology and ethics that exist in all versions of the *Anthropology* lectures, it is also the case, as Brandt notes, that "at times the anthropology lectures are presented explicitly as a counterpart [*Pendant*] of a priori ethics."[31] One such "counterpart passage" occurs early in *Mrongovius*:

> Anthropology is pragmatic, but contributes to [*dient*] moral knowledge of the human being because from it one must derive [*schöpfen*] the grounds of movement [*BewegungsGründe*] for [human] morality, and without it morality would be scholastic and not applicable to the world and not enjoyable [*nicht angenehm*]. Anthropology is to morality as spatial geometry is to geodesy. (25:1211; cf. *Pillau* 25:735, *Busolt* 25:1436)[32]

Similarly, in the opening section of *Friedländer* we read: "The reason that morals and sermons . . . have little effect is due to the lack [*Mangel*] of knowledge of the human being. Morals must [*muß*] be united with [*verbunden . . . mit*] knowledge of humanity" (25:471–72).

In both passages Kant is echoing well-known claims made in the *Groundwork* (morality "requires anthropology for its *application* to human beings," 4:412), the *Metaphysics of Morals* (moral anthropology deals with "subjective conditions in human nature that hinder human beings or help them in *carrying out* the laws of a metaphysics of morals," 6:217), as well as the *Moralphilosophie Collins* lectures ("morality cannot exist without anthropology, for one must first know the subject in order to know whether he is also capable of doing what is demanded of him," 27:244). And he is doing so in the context of his anthropology lectures.

Finally, it is also important to note that contemporaries of Kant who sought to make his philosophy more accessible to a wider audience clearly understood his anthropology as having a strong moral component. In 1797, one year before Kant's *Anthropology from a Pragmatic Point of View* appeared, Georg Samuel Albert Mellin published the first volume of his *Enzyclopädisches Wörterbuch der kritischen Philosophie*. In his preface, Mellin states that the "goal of this dictionary is to present the doctrines of the critical philosophy in their entire range, clearly, understandably, and convincingly."[33] At the beginning of his impressive six-page entry "Anthropology," the author notes that Kantian anthropology "divides into two parts, theoretical and practical." Practical anthropology, he elaborates later,

> in the wider sense of the term, is the application of morality to the characteristic condition and situation of the human faculty of desire—to the drives, inclinations, appetites, and passions of the human being, and the hindrances to the carrying-out of the moral law, and concerns virtues and vices. It is the empirical part of ethics, which can be called practical anthropology, a true doctrine of virtue [*eigentliche Tugendlehre*], or applied philosophy of ethics or morals [*angewandte Philosophie der Sitten oder Moral*].[34]

Mellin continues:

> The task of practical anthropology, is to determine how the human being shall [*soll*] be determined through the moral law; or what the moral laws are to which human beings under the hindrances of feelings, desires, and passions are subject. . . . No one yet, even from among the critical philosophers, has produced [*geliefert*] a practical anthropology from this single, correct point of view.[35]

Similarly, Carl Christian Erhard Schmid, in the fourth edition of his *Wörterbuch zum leichtern Gebrauch der kantischen Schriften* (1798), also subdivides Kantian anthropology into "theoretical" and "practical" parts. "Practical anthropology," he writes, is

> applied and empirical philosophy of morals, a true doctrine of virtue [*eigentliche Tugendlehre*]—it is the consideration of the moral law in relation to the human will, whose desires and drives are hindrances to the practicing of the moral law. It is supported in part by principles of pure ethics [*reine Moral*], or the metaphysics of morals; and in part by doctrines of theoretical psychology.[36]

Mellin's and Schmid's descriptions of the nature and aims of practical anthropology are both quite in line with the critical philosopher's. At the same time, Mellin's last sentence, though probably not intended as a criticism of the "deeply esteemed professor," also helps indicate why we do not find more explicit discussion of moral anthropology within Kant's *Anthropology* lectures. Kant did not see it as his task to develop a detailed moral anthropology. Though he states repeatedly that such a moral anthropology is necessary for the proper application of ethical theory, and while he gives numerous hints in a wide variety of different texts concerning what this moral anthropology should look like and what its aims should be, he himself does not produce it for us. It remains an uncompleted task for others to take "this single, correct point of view" and produce a viable practical anthropology.

Individual Character

In nearly every version of the *Anthropology* lectures, Kant includes a detailed discussion of "The Character of the Person." In most cases, it leads off the second, more applied half of the lectures, and is immediately followed by sections on "The Character of the Sexes," "The Character of Peoples," "The Character of Races," and "The Character of the Species" (*Anth* 7:124).[37] A similar sequence of topics is also followed in sections 2–4 of the *Observations on the Feeling of the Beautiful and the Sublime*. These various discussions of the character of the person in the *Anthropology* lectures constitute one direct link to a specifically moral anthropology.

In a general sense, the anthropology materials on individual character complement the discussions of moral character in Kant's moral philosophy writings. For instance, the former map on directly to the opening praise of the good will in the *Groundwork* (4:393) and the related later distinction between dignity and price (4:434–35; cf. *Menschenkunde* 25:1156–57). A key move in these discussions in the *Groundwork* and their anthropological analogues involves separating off the moral character of agents from their non-moral talents and temperaments. At the same time, as befits their setting within an anthropology lecture, there is more detailed discussion of the non-moral aspects of human character in the material from the anthropology lectures. A discussion and analysis of some specific themes follows.

Kant begins (in the 1798 version) by distinguishing physical from moral character. Physical character is "the mark of difference of a human being as a sensuous or natural being"; moral character is the mark of difference of a human being "as a rational being endowed with freedom" (*Anth* 7:285; cf. *Mrongovius* 25:1367–68). Immediately after this last definition comes a quintessential Kantian remark concerning moral character: "The man of principles [*Der Mann von Grundsätzen*],[38] of whom one definitely knows that he acts not from his instinct but rather from his will, has a character" (7:285). Kantian moral character necessarily concerns principled behavior; it is a *Denkungsart* or way of thinking (*Anth* 7:291; cf. *Mrongovius* 25:1385, *Busolt* 25:1530, Dohna, 270). As he remarks in two related *Reflexionen zur Anthropologie*: "Character proceeds on principles" (*Refl* 1156, 15:512); it "is that which brings all desires under a rule" (*Refl* 1222, 15:535).

Physical character is then subdivided into natural talents (or what he sometimes calls more broadly "the natural," *das Naturell*) and temperament. In Kant's discussion of "the natural" dimension of character, he makes several remarks about the person "who has a good heart" which expand on the famous critique of the naturally kindhearted person in the *Groundwork* (4:398). The person with such a disposition does have "an impulse [*Antrieb*] toward the practical good, although it is not practiced according to principles" (*Anth* 7:286; cf. *Menschenkunde* 25:1158). In allowing here that such people at least "aim in the right direction," Kant might seem to be judging them less severely than he does in the *Groundwork*. In the latter text he shocks many readers by asserting baldly that their actions simply possess no "genuine moral worth" at all (4:398). But they are not held up very highly in the *Anthropology* either. Because such persons act from impulse and inclination rather than reason, they are often moral chumps; "the good-natured and good-hearted are both people whom a crafty guest can use as he wants" (7:286). As the *Menschenkunde* version has it: "A good heart consists in the positive activity of doing good, though only from certain instincts; thus it is distinguished from character, which is the activity of doing good from principles" (25:1158). It is this non-reflective, purely instinctual nature of the kindhearted person's conduct that leads Kant to condemn it. "Morality consists not at all [*keineswegs*] in the good-naturedness of the heart, but rather in good character, and one is supposed to form it [*soll sie bilden*]" (*Refl* 1179, 15:521).

But this reference to the *formation* of moral character leads to a fundamental problem for Kant: *How* exactly is it to be formed? In *Anthropology from a Pragmatic Point of View* he echoes the strong "rebirth" language of *Religion within the Boundaries of Mere Reason* (6:47–48; cf. "Revolution" in chap. 2). The grounding of character, we are told, is

> identical to a kind of rebirth [*Wiedergeburt*], a certain solemn resolution which the person himself makes, [and] the resolution and the moment at which this transformation took place in him remain unforgettable to him, exactly like a new epoch. —Education [*Erziehung*], examples, and instruction generally cannot produce bit by bit this stability and perseverance in principles, but it can only be done through an explosion which takes place at once as a consequence of our weariness at the unsteady condition of instinct. (7:294)

However, in the *Menschenkunde* manuscript education and instruction are specifically singled out as means to the acquisition of character: "Education [*Erziehung*] and careful reflection are the means to acquire a character. To the means one can also add moral discourses [*moralische Unterredungen*], [for] the grasping [*Fassung*] of good, well-grounded principles" (25:1173 n. 1). And in *Friedländer* Kant's position on character formation is somewhere in between—here we are told that others cannot do it for us, but the emphasis now is on long-term effort rather than sudden conversion:

> It costs a great deal of effort and takes a very long time before one has become accustomed to act according to principles. It comes first with the years of mature reason. We all believe that we are educated in childhood, but we are not really educated. We must still lead ourselves to the result and form [*bilden*] our character ourselves. (25:633)

Although Kant does not present a totally consistent position concerning the means of moral character formation in the *Anthropology* lectures, his considered view is that moral character is an effect of freedom, which is beyond nature: "True character is character of *freedom*" (*Mrongovius* 25:1384). And just as no human being "can pass judgment in accordance with complete justice" (*KrV* A 551/B 579 n) on either his own or others' moral character due to lack of reliable information about inner freedom, so human knowledge of moral character *formation* is also fated to remain radically imperfect.

Kant's critique of naturally kindhearted people in the *Anthropology* lectures contains several other interesting twists. First, people of wicked character (who, in virtue of having character, at least reflect on their actions and motives, rather than respond instinctively) are more admirable than people without character; "a person of wicked character (like Sylla), although the violence of his fixed maxims fills one with disgust, is nevertheless an object of admiration, because we generally admire strength of soul [*Seelenstärke*] in comparison with kindness of soul [*Seelengüte*]" (*Anth* 7:293). A man of evil character is one who is "capable of acting according to principles. . . . thus he can also be improved through principles. But he who has no character at all, is not even in accord with himself" (*Friedländer* 25:631).

Second, moral imitators, precisely because they don't think for themselves, are not worthy of admiration. "The imitator (in ethics) is without character; for character consists precisely in the originality of the *Denkungsart*. It derives from a self-opened source [*selbst geöffnete Quelle*] of one's conduct" (*Anth* 7:293; cf. Starke II, 59). Kant's criticism of imitators applies both to those who mimic good people and those who copy evil people: both are "without character." At the same time, the person of character is not the type of "original thinker" who strikes others as strange. Such a person "must also not be an eccentric [*Sonderling*], indeed, he will never be, because he bases himself on principles which are valid for everyone" (*Anth* 7:293). "Principles which are valid for everyone" is of course a reference to the categorical imperative. But what is interesting here is the casualness of the reference. Kant doesn't belabor the point, and neither do people of character who ground their character on universalizable principles. Universalizability remains in the background, even though it is the structural basis of the moral person's character.[39]

Finally, although the naturally kindhearted person is subjected to much criticism in the anthropology lectures, there is one important passage which reveals that kindness is, on Kant's view, a necessary aspect of the morally good person's character. Immediately after the claim that strength of soul [*Seelenstärke*] is admired more than kindness of soul [*Seelengüte*] (cited earlier), Kant adds that "admittedly both [strength of soul and kindness of soul] must [*müssen*] be found united in the same subject in order to bring out what is more ideal than real, namely, the right to the title of magnanimity [*Seelengröße*]" (*Anth* 7:293). This passage helps serve as a correction to Schillerian misreadings of Kant's ethics which claim that the test of Kantian virtue is to do one's duty with aversion rather than gladness (cf. *Rel* 6:23–24 n).[40]

In Kant's 1798 version of his *Anthropology* lectures, the section entitled "The Character of the Person" runs eighteen pages. Only about three and a half pages of this material directly concerns *moral* character, or "what the human being makes of himself." The rest is about non-moral or physical character—"what nature makes of the human being" (7:292; cf. *Menschenkunde* 25:1157, Dohna, 324–25). Two dominant themes emerge from the remainder of this loosely arranged material.

Physiognomy

As noted earlier in this chapter ("Divisions of Anthropology"), the subtitle of the second part of the 1798 *Anthropology* is "On the Art of How to Recognize the Human Being's Interior from his Exterior" (7:283). This is essentially physiognomy (from the Greek *phusis*, nature + *gnōmōn*, judge, interpreter), which Kant himself defines as "the art [*Kunst*] of judging a person's disposition or way of thinking by his visible form [*sichtbare Gestalt*], consequently of judging the interior by the exterior" (*Anth* 7:295; cf. *Pillau* 25:826; *Mrongovius* 25:1376). Most people today do not admit to taking physiognomy seriously, and Kant himself does express more skepticism concerning its scientific status than did most of his contemporaries. For instance, he asserts that physiognomy "can never become a science [*Wissenschaft*]" (7:296)—note also that in the definition just cited he refers to it only as an art [*Kunst*];[41] and he concludes a long list of popular physiognomic inferences with the warning that "these are conjectures which permit only an uncertain interpretation" (7:299). Kant points out a related danger of physiognomic inferences (which we might call the "fallacy of unfamiliarity") when he remarks that "the unfamiliar faces of strangers are generally an object of ridicule for people who have never left their own country" (7:299).[42]

But it should also be kept in mind that physiognomy, despite its checkered career, has had a long list of notable defenders. Aristotle, for instance, discusses and endorses physiognomy in several different works (see, e.g., *Prior Analytics* 70b7, *History of Animals* 491b12–492a12, and the spurious Aristotelian work *Physiognomics* 805a1–806a18). And even Charles Darwin, in "his still highly important book" *The Expression of the Emotions in Man and Animals* (1872), argues that there are good grounds for associating physical expressions with character traits and habits of thought.[43]

Also, the temptation of physiognomy is particularly strong for moral theorists who, like Kant, emphasize the opacity of human motives. In the *Groundwork*, for instance, he writes that "in fact we can never, even by the most strenuous examination, completely get to the bottom of the secret impulses [*die geheimen Triebfedern*], because when moral value is in question it depends not on actions, which one sees, but on their inner principles, which one does not see" (4:407). And in a previously cited note in the first *Critique* he confesses: "The real morality of actions (merit and guilt), even that of our own conduct, remains entirely hidden [*ganz verborgen*] from us. Our imputations can only refer to the empirical character" (*KrV* A 551/B 579 n). How much easier things would be if one could infer reliably from the visible exterior to the invisible moral interior.

Human beings do not always wear their moral characters on their sleeves (or even on their faces). Still, because we are dealing with "inner principles, which one does not see" there exists a "natural impulse" (*Naturantrieb*) to look a man in the face—"first and foremost in the eyes"—when we are deciding whether to put our trust in him (*Anth* 7:296). What is repelling or attractive in his gestures, Kant continues, "determines our choice, or also makes us skeptical, before we have even inquired about his ethics [*seine Sitten*], and so it is not to be denied, that there is a physiognomic characterization" (7:296).

Kant is certainly not the only one who has tried to read moral character from facial expressions. But while he sometimes does appear to allow for the possibility of a *moral* physiognomy (*moralische Physiognomik*—cf. *Anth* 7:332), the art of physiognomic characteristics which he appeals to in the previous sentence would seem to be only a physiognomy of empirical character, not of moral character. For instance, lines and wrinkles on people's faces sometimes are caused by the repeated exercise of facial muscles which are associated with emotions, moods, and activities. And an accurate reading of these lines and wrinkles would (in the proper causal circumstances) tell us about these people's emotions and moods.[44] But such character traits and habits of thought are still, on Kant's view, signs of "mere nature and mistakes of temperament for which one is not responsible [*unverschuldete Fehler des Temperaments*]" (*KrV* A 551/B 579 n). They are not infallible signs of moral or intelligible character, which "we do not know, but indicate through appearances, which really only give immediate knowledge of the mode of sense (empirical character)" (*KrV* A 551/B 579). Epistemologically speaking, human beings have no other choice than to try and decipher each other's moral characters from appearances (e.g., facial expressions). But such deciphering efforts are not foolproof.

The Four Humors

An even odder portion of the discussion of individual character concerns a psychological application of the ancient doctrine of the four humors. In Kant's 1798 *Anthropology*, this portion occupies about one-third of the total discussion. The doctrine of the four humors is usually associated with Galen, although it appears to have started with Hippocrates. Kant's primary interest in it is as a theory of emotional temperament rather than of physical health, but these two aspects of the doctrine were in fact intertwined. According to the Galenic model,

> the four bodily humours were blood, phlegm, choler, and black bile, and they were endowed with the elementary qualities of heat and moisture. The preponderance of a particular humour determined a person's temperament, thus providing an early schema of psychosomatic or constitutional types. The theory was a comprehensive one in that it was able to account for health, temperament, and the type of illness to which a person was likely to succumb.[45]

For Kant, a large part of the attraction of this theory lay in its assumption of causal interaction between psychological and physical states. At the same time, he does not profess to know the details of this particular causal story: "[T]he temperaments, which we attribute merely to the soul, still probably have a secretly [*insgeheim*] cooperating cause in the physical condition of the human being" (*Anth* 7:286). As befits a pragmatic rather than physiological anthropologist, Kant is also not particularly interested in the "chemical blood-mixture" that warrants the designation of a certain property of temperament (7:287), even though he continues to use the traditional labels of "hot-blooded," "heavy-blooded," and so on in his later descriptions of the four basic character types.

Although Galenic theories were gradually being displaced by new medical discoveries during Kant's own life, the doctrine of the four humors was still a dominant paradigm within research on human personality in late eighteenth century Europe. One sign of this is that in his 1764 work *Observations on the Feeling of the Beautiful and Sublime*, which also makes extensive use of the four humors theory, Kant at one point says that he is merely examining the sublime and the beautiful "under the accepted classification of the temperaments [*unter der angenommenen Eintheilung der Temperamente*]" (2:220). Similarly, in another passage he says that he is merely looking at the temperaments themselves "as ordinarily classified" (2:218). Indeed, the influence of the ancient four humors doctrine persists even at present, as our own continued use of terms such as "melancholy" and "hot-blooded" indicates.

Kant divides the four temperaments into two groups: temperaments of feeling (the sanguine temperament of the light-blooded and the melancholic temperament of the heavy-blooded) and temperaments of activity (the choleric temperament of the hot-blooded and the phlegmatic temperament of the cold-blooded). Supposedly, there are "only four" temperaments: "one does not know what to make of the human being who claims to have a mixture of temperaments" (*Anth* 7:291; see also *Menschenkunde* 25:1158). Highlights of his comments on each of these four types follow.

The sanguine person, Kant writes,

> is carefree and of good cheer; he attaches a great importance to each thing for the moment, and in the following moment he may not think any further about it. He makes honest promises, but does not keep his word because he has not thought deeply enough beforehand whether he will be able to keep it. (*Anth* 7:287–88)

Similar descriptions occur in other versions of the anthropology lectures (e.g., *Menschenkunde* 25:1159–61, *Mrongovius* 25:1371–72, Dohna, 295) as well as in the *Observations* of 1764. In the *Observations*, for instance, he states that the person of sanguine frame of mind "loves change"—"his joys are laughing and lively," his "moral feeling[46] is beautiful, but without principles, and always depends immediately on the impression of the moment which objects make upon him" (2:222). In the Dohna *Anthropology*, Kant begins his description by saying that the "sanguine person is he who has a tendency toward cheerfulness before he even finds a reason for it" (295). In the *Menschenkunde* we are informed that the sanguine person "is good company, but a bad citizen" (25:1159–60).

The melancholic person, Kant holds, "attributes great importance to all things that concern him, finds cause for concern everywhere, and directs his attention first to the difficulties" (*Anth* 7:288). Or, as the Dohna version has it: "He does not promise easily, but keeps that which he has promised. Because before he does it, he always reflects on all the difficulties that he might find in carrying out the thing, and this goes so far that one usually names such people dealers in difficulties [*Diffikultätenkrämer*]" (Dohna, 297; cf. *Menschenkunde* 25: 1161–63, *Mrongovius* 25:1372–73; Starke II, 55).

In the *Observations* the human being of melancholic frame of mind is said to care "little for what others judge, what they consider good or true; he relies simply on his own insight in this matter" (2:221). At the same time, he "hates lies or dissimulation. He has a high feeling of the dignity of human nature" (2:221). And "genuine virtue from principles has something about it which seems to harmonize most with the *melancholic* frame of mind in the moderated understanding" (2:219).[47]

The choleric temperament is the first of the two temperaments of activity. "One says of him: he is hot, burns quickly like a straw-fire. . . . His activity is quick, but not lasting" (*Anth* 7:289; cf. *Mrongovius* 25:1373, Dohna, 300). In the *Menschenkunde*, we are told that the choleric "has an inclination to love of honor; he is pursued by an intense, burning fire, but it does not last long" (25:1163; cf. *Beob* 2:219–20). And in the second Starke manuscript, from Kant's anthropology course in the winter semester of 1790–91, it is said that the "activity of the choleric does not consist in the observation of duty, but simply in the influence that he wants to have on others" (56). Simply put, "his conduct is artful [*künstlich*]" (*Beob* 2:223).

Finally, the phlegmatic temperament of the cold-blooded person. As is still the case in contemporary English and German, we say that phlegmatic (*phlegmatisch*) people have a "tendency to inactivity" (*Anth* 7:289; cf. *Pillau* 25:821). Perhaps because of this lethargy, "in the phlegmatic mixture no ingredients of the sublime or beautiful usually enter in any particularly noticeable degree, and so this disposition does not belong in the context of our deliberations" (in the *Observations on the Feeling of the Sublime and the Beautiful*, 2:224). That is to say: the phlegmatic person does not exhibit much artistic taste (cf.. *Anth* 7:318). This is the downside. The upside is that he "warms up slowly, but holds the warmth longer. He does not get angry easily, but first considers whether he should get angry" (7:290). "Phlegm (taken in a good sense) is the temperament of cold reflection and perseverance in the pursuit of one's end, as well as tolerance of the hardship that is bound up with that pursuit" (7:318). As *Mrongovius* puts it: "Phlegm considered as a strength is the most distinguished temperament, because its activity is appropriate to its principles" (25:1374). Not surprisingly, it is Kant's judgment that the character of the German people is "phlegm combined with understanding; he [the German] does not argue about the already established order, nor does he try to think up a new one himself" (7:317; cf. *Friedländer* 25:647, *Mrongovius* 25:1409).

There are not a lot of surprises in this part of Kant's discussion of character, though it undoubtedly helped contribute to the strong popularity of his *Anthropology* lectures. But it is important to keep in mind that "one is talking here about sensuous impulses [*sinnliche Triebfedern*]"—not "moral causes [*moralische Ursachen*]" (*Anth* 7:288). Discussions of temperament concern only "what nature makes of the human being . . . (wherein the subject is largely passive)," not "what the human being makes of himself, and only the latter reveals whether he has a character" in the moral sense (7:292). "All the rest, what nature gave to the human being as predisposition, his *Naturell*, temperament, physiognomy, do not determine his true character. Character is the will of the human being in accordance with principles" (*Mrongovius* 25:1384–85).

However, there are clearly pragmatic uses to which knowledge of such material can be put. Knowledge of each other's temperament tells us a great deal about ourselves; those who possess such knowledge also easily learn "how one could use the other to his advantage" (*Anth* 7:312). And informed knowledge of a person's temperament can be important for moral evaluation as well. For instance, if we know that "nature had put little sympathy in this or that man's heart, if (being in other respects an honest man) he were of cold temperament" (*Gr* 4:398)—that is to say, if we are dealing with a phlegmatic person—we should adjust our judgments concerning his emotional responses accordingly.

Still, the strong dichotomy between natural temperament and moral character that Kant often defends in the *Anthropology* lectures is hard to swallow. Among other things, it would seem to follow from this position that agents are not ultimately responsible for many of their most basic moods and emotions. (E.g.: "Nature has admittedly put little sympathy in my heart, but that's not my problem. Anyway, this fact doesn't reveal whether I have moral character.") On the other hand, moods and emotions are also (under one description) "*capacities* . . . for furthering ends set by reason," and agents who fail to properly cultivate these capacities have also failed to heed the "unconditional (moral) imperative" of "*natural* [*physische*] perfection" (*MdS* 6:391–92). As a rational being a human being "necessarily wills that all capacities [*alle Vermögen*] in him will be developed, since they serve him and are given to him for all sorts of possible purposes" (*Gr* 4:423). At least in his less phlegmatic moods, Kant defends a more sensible theory of character.

Sex/Gender

> [W]hen the philosopher starts from experiences, it is extremely important that the facts which follow from them are grasped entirely correctly; for without this caution all syllogistic is wasted for nothing.
>
> Georg Forster, "Noch etwas über die Menschenraßen"

As noted earlier, a good portion of the applied, practical half of the *Anthropology* lectures consists of separate sections on the character of the sexes, peoples, and races. These are definitely among the most difficult topics within Kant's *Anthropology* to write about. Everyone agrees that he has many of his facts wrong here. But in these sections (unlike, say, the section "The Character of the Person"), the problem is not just that he is embracing theories that have fallen out of scientific favor. Here the ramifications of his errors run deeper, and the pitfalls of impure ethics become more evident. When a transcendental philosopher decides to go empirical, it is very easy to make mistakes. While the track records of other classical philosophers who are all supposedly closer to the material content of life than Kant are equally dismal in this area (e.g., Aristotle on women and slaves, Hume and Hegel on blacks, Marx on Jews), it is particularly depressing that someone who believes he is writing in "the genuine [*eigentliche*] age of criticism, to which everything must submit" (*KrV* A xii n) says some of the things he says. The tribunal of reason is apparently not so powerful after all.

For the most part Kant is not explicitly addressing questions of *moral* character in any of these sections, but rather empirical, physical character. Moral character, again, is an individual achievement—it is what a person makes of him or herself (cf. *Anth* 7:292).[48] But as I will show, he exhibits a disturbing tendency to slide into moral pronouncements throughout these sections, and the normative repercussions are impossible to ignore.

What is the rationale for this material? Knowledge of the characters of the human sexes, peoples, and races constitutes an integral part of our *Weltkenntnis*. As the only rational animal on the planet, it behooves us to know as much about our species and its major subdivisions as possible. From a pragmatic point of view, accurate empirical knowledge of the characteristic tendencies of sexes, peoples, and races, can aid us in our encounters with each other. We will know how to deal with each other, thus permitting "judgment about what each has to know about the other and how each one could use the other to his advantage" (7:312). But from a moral perspective, such *Weltkenntnis* is also important. We may learn whether there exist more specific subjective conditions that hinder or help members of these groups in carrying out the laws of a metaphysics of morals. Mellin, for instance, in his entry "Anthropologie" in the *Enzyclopädisches Wörterbuch der kritischen Philosophie*, states that "in practical anthropology either the human being in general or the human being in special circumstances and under subjective conditions will be considered, and accordingly it divides into two parts."[49] The material on sexes, peoples, and races in Kant's *Anthropology* lectures falls under Mellin's second part of practical anthropology; it is particular as opposed to general practical anthropology.

The opening section on the sexes, like much of the *Anthropology*, is marked by a strong teleological assumption that sharply constrains the range of the discussion.[50] Again and again Kant asks: What is nature's end [*Zweck*] in creating the female sex? In addition to injecting a positive moral judgment on all that he claims to find in nature ("everything which lies in nature is good"—*Menschenkunde* 25:1188; cf. *Friedländer* 25:698, Dohna, 333; *Refl* 1502, 15:794; *KrV* A 743/B 771), this brand of naive teleologism also does not always bother to stop and ask whether what it sees as a natural difference is perhaps only a contingent, socially constructed one.

As Kant sees it, nature actually has *two* distinct ends in creating women: 1) the preservation or maintenance [*Erhaltung*] of the species, and 2) the culture [*Kultur*] of society and its refinement (*Anth* 7:305–6; cf. *Menschenkunde* 25:1189, *Friedländer* 25:701, Starke II, 66). In the case of the first end, women are viewed as baby producers and nurturers, and many of the character traits discussed by Kant in this section (e.g., fear of physical injury, the ability to manage men) are understood by him to be natural adaptations that follow from this purpose. Women who, so to speak, seek to go against nature by denying this first end via careers in (e. g.) science come in for some particularly sarcastic criticism by Kant (more on this later).

The second goal of nature in creating women ties in more directly with ethics. According to Kant, women as a group serve as a moralizing force within society. Through interaction with women, men find themselves "brought, if not quite to morality itself, then at least to that which clothes it, ethical behavior [*gesitteter Anstand*], which is the preparation and recommendation [*Vorbereitung und Empfehlung*] to it" (*Anth* 7:306).

Here as elsewhere, the influence of Rousseau is detectable. In the Dohna *Anthropology* we read: "When Rousseau says that the culture of the male sex is based very much on the female sex, he speaks the truth" (342). In the following *Reflexion* he elaborates a bit more: "The important thought of Rousseau's, that the formation (*Bildung*) of character of girls by education would have the greatest influence on the male sex and on morals generally, is worth investigating. At present girls are merely trained [*dressiert*], but not formed [*gebildet*] to morals and a good way of thinking" (*Refl* 1281, 15:564).[51]

Within the larger scheme of Kant's philosophy of history, women in their influence on men thus play a role similar to that of education and culture on the species generally. All three function as preparatory steps in the ambitious

Übergang from nature to morality. Women as a group perform a proto-moralizing role in society, in so far as they bring into play "the legislation of taste and improved mores [*verfeinerte Sitten*] in society" (*Refl* 1317, 15:579). Women are "the judges of taste in social intercourse. Social intercourse without them is coarse, stormy, and unsociable" (*Friedländer* 25:705).

But despite women's strong moralizing potential, they are not to take an active role in society and politics. Unlike other *Aufklärer* who actively advocated the spreading of the rays of enlightenment beyond white, male burghers,[52] Kant for the most part embraces traditional prejudices concerning women. As is well known, in his political writings he explicitly denies women the right to vote, claiming in one notorious passage that the fact of being a woman itself constitutes a sufficient reason for denial of citizenship.[53] In *Mrongovius* we are informed that "in addition to his private interests man also has interest in public matters, but woman has an interest only for her home" (25:1394–95). Women are therefore to work only behind the scenes in private life, exerting their moralizing force in the home and at social gatherings (cf. *Anth* 7:313; *Friedländer* 25:704).

It is often argued that Kant "asserts that women's character, in contrast to men's, is wholly defined by natural needs. Women's lack of self-determination, in his view, is intrinsic to their nature."[54] Similarly, Kant allegedly denies "that woman's nature has a connection with reason. Woman's nature is identified with inclination, and it is for this reason that she must submit herself to man. It would appear that in the kingdom of rational beings there are only adult males."[55]

Even Kant's seemingly inclusive use of the term "humanity" (*Menschheit*) fails to convince some critics, who argue that the only Kantian *Menschen* are *Männer*:

> Kant's use of the concept "humanity" [*Menschheit*] . . . appears to be aimed at all human beings, but this appearance deceives. It often emerges from the context that what should be valid for *humanity* is not valid for *women*. . . . Progress is carried by men: *they* are the ones whom progress in the area of the arts and sciences, law, religion, and even education brings further.[56]

But it is not quite this simple. In the opening paragraph of "The Character of the Sexes" in the 1798 *Anthropology* Kant explicitly refers to "both" (*beide*) man and woman as "rational beings" and as "rational animals" (7:303). And in the *Observations* he says that "the fair sex has just as much understanding as the male [*eben so wohl Verstand als das männliche*]"—albeit while holding that the latter is "deep" and the former only "beautiful" (2:229). One can and should infer from these passages that women on Kant's view are definitely included within the class of rational beings. But although he views them as members of the class of rational beings, he also holds that women do not yet exercise their rational capacities properly. At the beginning of his famous essay "An Answer to the Question: What is Enlightenment?" he defines "enlightenment" as follows: "*Enlightenment* [*Aufklärung*] *is the human being's exit* [*Ausgang*] *from his self-incurred immaturity* [*Unmündigkeit*]. *Immaturity is the inability to make use one's own understanding without direction* [*Leitung*] *from another*" (8:35). In the second paragraph we are informed that "the far greater part of humanity (including the entire fairer sex [*das ganze schöne Geschlecht*]) regard taking the step to maturity [*Mündigkeit*] as very dangerous, and difficult as well" (8:35).[57] Although no further discussion of women's particular efforts to exit from *Unmündigkeit* occurs in this essay, the same term is used in connection with women in the 1798 *Anthropology*. In part of a section called "On Mental Weaknesses [*Gemütsschwächen*] in the Cognitive Power" (7:204), Kant writes: "A sound understanding (without mental weakness) can also be accompanied by weakness with regard to its exercise [*Ausübung*]" (7:208). In the case of children, this weakness is merely temporary. But "*woman*, whatever her age, is declared to be civilly immature [*bürgerlich-unmündig*]; the husband is her natural curator" (7:208–09). In a parallel passage in *Menschenkunde*, Kant baldly asserts that "certain insights and transactions are entirely outside the sphere of women. They may not make use of their own reason, but must submit themselves to the judgment of a foreign reason" (25:1046–47). Women as a group are therefore declared to still be in a state of *Unmündigkeit*: they do not yet exercise their reason properly, and thus need to be legally represented by men.

Though nothing specific is said here about the causes or sources of the alleged weak exercise of women's reason, it is clear that Kant believes that they do not think sufficiently for themselves. In the language of the *Aufklärung* essay, women do not yet have "the courage to use their own understanding" (cf. 8:35). Oddly enough, even those women who would appear to be trying to think for themselves in pursuing careers in science and scholarship rather than staying home to tend to the maintenance of the species are criticized by Kant precisely for being too dependent on the judgment of others. As he puts it in one of his favorite quips: "As for scholarly women, they use their *books* somewhat like their *watch*; that is, they wear it so that people can see that they have one, though it is usually not running or not set by the sun" (*Anth* 7:307; cf. Dohna, 345; *Refl* 1299, 15:572; *Beob* 2:229–30). Women do not take science seriously: "The sciences serve them only in so far as they are an entertainment and a game [*ein Spiel*] for them" (*Friedländer* 25:706).

However, since the ability to think for oneself is also a necessary part of Kant's own conception of *moral* character (see, e.g., *Anth* 7:292), the charge of weak exercise of reason appears to entail not only a lack of legal rights but of moral character as well. There are numerous remarks in the *Anthropology* materials which speak to this point. In the 1798 version, for instance, Kant asserts: "Man has taste for himself, woman makes herself into the object of taste for everyone. —'What the world says is true, and what the world does is good' is a feminine principle which is difficult to unite with character in the narrow sense of the term" (7:308). Though this passage concerns judgments of taste (*Geschmack*) rather than morality, "character in the narrow sense of the term" clearly refers to *moral* character. And his implicit claim is simply that men form their own judgments in this area while women do not. While Kant does not quite explicitly deny that women have moral character here, the assertion that it is "difficult to unite [*schwer . . . (zu) vereinigen*]" the feminine principle with character in the narrow sense does head in that direction.

More specific remarks about women's *moral* character do occur elsewhere in the *Anthropology* writings. One of the *Reflexionen* reads: "One must begin male education right away with the concept of duty; but female education must be grounded in the concept of honor" (*Refl* 1331, 15:582). The sentence is repeated virtually word for word in many of the *Nachschriften*. For example, in Starke II we read: "Male education must be grounded right away on the concept of duty; female education merely [*bloß*] on the concept of honor" (67; cf. *Friedländer* 25:722, *Menschenkunde* 25:1190, 1193, *Mrongovius* 25:1392).[58] And a few pages later: "The principle of male ethics is virtue, but that of female ethics is honor. What the world does, woman does also" (72). Honor [*Ehre*] is certainly not the worst of human motives (see, e.g., *MdS* 6:333–34, where Kant praises the "man [*Mann*] of honor"), but on Kant's view it suffers two crucial defects. First, the desire for honor engages only inclination rather than reason; second, it is too other-dependent and thus insufficiently autonomous. In his critique of the naturally kindhearted person early in the *Groundwork*, the first defect of honor is articulated as follows: "[T]he inclination to honor, which if fortunate enough to hit on something which is in fact useful and in accord with duty and consequently honorable, deserves praise and encouragement but not esteem, because the maxim lacks moral content, namely the doing of such actions not from inclination but *from duty*" (4:398).

This first criticism of the motive of honor is not very convincing. Why couldn't one act from *reasons* of honor rather than from the inclination to honor? In cases where the motive of honor involves reflection rather than mere unthinking inclination (e.g., a situation where someone is tempted to run away, but for the sake of honor stays to defend herself), Kant's first criticism becomes irrelevant. At the same time, the mere fact that he construes honor as stemming from inclination rather than reason does serve to explain part of his skepticism about women's character: they are too inclination-dependent. As he puts it in the *Menschenkunde*, "with women feelings of honor [*Gefühle der Ehre*] must take the place of principles" (25:1170). Another favorite formula which crops up in many versions of the *Anthropology* lectures illustrates this assumption; "woman should reign [*herrschen*] and man should govern [*regieren*]; because inclination [*Neigung*] rules and understanding [*Verstand*] governs" (*Anth* 7:309; cf. *Menschenkunde* 25:1193; *Friedländer* 25:717; *Collins* 25:234; *Parow* 25:459, Starke II, 74). In this formula woman is essentially identified with the exercise of inclination; man with that of understanding.

A hint of Kant's second criticism of the motive of honor is present in remarks such as the following: "[W]omen's entire worth is determined through the opinion of men. . . . Men can give their worth to themselves" (*Collins* 25:238; cf. *Parow* 25:462, Starke II, 72). Women are allegedly too dependent on the judgments of others. The connection of this other-dependence to the motive of honor is perhaps brought out best in Aristotle's famous rejection of honor as a candidate for the good. "Honor [*timē*]," he writes, "seems too superficial to be what we are looking for, since it is thought to depend on those who bestow honor rather than on him who receives it, but the good we divine to be something proper to a man and not easily taken away from him" (*EN* 1.5 1095b23–26).[59]

Perhaps Kant's strongest condemnation of women's moral character occurs in passages where he claims either that they don't care about cultivating character

("Woman is absolutely no authority on character (she is indifferent to it)," *Refl* 1282, 15:564), and/or that it is somehow contrary to their nature to develop character: "With the female sex one sees that so far [*schon*] it is not so appropriate to their nature to have a character at all [*überhaupt*]" (*Friedländer* 25:631).

Kant seems to have never shaken entirely loose from his early quip that in discussing the sexes we are dealing with "two species of human beings [*zwei Menschengattungen*]. . . . [H]ere it is not enough to imagine that one is dealing with human beings [*Menschen*]; one must at the same time not disregard the fact that these human beings are not of the same kind [*nicht von einerlei Art sind*]" (*Beob* 2:228). On his view nature has programmed qualitatively different roles within the sexes of the human species; roles which are in turn to receive cultural backing within human society. In some places, he even seems to be comfortable referring to "male ethics" (*männliche Sitten*) and "female [*weibliche*] ethics" (Starke II, 72)—though *Sitten* is perhaps better rendered here as "mores" or "customs." Kant views those of his contemporaries who are women (however, in this respect they are not different from most men—cf. 8:35) as still being in a state of *Unmündigkeit*: they do not yet have the courage to use their own reason. The question of whether women as a group require different strategies for achieving enlightenment (e.g., strategies involving increased education, legal and political rights, professional and career opportunities) is not one he addresses. At the same time, as members of the human race women do in his view share in humanity's destiny: the moral perfection of the species (see "'The Whole Human Race': Kant and Moral Universality" later in this chapter). But while Kant does not view women's tutelage as a permanent condition, he was also not personally interested in trying to alleviate it. Women who tried to discuss philosophy or politics with him found themselves talking about food recipes instead. According to Stuckenberg, one female guest reportedly exclaimed: "It really seems, dear professor, as if you regarded all of us as mere cooks."[60] As I will show later, examples of this tension between Kant's commitment to the moral perfection of the species as a whole and his derogatory remarks about different subgroups within the species occur repeatedly throughout the applied half of the *Anthropology* lectures.

Schleiermacher, in his 1799 review of Kant's *Anthropology from a Pragmatic Point of View*, labeled it "a collection of trivialities" and "not anthropology, but the negation of all anthropology." To his credit, one of the reasons behind his brash dismissal of the work lay in his objection to Kant's "handling of the female sex as an abnormality [*als einer Abart*]."[61]

Peoples

In Kant's 1798 *Anthropology*, the section following his discussion of the character of the sexes is entitled "Der Charakter des Volks." Although Kant's use of the German term *Volk* is not quite as mysterious as that of certain other German writers, it is nevertheless difficult to convey in contemporary English. Let us start with his own definition:

Under the word *Volk* [*populus*] one understands the united group [*vereinigte Menge*] of human beings in a region, in so far as they make up a whole [*ein Ganzes*]. The ones of the group or also a part of the same which recognize themselves as being united into a civil whole through common descent [*durch gemeinschaftliche Abstammung*] are called a *nation* [*Nation*] (*gens*). (*Anth* 7:311)

The most direct English translation of *Volk* would of course be "folk," and the first entry under this term in the *Oxford English Dictionary* in fact reads: "a people, nation, race, tribe." But this meaning is also listed as obsolete. Victor Lyle Dowdell, in his translation of *Anthropology from a Pragmatic Point of View*, renders *Volk* as "nation." However, in the preceding citation, a *Nation* is defined as a subset of a *Volk*. On the other hand, in the Dohna version the title of the parallel section runs *Charakter des Volkes oder der Nationen* (347); in *Collins* it is *Vom National Charackter* (25:232); and in both *Menschenkunde* and *Mrongovius* Kant is concerned, as his titles indicate, with the *Charackter der Nationen* (25:1181, 1398). Even in his own 1798 *Anthropology* he moves casually from a phrase like *Die französische Nation* (7:313) to *Das englische Volk* (7:314). In other words, even though *Nation* is defined formally as a subset of *Volk* at the beginning of the 1798 discussion, Kant often seems to use the terms *Volk* and *Nation* interchangeably. And there is a sense of "nation" (from the Latin *nasci*, to be born) which does fit very well here. The first *OED* entry under "nation" reads: "An extensive aggregate of persons, so closely associated with each other by common descent, language, or history, as to form a distinct race or people, usually organized as a separate political state and occupying a definite territory." But this particular sense of "nation" seems dated, current ethnic conflicts notwithstanding. (As the *OED* puts it: "In early examples the racial idea is usually stronger than the political; in recent use the notion of political unity and independence is more prominent.") For most of us, the word "nation" at present connotes more a common form of government rather than common ethnic ties. And Kant is also clear in stating that the particular form of government which a *Volk* has does not necessarily help to explain its character: "To say that everything which the character of a people has comes from the form of government [*Regierungsart*] is an ungrounded assertion that clarifies nothing, for from where does the government itself get its own character?" (*Anth* 7:313). In the Dohna *Anthropology*, after claiming (erroneously) that "Hume and many others have wanted to deny completely that there is national character[62] [*Nationalcharakter*]" (347; cf. *Collins* 25:232; *Parow* 25:450), he asks: "Therefore the question remains: does each *Volk* have a character, something general, innate [*angeboren*], which is not dependent on chance impressions or at all on the form of government [*Regierungsform*]?" (347).

For these reasons, "nation" is not the best choice as a translation of *Volk*. I have chosen to render *Volk* as "people" (from the Latin *populum*), which does hook up etymologically with the beginning of Kant's own definition at *Anth* 7:311 (cited earlier). What he is attempting to delineate in this section are collective character traits shared by a majority of persons[63] who live in the same region and who possess a common ethnic background, as revealed in (e.g.) their language, culture, social mores, religion, and history.

It is important to note that while Kant (like many others) does include "common descent" (*gemeinschaftliche Abstammung*) in his definition of *Volk*, a *Volk* is not necessarily the same as a race. Although he professes to be talking about "an innate [*angeborene*], natural character, which so to speak lies in the blood mixture [*Blutmischung*] of human beings" (*Anth* 7:319; cf. *Friedländer* 25:654–55), a *Volk* is not a *Rasse* for two simple reasons: 1) some peoples are themselves a mixture of different races, and 2) a variety of different national characters may be present within a single race. "The *Spaniard*," for instance, according to Kant, "arose out of the mixture of European with Arabian (Moorian) blood" (*Anth* 7:316). On the other hand, "all of Europe, the Turks, and the Kalmucks belong to the white race" (*Menschenkunde* 25:1188). At any rate, Kant's dual emphases on common descent and geographic proximity mean that his descriptions of national character will have little relevance to large nation-states whose members possess a variety of different ethnic and racial backgrounds. And such societies are increasingly the norm (though they have also been with us from the beginning). Although Kant holds that people "bring their *Volkscharakter* with them," so to speak, when they move from one country to the next ("climate and soil do not furnish the key [to national character],[64] since migrations of entire peoples have shown that they did not change their character because of the new location," *Anth* 7:313), the sort of multi-*Volkscharakter* background of many of us at present (e.g., in my own daughters' cases: Scottish, Russian, Latvian, German, French . . .) is clearly not what he is talking about. There are very few true *Völker* around any more, in Kant's sense of the term.

Kant's litany of national characters is of course very western-Eurocentric. In the 1798 *Anthropology*, the only *Völker* featured are the French, English, Spanish, Italians, and Germans. Russia, we are informed at the end of the discussion, "has not yet developed a definite concept from its natural predisposition"; Poland "no longer has a *Volkscharakter*"; and the "nationals of European Turkey neither had nor will have what is necessary for the acquisition of a definite *Volkscharakter*" (*Anth* 7:319). After the mandatory survey of the "big five" in some of the other versions of the lectures, he makes brief mention of other *Völker*, but the character traits mentioned (they are not analyzed in any detail) are for the most part negative. The Poles, we are told, "have very little culture, with respect both to the arts and also to the sciences" (Dohna, 358)—"we find no good, original writers among them" (*Mrongovius* 25:1412; cf. *Pillau* 25:835, *Menschenkunde* 25:1185). The Russians "are imitators and as a result can learn everything, but cannot teach anything to others—imitate everything—but do not do anything themselves. They can paint well, but cannot invent anything themselves. Their teachers gladly take from other lands. Although Russia has been in a condition of civilization for eighty years, not a single great mind has distinguished itself in their universities" (Dohna, 359–60). The Russians fare even worse in *Menschenkunde*: "the Russian nation is . . . not civilized at all, and is moralized even less than any other [*irgendein*] people in the world" (25:1186; cf. *Mrongovius* 25:1412–13).

As for the people of Turkey, "they always demand gifts. Every governor demands them from travelers. The characteristic feature of a raw, barbaric people is when they have no respect for law. They seek their salvation in lawlessness"

(Dohna, 361). The Turks "do not want to accept any culture, least of all discipline" (*Mrongovius* 25:1414).

Given such ethnic slurs against non-western European peoples, one might think that other western European peoples outside of the big five would receive relatively favorable treatment. But they are virtually ignored. In *Mrongovius* we read: "We now pass by the Danes, the Swedes, the Dutch, and the Swiss because these are German nations" (25:1412; cf. 1398). *Friedländer* starts promisingly with the compliment that "the Nordic peoples of Europe have a great talent of concepts" (25:657), but in the next sentence of the manuscript the author moves on to another topic.

In the *Menschenkunde* we are told that the Poles and Russians "do not appear to be properly capable [*nicht recht fähig*] of civilization," and that they "have more of an oriental mixture than all the other nations of Europe" (25:1185; cf. *Friedländer* 25:661; *Mrongovius* 25:1412). This last remark leads to a further question: What does Kant tells us about non-European peoples in his discussions of *Volkscharakter*? In most versions of the *Anthropology* lectures, they are not regarded as proper *Völker* at all, though as I will show later, in his various discussions of race much is said about non-European peoples. However, in some of the anthropology materials dealing with peoples we do find material on non-European nations. *Pillau* tells us: "We find with all oriental peoples that they have no *Geist*; they are not capable of acting according to concepts" (25:833). *Friedländer* adds: "The beauty of music is missing entirely among the Oriental peoples, they do not understand at all that when many instruments play harmonically together in different tones, there is beauty within—they think it is confusion" (25:655; cf. *Refl* 1372, 15:598).[65]

In *Anthropology from a Pragmatic Point of View*, Kant warns that he is sketching his portraits of the various national characters "somewhat more from the side of their defects and deviation from the rule than from the prettier [*schönere*] side," on the ground that "flattery ruins, criticism on the other hand improves" (7:313).[66] One might be tempted to read his unflattering portraits of non–western European peoples in this light, but unfortunately there is more to it. As the preceding quotations reveal, there are further normative assumptions behind his concept of *Volk* which are not explicitly laid out in his initial definition at *Anth* 7:311. If all that is meant by *Volkscharakter* are the social mores, religion, history, language, and general collective habits of a people who live together in a certain area and share a common ethnic background, one would also expect to see a sketch of the portraits of the *Volkscharakter* of (e.g.) the various tribes of Native Americans. The fact that one does not encounter these additional sketches is a further clue that a certain level and kind of cultural and political development is presupposed in Kant's sense of *Volk*.

What additional normative assumptions are operative? Although Kant does not address this question directly in the 1798 *Anthropology*, other versions of the lectures are quite explicit. Toward the end of the discussion of *Volkscharakter* in Starke II we read: "One can only call those nations cultivated in which external freedom, a civil constitution—that is to say a restriction of the freedom of each in so far as it is compatible with the freedom of others—and an authority by which the laws are secured, all exist" (117; cf. *Pillau* 25:843). In the case of

Turkey, "one finds to be sure authority, but it is without freedom and without law. With the Poles one finds freedom and law, but no authority . . . [and] with the Russians one finds authority and law, but no freedom" (117–18; cf. Dohna, 357, 358, 361; *Refl* 1367–69, 15:595–96). It seems then (despite Kant's remarks to the contrary—see *Anth* 7:313; Dohna, 347) that *Volkscharakter* is after all in a fundamental way "dependent on the form of government." The kind of government which a people has serves as an entrance requirement, so to speak, into the more exclusive club of nations or *Völker* proper. Similarly, unarticulated norms and biases are behind Kant's remarks that that Native Americans "do not accept any culture at all" (*Refl* 1520, 15:877). Some socially transmitted behavior patterns count as contributions to culture, and some do not, but the criteria of differentiation are not made explicit.

Granted, Kant does occasionally use the term *"Völker"* in a less restrictive sense. In one revealing *Reflexion* we read: "Many *Völker* do not progress further by themselves. Greenlanders. Asians. It must come from Europe" (*Refl* 1499, 15:781). Here the peoples of Greenland and Asia are at least included in the *Völker* club, even though they are held to be incapable of self-progress. But in his official discussions of *Volkscharakter*, Kant employs the term *"Volk"* in a narrower, normative sense. Culture and civilization (two crucial steps in the destiny of the species toward moralization) are themselves only possible under certain forms of government; that is, ones which grant constitutionally protected freedoms to all citizens.

I have said nothing thus far concerning Kant's portraits of the *Volkscharakter* of the five western European peoples that occupy the bulk of his discussion in all versions of the *Anthropology* lectures. Here are a few highlights:

The French

The French communicate

> not out of interest but out of an immediate demand of taste. . . . [A]nd it cannot be disputed at all that an inclination of such a manner must also have influence on the ready willingness in rendering services, helpful benevolence, and the gradual development of universal human kindness according to principles [*allgemeine Menschenliebe nach Grundsätzen*] (*Anth* 7:313).

In other words, the good taste of the French (like that of the female sex) is itself contributing to the moralization of humanity: "We are in debt to them for many good customs [*Sitten*]; e.g., bringing women into society . . . in morality [*Moralitaet*] we have much to thank this nation" (*Pillau* 25:833; cf. *Friedländer* 25:657). On the other hand, the French people suffer from "an infectious *spirit of freedom* which probably pulls reason itself into its game, and, as concerns the relation of the people to the state, creates a shocking enthusiasm which goes beyond all bounds" (*Anth* 7:313–14; cf. Dohna 348–50; *Menschenkunde* 25:1182–83, *Mrongovius* 25:1399–1403, Starke II, 111–13; *Refl* 1359–65, 15:593–94). Here Kant reveals once again his own ambivalent attitude toward the French Revolution of 1789.[67]

The English

In direct contrast to the French, the English renounce "all kindness . . . and merely make a claim to respect," so that each can live according to his own lights (*Anth* 7:314). At the same time, in England "knowledge extends out to the most common man" (*Menschenkunde* 25:1184); thus "the entire nation is more cultivated" (Dohna, 353; cf. *Refl* 1358, 1366, 15:595). The Englishman "works hard and nimbly, but only until dinner. After that he goes in the pub and argues about politics and religion" (*Mrongovius* 25:1407).

The Spanish

The Spaniard "is moderate (*mäßig*), [and] wholeheartedly obedient to the laws, especially those of his ancient religion" (*Anth* 7:316). This is his good side. The bad news is that "he does not learn from foreigners, does not travel in order to get to know other peoples, lags centuries behind in the sciences, resists all reform, [and] is proud of not having to work" (7:316). "All of their literature is restricted to religion" (Dohna, 351). "They have a great national pride, and accordingly they must be lazy, because all nations that place their pride in blood are lazy" (*Pillau* 25:834; cf. *Menschenkunde* 25:1183–84, *Mrongovius* 25:1403–05, Starke II, 113–14).

The Italians

The Italian "unites French liveliness (cheerfulness) with Spanish seriousness (firmness)" (*Anth* 7:316). The Italian people are also well experienced in business: "Banks, bookkeeping,[68] lotteries, bills of exchange, and so on are discoveries of the Italians. Italian bookkeeping is a special, very well-conceived [work of] order" (Dohna, 352). But their practical skill has a darker side. "Italy is the land of crafty heads [*Schlauköpfe*]" (*Menschenkunde* 25:1185; cf. *Pillau* 25:834); "they have systematic deceitfulness or deep-lying craftiness" (Dohna, 352; cf. *Mrongovius* 25:1405–6).

The Germans

Finally, the Germans. As we saw earlier in our discussion of the doctrine of the four humors, Kant sees a great deal of phlegm in the German *Volscharakter*: "Here the phlegmatic temperament rules" (*Mrongovius* 25:1409; cf. *Anth* 7:317, *Menschenkunde* 25:1185, Dohna, 355). But he also lists several German character traits which almost sound like Hegelian criticisms of Kantian ethics: "The Germans possess great diligence and all the skills to which industry and sustained, patient diligence belong; with them the spirit of order and method rules. But they stay so much with the formula that they forget the material; this shows itself especially in school education" (Starke II, 116). Or, as he puts it in his own 1798 *Anthropology*, the Germans possess "a certain mania for method [*eine gewisse Methodensucht*]," and this "need for methodical classification, in order to grasp a whole under a concept, betrays the limitation of the German's innate talent" (*Anth* 7:319; cf. *Mrongovius* 25:1409–12). The German's love of rules makes him "the pedant in the world"; but unfortunately he reveals a "lack of wisdom and power of judgment in applying these rules" (*Friedländer* 25:659).

Like much of the *Anthropology*, the material on *Volkscharakter* is very loosely arranged and unsystematically developed. Though one senses that Kant enjoyed relaying these anecdotes about foreign peoples to his audience, there are darker sides to many of his remarks of which he seems blissfully unaware. Odd, too, that one finds no clear espousal in this section of the value and necessity of different forms of human cultural life. There is an assumption of unilinear cultural development throughout, which is then supposed to extend gradually outward from western Europe: "We must look in the Occident for the continual progress of the human race [*das menschliche Geschlecht*] to perfection and from there the spreading around the world [*die Verbreitung auf der Erde*]" (*Refl* 1501, 15:789). Essentially, Kant holds that sexual and racial differences are preprogrammed into the species in order to help insure that the race as a whole achieves its collective destiny, regardless of what environmental circumstances individual members find themselves in. Why isn't a similar (pluralistic) teleology of culture also needed; namely, a conviction that nature requires a plurality of cultures in order to reach her goal for the human species? Kant's formal definition of "culture" in the *Critique of Judgment*—"the production of an aptitude in a rational being for any ends whatever that are to one's own liking [*beliebige Zwecken überhaupt*]" (5:431)—is extremely open-ended, and certainly allows plenty of room for non-western cultures. Exposure to and participation in *some sort* of culture is a necessary preparatory step to moralization (cf. *KU* 5:433). But it is not the case, contrary to what Kant sometimes asserts in his *Anthropology* lectures, that only one particular kind of culture satisfies this requirement.

Despite these and other shortcomings of Kant's anthropological discussions of peoples and cultures, it remains the case that in his popular lectures he succeeds in doing something that he firmly resists in his theoretical writings on ethics—namely, discussing an *Übergang* from pure moral principles to their application in human life via an examination of the situations of subgroups within the human species. The statement "Completeness of the division of the empirical is impossible" (*MdS* 6:205), though true, can also put a stop to all empirical investigations if too high a premium is placed on completeness. When Kant is operating outside the confines of "the pure system of ethics" (cf. *MdS* 6:468) he clearly does not let a concern for completeness stand in the way. On the contrary, he is convinced that knowledge of *Volkscharakter* "is always a necessary prerequisite of *Weltkenntnis*, and this is also the final end with all histories which we read, and with all travels, where we get to know nations" (*Pillau* 25:831).

Races

The rubber is good, the pepper is good,
Three hundred sacks and barrels.

I have gold dust and ivory tusks—
The black goods are better.

> Heinrich Heine,
> "Das Sklavenschiff"

In Kant's *Anthropology from a Pragmatic Point of View*, the section entitled "Der Charakter der Rasse" is extremely short (less than one full page of the Academy Edition) and rather innocent-looking (7:320–21). If this were Kant's only statement on the issue of race, one might easily infer that the topic does not play much of a role in his anthropology. But other versions of the *Anthropology* lectures contain more extensive remarks on race, and the issue of race also looms large in three separately published essays.[69] Additionally, an important section of the *Physical Geography* lectures also deals with race.[70] The issue of race is accordingly much more central to the empirical part of Kant's study of human nature than the text *Anthropology from a Pragmatic Point of View* would lead one to believe. And this makes sense, since, as many commentators have noted, race was one of the principal preoccupations of eighteenth century European armchair anthropologists.

Part of Kant's problem seems to be where to place this material (indeed, whether to use it at all). Does it fit under physical geography or under anthropology?[71] And if the latter, is it properly part of "pragmatic" anthropology or only "physiological" anthropology? In the preface to *Anthropology from a Pragmatic Point of View*, Kant situates the study of "the human races, which are regarded as products of the play of nature," as "not yet pragmatic, but only *theoretische Weltkenntnis*" (7:120). Because it is a viewed as a product of the play of nature (*Spiel der Natur*), race falls under the "physiological knowledge of the human being," a type of knowledge which "aims at the investigation of what nature makes of the human being." On the other hand, as noted earlier, pragmatic knowledge of the human being "aims at what the human being makes, or can and should make of himself as a freely acting being" (7:119). This may serve to explain why there is so little discussion of race in most versions of the anthropology lectures (cf. n. 71)—though strictly speaking one would not expect to see any discussion at all.

Physical geography as construed by Kant also studies human beings, in so far as they are natural beings found on earth who are affected by (e.g.) changes of climate and temperature. Indeed, in Kant's first published description of his physical geography course (published in 1757 as part of the "West Winds" essay), he states that a "particular part" of geography "considers the animal kingdom in a comparative manner, [and] within it the human being according to the differences of his natural formation and color [*natürliche Bildung und Farbe*] in different regions of the earth" (2:9). This remark helps explain the presence of the fairly detailed section entitled "Of the Human Being" in Rink's edited version of Kant's *Physical Geography* lectures, a text which in the judgment of Adickes "consists of two parts of completely different origin" and to which Rink himself added "many stylistic changes."[72] An important part of physical geography as construed by Kant simply concerns the physical description of human beings qua natural objects which are "found on the earth" (cf. 9:311).

However, ultimately the placement issue is perhaps not terribly important, since Kantian anthropology and geography are viewed as intersecting halves of a larger whole. The goal, again, is to acquire pragmatic, cosmopolitan *Weltkenntnis*, a kind of knowledge that will be "useful not merely for school but rather for *life*, and through which the accomplished student is introduced to the stage of his destiny, namely, the *world*" (*Racen* 2:443 n; cf. *Anth* 7:120). "*Nature* and the *human being*" themselves constitute "the two-fold field [*das zweifaches Feld*]" of *Weltkenntnis* (2:443 n). "In physical geography we consider nature; in anthropology the human being, or human nature in all of its situations. Both of these sciences (*Wissenschaften*) make up *Weltkenntnis*" (*Pillau* 25:733). But in the quest for *Weltkenntnis* pride of place is always given to *Menschenkenntnis* over mere *Naturkenntnis*: "The human being therefore interests us more than nature, since nature exists for the sake of [*wegen*] the human being. The human being is the end of nature" (*Friedländer* 25:470).

A study of the character of the human races construed as a "products of the play of nature" (cf. *Anth* 7:120) means that what is supposedly being studied is not *moral* character but physical characteristics. Moral character, again, concerns "what the human being makes of himself" (*Anth* 7:292). Race would seem to be a paradigm instance of what "nature makes of the human being" (7:292). However, here too (as was also the case in his discussion of the character of the sexes), Kant exhibits a frequent tendency to slip in moral pronouncements about race in the midst of his allegedly descriptive accounts of these "products of the play of nature." One can of course undertake a *descriptive*, comparative account of human moral communities, and in fact Kant often suggests that part of physical geography's task is to formulate just such a comparative, descriptive ethics. For instance, in the section of the 1765 *Nachricht* dealing with physical geography we read:

> The *second* part of the subject [of physical geography] considers *the human being*, throughout the whole world, from the point of view of the variety of his natural properties and the difference in that feature of the human being which is moral [*was an ihm moralisch ist*]. The consideration of these things is at once very important and also highly stimulating as well, and unless these matters are considered universal judgments about the human being would scarcely be possible. The comparison of human beings among each other [at present] and with the moral state [*moralischer Zustand*] of the human being in earlier times furnishes us with a comprehensive map of the human race. (2:312–13)

Here the terms "consideration" (*Betrachtung*), "comparison" (*Vergleichung*), and "map" (*Karte*) suggest a descriptive enterprise. Similarly, toward the end of the Introduction to the *Physical Geography* lectures, Kant states that physical geography also serves as the ground "of all other possible geographies." One of these other possible geographies, "which must be dealt with briefly," is "moral geography [*moralische Geographie*], in which the different customs and characters [*Sitten und Charakteren*] of human beings are discussed" (9:164). Here too, the language employed suggests that the promised section on moral geography (which, alas, does not materialize in Rink's text; the closest we get is the section entitled "Concerning Human Beings") will be a descriptive account of ethics. However, as I will show later, this turns out not to be the case.

Although it is the practical applications and implications of Kant's theory of race which are of primary interest here, it is necessary first to sketch some of its basic conceptual commitments. A good place to begin is Buffon's rule, which Kant discusses at the beginning of the 1775 "Racen" essay. Georges Louis Leclerc, Comte de Buffon (1707–88), praised by Kant elsewhere as "the great author of the system of nature" (*Anth* 7:221), was author of the forty-four-volume opus *Histoire naturelle, générale et particulière* (1749). According to Buffon's rule, "animals which produce fertile young with one another . . . belong to one and the same physical species" (2:429). Kant endorses Buffon's naturalistic conception of a species, stressing that it "must actually be regarded simply as the definition of a natural species [*Naturgattung*] of animals in general" (2:429), and it is still generally accepted at present that all individuals who are potentially or actually capable of interbreeding with one another are members of the same natural species. It is important to note here that *all* human beings must be regarded as members of the *same* species if Buffon's definition of species is used. As Kant himself puts it, "all human beings on the wide earth [*alle Menschen auf der weiten Erde*] belong to one and the same natural species, because they consistently produce fertile children with one another, no matter what great differences may otherwise be encountered in their shape [*Gestalt*]" (2:429).[73]

This means that Kant's own account of the human species and its races is a monogenetic rather than polygenetic one: that is, he maintains that all races within the human species share the same genetic origins. Kant is a firm believer in the unity of the human species, at least in the sense that he rejects all accounts of race which hold that the human races originate from a plurality of different, independent sources. "All kinds [*Arten*] of human beings are fertile with another race when they have copulated with each other. This makes us also believe that they descend from a single phylum [*Stamm*]" (*Menschenkunde* 25:1187). Historically, polygeneticism, the positing of diverse origins of races, has been a favorite strategy of racists. If the various races do indeed stem from different, independent genetic sources (and if "different" is interpreted, as is normally the case in such contexts, as meaning "unequal"), we are provided a means of asserting a basis for permanent inequalities between peoples.[74] The fight against polygeneticism was in fact one of Kant's main motives for writing his third and most philosophically sophisticated essay dealing with race, "On the Use of Teleological Principles in Philosophy" (1788). This essay was a reply to Georg Forster's earlier attack on Kant's theory of race, "Noch etwas über die Menschenraßen," originally published in the *Teutsche Merkur* in 1786. Forster advocated a polygenetic account of the races; Kant a monogenetic one.[75]

In addition to this naturalistic, Buffonian influence, there is also a very strong teleological dimension to Kant's theory of race. In his first essay on race he writes:

> The human being was destined [*bestimmt*] for all climates and for every soil condition; consequently, various germs [*Keime*] and natural predispositions [*Naturanlagen*] must lie ready in him to be on occasion either unfolded or restrained, so that he would become adapted to his place in the world and over

the course of generations would appear to be as it were native and made for that place. (2:435; cf. *Menschenrace* 8:93; *Gebrauch* 8:166; *Päd* 9:445)

According to this teleological view, racial characteristics are present in the human species because they help us reach our collective destiny. The same potential skin colors were preprogrammed into each one of our ancestors from the beginning to help them cope with different environments as a means of better ensuring that the development and future perfection of all human talents would occur, regardless of what natural obstacles stood in the way. We were all potentially black, red, yellow, and white. Racial differences emerged gradually with the dispersal of human beings to different climatic conditions. "The end of providence is this: God wills that human beings should populate the entire earth. All animals have their special climates, but human beings are to be found everywhere" (*Friedländer* 25:679).

It is precisely this teleological assumption concerning the various latent "germs and natural predispositions" in all human beings that leads Kant to argue against both eugenics and intermarriage. Eugenics is inadvisable because it short-circuits the plan of "a wiser nature" that allows humanity to develop "all its talents and to approach the perfection of its destiny" (*Racen* 2:431). Similarly, intermarriage [*Vermischung*] is wrong because nature "does not want the old forms to be always reproduced again, but wants rather that all the diversity [*Mannigfaltigkeit*] be brought out which it had placed in the original germs [*Keime*] of the human phylum" (*Gebrauch* 8:167). Nature has compelling reasons for seeking diversity in the human species, and we reject these reasons at our own peril.

Race as Kant construes it is thus a set of latent predispositions that reside in all members of the species, parts of which then get activated depending on what sort of climate an individual lives in (and what length of time one spends in this climate). Again, according to this view, *all* human beings were potentially black, red, yellow, and white. (On Kant's view there are only four races.) Our ancestors actually became black, yellow, red, or white only by moving to a region of the earth whose climatic conditions triggered the appropriate "race germ" to actualize itself—after which point "the other germs obligingly retire[d] into inactivity."[76]

Kant defines "races" in his 1775 essay as "hereditary [*erbliche*] distinctions in animals which belong to a single phylum," distinctions that "constantly preserve themselves in all transplantations [*Verpflanzungen*] (transpositions to other regions) over prolonged generations and which always produce half-breed [*halbschlächtig*] young in the intermingling with other variations of the same phylum" (2:430; cf. *Menschenrace* 8:99–100, *Gebrauch* 8: 165). "Race," in other words, is used by Kant to refer to invariably inherited characteristics which do not belong to the species as such. Race is distinguished from non-racial inherited characteristics such as eye color in that it is *invariably* inherited from *both* parents. For example, the child of a white mother will necessarily be at least partly white in color; the child of a brown-eyed father will not necessarily have brown eyes at all (cf. 8:95, 102, 2:430).

Skin color, according to Kant, is the sole defining characteristic of race. The title of section 3 of his second essay on race ("Determination of the Concept of a Human Race") reads: "No other characteristic property is *necessarily hereditary* [*nothwendig erblich*] in the class of the whites other than what belongs to the human species in general; and so with the other classes as well" (8:94). Since Kant views skin color alone as being the only unfailingly hereditary property found in the various races ("other than what belongs to the human species in general"), it follows that other allegedly hereditary properties that loom large in some theories of race (e.g., intelligence, moral capacity, or the ability to produce culture) cannot be a part of Kant's account of race.[77]

The foregoing general outline of a race theory, though for the most part not unique to Kant,[78] also appears fairly tame. Following Buffon, Kant insists that all human beings, regardless of race, belong to the same species; we share a common origin. "Race" is defined by skin color alone, and skin color (as Leibniz, Montesquieu, and others had argued earlier) is caused by climate. Mental characteristics such as intelligence, personality, and character are not to be equated with race. Finally, Kant's own teleological twist on the race theories of his day: the human being was "destined for all climates and every soil condition" (2:435). Race (that is, skin color) was programmed into all members of the species from the beginning to help them cope with different environments as a means of better insuring that the development and perfection of all human talents would occur, regardless of what climatic conditions people found themselves in.

However, many of Kant's more specific remarks about race are not nearly as tame, and in recent years a number of criticisms have been leveled at them. One critic has concluded that "the specific Kantian variety of humanism is tied together [*verknüpft*] with an *implicit* racism."[79] Another argues that skin color "for Kant is evidence of superior, inferior, or no 'gift' of 'talent', or the capacity to realize reason and rational-moral perfectibility through education."[80] Reinhard Brandt reaches a similar conclusion:

> Kant's remarks . . . leave no doubt that [he, namely Kant, believes that] the white race is intellectually and morally superior to the remaining three not only in degree but qualitatively; only whites are capable of progress; only whites can act from moral principles, and, as a result, do justice to the demand of the categorical imperative. Whites, that is to say clearly and exclusively: the white man and not also the white woman.[81]

What does Kant say about race that leads people to such conclusions? Some of his more disturbing remarks are as follows.

Sensitivity

Some of the races are allegedly less sensitive than others. This judgment is usually aimed at Native Americans or *die Wilden* ("savages," "the wild ones"), as in the following passage from the *Nachlaß* of the 1780s: "Americans [are] insensitive [*unempfindlich*], without affect and passion for anything more than revenge. . . . [D]o not love anything, do not care for anything" (*Refl* 1520, 15:877; cf. *Parow* 25:451, *Pillau* 25:833). Similarly, in the *Menschenkunde* transcript Kant states that Native Americans "have no drives [*keine Triebfedern*], for they have no affect and passion" (25:1187; cf. Starke II, 119, Dohna, 363).

In the 1764 *Observations* he makes a similar judgment about blacks: "The Negroes of Africa have by nature [*von der Natur*] no feeling that rises above the trifling" (2:253). However, later remarks about blacks inexplicably grant them a new-found sensitivity: "Negroes. Exactly the opposite [of the Native Americans]: they are lively [*lebhaft*], full of affect and passion. Chattering, vain, devoted to pleasure" (*Refl* 1520, 15:877; cf. *Parow* 25:451). A parallel passage occurs in *Menschenkunde*: "The race of the Negroes, one could say, is entirely the opposite of the Americans; they are full of affect and passion, very lively, talkative, and vain" (25:1187; cf. Starke II, 119; Dohna, 363).

Intelligence

In the *Observations*, Kant endorses Hume's notorious claim[82] that "not a single Negro was ever found who presented anything great in art or science or any other praiseworthy quality, even though among the whites some continually rise aloft from the lowest rabble, and through superior gifts [*vorzügliche Gaben*] earn respect in the world. So fundamental is the difference between these two races of human beings [*diese zwei Menschengeschlechter*], and it appears to be as great in regard to mental capacities [*Gemüthsfähigkeiten*] as in color" (2:253; cf. *Gebrauch* 8:174 n).

In the *Physical Geography* lectures, we are told that Native Americans "become prudent [*klug*] very early, but their understanding [*Verstand*] does not continue to grow at the same rate thereafter. . . . The tiredness of their minds [*Die Erschlaffung ihrer Geister*] looks for a stimulus in brandy, tobacco, opium, and other strong things" (9:316, cf. *Racen* 2:438).

Talents

Perhaps Kant's most notorious passage on race is the following, from Rink's edited version of the *Physical Geography* lectures: "Humanity is in its greatest perfection in the white race. The yellow Indians already have a lesser talent. The Negroes are much lower, and lowest of all is part of the American peoples" (9:316). In a related *Reflexion* Kant claims that whites "contain all drives of nature in affects and passions, all talents, all predispositions to culture and civilization and can obey as well as rule. They are the only ones [*die einzige*] who always progress toward perfection" (*Refl* 1520, 15:878; cf. *Menschenkunde* 25: 1187).

Culture

As the previous quotation indicates, Kant's view is that some races are culture producers while others are not. Here too, Native Americans fare extremely poorly. In the "Teleology" essay he writes:

That their [Native Americans'] natural aptitude [*Naturell*] did not achieve a *perfect* fitness with any climate, can be seen from the circumstance that hardly another reason can be given for why this race, which is too weak for hard labor, too indifferent for industry, and incapable of any culture [unfähig zu aller Cultur]. (8:175–76; cf. Pillau 25:843)

A description of Native Americans in the Reflexionen zur Anthropologie ends on the same note; "they accept no culture at all [nehmen gar keine Cultur an]" (Refl 1520, 15:877; cf. Menschenkunde 25:1187, Starke II, 119). Blacks fare only marginally better as culture producers: "They accept the culture of slaves, but not of free people, and they are incapable of leading themselves [unfähig sich selbst zu führen]" (Refl 1520, 15:877; cf. Menschenkunde 25:1187, Dohna, 363). Blacks and Americans (that is to say, die Wilden in Amerika), we are informed in Starke II, will "never be able to create for themselves an orderly civil society" (119). In the essay "Teleology" Kant attempts to offer a causal explanation for Native Americans' alleged multiple shortcomings. Due to their frequent migrations into different climates, they have become a race which "is not suited to any climate" (8:175). Native Americans now lack a sufficient "drive to activity [Trieb zur Thätigkeit] . . . which is especially interwoven with certain natural predispositions [Naturanlagen]" (8:174 n; cf. Menschenrace 8:104). Once such predispositions are developed, they apparently cannot be altered, and a predisposition that was suitable for (e.g.) a warm, southern climate will be unsuitable for a cold, northern one.

Hierarchy and the Stammgattung

Finally, despite Kant's assertion that the same race potentialities were originally programmed into all human beings (2:435), other remarks of his concerning ancient peoples have led critics to conclude that his considered view is that the white race alone comes closest to the original type of human being; the other races being "merely degenerative developments from the white original."[83] For instance, in his 1775 essay he speculates that the Stammgattung or phyletic species is most likely to be found "in the thirty-first to the fifty-second degree of latitude in the ancient world. . . . Now here to be sure we do find inhabitants that are white, but they are brunette [brunette]; therefore we wish to assume this shape [Gestalt] to be the one closest to that of the Stammgattung" (2:440–41).[84]

A different (but ultimately related) kind of racial hierarchy is also present in his classification of races in the Physical Geography lectures, the Reflexionen zur Anthropologie, Menschenkunde, Starke II, and the Dohna Anthropology, all of which have been referred to earlier. White is always at the top, followed by yellow, black, and red. Again: "Humanity is in its greatest perfection in the white race. The yellow Indians already have a lesser talent. The Negroes are much lower, and lowest of all is part of the American peoples" (Geo 9:316; cf. Refl 1520, 15:878; Menschenkunde 25:1187; Starke II, 119; Dohna, 363).[85]

In classic works dealing with race, Kant is often touted as a progressive voice who emphasizes "the unity of mankind";[86] one whose "'humanitarian' and 'equalitarian' ideas" are "not only entirely unintelligible to Gobineau, but simply intolerable."[87] The facts appear to be otherwise. Not all Kant's ideas about race are entirely "humanitarian" and "equalitarian," and the gap between Gobineau and Kant is unfortunately not always as wide as one would like it to be.

"The Whole Human Race":
Kant and Moral Universality

> The language of true reason is humble. All human beings are
> equal to one another.
>
> *Moralphilosophie Collins*

After examining both individual character as well as various kinds of group character among human beings, Kant concludes most of the later versions of his lectures[88] with an examination of the character of the species. However, this problem of describing the character of the species as a whole appears to be "absolutely insoluble [*schlechterdings unauflöslich*], because the solution must turn on the comparison of two species of rational beings through experience, which experience does not offer us" (*Anth* 7:321).[89] Because experience does not present us with a second species of rational being with which to compare ourselves, all that we can safely say is that the human being "has a character, which he himself creates [*sich selbst schafft*]" (7:321; cf. 329). Here, however, "character" is clearly being used in a moral sense (cf. 7:292), whereas in the earlier sections on individual and group character it is primarily nonmoral dimensions of character that are under discussion.

But what one in fact finds in the last part of the lectures is not so much a description of the character of the human species as it exists at present as a sketch of its historical destiny. (In this respect the title of the last chapter of Starke II is more accurate: "The Character of the Human Race and the Task which it has to Solve on this Earth" [x].) Kant's *Anthropology* lectures, like his *Pedagogy* lectures and other texts which I examine in later chapters, ends on a strong teleological note concerning the destiny of the human species. This teleological dimension injects both an underlying unity to the earlier sections (many of which, as I have shown, are very loosely arranged, and do not always fit together well with one another) as well as a strong moral rationale for the entire work.

What is the destiny of the human species? The following well-known summary from the 1798 *Anthropology* is still the best formulation:

> The sum total of pragmatic anthropology in respect to the destiny [*Bestimmung*] of the human being and the characterization of his formation [*Ausbildung*] is as follows. The human being is destined through his reason to be in a society with human beings and through art and the sciences to cultivate, civilize, and moralize [*moralisieren*] himself in it. (7:324; cf. *Pillau* 25:847; *Menschenkunde* 25:1198; *Mrongovius* 25:1426; Dohna, 369; Starke II, 121; *Refl* 1524, 15:897)

This final goal of *Moralisierung* is essentially a secularizing of the biblical theme of the kingdom of God. As Kant asserts in a *Reflexion*: "The kingdom [*Reich*] of God on earth: this is the final destiny of the human being" (*Refl* 1396, 15:608; cf. *Friedländer* 25:695, *Rel* 6:93–147, Matthew 6:33). As I have shown (see "The Education of Humanity" in chap. 2), humanity in Kant's judgment has still not reached the crucial step of moralization. Much more needs to be achieved in the fields of education, government, law, and religion before we will be ready for it, and the *Weltkenntnis* we acquire from anthropology is itself designed to be applied toward this fundamental transformation:

> We human beings are . . . in the second degree of progress toward perfection, certainly cultivated and civilized, but not moralized. We have the highest degree of culture that we can possess without morality, civility also has its maximum. The lack [*Bedürfnis*] in both will eventually force moralization, namely through education, a federal constitution [*Staatsverfassung*], and religion. (*Refl* 1460, 15:641; cf. *Refl* 1524, 15:897, *Pillau* 25:847, *Menschenkunde* 25:1198, *Mrongovius* 25:1427)

This last step will also be the most difficult: "The worst condition of the human race is the *Übergang* from civilization to moralization" (Starke II, 124). However, we still have a very long way to go, since "the majority of human beings are still raw and the proper development of our talents is still lacking" (*Mrongovius* 25:1426). Furthermore, with respect to the primary means of human moral improvement (education, legislation, and religion) we are "so to speak in a threefold immaturity (*Unmündigkeit*)" (25:1427; cf. *Menschenkunde* 25:1198).

But now comes the difficult question: Who is the "we" that is progressing toward perfection? As I have shown, Kant's *Anthropology* lectures are riddled with western-Eurocentric prejudices. Are all human beings to share in the destiny of the species or only some? Brandt writes:

> [Kant's] anthropology must . . . demand from moral philosophy that it speak not of the human being in general but of a class-division between rational beings (or rather human beings) capable of maturity [*mündigkeitsfähig*] and incapable [-*nichtfähig*] of maturity, and that it apply the [categorical] imperative qua imperative only to the first class. Anthropology does not thereby destroy moral philosophy; however, it does demand a sensitive restriction [*empfindliche Einschränkung*] from it.[90]

This claim is erroneous in two respects. First, it is not the case that "the *Anthropology*, particularly in the lecture manuscripts and *Reflexionen* . . . demands a specification not foreseen in the practical philosophy."[91] The various versions of the *Anthropology* lectures do not contain any huge surprises on this point; they do not "demand a sensitive restriction" from pure ethics concerning the class of moral agency. Kant's views concerning women, people of color, and indeed, all non–western European peoples generally, are abhorrent. But one does not need to delve into his *Anthropology* lectures to find this out. It is not the case that Kant presents contradictory models (a universalist one in his theoretical writings on moral philosophy; a narrower picture in the *Anthropology* writings). As befits the project of pure ethics, he does not discuss issues of gender and race in any detail in his theoretical writings on moral philosophy. But as I showed earlier, the few remarks that he does make on these topics are (unfortunately) consistent with what we find in the *Anthropology*. Also, Kant makes numerous statements on race and gender elsewhere (e.g., in the *Observations*, the three essays on race, and "Theory and Practice") which are consistent with his position within the *Anthropology*. These other texts, though not strictly speaking part of Kant's "moral philosophy" in a narrow sense, nevertheless serve to further discredit the notion that we are somehow being presented with an unforeseen specification of moral agency in the *Anthropology* lectures.

As concerns women, for instance, we are informed in the *Metaphysics of Morals* that "all women . . . lack civil personality, and their existence is, as it were, only inherence" (6:314, cf. *Gemeinspruch* 8:295). And in the *Observations*, Kant states that woman's "philosophy [*Weltweisheit*] is not reasoning [*Vernünfteln*], but feeling [*Empfinden*]"; and he doubts whether "the fair sex is capable [*fähig*] of principles" (2:230, 232, cf. 8:35). All these statements are quite in line with the picture of women presented in the various versions of the *Anthropology* lectures.

Remarks about race seldom occur in Kant's theoretical writings on moral philosophy. But the following seldom-discussed passage from the *Groundwork* is relevant. In his illustration of the duty to develop one's talents using the formula of the law of nature, he disparages the South Sea islanders who let their talents rust and are bent on devoting their lives "merely to idleness, amusement, procreation—in a word, to enjoyment" (4:423, cf. *Herder* 8:65). This comment is quite consistent with the strong western-Eurocentrism of the *Anthropology* writings.[92] And then of course there are the racist remarks in the *Observations* and in the three essays on race. Again, in the *Observations* Kant (following Hume) asserts: "So fundamental is the difference between these two races of human beings, and it appears to be as great in regard to mental capacities as in color" (2:253). And in the essay "Teleology" we are told that Native Americans are "incapable of any culture [*unfähig zur aller Kultur*]" (8:176) and that Blacks, Native Americans, Indians, and gypsies[93] lack the "capacity to work" and the "drive to activity" (8:174 n). All of these statements are quite consistent with the racist side of Kant's account of the character of the races in the *Anthropology* lectures.

The second and more fundamental respect in which Brandt's claim is erroneous is that it misconstrues Kant's views concerning which human beings are to participate in the moral progress of the species. As Brandt sees it, Kant's position is not just that women and people of color are presently or temporarily "incapable of maturity" (*mündigkeitsnichtfähig*), but rather that "they are and remain [*sind und bleiben*] passive citizens in the kingdom of ethics"; they "cannot become active, lawgiving citizens in the kingdom of ends, because by nature they act not according to principles but according to examples and feelings."[94] However, when Kant refers to the moral destiny of the human species, he clearly means that the *whole* race progresses toward this destiny. The following three arguments articulate the universal intent of his applied ethics.

The Unity of the Human Family

As we have seen, Kant's human species concept is straightforwardly naturalistic; "animals which produce fertile young with one another . . . belong to one and the same physical species. . . . According to this concept [of a natural species], all human beings on the wide earth belong to one and the same natural species" (*Racen* 2:429; cf. *Menschenkunde* 25:1187). It follows from this definition that both women and people of color are members of the human species. Kant's human species concept is also monogenetic, not polygenetic—that is, he maintains that all human beings "descend from one phylum" (*Menschenkunde* 25:1187). But here as elsewhere, teleological and moral assumptions play major roles. In one essay he remarks that "if there were diversity of descent," one could rightly accuse nature of having erred "regarding the most appropriate organization toward sociability as the highest end of human destiny, for the unity of the family [*Einheit der Familie*] from which all human beings should descend was without doubt the best arrangement for this purpose" (*Anfang* 8:110). All human beings "are from one family" (*Refl* 1499, 15:782), and we reject this assumption on pain of making nature—who "does nothing superfluous and is not wasteful in the use of means towards her ends"—look stupid (*Idee* 8:19). This assumption of "the unity of the human species [*die Einheit der menschlichen Gattung*]" (*Menschenkunde* 25:1195), as Rotenstreich remarks, "has both a biological and a moral meaning,"[95] one that is central to all of Kant's explorations of race.

Again, racial characteristics are present because they are allegedly instrumental in helping the species reach its destiny: "The human being was destined for all climates and for every soil condition; consequently, various germs [*Keime*] and natural predispositions must lie restrained in him to be on occasion either unfolded or restrained, so that he would become adapted to his place in the world" (*Racen* 2:435; cf. *Friedländer* 25:679). According to this view, the same potential skin colors were preprogrammed into each one of our ancestors from the beginning to help them cope with different environments as a means of better ensuring that the development and future perfection of all human talents would occur, regardless of what climatic conditions were encountered. We were all potentially black, red, yellow, and white.

"The Whole Human Race"

When Kant speaks of the moral destiny of the species, he stresses repeatedly that the *entire* species must eventually participate in progress toward perfection. What we want to know is "whether the human *race* (in its entirety) [*das menschliche Geschlecht (im Großen)*] is continually improving" (*Streit* 7:79). In order to know this, we must find a "*historical sign* that could prove the *tendency* of the human race as a *whole* [*das menschliche Geschlecht im Ganzen*]" (7:84). We are looking for "a way of thinking" (namely, in public reaction to the French Revolution) that, "because of its universality," "proves a character of the whole human race [*das Menschengeschlecht im Ganzen*], and at the same time (because of its disinterestedness), a moral character of the race, at least in the predisposition" (7:85).

Similarly, in his review of Herder Kant informs readers that he believes he "knows pretty well the materials for an anthropology . . . in attempting a history of the destiny of humanity in its entirety [*die Menschheit im Ganzen*]" (8:56). And at the end of the review he emphasizes that the concept of a human species properly "refers to the *whole* [*das Ganze*] of a series of generations running into infinity (the indeterminable)" (8:65). Also in the *Religion* he maintains that human beings can only hope for a victory of good over evil "through the setting up and spreading [*Ausbreitung*] of a society in accordance with, and for the sake of, the laws of virtue—a society which reason makes it a task and duty of the entire human race [*die ganze Menschengeschlecht*] to determine in its full scope" (6:94).

Kant thus clearly holds that "what is special about humanity is that . . . the entire species progresses in perfection" (*Refl* 1499, 15:784). And because he believes that the entire species progresses in perfection, he must also accept that the entire species is destined to eventually work its way through the preparatory steps of culture and civilization to moralization. It therefore cannot be the case, Brandt and other critics to the contrary, that women or people of color will always remain mere passive citizens in the realm of ethics. This assertion contradicts the core assumptions of his theory of human moral development.

"The Spreading over All Peoples of the Earth"

A third indication that Kantian moral progress must eventually include more than western European white men who manage their own businesses (cf. *MdS* 6:314) is that Kant frequently uses expressions such as "the spreading over all peoples of the earth" in describing this progress. A proper concern for human progress requires that one "not simply consider what may happen with any one people [*Volk*], but consider also the spreading [*die Verbreitung*] over all peoples of the earth, who will gradually come to participate in progress" (*Streit* 7:89; cf. *Rel* 6:94). A critical perspective on progress enables one to discover "a regular course of improvement in the constitutions of states in our part of the world (which will probably give laws eventually to all others)" (*Idee* 8:29).

Kant is convinced that we "must search for the continual progress of the human race in the Occident, and from there the spreading [*Verbreitung*] around the world" (*Refl* 1501, 15:788–89). Clearly a strong faith in moral *gradualism* is indicated here, albeit one that sees the source of progress as always lying in western Europe, and one that sees certain population groups which do not advance culturally as eventually dying out (cf. n. 92). But eventually, as more and more nations develop appropriate civil constitutions and social infrastructures, moral progress will take root everywhere, and "the peoples of the earth" will enter into the kind of moral community where "a violation of rights in *one* part of the world is felt *everywhere*" (*Frieden* 8:360).[96] The long-term goal is thus a "broadened way of thinking [*erweiterte Denkungsart*]"; one that enables everyone eventually "to think from the standpoint of everyone else" (*KU* 5:294).

These three interrelated arguments show that Kant is logically committed to the belief that the entire human species must eventually share in the destiny of the species: moral perfection. "Logically" but perhaps not "personally." Kant's writings do exhibit many private prejudices and contradictory tendencies. It may well be that the Kant who wrote that "the Negro can be disciplined and cultivated but never genuinely civilized" (*Refl* 1520, 15:878); and who "hardly believes the fair sex is capable of principles" (*Beob* 2:232), would not accept these logical implications of his own theory. But Kant's theory is fortunately stronger than his prejudices, and it is the theory on which philosophers should focus. We should not hide or suppress the prejudices, but neither should we overvalue them or try to inflate them into something they are not.

Properly understood, the core value of universality in Kant's ethics is much more than an esoteric head-game of scrutinizing maxims. Rather, it refers to the hard and painful work of making the world moral—of figuring out what changes in human institutions and practices need to be made so that all members of the species will be brought into the moral community. This ideal of a truly universal moral community where all people count remains the most important single legacy of Kant's ethics. The "redemption of the hopes of the past"[97] is still a task worth pursuing, and we should not let ourselves be deceived by self-serving distortions of these hopes. Finally, Kant's writings in anthropology and empirical ethics do not tarnish this legacy. On the contrary, they show us what we need to do to make it real. At the same time, the underlying vision of gradual moral universality in these texts also reveals that the true intent of Kantian anthropology lies somewhere between transcendental and merely empirical concerns. In his lectures on anthropology Kant is not trying to make good on the ambitious claim that all philosophical questions are at bottom anthropological questions concerning the human subject (cf. 9:25), but neither is he simply engaged in a descriptive account of human cultures. Rather, his aim is to offer the species a moral map that they can use to move toward their collective destiny.

4

ART AND RELIGION

The chief texts to be examined in this chapter are Kant's *Critique of Judgment* (1790) and *Religion Within the Boundaries of Mere Reason* (1793). Both of these works are quite different from the Kantian lecture materials on education and anthropology examined in previous chapters in that they: (1) were published by Kant himself, (2) are mature works of the critical period, and (3) are intended primarily as contributions to his project of critical philosophy rather than that of popular, applied philosophy. Additionally, there is much more secondary literature on Kant's aesthetics and religion than there is on his pedagogy and anthropology, and some of the former does cast considerable light on a variety of Kantian moral themes, for example, the role of feeling in relation to morality.[1] However, to my knowledge, no one has yet analyzed Kant's aesthetics or religion from the particular perspective of impure ethics. The fields of art and religion are treated together in this chapter primarily because (1) they address similar issues in empirical ethics and (2) neither domain on its own makes quite as direct or as large a contribution to the second part of ethics as do those domains explored in other chapters. The first four sections treat art, while the final two sections concern religion.

In what follows I am not primarily interested in the myriad details of either Kant's aesthetics or philosophy of religion as traditionally conceived. Rather, my aim is to approach both texts from the particular perspective of impure ethics: What do they tell us about ethics for human beings? What specific claims and insights into human morality do we find in these two interconnected aspects of the Kantian corpus that help us to fill out our picture of the second part of his ethics, "to which the empirical principles belong" (*Moral Mrongovius II* 29:599)? The following discussion is also highly selective; it makes no claim to systematic completeness. Rather, my aim is merely to mark out the major intersecting points between both Kant's aesthetics and empirical ethics and his religion and empirical ethics, and to then show how these materials tie in with specific issues raised in previous chapters. I hope to convince the reader that each text has a much more pronounced moral anthropological orientation to it than has often been realized, an orientation that, when supplemented by those found in the writings on pedagogy, anthropology, and history, results in an extremely rich and detailed applied ethics for human beings.

Art as a Human Phenomenon

> Die *Kunst*, o Mensch, hast du allein.
> Schiller,
"Die Künstler"

In Kant's writings on education, the claim that the human being is a particular type of creature who requires education (education in a *very* big way) stands out: "The human being can only become human through education. He is nothing except what education makes of him" (*Päd* 9:443). Other living creatures on earth, according to Kant, require no education; and how it may be with other rational beings elsewhere in the universe in this regard we do not know. Human beings are not "ready made" or even self-actualizing creatures; they require extensive care, discipline, training, and enculturation in order to realize their capacities. And the most difficult aspect of this process is that which educates them *into morality.*

In Kant's lectures on anthropology we are offered one specification and provision of the kind of knowledge human beings need for their moralization. We need *Weltkenntnis*, pragmatically and cosmologically conceived. That is to say, we need to know about the world around us, particularly human beings' place within it, and we need to understand human beings not just as natural objects but as freely acting beings who act according to ends they have set for themselves.

In Kant's writings on aesthetics we find a second specification of the kind of education and preparation human beings need for morality. Human beings are not just rational beings but sensuously affected, embodied rational beings. Our sensory experiences and the feelings and thoughts aroused by these experiences form an integral part of our identity; a part that in turn plays multiple roles in human morality.

The *Critique of Judgment* does contribute many further details to impure ethics, partly because it is Kant's view that beauty (unlike the good) applies "only to human beings," and partly because this allegedly humans-only encounter with beauty helps prepares us for the not exclusively human encounter with moral concepts. On the first point Kant writes:

> Agreeableness applies [*gilt*] also to irrational animals; beauty only to human beings [*nur für Menschen*], that is, animal and yet rational beings, but also not simply rational beings as such (for instance, spirits [*Geister*]), but animal as well; the good however applies to every rational being in general [*jedes vernünftige Wesen überhaupt*]. (*KU* 5:210)

Similarly, in regard to both beauty and sublimity (this second aesthetic category, as I will show later, is particularly important for Kant's ethics) he writes: "[T]hese are aesthetic modes of representation that we would never come across in ourselves if we were merely pure intelligences (or even if we were to transfer ourselves in thoughts into this quality)" (5:271; cf. 233). In Kant's writings on pure ethics he is usually concerned with concepts that he believes apply to all rational beings. *The Critique of Judgment*, though officially part of Kant's transcendental philosophy and not part of his applied, popular philosophy in the way that the *Anthropology* and *Education* lectures are, nevertheless does have the narrower "for humans only" scope of the latter. If we approach the *Critique of Judgment* primarily with an eye toward impure ethics rather than art (or, more precisely, with a focus on the key intersections between art and impure ethics), we are thus presented with a rare opportunity to explore Kant's conception of the human side of ethics, particularly as concerns our sensuous, affective (animal) side.

In the following examination of connecting points between aesthetics and human morality, my aim is to look critically at what I believe are Kant's three major claims regarding the intersection of art and human morality: (1) art serves as an important and necessary preparation for morality in the lives of human beings; (2) for human beings beauty serves as a necessary symbol of the morally good; (3) for human beings the experience of the sublime in nature constitutes a second (and superior) symbol of the morally good.

Art as Preparation for Morality

In Kant's writings on education surprisingly little is said about aesthetic education. One paragraph in the *Lectures on Pedagogy* begins promisingly with the declaration: "The formation [*Bildung*] of the feeling of pleasure or displeasure[2] also belongs here" (*Päd* 9:477). However, the hope that a discussion of aesthetics' positive contributions to moral education will follow is dashed immediately by the next sentence: "That formation must be negative and the feeling itself must not be coddled" (9:477). The only other explicit reference to aesthetic education occurs a bit earlier where Kant is summarizing a recommended course of study for children. He concludes by saying: "Thus one prepares the way for a *correct* [*richtiger*] taste rather than a *fine* [*feiner*] or *delicate* taste" (9:474).[3]

But in the *Critique of Judgment* and related works Kant discusses the formation and development of aesthetic experience and its role in moral development in some detail.[4] "The beautiful," he tells us, "prepares us [*bereitet uns vor*] to love something, even nature, without interest" (*KU* 5:267). Similarly, in a *Reflexion* that probably dates from 1788–89 he writes: "The culture of taste is a preliminary exercise [*Vorübung*] for morality" (*Refl* 993, 15:438). And in preparing us to love something without interest, taste (the faculty by means of which we discern what is beautiful) "makes possible the *Übergang*, so to speak, from the charm of sense to habitual moral interest without too violent a leap" (*KU* 5:354). How exactly does the experience of beauty prepare us to love something without interest, and what does such preparation have to do with morality?

"Disinterestedness" is commonly taken to be the core of Kant's aesthetic theory, but what exactly he means by this concept is still being debated.[5] At first glance, the assertion that taste estimates its objects "through a delight or displeasure *without any interest*" (*KU* 5:211) might seem to detach it entirely from morality. How can people who are so seemingly detached from things that they show no interest in them be said to be preparing themselves for morality? For the moral good on Kant's view "carries with it the highest interest" (*KU* 5:209). Moral interests always have primacy over all others (cf. *KpV* 5:121), and if in our aesthetic contemplations of beautiful objects we are temporarily cut loose from consideration of any and all interests (including the most important ones, namely, moral), it is difficult to see how the experience of beauty can be said to prepare us for morality.

This particular side of Kant's emphasis on disinterestedness is what has led so many interpreters to view him as the father of aesthetic formalism and of art for art's sake—the view that art serves no other masters than its own, and that aesthetic judgment must not kowtow to extraneous theoretical or practical concerns (of either a moral or nonmoral variety) of any kind. But there is clearly something else going on in the preceding passages. Paul Guyer writes:

> what he [Kant] actually argued is that paradigmatic judgments of taste are disinterested in their origin but can serve the supreme interest of morality precisely in virtue of their disinterestedness. At the most immediate level of response, aesthetic judgment must be free of external constraints, including the constraints of morality, but in virtue of this freedom the experience of aesthetic judgment can represent and in some degree prepare us for the exercise of freedom in morality itself. For Kant, the autonomy of the aesthetic is in the service of the primacy of practical reason, but the aesthetic serves practical reason in virtue of nothing less than its freedom from constraint by practical as well as theoretical reason.[6]

On this view, it is the initial experience of freedom within aesthetic judgment (the sense that while we are enjoying objects of beauty we are properly not constrained by extraneous theoretical or practical concerns of any sort) that helps prepare the way for morality. And Kant does make similar claims on behalf of aesthetics in his moral writings as well. For instance, in the *Metaphysics of Morals* he refers to a

> feeling in the human being which, though not of itself moral, is still a disposition of sensibility [*Stimmung der Sinnlichkeit*] that greatly promotes [*sehr befördert*] morality or at least prepares the way [*vorbereitet*] for it—the disposition, namely, to love something (e.g., beautiful crystal formations, the indescribable beauty of plants) even apart from any intention to use it. (6:443)

It is by means of this feeling we experience when appreciating objects of beauty that moral freedom is made tangible or (to use one of Guyer's favorite terms) "palpable" to us:

> the heart of Kant's connection between aesthetics and morality is the view that it is only by preserving its freedom from direct constraint by concepts, even didactic concepts of morality itself, that the experience of beauty can

serve the purpose of giving us a palpable experience of freedom, which is its deepest service to the needs of morality.[7]

A second important service that the experience of beauty provides to the needs of morality, one that has not received as much attention from scholars, concerns the inter-related feelings of love, delight, and pleasure that accompany this experience. As noted earlier, it is Kant's view that the beautiful "prepares us to love [*lieben*] something" (5:267). The related passage at *KU* 5:354 also stresses the "free delight [*freies Wohlgefallen*]" or satisfaction that taste represents to the imagination. Similarly, in a famous passage in part 2 of the *Critique of Judgment* he writes:

> Fine art and sciences, if they do not make the human being morally better [*sittlich besser*], yet, through a pleasure [*Lust*] that allows itself to be universally shared, and through polish and refinement for society, still make him civilized [*gesittet*], and do much to overcome the tyranny of the senses and prepare the human being for a sovereignty in which reason alone shall have power. (5:433)

And in a related passage from *Anthropology from a Pragmatic Point of View* (which occurs in a section entitled "Taste Contains a Tendency toward External Promotion [*äußere Beförderung*] of Morality"), Kant also stresses that taste "concerns the communication of one's feeling of pleasure or displeasure to others and contains a receptivity, which through this communication affects others with the pleasure [*Lust*] of feeling a satisfaction [*complacentia*] in common about it (that is, sociably)" (7:244). In all of these passages we see a pronounced stress on feelings of pleasure, satisfaction, and love, along with the joint claims that: (1) the experience of beauty itself can produce these feelings, and (2) the presence of such feelings is also necessary and important in ethics. The second claim has of course often been asserted to have no place in Kant's ethics, and, admittedly, his praise in the *Groundwork* of the "genuine moral worth" of the actions of a man in whom "all sympathy with the fate of others has been extinguished" due to a "deadly insensibility" (4:398) might seem to support such a reading.[8] But when he is careful, Kant is clear in asserting that certain feelings have a necessary and positive contribution to make to human moral character. Perhaps the clearest text occurs in a famous footnote early in the *Religion*, discussed earlier, where Kant defends his own self-proclaimed moral rigorism against Schiller:

> Now if one asks: what is the *aesthetic* quality, the *temperament of virtue* as it were, brave and thus *cheerful* [*fröhlich*], or bent with fear and beaten down? then an answer is hardly necessary. The latter slavish frame of mind can never take place without a hidden *hatred* of the law, and the cheerful heart in *following* its duty (not complacency in the *acknowledgment* of it) is a sign of genuineness in virtuous disposition. (6:23–24 n; cf. "Divisions of the *Methodenlehre*" in chap. 2.)

Here the same emphasis on aesthetic quality or feeling is present (the term of choice this time is *fröhlich*, cheerful, joyous, happy; but it is in the same general emotional neighborhood as Kant's earlier emphases on *Wohlgefallen*, *Liebe*, and *Lust*). However, now the place of this feeling in ethics is paramount: the presence of joyousness is "a sign of genuineness in virtuous disposition." The proper goal of human moral character development is not to eradicate feelings and sensibilities, but rather to teach them to work in harmony with reason. And it is a central doctrine of Kant's aesthetic theory (a doctrine repeated elsewhere in his applied ethics) that art serves as a preparation for morality by properly cultivating the feeling of joyousness.

Finally, a third related aspect of art's preparation for morality concerns universality and necessity. According to Kant, a judgment of taste "must involve a claim to validity for everyone . . . that is, there must be joined with it a claim to subjective universality" (*KU* 5:212; cf. 354). The universality of a judgment of taste is subjective rather than objective, that is, it rests "not on any concept" (5:215) but rather on shared feelings. The objective principles of morality, on the other hand, are "knowable through a universal concept" (5:354). This means that the universality of aesthetic judgments is in effect smaller than that of moral judgments. The possibility of aesthetic judgments rests on the feelings of the perceiving subject. Such judgments cannot be conceptualized, and so other rational beings whose bodies and sense organs (if they have any) differ substantially from ours will not be capable of experiencing them. Moral universality, on the other hand, supposedly stretches beyond the merely human. But it is precisely this subjective, all too human universality of aesthetic experience that enables us to make the *Übergang* to morality "without too violent a leap" (5:354). The shared perception and shared pleasure that aesthetic experience makes possible among human beings is not quite (*contra* Stuart Hampshire) "as potentially universal as reason itself,"[9] for again, aesthetic experience on Kant's view generates merely a subjective claim to species-specific universality rather than objective, species-transcendent universality. Still, as forms of perception and pleasure that we can share with *all* other members of our species, these aesthetic experiences do help move us into morality. As Kant notes:

> Humanity [*Humanität*] signifies, on the one hand, the universal *feeling of sympathy*, and, on the other, the faculty of being able to *communicate* universally one's inmost self; properties which, taken together, constitute the proper sociability [*Geselligkeit*][10] of humanity [*Menschheit*], by means of which human beings are distinguished from the limitation of animals. (5:355)

The same holds for the related concept of necessity. The necessity involved in aesthetic judgments is what Kant calls 'exemplary' rather than 'practical' necessity; agents are not supplied with a rule or principle by means of which they can make the judgment (5:236–37). But this weaker necessity still allows Kant to speak of species-specific 'oughts' in aesthetics, for example, when he remarks that "the feeling in the judgment of taste comes to be exacted from everyone so to speak as duty [*gleichsam als Pflicht*]" (5:296). So the experience of necessity in aesthetic judgment (and this is also true for each of the related experiences of freedom, joy, and species-universality) amounts to a further argument in support of the claim that art enables human beings to make the *Übergang* to morality without too violent a leap.

Many other philosophers and educational theorists have also argued that art has an important role to play in moral education; Kant's claims here are for the most part not new. But when considered within the context of his own ethical theory, they do serve as a clear corrective to the still popular interpretive tendency to read this theory as one that denies the positive role of feelings in ethics. Still, there are several puzzling features to Kant's advocacy of art as preparation for morality.

First, he seems to have trouble making up his mind about the proper causal relationship between art and morality. In the following passage from the *Critique of Judgment* he asserts not that art prepares us for morality but rather the opposite: "[T]he true propaedeutic for the grounding of taste is the development of ethical ideas [*sittliche Ideen*] and the culture of the moral feeling [*Kultur des moralischen Gefühls*]" (5:356). How can he have it both ways? Is art a propaedeutic for morality or vice versa? Guyer argues that "the very fact that either the disposition to moral feeling or the disposition to aesthetic response can be regarded as the propaedeutic to the other shows how intimately connected the two dispositions are and how the perfection of each goes hand in hand with that of the other."[11] But if we resolve the apparent contradiction in this comfortable manner, many of Kant's remarks quoted earlier about how art prepares human beings for morality "without making too violent a leap" no longer make sense. The contrasts he seeks to establish between art and morality (e.g., the merely human universality of the former, the "valid for all rational beings" universality of the latter) disappear. Also, it is important to keep in mind that Kant's conviction that art (along with culture and science generally) prepares human beings for morality appears not only in *KU* but in other texts as well (see, e.g., *Anth* 7:324, quoted earlier). For Kant, the ultimate destiny of the human species is clearly moral rather than aesthetic. Kant's remark at *KU* 5:356 concerning morality's serving as a propaedeutic to art must not be read in such as way as to negate one of the most fundamental themes in his philosophy of history.

Which leads to a further worry: Does Kant's talk of art as a preparation for morality demean the value of art, giving it only an instrumental status? Once human beings make the *Übergang*, will they even need art any more? When the "sovereignty of reason alone has authority" and we have succeeded in overcoming "the tyranny of the senses" (5:434), will we still be in a position to even make aesthetic judgments? The moralistic tendencies of Kant's aesthetics are impossible to ignore, but this is properly a source of worry more for theorists of aesthetics rather than ethics.

Finally, in Kant's more expansive historical moods art is usually only mentioned in conjunction with "the sciences" (cf. *Anth* 7:324, *KU* 5:434), and this suggests that art on his view may not even have a unique instrumental status. It shares only double billing with the sciences as a civilizing and proto-moralizing force. In such passages the "art as preparation" language demotes art even further, to a non-unique instrumental role.

These seem to me to be unresolved problems for Kant. Still, the art-as-preparation dimension of his aesthetic theory does add a great deal to his rough sketch of impure ethics. We are mixed beings, and the natural language of art is able to speak to this condition like perhaps no other.[12] Human beings, precisely because they are human beings rather than simply rational beings, need to properly cultivate their sentiments and feelings in order to grasp or "make sense of" morality. Art helps us do this.

Beauty as Symbol of Morality

In the previous section I examined a dimension of Kant's position on the connection between aesthetics and ethics that is primarily psychological and educational in nature. Human beings need to properly educate their feelings to prepare for morality, and one of the most effective ways of acquiring this necessary education of the sentiments is through aesthetic experience. But there is also an important epistemological side to Kant's views on the relationship between aesthetics and ethics, a side that comes out most clearly in section 59 of the *Critique of Judgment*, "Of Beauty as Symbol of Morality" (5:351).[13] Aesthetic objects and experiences also make abstract moral ideas more tangible for human beings, and, precisely because we are at once both rational and animal beings (cf. 5:210), our mixed nature requires that we search for more palpable, concrete ways of representing moral ideas to ourselves.

This epistemological side of Kant's position on the relationship between aesthetics and ethics makes an even stronger case for the importance of art to ethics, in so far as it clearly implies that aesthetic experience serves not merely as a preparatory step toward morality that human civilization in its adolescence needs to make, but rather as a permanent access to it. If we were purely rational beings rather than human beings, we would not require the sensible representation of moral ideas afforded by beauty. But it is the fully formed (adult) human condition itself (rather than, say, facts of human development as considered by theories of moral education and developmental psychology) that necessitates the epistemological side of the doctrine.

Section 59 begins with the claim that "intuitions are always required in order to demonstrate [*dartun*] the reality of our concepts" (5:531), an assertion which echoes Kant's famous maxim in the first *Critique*: "Thoughts without content are empty, intuitions without concepts are blind" (*KrV* A 51/B 75). However, moral concepts are *Vernunftbegriffe* (concepts of reason), and for abstract, non-empirical concepts of this sort "absolutely no intuition adequate to them can be given" (5:351). Moral ideas cannot be directly presented to the senses. So a compromise needs to be made. Instead of searching in vain for direct intuitions of moral concepts, we need to represent these concepts indirectly, by means of analogy.

Kant calls this strategy of analogy or indirectness 'symbolic', and contrasts it with direct or 'schematic' presentations of concepts to the senses. A presentation of a concept to the senses is schematic if properties specified by the concept are given directly to the senses (e.g., representing the concept of a circle by means of a round plate—cf. *KrV* A 137/B 176); such a presentation is symbolic if the properties presented are merely analogous to those specified by the concept. Kant gives a double example of the latter in section 59 when he represents a monarchical state as an animate body when it is ruled by constitutional law, but as "a mere machine (something like a hand-mill)" when it is ruled by a single absolute will. In both cases the representation is *nur symbolisch* (5:352)—that is, none of the defining properties specified by the concept of a monarchical state are actually present in either animate bodies or machines. Nevertheless, there are certain analogous features contained in the latter (e.g., connections between parts) that supposedly help us to better understand the former.

Moral ideas cannot be presented directly to the senses, but "the beautiful is the [*das*]¹⁴ symbol of the morally good" (5:353). What features in the human experience of beauty are sufficiently analogous to the concept of the morally good, such that the former is entitled to serve as a symbol of the latter? Kant summarizes the main features of the analogy (without "letting the differences go unnoticed") as follows:

> 1) The beautiful pleases *immediately* (but only in the reflecting intuition—not, like morality, in concepts). 2) It pleases *without any interest* (the morally good is to be sure necessarily connected with an interest, but not one of the kind that precedes the judgment; rather with one that is first of all produced by it). 3) The *freedom* of the power of imagination (therefore of our faculty in respect of its sensibility) is represented as harmonious with the lawfulness of the understanding in the estimation of the beautiful (in moral judgments the freedom of the will is conceived of as the agreement of the latter with itself according to universal laws of reason). 4) The subjective principle of the estimation of the beautiful is represented as *universal*, that is, as valid for everyone, but not as cognizable by a universal concept (the objective principle of morality is also set forth as universal, that is, for all subjects and at the same time for all actions of the same subject, and thereby as cognizable through a universal concept). (5:353–54)

In other words, there are four key respects in which the experience of beauty and judgments concerning the morally good are both strikingly similar and nevertheless somewhat different. (1) Both produce a feeling of pleasure. As I argued previously, this emphasis on the rightful place of pleasure in human moral experience serves to correct overly ascetic interpretations of Kant's ethics. At the same time, as I will show later in this chapter (see "Morality and the Sublime"), pleasure is not the only feeling that accompanies moral judgment. (2) Beauty and morality both please without interest, or rather, without an *antecedent* desire for the object. (Moral judgment does produce an interest, that is, a desire and duty to realize the highest good. But this interest is determined by moral judgment itself.) (3) Both beauty and morality involve the experience of freedom—neither is determined by heteronomous forces. (However, the kind of freedom involved in each case is somewhat different. The freedom of the imagination in responding to beauty is felt; the freedom of the will is thought through concepts.) (4) Finally, both the experience of beauty and judgments concerning the morally good involve claims that are universally valid. Again, however, the universality of aesthetic judgment is a humans-only, inter-subjective kind of agreement, while the universality of moral judgments supposedly holds for all rational beings. Also, the former is not cognizable through concepts; the latter is.

In analyzing this analogy, it is important to note that Kant does not assert that the beautiful itself requires any moral content at all in order to serve as a symbol of the moral good. Rather, the claim is that the human response to aesthetic experience itself is morally significant in so far as it is strongly analogous to the state of mind produced by moral judgment in each of the just given four ways. Aesthetic experience offers human beings tangible access to concepts of pure ethics, and we need this access if we are to make ethics comprehensible or "graspable [*faßlich*]" (cf. *Rel* 6:65, n) to ourselves. Also, just as Kant holds that his justification of moral principles is itself reached through a descriptive analysis of what "common human reason [*gemeine Menschenvernunft*]" already holds to be true (see, e.g., *Gr* 4:389, 397, 403),[15] so his analogy between art and morality is also offered as one that "common understanding [*gemeiner Verstand*] normally considers" (5:354). That is, Kant holds that he is merely describing a relationship "that is natural to everyone [*jedermann näturlich*]" (5:353). Human beings commonly apply normative moral terms to aesthetic experiences, and this fact itself indicates that most people already assume that such experiences themselves "excite sensations that contain something analogous with the consciousness of the state of mind produced by moral judgments" (5:354).

Kant also draws a strong and rather unexpected inference from this analogy between aesthetic experience and morality. The fact that the experience of beauty symbolizes the morally good (a fact, again, that is supposedly already acknowledged by common human understanding) gives everyone sufficient ground "to expect [*zumutet*] [an acknowledgement of] this relationship from others as duty [*als Pflicht*]" (5:353, cf. 5:296). In other words, human beings can rightfully demand from one another that everyone acquire aesthetic experience precisely because this experience provides a crucial, sensuously graspable inroad into morality. We have a duty to properly appreciate beauty because the aesthetic experience of beauty gives us a better grip on intangible morality.

But is Kant really claiming here that each of us has a moral duty to increase our aesthetic awareness? Among other things, he appears (once again) to be in danger of valuing art only for its ability to help us make the *Übergang* into the moral realm. Such an instrumentalist, crudely moralistic approach to aesthetics represents a throwback to an earlier era; one that the critical philosopher would presumably reject.

The claim that human beings have a (moral) duty to cultivate taste and aesthetic awareness presupposes that the aesthetic is *indispensable* in cultivating human moral virtue.[16] The underlying idea is that human beings absolutely need aesthetic experience in order to gain access to morality—without successfully cultivating the former, they cannot get to the latter. I have already indicated some of the grounds for my own skepticism regarding the even stronger claim that beauty is the *only* symbol of morality (see n. 13). Let me now respond briefly to the milder claim that beauty is indispensable for human morality.

Among authors who defend the indispensability claim, the most intriguing defense strategy consists of bringing the moral argument in behalf of taste under the larger rubric of our duty to perfect our natural powers. In the *Metaphysics of Morals* Kant writes:

> The cultivation [*Anbau*] (*cultura*) of his natural powers (powers of spirit, mind, and body) as means to all sorts of possible ends is a duty of the human being to himself. —The human being owes it to himself (as a rational being) not to

leave unused [*unbenutzt*] and, as it were, rusting away the natural predispositions and capacities of which his reason can someday make use. (6:444)

Both 'imagination' (*Einbildungskraft*) and 'taste' (*Geschmack*) are included among
the various "powers of mind" (*Seelenkräfte*) that all human beings have a duty
to develop (6:445). But does this claim concerning our duty to develop our powers of mind actually entail that each of us has a moral duty to cultivate aesthetic
taste? (Does everyone, so to speak, need to present evidence of having attained
a satisfactory proficiency level in art appreciation?) Kant's argument here is
open-ended in several different ways, each of which makes a conclusive interpretation difficult. Note first that the claim is only that reason might "someday
[*dereinst*] make use of" these powers. A related remark occurs earlier in *MdS*:

> No rational principle prescribes specifically *how* far one should go in cultiva-
> tion [*Bearbeitung*] (enlargement or correction of one's capacity for understand-
> ing, i.e., in knowledge or technical ability). Also, the variety of circumstances
> in which human beings may find themselves makes very optional [*sehr willkür-
> lich*] the choice of the kind of occupation for which one should cultivate his
> talent. —There is therefore no law of reason here for actions, but merely for
> the maxims of actions, which runs as follows: "Cultivate your powers of mind
> and body so that they are fit to realize all ends [*alle Zwecke*] you might hit
> upon, however uncertain you are which of them could sometime become
> yours." (6:392)

The stress here is on our inability to know what lies ahead, and the subsequent
advice is: "Be prepared." For example, how do we know that we won't someday
be in a situation where a strong sense of aesthetic appreciation is absolutely
needed? We don't, which is what leads Guyer to conclude "that the range of the
powers of mind which can be helpful to moral ends must in fact be determined
by experience, not *a priori* theory."[17] At the same time, it is not at all clear that
Kant is recommending here that everyone set out to become a Renaissance person, that is, develop the entire range of human talents. There is a realistic acknowledgment that individuals aspire to different ways of life, or *Lebensarten* (cf.
6:445), and that not all ways are open to all people. Still, the emphasis at *MdS*
6:445 on not leaving one's powers unused or idle (*unbenutzt*) "and, as it were,
rusting away" does suggest a sort of minimum threshold requirement for everyone concerning all natural powers. Someone who chooses art as a profession
will need to develop more *Geschmack* than will someone who sets out to be a tax
lawyer, but both individuals will need to develop all of their natural powers to
some minimal functional level. (And 'all' of course does mean 'all'; aspiring art-
ists also will need to develop, e.g., their "powers of body" (*Leibeskräfte*) to the
minimum threshold level so that these specific powers don't rust away.)

A second (related) sense of open-endedness in Kant's position here concerns
his acknowledgement that ultimately it is up to each of us to choose best how
to develop our own natural powers:

> Which of these natural perfections should take *priority* and in what proportion,
> in comparison with one another, it may be the human being's duty to himself
> to make his end, are matters left for him to choose in accordance with his

own rational reflection with respect to his desire for a certain way of life [*Lust zu einer gewissen Lebensart*], together with an evaluation of the powers necessary for it (*MdS* 6:445).

As an imperfect duty, our duty to ourselves to develop our natural powers allows playroom or latitude [*Spielraum*] for free choice (cf. 6:446, 392). But this *Spielraum* leaves it to us only to determine how and to what extent—not whether—we will develop our natural powers (cf. 6:390).

When the moral argument to develop taste is situated within the comprehensive duty to perfect our natural powers, it has to share the spotlight with the full cast of human natural powers. This does not mean that it disappears, or that we no longer have a duty to cultivate it. Quite the contrary. Again, we are not to leave this power *unbenutzt*. All human beings have a duty to cultivate a certain minimum level of aesthetic awareness, but this duty (at least for those of us who do not choose art as a way of life) does not take priority over our duty to develop our other natural powers. The cultivation of aesthetic experience, while certainly conducive to moral virtue in human beings, is not the only thing that is conducive to it.

Morality and the Sublime

A third major connecting point between aesthetics and ethics in the *Critique of Judgment* is the sublime. Following the lead of Edmund Burke (*A Philosophical Inquiry into the Origins of Our Ideas of the Sublime and Beautiful*, 1757) and other eighteenth century authors, Kant regards the sublime and the beautiful as the two most basic forms of aesthetic merit. Although Kant's discussion of the sublime was often ignored or dismissed in Anglo-American studies of his aesthetics published as recently as the 1970s, since then the topic has returned with a vengeance—albeit in ways that seldom cast light on its role in his ethics.[18]

In this section I examine briefly Kant's discussion of the sublime from the perspective of impure ethics. What further details does the material on the sublime in the *Critique of Judgment* add to our picture of the second part of ethics?

First of all, the sublime (in this respect like the beautiful—cf. 5:210) on Kant's view is a uniquely human experience. Other rational beings who do not share our biology and psychology are supposedly unable to experience the sublime. Nothing in principle would prevent these other beings from employing a term that is in roughly the same conceptual neighborhood as 'sublimity (*Erhabenheit*)', but the precise psychological states that human beings undergo when they experience what Kant means by the sublime would be unavailable to them. The sublime as Kant understands it has very much to do with species-specific facts of human psychology and with human ways (and particularly limits) of cognition. Again, both the beautiful and the sublime are "aesthetic modes of representations that we would never come across in ourselves if we were merely pure intelligences (or even if we were to transfer ourselves in thoughts into this quality)" (5:271).

Second, the human capacity for the experience of the sublime lies directly in our own predisposition for feeling moral ideas. Without this moral predisposition we would not be able to experience the sublime. Kant underscores both points one and two when he remarks that

> the sublime has its foundation in human nature [*hat seine Grundlage in der menschlichen Natur*] and, in fact, in that which, at once with sound understanding, one may expect [*ansinnen*] of everyone and can demand [*fordern kann*] from everyone, namely, the predisposition [*Anlage*] for the feeling for (practical) ideas, that is, moral feeling. (5:265)

The second point is reasserted a few pages later when he claims that "in fact it is difficult to think of a feeling for the sublime in nature without connecting it to an attitude of mind [*Stimmung des Gemüths*] that is similar to the moral" (5:268).

Third, while beauty remains *a* symbol of the morally good, Kant's considered view is that the experience of the sublime is in fact a superior symbol of the morally good:

> [A]lthough the immediate pleasure [we take] in the beautiful in nature presupposes and cultivates a certain *liberality* in the way of thinking, i.e., independence of pleasure from mere sensual enjoyments, freedom is here still represented more as in *play* than as under a lawful *business* [*unter einem gesetzlichen Geschäfte*]. But the latter is the genuine characteristic of the morality of the human being, where reason must apply force on sensibility [*wo die Vernunft der Sinnlichkeit Gewalt antun muß*], only in the aesthetic judgment on the sublime this force is represented as exercised by the imagination itself, as through an instrument of reason. (5:268–69)

Beauty, it seems, is not serious enough to be the best symbolic representation of morality for human beings: we need a more earnest symbol. And the sublime fits the bill, for it is an emotion "that appears not to be a game [*kein Spiel*], but seriousness [*Ernst*] in the activity of the imagination" (5:245; cf. *Beob* 2:209). The superiority of the sublime as moral symbol comes out even more strongly in the following related passage:

> [T]the intellectual and intrinsically purposive (morally) good, aesthetically estimated, must not be represented as beautiful but rather as sublime, so that it arouses more the feeling of respect (which scorns charm) than of love and intimate affection. For human nature does not accord with the good of itself, but only by means of the force which reason applies to sensibility. (5:271; cf. 2:208–09)

These passages offer still another refutation of the claim that "the beautiful is the [only] symbol of the morally good," although now the competition at least comes from within the field of aesthetic categories. But how friendly is this competition between the beautiful and the sublime concerning which experience better represents morality for human beings? One can (try to) finesse the matter by saying that the beautiful and the sublime are each symbols of "different aspects of morality."[19] However, Kant himself does not take this route. Beauty is clearly demoted to a secondary position. It is too playful and lacking in seriousness, too strongly identified with the charms of sensuous enjoyment, to serve as our best symbol of morality. "The value of life for us, when measured simply by *what one enjoys . . .* is easy to decide. It sinks below zero. . . . What value life has . . . consists in *what one does* (not what one simply enjoys)" (5:434 n).

But perhaps I am jumping too far ahead. In order to assess critically Kant's claim that the sublime is our best symbol of morality, we need a clearer understanding of what exactly the Kantian sublime is. For starters, with what kinds of objects is the experience of the sublime concerned? Essentially, Kant's answer is that the experience of the sublime always concerns certain objects or events of 'raw' nature rather than conventional objects of art:

> [O]ne must point to the sublime not in art products (e.g., buildings, columns, and so forth) where a human end determines the form as well as the magnitude, nor in natural things, *whose concept already conveys a determinate end* (e.g., animals of a recognized natural order [*Naturbestimmung*]), but rather in raw nature merely insofar as it contains magnitude (and even in this only insofar as it does not convey any charm, nor any emotion arising from real danger). (5:252–53)

Paradigmatic Kantian examples of the sublime (and on this point he is also echoing many other eighteenth century writers) would thus include "the starry heavens above" (*KpV* 5:161), "the boundless ocean" (*KU* 5:261), and the sight of "a mountain whose snow-covered peak rises above the clouds" (*Beob* 2:208). Human art works are too conceptually constrained ("a human end determines [their] form as well as magnitude") to trigger the experience of the sublime within us. We experience the sublime when we witness that which exceeds our grasp.

However, strictly speaking (and in the preceding passage at 5:252–53 he is not speaking strictly), Kant's view is that objects and events of raw nature are *not* in fact sublime. No physical object, natural or conventional, can be sublime, for the sublime ultimately concerns the super-sensible. The sublime is not in nature, but rather in us; that is, in our noumenal character. Sublimity "is not contained in any thing of nature, but only in our mind [*nur in unserm Gemüthe*], insofar as we think about and can become conscious of our superiority to nature within us and thereby also to nature outside of us (in so far as it has influence on us)" (5:264). The following passage brings this "only-in-our-mind" claim out very clearly:

> [W]e express ourselves altogether incorrectly if we call any *object of nature* sublime, although we may perfectly correctly call many of the same objects beautiful. . . . We can say nothing more than that the object is suitable for a presentation of sublimity that can be met in the mind [*im Gemüthe*]; for the actual sublime can not be contained in any sensuous form, but rather concerns only ideas of reason, which, although no adequate presentation of them is possible, may be stirred [*sich . . . regt*] and called into the mind exactly by this inadequacy, which does allow itself to be sensuously presented. (5:245)

The sublime is therefore "not to be looked for in the things of nature, but only in our ideas" (5:250). Still, it is the things of nature (again, *raw* things of nature) that trigger or stir up our ideas of the sublime. Our experience of the former gives us access to the latter.

In effect, Kant's position is that human beings are guilty of a fallacious inference when they contemplate a snow-covered mountain peak jutting above the clouds and call it sublime. As he asserts:

[T]he feeling of the sublime in nature is respect for our own destiny [*Achtung für unsere eigene Bestimmung*], which we show to an object of nature through a certain subreption [mixing up (*Verwechselung*) of a respect for the object instead of for the idea of humanity in our subject], which as it were makes intuitable [*anschaulich*] the superiority of the destiny of reason in our cognitive capacities over the greatest capacity of sensibility. (5:257; cf. *De mundi* 2:412, 417)

John Zammito overstates the case somewhat when he declares that "Kant's whole theory of the sublime revolved around 'subreption'—viewing an object of nature as though it were the ground of a feeling which in fact had its source in the self."[20] But this mixing up or *Verwechselung*, by which we project a sublimity onto an object of nature that actually exists only in ourselves, certainly plays a major role in Kant's account of the sublime. And these experiences of what is "*absolutely great (schlechthin groß)*" in raw nature (5:248) provide human beings with one more way of making abstract moral concepts intuitable or graphic (*anschaulich*) to themselves. So even though there is a false inference involved in the experience of the sublime, by means of which conditions "which are peculiar to the *subject* . . . are rashly transferred to *objects*" (*De mundi* 2:417), it is an all too human error that appears to be triggered by our own cognitive limitations and psychology.

What kinds of experiences of raw nature trigger the sublime in us? Here Kant's distinction between the so-called mathematically sublime and dynamically sublime comes into play. The experience of the mathematically sublime occurs "when we encounter and reflect upon a natural object whose size or magnitude is exceedingly great, such as the sea, huge mountains, vast deserts, the night sky."[21] When we encounter limitless (or even seemingly limitless) magnitudes in nature, our imagination is boggled and overwhelmed—we cannot get a conceptual grip on what we are sensing.

We experience the dynamically sublime, on the other hand, when we encounter and reflect on "extremely powerful natural objects and phenomena that are capable of exciting fear."[22] Kant's own examples are as follows:

Bold, overhanging, and, as it were, threatening rocks; thunderclouds piled up in the sky, pulled along with lightening flashes and thunder crashes; volcanoes in all their destructive violence; hurricanes with the devastation they leave behind; the boundless ocean in a state of tumult; a high waterfall of a mighty river. (5:261)

Some of these examples would also seem to be good candidates for the mathematically sublime—for example, the boundless (*gränzenlos*) ocean. The fact that it not only appears to be boundless but is also in a state of tumult when viewed is what brings it over to the dynamically sublime. On a calm day, the boundless ocean would presumably invoke merely the mathematically sublime. But the basic difference seems clear enough. And from the psychological side, the human experiences of these two different kinds of sublime are structurally identical.

In both cases we find an initial feeling of displeasure and then a sudden, radical shift to pleasure.[23] This shift or movement from displeasure to pleasure, and the resulting complexity of the feeling of the sublime, marks another sharp difference between it and the simpler, more peaceful feeling of the beautiful: "The mind feels itself *moved* [*fühlt sich . . . bewegt*] in the representation of the sublime in nature; while in the aesthetic judgment about the beautiful it is in *peaceful* [*ruhige*] contemplation" (5:258). Or, as he puts it in the *Observations*: "The sublime *moves* [*rührt*], the beautiful *charms*" (2:209). Again, this sense of rapid movement or stirring begins with displeasure (terror, fear, awe) and then immediately jumps over to pleasure:

> The feeling of the sublime is . . . a feeling of displeasure from the inadequacy of the power of imagination in the aesthetic estimation of magnitude to attain the estimation through reason and then at the same time [*zugleich*] an awakened pleasure from the agreement of exactly this judgment of inadequacy of the greatest capacity of sense with ideas of reason, insofar as striving toward them is still for us a law. (5:257)

Because this particular description of the sequential feelings of displeasure and pleasure focuses on the imagination's inability to measure magnitude, it might seem to fit only the experience of the mathematically sublime and not the dynamically sublime. But the same shift of feelings occurs in the latter case as well. In experiencing the dynamically sublime, the displeasure ('displeasure' seems ludicrously weak here, but on Kant's view there are in fact only two basic feelings—namely, pain and pleasure; all other feelings are then analyzed in terms of them) is caused by our initial sense of helplessness and fear "against the seeming omnipotence of nature" (5:261). The consequent pleasure comes when we realize that the immense destructive power of nature nevertheless "has no dominion over us" (5:260), that is, over our moral personality.

When he is careful, Kant qualifies the particular kind of pleasure that is involved in the experience of the sublime by tagging it as a *negative* pleasure: "The delight [*Wohlgefallen*] in the sublime in nature is . . . only *negative* (instead the delight in the beautiful is *positive*)" (5:269). Or, as he remarks earlier: "the delight in the sublime does not so much contain positive pleasure as admiration or respect [*Bewunderung oder Achtung*], that is, deserves to be called negative pleasure" (5:245). This reference to respect or *Achtung* provides us with the strongest link between morality and the sublime, a link that is nevertheless difficult to articulate clearly. First of all, it is definitely the case (particularly in *KpV*) that "the sublime (*das Erhabene*)" and "sublimity (*Erhabenheit*)" are both frequently invoked by Kant in his own descriptions of duty, the moral law, and moral personality. For instance, his famous encomium to duty begins: "Duty! Sublime [*erhabene*], mighty name that embraces nothing charming [*Beliebtes*] that leads to ingratiation, but demands submission" (5:86). The language here, particularly the term *Beliebtes*, indicates that peaceful talk of beauty is clearly out of place in describing duty (cf. *Beob* 2:209). Similarly, the idea of moral personality which awakens respect in us "places before our eyes the sublimity [*Erhabenheit*] of our own nature (in its destiny)" (5:87). And the "pure moral law itself . . . allows us to feel [*spüren*] the *Erhabenheit* of our own supersensuous existence" (5:88). Later he tells us that it is "something *sehr Erhabenes* in human nature to be determined directly to actions through a pure law of reason" (5:117). Finally, the celebrated conclusion to the second *Critique*, in which the two realms of theoretical and practical reason are juxtaposed with one another, also invokes the language of the sublime within a moral context (5:161–62).[24]

In the *Groundwork* we also find occasional employment of the language of the sublime in describing morality. At 4:439 Kant asserts that the *Erhabenheit* of a maxim "consists in the independence of the maxim from all . . . incentives"— namely, incentives stemming from the thought of achievable ends or personal advantages, not including the categorical command to promote the kingdom of ends. And on the next page he states that we picture the person "who fulfills all his duties . . . as having a certain *Erhabenheit* and *dignity*. For it is not in so far as he is *subject* to the moral law that he has *Erhabenheit*, but rather in so far as, in respect to this very same law, he is at the same time *lawgiving* and is subordinated to it only for this reason" (4:440).[25]

Finally, in the *Metaphysics of Morals*, Kant also refers to "the feeling of *Erhabenheit*" that the human being has "for his destiny, that is, the *elation of spirit* [*elatio animi*] as esteem for himself" (6:437). So the language of the aesthetics of the sublime is invoked at crucial junctures in all three of Kant's major writings in moral philosophy. The sublimity of the moral law, as Beck rightly notes, "is more than a metaphor for Kant."[26] Furthermore, Kant also invokes the moral language of *Achtung* at key places in his analysis of the sublime in the *Critique of Judgment*. As noted earlier, the delight in the *Erhabene* "contains not so much positive pleasure as admiration or *Achtung*, that is, deserves to be called negative pleasure" (5:245).[27] When we pronounce objects to be "great without qualification" (the defining feature of the mathematically sublime), "we then always join with the representation a kind of *Achtung*" (5:249). And once we get past the mix-up of the subreption, we see that the feeling of the sublime in nature in fact "is *Achtung* for our own destiny" (5:257). Section 27, from which the previous quotation is taken, also begins with the telling remark: "The feeling of the inadequacy of our capacity to reach an idea, *that is a law for us*, is *respect*" (5:257). Here the language of law, duty (a law "for us"), and respect all appear within the context of a discussion of the aesthetics of the sublime. And finally, in one of the key passages where Kant asserts that the sublime is a better symbol of morality than the beautiful, he says that the sublime "arouses more the feeling of *Achtung* (which disdains charm) than of love and intimate affection" (5:271).

So not only is the aesthetic language of the sublime employed frequently in Kant's descriptions of morality in his three major texts in moral philosophy, but the key moral term of "respect" (or "moral feeling," albeit a feeling "produced solely by reason"—*KpV* 5:76), is also frequently invoked in his analysis of the sublime in the *Critique of Judgment*. And this is hardly surprising, once we realize the strong psychological parallels that exist between the two feelings of respect and of the sublime, as Kant understands them. Both begin in pain, fear, and humiliation. In the case of the mathematically sublime, we experience pain in our imagination's inability to estimate the magnitude of objects of raw nature (5:257); in the case of the dynamically sublime, fear over the crushing power of nature (5:260). In confronting the moral law, we experience a sense of humiliation that "strikes down self-conceit" (*KpV* 5:73) and "undermines . . . self-love" (*Gr* 4:401 n). But in all three experiences the pain is then transformed into elation and admiration. With the sublime, pleasure comes when we find within ourselves a power greater than nature; whereas in the moral experience of respect the positive feeling of admiration takes over when we realize that we as rational beings are creators of the very same law to which we must submit ourselves and by means of which we must govern our inclinations. So both respect and the sublime are complex feelings involving radical mental movement from pain to pleasure. Neither is a peaceful feeling at rest with itself, and in this respect both differ strongly from the experience of the beautiful (cf. 5:226, 258).

How then do respect and the sublime differ? Zammito suggests that one difference lies in Kant's claim that "respect applies always only to persons, never to things" (*KpV* 5:76).[28] However, this can't be right, since (as we saw earlier) Kant also states repeatedly in *KU* that "true sublimity must be sought only in the mind of the judging subject, and not in the object of nature that occasions this mood" (5:256; cf. 245, 250, 264). Sublimity, in other words, also applies "only to persons, never to things." And to complicate matters still further, Kant also emphasizes in both *KpV* and *Gr* that the respect that we have for a person is really respect "for the law that his example holds before us" (5:78; cf. 4:402 n). Virtuous individuals can be said to embody the moral law *for us* (which is yet another way of making epistemological allowance for "the 'conditions' of our agency"),[29] but strictly speaking, we respect the law rather than persons.

According to Zammito, a second alleged difference stems from Kant's claim that "respect can never have other than a moral ground" (*KpV* 5:81 n).[30] Here I think he has located a difference, though not a big one. Yes, the feeling of respect always has a moral ground; in reflecting on the moral law and its significance (or, again, on a virtuous individual, who for us can serve as an example of the law), human beings feel respect. The sublime, on the other hand, is a feeling human beings experience when reflecting on either the power or majesty of raw nature. However, as we have seen, the whole point of the Kantian sublime is to awaken "the feeling of a supersensible faculty [*ein übersinnliches Vermögen*] within us" (5:250). "The feeling of the sublime in nature"—once we, so to speak, figure out what is behind the *Verwechselung*—"is respect for our destiny" (5:257). The feeling of the sublime is triggered by certain experiences of nature. But does the sublime have its 'ground' in nature or in the moral law (more specifically, in the human subject who is viewing nature)? Perhaps we should say, with apologies to Aristotle, that while its efficient cause lies in nature, its final cause is moral. The experience of the sublime always connects us directly to morality. In reminding us to have respect for our destiny as rational beings who are authors of the moral law, the experience of the sublime points to a moral ground. So while respect and the sublime do seem to differ with respect to what initially triggers them, ultimately they both refer to moral ideas.

Still, despite their shared moral ground, there remains an important difference between these feelings. The primary difference between respect and the sublime lies in the indirect strategy of subreption that we find in the latter. In the case of respect we know immediately the ground and the referent of our feeling; there is no mix-up. In the case of the sublime, we mistakenly direct our awe at nature rather than our own noumenal moral character. Beck writes:

> [W]hereas a subreption necessarily occurs in the sublime feelings, so that we attribute to the object a sublimity which actually exists only in ourselves, the feeling of respect is directed to a law, which is a law of our own freedom, self-imposed and not imposed on us from without, and to persons, ourselves or others, who embody this law. Hence respect for the law and respect for our own personality are not distinct and even competing feelings, as are the two feelings which merge in our experience of the sublime.[31]

Kant's *Critique of Judgment* is an extremely rich and multi-dimensional text, and in a study focusing solely on connections between aesthetics and ethics one would rightfully expect to find further explorations of still more connecting themes between art and morality hinted at by Kant in this text. Promising candidates in a more detailed study of this sort would include investigations of the moral ramifications of Kant's analyses of teleology, judgment, imagination, and genius as presented in *KU*.[32] But our present task is a broader, more varied one. We are examining multiple "fields of impurity" (of which human aesthetic experience is only one), in order to fill out Kant's incomplete sketch of the second part of ethics.

Although Kant himself does not make explicit references to moral anthropology or empirical ethics in the *Critique of Judgment*, it is very difficult to read this text without oneself making connections to Kant's project in moral anthropology. Indeed, Guyer goes as far as claiming that Kant's aesthetic theory is "ultimately, part of . . . [his] moral anthropology," while at the same time suggesting that "the *Anthropology* [*from a Pragmatic Point of View*], intended only as a handbook for Kant's undergraduate lectures, may be a less useful source for Kant's moral anthropology than [one might wish]."[33] And Reinhard Brandt reminds us that "both parts of the *Critique of Judgment* conclude with references to the practical philosophy. . . . Art and culture . . . are for Kant only valuable, or indeed real, on the basis of morality."[34] In this particular portion of the Kantian corpus, we receive detailed defenses of the dual claims that certain feelings are necessary and important in (human) morality, and that human beings require tangible representations of moral concepts. As I have tried to show, the story is complicated and at times paradoxical, for part of the message (particularly in his analysis of the sublime) is that we must use our feelings in order to recognize (and then pay proper respect toward) the non-sensuous side of our character. But the "must" here (as elsewhere in his aesthetic theory) is a species-specific must. This is part of who we are.

The Church as Moral Community

> But with the human being the invisible needs to be represented
> through something visible (sensible).
>
> *Religion within the Boundaries*
> *of Mere Reason*

The strongest and clearest connecting point to the concerns of impure ethics to be found in *Religion within the Boundaries of Mere Reason* is Kant's discussion of the church as moral community or ethical commonwealth (*ethisches gemeines Wesen*) (cf. 6:94). For in presenting his case for the church as a means of promoting the goal of universal moral community, Kant makes frequent references to particularities of human nature. For instance, it is "only due to a special weakness [*besondere Schwäche*] of human nature that pure faith can never be counted on as much as it deserves, namely to ground a church on it alone" (6:103). And "the requirement of human beings demands [*fordert das Bedürfnis der Menschen*]" that the spreading of pure religious faith via historical faith be carried out "only through *scripture*," in order that people may be sure of their duty in divine service (6:107). Similarly,

> because of the natural requirement of all human beings to always demand for even the highest concepts of reason and grounds of reason something *sensuously graspable* [*etwas Sinnlich-Haltbares*], a confirmation of some sort from experience and the like ... some historical ecclesiastical faith or other, which one usually finds before oneself, must be used. (6:109)

Finally, it is "in accordance with the unavoidable limitation of human reason [*die unvermeidliche Einschränkung der menschlichen Vernunft*]" that historical belief "attaches itself to pure religion as its vehicle" (6:115).

The implication of each of these passages is that there is something peculiar or special about human beings that requires them to seek moral community through the institution of the church. Other kinds of rational beings may well have their own species-specific means of promoting moral community, means that do not involve sensuously graspable buildings, liturgies, symbols, and so on. But human beings require these visual cues.

What specific sorts of human particularities does Kant have in mind? Michel Despland suggests that in such passages Kant's argument rests "more upon observed facts of history than upon results of an analysis of human nature."[35] But it is very difficult to see which (if any) "observed facts of history" could support Kant's ambitious *Aufklärung* claim that the various historical faiths have all attached themselves to pure religion as its vehicles, or even that human beings need churches in the first place. Historians approaching such topics without Kant's own religious assumptions could hardly be expected to reach this conclusion. More recently, Hans Michael Baumgartner has claimed that Kant's references to human weakness and limitation in this context "must have to do with the [human] propensity to evil."[36] True, Kant does hold that, "as far as we can see," a victory of the good over the evil principle "is not otherwise attainable [*nicht anders erreichbar*]" except by the establishment and spreading of a commonwealth of virtue as represented by visible churches (6:94). The church is necessary as a collective human response to the problem of moral evil—indeed, it appears to be our only reliable means for overcoming evil. But the kind of weakness and limitation Kant is referring to in the preceding passages is clearly epistemological and psychological, not moral. It is "the unavoidable limitation of human *reason*" (my emphasis) to which he draws our attention; and to "the natural requirement of all human beings to always demand something sensuously graspable." In other words (*contra* Despland), it is precisely Kant's "analysis of human nature" on which his case for the historical church as vehicle for moral community rests.

Kant's claims in the preceding passages concerning particularities of human nature are not nearly as unintuitive and paradoxical as commentators have made them out to be. Indeed, they are quite in line with remarks he makes in other works, particularly the *Critique of Judgment*. Human understanding is a "discursive understanding that needs images [*Bilder*]" (*KU* 5:408). We need something solid that we can see and touch. In religion (as in aesthetics and moral education as well), a large part of the project of impure ethics consists in finding concrete ways to make the message of pure ethics graspable to human beings. In order for moral principles to be efficacious in human life, human beings must be presented with tangible symbols of what it is that they are being asked to uphold and promote. Kant has multiple strategies here, strategies that mutually reinforce one another in their pursuit of a common goal. As James Collins notes, in the *Religion* Kant rightly emphasizes that because human beings are

> the composite, experience-bound agents that they are, this moral union of hearts in the invisible church does not, in fact, suffice for the ordering of our practical life. . . . Kant recognizes that the passage from the pure moral belief in God to a faith involving history and rites and public statutes, i.e., the passage from the invisible to the *visible church*, does respond to a need of our actually constituted human reality.[37]

But while much of the motivation behind the idea of historical churches as builders of moral community focuses on particularities of human nature (particularities which, I have argued, are primarily epistemological and psychological), Kant also places a very strong emphasis on universality in this discussion. The church aims at "the establishment and spreading of a society in accordance with, and for the sake of, laws of virtue," a society that will eventually encompass "the entire human race in its scope [*das ganze Menschengeschlecht in ihrem Umfang*]" (6:94). As noted earlier, the tail end of this passage adds crucial support to the claim that eventually the entire human race, rather than (as Reinhard Brandt and others hold) merely a privileged part of it, must assume active membership in the Kantian moral community. (See " 'The Whole Human Race' " in chap. 3.) But the eventual intended scope of this moral community is actually supra-human. Because duties of virtue

> concern the entire human race [*das ganze menschliche Geschlecht*], the concept of an ethical commonwealth always refers to the ideal of a whole of all human beings [*ein Ganzes aller Menschen*], and in this respect distinguishes itself from the concept of a political commonwealth. Therefore a multitude of human beings united in that purpose cannot yet be called the ethical commonwealth itself, but only a particular society that strives toward consensus [*Einhelligkeit*] with all human beings (indeed, all finite rational beings) [*alle endlichen vernünftigen Wesen*], in order to establish an absolute ethical whole, of which every partial society is only a representation or schema. (6:96)

Similarly, the duty that human beings have to promote this community is a duty "not of human beings toward human beings, but of the human race toward itself. For every species of rational being [*jede Gattung vernünftiger Wesen*] is objectively, in the idea of reason, destined to a common end, namely the promotion of the highest good as a good common to all" (6:97). Nevertheless, whatever species-specific means of promoting this universal common end other species of rational beings may have at their disposal, historical churches constitute a necessary and important path toward it for human beings on earth. Human beings cannot expect to achieve their moral destiny outside of organized religion.

What *kind* of community is the human church supposed to be? Not a political community that employs "coercive laws [*Zwangsgesetze*]" designed to insure external legality in action via the threat of punishment, but rather a moral community whose members "are united under coercion-free laws, i.e., under mere *laws of virtue*" (6:95). The aim is a "voluntary, universal, and enduring union of hearts"; and such a community has, "as regards its basic principles, actually nothing that resembles a political constitution" (6:102). However, though the church as voluntary moral community rejects the coercive laws of political states, "there is a certain analogy between both of them, when regarded in general as two commonwealths" (6:94; cf. 124 n). Political states are the empirical ectype of a realm of external justice; historical churches the empirical form of the universal ethical community. And both are destined to eventually encompass all peoples of the earth in their respective communities. The respective 'interior' and 'exterior' strategies of churches and states thus complement one another in promoting the larger goal of universal moral community founded on principles of justice. Indeed, political and moral progress are eventually to converge on the same goal of perpetual peace, the securement of which will remain elusive without the moral improvement of humanity. The church itself is to play an important and necessary role in bringing about this moral advancement of the species.[38]

In rejecting political models, Kant resorts to the analogy of the family to describe the sort of community he has in mind in his discussion of the church. A moral community in the form of a church, he holds, "could best of all be likened to that of a household (family) under a common, though invisible, moral father" (6:102). Kant's strongly patriarchal conception of the family is unlikely to win over many contemporary readers, and, to make matters worse, his terse analogy also gives us very few clues concerning *how* exactly he thinks the church as voluntary association is to foster moral community. Unfortunately, Kant's more detailed treatments of familial and household relationships in the *Metaphysics of Morals* (6:277–84) and in *Anthropology from a Pragmatic Point of View* (7:303–11), with their heavy-handed emphases on possession, right, and power, are also of little help on this point.[39] In his discussion of the church Kant himself at one point presses the important question of "what preparations people now have to make" in order that the kingdom of God be established on earth (6:101), but the question remains largely unanswered; the specific ways in which the institution of the church might address this crucial question of means are surprisingly not addressed.[40]

As is also the case with followers of Bahaism, Kant holds that underneath the apparent surface differences of the various world religions we find an identical core truth. "There is only *one* (true) *religion*; but there can be various kinds of *faith*" (6:107). As he remarks in "Perpetual Peace":

> *Difference of religions*: an odd expression! Just as if one were to speak of different *moralities*. There can certainly be different kinds of historical *faiths*, though these do not pertain to religion, but only to the history of the means used to promote it. . . . [T]here is only a single *religion*, valid for all human beings and in all times. (8:367 n)

Ecclesiastical faith is thus merely the humanly necessary "vehicle" (*Vehikel*) (6:106; 123 n, 135 n) or "leading-string" (*Leitband*) (6:121) for pure religious faith; the cover or "shell" (*Hülle*) (6:135 n; cf. 121) inside of which lies the rational kernel of pure religious faith. At the same time, all of the various ecclesiastical faiths are themselves to a greater or lesser degree faulty vehicles of the one true religion. They are subject to illusion (*Wahn*) when they mistakenly assert that their own "arbitrary and contingent" worship formats are "essential [*wesentlich*] to the service of God generally" (6:168); they are guilty of superstition (*Aberglaube*) when they assert that their members can justify themselves to God through religious acts of worship (6:174); and they fall into pseudo-service (*Afterdienst, cultus spurius*) when they fail to focus on the universal goal of pure rational faith that has only the principle of "good life-conduct" (*guter Lebenswandel*) as its real end (6:175; cf. 176, 191). It is this moral end alone which on Kant's view serves as the true justification of all historical faiths.

True religious faith must therefore eventually be set free from its present shell (cf. 6:135 n), so that the self-developing and self-pollinating seed that lies invisibly within the various world faiths "shall one day enlighten the world and rule over it" (6:122). But doesn't this goal of shell-shedding imply

> that the concept of the visible church remains ambiguous for Kant: the visible church with its historical ecclesiastical faith, statutes, and organization is necessary for the human being in this (sensuous) world, and at the same time it should already dissolve into the invisible church in this world (therefore into an idea) [?][41]

Although the more gung-ho *Aufklärung* side of Kant does speak optimistically of shedding the exterior shell of religion and resting content with its inner moral core, his more realistic side recognizes that the various historical manifestations of religious faith will always remain humanly necessary. In an important footnote concerning the historical church he writes: "Not that it will come to an end [*aufhöre*] (for as a vehicle it may perhaps always be useful and necessary); but that it can come to an end, by which is meant merely the inner stability of pure moral faith" (6:135 n). This suggests that human beings will eventually "see through" the various historical churches, so to speak, and realize that their trappings are merely all-too-human vehicles or conducting agents for truth rather than truth itself. However, we will still need these trappings, for our image-dependent nature requires us to hold onto them. Kant exhorts us to "work diligently even now" for "the continuous development of the pure religion of reason from its not yet dispensable shell" (6:135 n), but he also states that the visible forms of historical churches will be dissolved only when "all earthly life comes to an end" (6:135). (At which point our epistemological and psychological condition will change?) In other words, ecclesiastical faith is not to be "*abolished* by progress. Rather, it is to come to an understanding of itself as a vehicle for pure religious faith, so better to serve the pure faith which is its essence."[42] Similarly, as Michalson argues, the empirical, historical aspects of religion

> apparently cannot be reduced away at any given point, leaving a pure moral core; only if man were not subject to conditions of finitude and the corruption of his will could this be possible. Rather, precisely because man is limited in certain crucial ways, the historical dimensions of religion assume a significant systematic role in [Kant's] *Religion*.[43]

However, there remains a different, more disturbing sort of ambiguity in Kant's discussion of the church. Sometimes he implies that "all historical faiths are equal," in so far as they are all mere vehicles for the one true religion. His seemingly flippant remarks that "some historical faith or other [*irgend ein*], that one usually finds before oneself, must be used" (6:109), and that "the historical element [of faith] . . . is something that in itself is completely indifferent [*ganz Gleichgültiges*], with which one can do what one wants" (6:111) lean in this direction, as does the previously cited claim that there is "only *one* true *religion*; but there can be many kinds of *faith*" (6:107). But in other passages it is clear that he is privileging Christianity in a not entirely subtle manner. To be sure, Kant does not offer readers a developed world-historical account of religious progress; his occasional remarks about non-Christian faiths are scattered and unsystematic. But it is evident that he is assuming a ranking of historical faiths throughout his presentation, and that he thinks it is obvious that Christianity is the most developed religion.[44] Just as Kant's attempt in his *Anthropology* lectures to track humanity's cultural progress reveals a strongly western Eurocentric slant (see "Peoples" in chap. 3), so too in the *Religion* we find an unmistakably Christian bias in his discussion of historical faiths. On both the cultural as well as the religious front, his considered view is not that universal moral community will arise out of the interaction and reconciliation between different cultural and religious traditions, but rather that the ways of the West will gradually be adopted throughout the planet. "We must look in the Occident for the continual progress of the human race to perfection and from there the spreading around the world" (*Refl* 1501, 15:789).

How do the different historical faiths stack up against one another? Concerning Christianity, Kant writes that "of all the public religions that have ever existed, the Christian religion alone is a moral religion" (6:51–52). Christianity, in comparison with all other historical faiths, "treads in the closest proximity to reason" (6:167), and its members consist of "that part of the human race in which the predisposition to the unity of the universal church has already been brought close to its development" (6:124). Judaism, on the other hand, "is actually not a religion at all [*eigentlich gar keine Religion*], but merely a union of a number of people, who, since they belonged to a particular tribe [*Stamm*], formed themselves into a commonwealth under merely political laws, hence not into a church" (6:125).[45] As Kant sees it, Judaism is merely political, not religious; the Ten Commandments "concern merely external acts"; and all rewards or punishments for fulfilling these commandments "are limited to those alone which can be allotted to everyone in this world, and not even these are allotted according to ethical concepts" (6:126).[46] Judaism is *"garments without a man* (a church without religion)" (*Streit* 7:53), and in order to become a religion it must allow "purified religious concepts to awaken" its members so that they "throw off the garments of the ancient cult" (7:52–53). Switching metaphors, he adds:

> The euthanasia of Judaism is pure moral religion, freed from all ancient statutory teachings, some of which admittedly must have remained in Christianity (as a messianic faith). But this difference of sects [*Sectenunterschied*] must also eventually disappear, leading, at least in spirit, to what one calls the conclusion of the great drama of religious change on earth (the restoration of all things), when there will be one shepherd and one flock. (7:53; cf. *Rel* 6:166 n, *Vorarbeitungen* 23:114)[47]

Other non-Christian historical faiths also fare poorly by Kant. Islam "distinguishes itself through *pride*, because it finds the confirmation of its faith in victories and the subjugation of many peoples instead of in miracles, and its devotional practices are all of the fierce kind" (6:184 n; cf. *Geo* 9:399–400). Islam with its five commands of "washing, praying, fasting, almsgiving, and pilgrimage to Mecca" also engages in *"fetish-faith (Fetischglaube),"* namely, the belief that "that which through neither *natural* nor moral laws of reason can effect anything still on its own effects what is wished for, if one merely believes firmly that it will do so and then joins this belief with certain formalities" (6:193). In Christianity, on the other hand, similar practices are (surprise, surprise) "related to concepts of practical reason and their appropriate dispositions" (6:193).

The Hindu religion "consists of grotesqueries" (*Beob* 2:252), and gives its members "the character of *faint-heartedness* [*Kleinmüthigkeit*], for reasons which are directly opposed" to those of Islam (*Rel* 6:184 n). Religion in India also "remains unchanged" (Dohna, 364), which implies that the Hindus are not making any progress in shedding the exterior shell of their historical faith. And Buddhism, Kant informs us in a lecture, teaches "that nothingness is the source and end of all things, and that as a result absence of feeling [*Fühllosigkeit*] and renunciation of all work for some time are pious actions."[48] Listeners are expected to infer that Buddhism therefore teaches a false ethics.

To be sure, Christianity considered as a historical rather than rational faith also comes in for its share of criticism. The history of Christianity, when viewed in terms of "the beneficial effect that one can rightly expect of a moral religion, has nothing in any way to recommend it" (6:130). Nevertheless, there is more than a grain of truth in Nietzsche's remark that in the end Kant was "an underhanded Christian."[49]

Metaphors of shell-shedding and conducting substances aside, Kant holds fast to his conviction that "Christianity is indeed *destined* [*bestimmt*] to be the universal world religion" (*Ende* 8:339). Again, the time when there will be "only one shepherd and one flock" is to be reached not through reconciliation and dialogue among the various historical faiths but rather through the eventual domination of one (albeit in its yet-to-be-witnessed morally purified form). Though Kant believes that "the predisposition [*Anlage*] to moral religion" lies "hidden in human reason" and thus precedes all historical faiths (6:111), he is also convinced that "the *Anlage* to the unity of the universal church" is approaching complete development only in a privileged "part of the human race," namely, Christians (6:124).

The chief weaknesses of Kant's account of the church, as I see it, are: (1) its lack of specificity in describing how the church as a social institution is to be structured, and in explaining what it must do, in order effectively to promote moral universal community;[50] and (2) its tendency to over-identify the "one true religion" whose real end is simply "good life-conduct" with historical Christianity. Nevertheless, when approached from the perspective of impure ethics, the discussion of the church in part 3 of the *Religion* provides additional evidence that Kant (contrary to what his critics and even some of his friends have held) was deeply concerned with addressing the obstacles that human beings as a particular sort of creature face in pursuing moral ends, and that he also tried to confront these obstacles by advocating what he thought were appropriate changes in our institutional practices.

"On the Radical Evil in Human Nature"

A second strong connecting point to the concerns of impure ethics in Kant's *Religion* (albeit one whose details are not as straightforward as those found in the discussion of the church) is his analysis of radical evil in human nature. As we have seen, a key task of "the other member of the division of practical philosophy as a whole" is to determine the "subjective, hindering [*hindernde*] . . . conditions in human nature" that impede the carrying out of the laws of pure ethics (*MdS* 6:217). Obviously, if human nature is indeed radically evil, this would certainly qualify as a hindrance of major proportions.

Many readers (and more than a few commentators) are surprised to find that Kant's argument concerning the presence of evil in human nature is strongly anthropological, and indeed, empirical in nature.[51] For instance, we find either the term "human nature" (*menschliche Natur*) or "human being" (*Mensch*) not only in the title of part 1 but in all four section titles of part 1 as well.[52] By means of this repetition Kant makes it very clear that throughout his discussion of radical evil he is concerned specifically and solely with the moral psychology of human beings and not that of any other kind of rational being. Early in part 1 he also explicitly pins his hopes on progress in "anthropological research," which will eventually provide sufficient data to entitle us to attribute good or evil dispositions to "the whole species [*die ganze Gattung*]" rather than to single individuals (6:25). It is, as he states earlier, "the difference of the human being from other possible rational beings" (6:21) that he seeks to delineate here. What is "the character of the human being's species [*Charakter seiner Gattung*]" (6:21)?

This anthropological character of parts 1 and 2 of the *Religion* also at times has a strong empirical, inductive slant to it.[53] As Pierre Laberge notes in the opening sentence of his essay "Das radikale Böse und der Völkerzustand": "In

Kant's opinion the proposition "The human being is evil by nature" (6:32) needs no formal proof. Indeed, experience offers us more than enough glaring examples of the manifestation of radical wickedness."[54] And in fact he is merely paraphrasing Kant at this point: "We can see by the multitude of glaring examples of *the deeds* of human beings which experience sets before our eyes that such a corrupt tendency must be rooted [*gewurzelt*] in the human being, and spare ourselves the formal proof" (6:32–33). Whether one looks at the actions of human beings in the "so-called *state of nature* [*sogenannte Naturzustand*],"[55] "the civilized state [*gesitteter Zustand*]," or on the international plane concerning "the state of peoples in external relation to one another [*äußerer Völkerzustand*],"[56] the result is sadly the same; we see people repeatedly committing horrendous, unprovoked acts of evil against one another (6:33–34).

Further evidence of the strong empirical side of Kant's argument in defense of the claim that human beings are evil by nature can be found in the opening sentence of *Religion*: "That the world lies in evil is a complaint as old as history, older even than the still older art of poetry; indeed, exactly as old as the oldest of all fictions [*Dichtungen*], the religion of the priests" (6:19).[57] Kant begins by appealing to the collective testimony of the ages in support of the thesis that human beings are evil by nature, and in the second paragraph he quickly parts ways with his overly-optimistic *Aufklärung* brethren who believe that the world is steadily moving from bad to better. And experience is once again invoked to defend this parting of the ways. If value terms such as 'bad' and 'better' are meant in a *moral* sense, Kant notes, the subscribers to the optimistic proposition "have certainly not drawn this opinion from experience [*sicherlich nicht aus der Erfahrung geschöpft*]" (6:20).[58]

Finally, in explaining what he means in asserting that the human being is evil "by nature," Kant states:

> The human being is evil *by nature* means the same as: being evil applies to him considered in his species [*in seiner Gattung betrachtet*]. Not that such a quality may be inferred from the concept of his species [*Gattungsbegriff*] (out of the human being in general)—for then the quality would be necessary, but rather that, as one knows him through experience he cannot be judged otherwise [*wie man ihn durch Erfahrung kennt, nicht anders beurtheilt werden*], or that one can presuppose it to be subjectively necessary in every human being, even the best. (6:32; cf. 20–21)

We cannot infer automatically from the mere concept of the human species that all human beings are necessarily radically evil. In principle, it is possible that some people might not be evil. But the only solid inference to be drawn from experience is that all human beings are indeed evil. As Michalson notes: "Invariably—but not necessarily—a capacity for evil becomes the production of evil in fact"[59] in the lives of all human beings.

Kant's endorsement of the claim that human nature is radically evil has surprised many readers over the years. Schiller, for instance, in a letter to Christian Gottfried Körner of February 28, 1793, writes:

> [O]ne of the first principles in the work [Kant's *Religion*] drives my feelings into revolt, and probably also yours. He maintains, that is to say, that there exists

a propensity of the human heart to evil, which he calls radical evil, and that this may not be confused at all with the provocations of sensibility [*Reizungen der Sinnlichkeit*].[60]

And Goethe, in a frequently cited letter to Herder of June 7, 1793, accuses Kant of ulterior motivations: "Kant, who required a long life to purify [*reinigen*] his philosophical mantle from all sorts of slovenly prejudices, has wantonly tainted it with the stain of radical evil, so that Christians too might be attracted to kiss the hem."[61] More recently, Karl Barth, in *Protestant Thought: From Rousseau to Ritschl*, has written: "One certainly does not expect, having a knowledge of Kant's ethics from his earlier writings . . . to be met here [in the *Religion*] immediately on the doorstep with a detailed doctrine of the problem of evil. . . . It is in fact the last thing one would expect."[62]

Although it is not hard to see why so many readers have concluded that Kant's discussion of radical evil in the *Religion* constitutes "a repudiation of aspects of his 'enlightened' past,"[63] a careful perusal of the evidence suggests rather that in this late work he is working out implications of a long-held theory of the will. One text often cited in support of the claim that Kant was committed to a "Leibnizian instrumentalist" view of evil before he wrote *Religion* is found in Pölitz's edition of Kant's *Lectures on the Philosophical Doctrine of Religion*. These lectures, though not published by Ludwig Pölitz until 1817, were delivered by Kant in the early or middle 1780s. In the *Lectures* we are told that evil is

> the *incomplete development of the germ* [*Keim*] *toward the good*. Evil has *no special germ at all* [*gar keinen besondern Keim*]; for it is *mere negation*, and consists only in the *limitation of the good*. Evil is nothing further than the incompleteness of the development of the germ for the good out of rawness [*Rohheit*]. (28: 1078)[64]

A quite similar Leibnizian sentiment occurs in Rink's edition of Kant's *Pädagogik* lectures: "In the human being lie only germs toward the good [*nur Keime zum Guten*]" (9:448). Rink himself adds a footnote here, instructing the reader to "see further" Kant's discussion in part 1 of the *Religion* (9:448 n), without even commenting on the stark differences in the two accounts of evil.

However, it is not the case that Kant unequivocally held onto this particular strand of Leibnizian optimism up until the publication of *Religion* in 1793. In his *Attempt to Introduce the Concept of Negative Magnitudes into Philosophy* (1763), he makes a fundamental distinction between what he calls "logical" and "real" opposition. In the former case, we have a contradiction: the consequence of the logical conjunction of the two things "is *nothing at all* [*nihil negativum irrepräsentabile*]" (2:171)—a negative nothing which is incapable of being represented. But in the case of real opposition between two things, "the consequence is *something* [*cogitabile*]" (2:171)—it is capable of being thought. In this latter case, the conjunction of the two forces is something real, since neither of the two things is the mere negation of the other. In applying this distinction to evils (*Übel*), Kant specifically criticizes those philosophers who "treat evils like mere negations" (2:182). Some evils, he holds, are not the mere absence or negation of good but are real and irreducible forces. A key move in the later *Religion* discussion also involves the claim that evil is not "the mere absence of a ground of the good"

(6:22 n), but an independently existing force that is in opposition to the moral law. This is not an idea that Kant suddenly came up with while writing *Religion*.

Also, in *A New Elucidation of the First Principles of Metaphysical Cognition* (1755) Kant asserts that the origin of evil lies not in God but in "the will of beings endowed with understanding and the spontaneous power itself of self-determination . . . from conscious desires and from a choice of one of the alternatives according to the freedom of the power of choice" (1:404). This emphasis on the conscious choosing of evil is also a major ingredient in his later discussion of radical evil.

The following two *Reflexionen zur Anthropologie* (both of which are included in Weisskopf's list of *Parallelstellen* to *Päd* 9:448, cited earlier) also argue for the real and irreducible character of evil: "The human being is evil by nature [*von Natur böse*]" (*Refl* 1425, 15:622). "The human being is evil by nature; but if he did not have the seed of good in him (a universal good will), then one would not be able to hope for improvement from him" (*Refl* 1426, 15:622–23). Both of these *Reflexionen* predate the *Religion*. So at best the evidence is ambiguous. While there are some pre-*Religion* texts in which Kant does commit himself to a Leibnizian instrumentalist view of evil, there are many others where he rejects this position. It is certainly not the case that Kant was totally unreceptive to the idea of radical evil before he wrote part 1 of *Religion*.

But while claims such as that in *"Religion within the Limits of Reason Alone . . .* Kant for the first time explicitly thematizes about evil" and before 1793 he "had not spoken of radical evil"[65] are all clearly false, it is understandable that readers who are familiar with, say, the *Groundwork* but not some of the less central works cited earlier might be surprised at his defense of radical evil in the *Religion*. For in the former text Kant asserts that "a free will and a will under moral laws are one and the same [*einerlei*]" (4:447; cf. *KpV* 5:29). This strong identification of freedom and morality has led many readers (among them Henry Sidgwick)[66] to infer that it is Kant's considered view that only morally good actions are really free; that is, that we are not morally responsible for the evil actions that we do. Although this was never actually Kant's position (as Paton points out, a will "under moral laws" and a will which always obeys moral laws are two quite different wills; even a bad will is under moral laws and is free—a point that Kant later makes explicit in *KU* 5:448 n),[67] Kant's manner of expression in the *Groundwork* is admittedly ambiguous and thus partly to blame.

When Kant calls the evil in human nature "radical" he does not mean (as Hannah Arendt did in her early work *The Origins of Totalitarianism*) that it is "beyond measurement," "beyond comprehension," or "qualitatively distinct from all else that has preceded it." Arendt, for instance, characterized the evil perpetrated by the regimes of Hitler and Stalin as "radical" in the sense of being "beyond the pale of human sinfulness."[68] But for Kant "radical" is meant in the more straight-ahead, etymological sense of "roots" (from the Latin *rādic-*, "root"). The kind of evil he is analyzing is one that is allegedly "interwoven [*verwebt*] with, and as it were, rooted [*gewurzelt*] in humanity itself"; it "must be rooted in the human being [*im Menschen gewurzelt*]" (6:32). More specifically, the human "way of thinking (what concerns the moral disposition) is corrupt in its root [*in ihrer Wurzel . . . verderbt*]" (6:30). This means that *all* human beings, to a greater or lesser degree, share in this evil; it is not a quality that only a few demonic individuals possess. Rather, "the propensity to evil is here established (as concerns conduct) in the human being, even the best, which must be the case if the universality of the propensity to evil is to be proved, or, which here means the same thing, that it is interwoven with human nature" (6:30).

Kantian radical evil is also (contra Goethe) not to be equated with Christian original sin. In the classical Augustinian version, all descendants of Adam inherit by causal transmission both an innate propensity to sin and an innate guilt. But in Kant's view, "it is not necessary, and also not feasible," to track the causes of evil back "to the first man" (6:43). Radical evil must be something for which each agent is responsible; it is "brought upon us by ourselves" (6:32). The disposition to evil or to good "itself must have been adopted through free choice [durch freie Willkür], for otherwise it could not be imputed [zugerechnet]" (6:25). Nothing "is morally evil (i. e., capable of being imputed) except that which is our own *deed*" (6:31). The kind of evil Kant is concerned with "is possible only as a determination of free choice [freie Willkür]" (6:29).

However, at this point a paradox in Kant's own position makes an appearance. Although evil is freely chosen, he also asserts repeatedly that it is "innate" (angeboren) (6:25, cf. 29, 31, 32, 38, 42, 43). Similarly, he defends the proposition that the human being is evil "by nature" (6:32; cf. 25). How can something that is freely chosen also be innate? Unless the evil that we do is freely chosen, it cannot be imputed to us. This much is clear. But why the repeated assertion that moral evil is innate? Part of his answer is that unless we do so we will not be able to claim that the attribution of evil applies to "*die ganze Gattung*" rather than only to particular members of the species (6:25, cf. 29). The inference is correct, but now the presupposition that evil is "subjectively necessarily in every human being, even the best" (6:32) is revealed for what it is: something assumed rather than argued for. And in drawing attention to this presupposition of universal evil, the seriousness of the empirical, inductive side of his argument concerning radical evil is called into question.

A more fundamental reply to the innateness issue can be extracted from Kant's discussion of disposition (Gesinnung). By this term Kant means the ultimate source of a person's moral character, "the underlying common ground in the subject of all particular morally-evil maxims, which itself again is a maxim" (6:20). "Disposition" in this sense thus refers to "the supreme maxim [die oberste Maxime]" (6:31) or what Michalson calls "a kind of 'mega-maxim' . . . that arises out of a free act and gives characteristic tendencies or patterns to our various acts of maxim-making."[69] But Gesinnung is also not observable by human beings—we can only make fallible inferences about it from particular maxims. And these particular maxims themselves are also not observable. They in turn must be inferred from the particular observable acts of which they serve as underlying policies. All of which is to say that we should always exercise extreme caution when judging character; we can never get directly to its source. Outer experience "does not uncover the interior of the disposition, but merely allows one to make a conclusion about it, although not with strict certainty [nicht mit strenger Gewißheit]" (6:63). Again, though, Gesinnung also refers to the underlying unity and continuity of each agent's character; it is not simply an aggregate of particular maxims inferred from isolated acts, but is rather "the first subjective ground of the adoption of maxims, can only be a single one [*kann nur eine einzige sein*], and applies universally to the whole use of freedom" (6:25).

The double claim that *Gesinnung* is both (1) invisible to the human eye, and (2) the source of our moral character may help explain Kant's ambiguous appeal to experience in defending the claim that all human beings are evil. On the one hand, he insists that the propensity to evil in human nature "can be demonstrated [*dargethan werden kann*]" "through experiential proofs [*durch Erfahrungsbeweise*]." But such proofs, he immediately adds, "do not teach us the real nature" of the propensity or "the ground" of the will's resistance to moral law (6:35). Empirical data play a necessary and important role in making the case for human evil, for in a sense they are all that we have. But they always stand in need of a non-empirical background theory of moral character if they are to be employed in moral argument.

Now since *Gesinnung* is the ultimate unifying source, so to speak, of moral character, and since we cannot derive ĭt directly from nature, we must (if we are going to call people evil) therefore posit evil in it too. This positing of evil within the *Gesinnung* itself seems ultimately to be primarily what Kant intends with the dubious language of "innate" and "by nature." As he puts it: "Since, therefore, we are unable to derive this disposition, or rather its supreme ground, from any sort of first act of the will in time, we call it a property of the will which is due to it by nature [*von Natur zukommt*] (although actually it is grounded in freedom [*in der That in der Freiheit gegründet*])"(6:25).[70]

However, in this last parenthetical remark Kant indicates that he himself is not entirely comfortable with the language of "from nature" and "innate"—he certainly does not mean these terms in a literal sense. *Gesinnung* as he uses it does not refer to a fixed state or essence of human nature that can be empirically examined. Rather, it is the noumenal source of character, "according to which one's life must be judged (as something transcending the senses [*etwas übersinnliches*]) (6:70 n). A parallel misgiving about the language of innateness is expressed a bit earlier in the text:

> But since the first ground of the adoption of our maxims, which must itself always lie in free choice, cannot be a fact that could be given in experience, the good or evil in the human being (as the subjective first ground of the adoption of this or that maxim with reference to the moral law) is called innate only in *the* sense that it is posited as the ground that comes before every use of freedom given in experience (in earliest youth as far back as birth) and is thus represented as present in the human being simultaneously with birth: not that birth is exactly [*eben*] the cause of it. (6:21–22)

A further core feature of Kantian radical evil that has surprised some readers is his straightforward claim that our sensible nature is not the cause of evil.[71] Near the beginning of part 2 there appears a passage that almost sounds as though it were lifted out of Aristotle's *Ethics*:

> Natural inclinations, *considered in themselves*, are *good*, that is, not reprehensible [*unverwerflich*], and to want to wipe them out would not only be futile but

also be harmful and blameworthy; one must rather only restrain them, so that they do not wear each other out, but rather are harmonized into a whole, called happiness. (6:58)

Radical evil as Kant understands it has no necessary connection to our natural impulses and inclinations: the ground of evil "cannot lie . . . in any natural impulses" (6:21).

What then is radical evil? Simply put, it refers to our propensity knowingly to choose maxims contrary to the moral law. "The statement 'The human being is *evil*' . . . can mean only: he is conscious of the moral law and yet has incorporated into his maxim the (occasional) deviation from it" (6:32; cf. 29). And (again), this propensity to deviate from the moral law is not the exclusive property of a few demonic individuals, but refers rather to the common root of all human evil, whatever its extent. Nevertheless, three distinct steps or *Stufen* of the propensity to evil may be distinguished from one another, and within each level there are also important differences of degree to be detected.

The first level is "frailty" (*Gebrechlichkeit, fragilitas*), and corresponds to what is traditionally known as "weakness of will." Indeed, in describing this first level of evil Kant paraphrases Paul: "I have the wanting perfectly well, but the performance is missing" (6:29; cf. *Romans* 7:15). The agent intends to act from a moral motive but at the last minute weakens his or her resolve and acts from a non-moral motive.

The second level is what Kant calls "impurity" (*Unlauterkeit, impuritas, improbitas*). As noted earlier, his use of "impurity" here is not the same as our own term, "impure" (cf. "Degrees and Kinds of Impurity" in chap. 1). We use "impure" to refer to the second, empirical part of ethics. "Impurity" in the present sense refers to a lack of single-mindedness or integrity in action. An agent knows that X is morally required, but seeks out and acts on additional reasons (other than the fact that X is morally required) as the sufficient motive of action. The agent's motive in such cases is thus "*nicht rein moralisch*" (6:30); he or she stands in constant need of additional, non-moral incentives.[72]

Finally, the most severe level of the propensity to evil: "wickedness" (*Bösartigkeit, vitiositas, pravitas*). At this last stage, agents intentionally, regularly, and with what lawyers call "malice aforethought" act on non-moral motives (indeed, mostly immoral ones, though Kant also states that actions which are "legally good (legal) [*gesetzlich gut (legale)*]" can also exist at this level) (6:30).

Kant also labels this third level "perversity" (*Verkehrtheit, perversitas*—the German term also connotes a sense of going in the wrong direction), since here the human heart "reverses [*umkehrt*] the ethical order in respect to the incentives of a *free* choice" (6:30). However, strictly speaking all three levels of the propensity to evil involve a reversal of priorities, insofar as agents who exhibit each kind of evil have non-moral rather than moral reasons as the sufficient motive of their actions. (This is why they are different degrees of the same propensity.) It is not only the wicked who have reversed priorities; all human beings (even the best) are evil only because they have reversed the moral order of their incentives in incorporating them into their maxims (cf. 6:36). And even the most wicked person does not possess "an absolutely [*schlechthin*] evil will"—the term "*diabolical* being" is not applicable to human beings (6:35; cf. 36). Wicked human beings are still rational beings, and as such they still possess the ability to understand their moral obligations and to recognize that these obligations may serve as incentives for action. If we strip them of their rationality, we also forfeit our own right to impute evil to them.[73]

Still, there are significant moral differences between these three degrees of the propensity to evil. Wicked people regularly and deliberately act on non-moral (again, usually grossly immoral) motives, even while maintaining the basic ability to recognize and act on moral ones. Frail or weak-willed persons give in to non-moral motives only occasionally, and when they do so it is at the very last moment—they are not deliberately plotting evil with malice aforethought. And the agent with an impure heart is at least a law-abiding *Bürger*—his actions are *pflichtmäßig* (or at least *gesetzmäßig*—cf. 6:30). But like the infamous grocer in Kant's *Groundwork* example, he has ulterior motives for obeying the law (*Gr* 4: 397–98).

Finally, the non-moral incentives in question are very broad in scope (the possibilities for evil are infinite). It is not the case, as Allison claims, that Kantian radical evil consists simply in "the propensity to subordinate moral considerations to those stemming from self-love."[74] All that is necessary for evil to occur is that agents act on "incentives other than the law (for example, ambition, self-love in general, yes, even a good-hearted instinct such as compassion [*Mitleiden*]" (6:30–31). People are evil for many different reasons, but all of these reasons share a common root: we don't put the moral law first.

Over the years, people have objected to Kant's doctrine of radical evil for allegedly caving in to Christian doctrine when it was politically prudent to do so (Goethe), for naively overlooking the true demonic depths of human evil (Silber), for advocating "a fundamental optimism or rationalism . . . [that] leaves our absolute freedom untouched" (Despland),[75] or simply on the ground the it ultimately leaves our ability to understand why we are evil "inscrutable" (Michalson). Each of these objections, I think it is fair to say, points more to the predilections of its author than to weaknesses in Kant's own position. What Kant means by "radical evil" is clearly different than what some other theologians and philosophers have meant by the term, but the referent of his own term is unfortunately an extremely pervasive feature of human experience. In drawing our attention to this feature, Kant is also indicating that the hoped-for *Übergang* to the moralization of human life will be much harder to achieve than many of us would like to think.

5

HISTORY

Kant's writings on history occupy a middle position between the texts examined in earlier chapters, in the sense that they are neither edited versions of lectures he gave in various seminars nor large, systematic works that he published himself. Rather, his views on the philosophy of history for the most part are presented in short, informal essays published between the mid-1780s and mid-1790s, many of which first appeared in journals. Among the most important of these writings are: (1) "Idea for a Universal History from a Cosmopolitan Point of View" (first published in 1784 in the *Berlinische Monatschrift*), (2) reviews of parts 1 and 2 of Herder's book *Ideas for a Philosophy of the History of Humanity* (first published in 1785 in separate issues of the *Jenaische Allgemeine Literaturzeitung*), (3) "Conjectural Beginnings of Human History" (1786, *Berlinische Monatschrift*), (4) "The End of All Things" (1794, *Berlinische Monatschrift*), (5) "An Old Question Raised Again: Is the Human Race Constantly Improving?" (probably written in 1795),[1] and (6) "Perpetual Peace" (published separately as an essay by Kant in 1795). Additionally, sections 83–84 of the *Critique of Judgment* also count as being among Kant's most important discussions of the philosophy of history.

In part because of its (seemingly) unsystematic and informal mode of presentation, Kant's philosophy of history has suffered relative neglect in the hands of philosophically oriented Kant commentators. Over fifty years ago, Ludwig Landgrebe opened his essay "Die Geschichte im Denken Kants" by observing that "for a long time it has been a fixed opinion that Kant's philosophy is 'unhistorical [*ungeschichtlich*]' and that particularly in his philosophy of history he remains on the soil of the Enlightenment and its optimism of reason, which in his Critiques he had already overcome."[2] Similarly, Emil L. Fackenheim began his 1957 essay "Kant's Concept of History" by noting that few expositors treat Kant's philosophy of history seriously: "Many treat it, for it is popular and attractive;

few treat it seriously, for it seems unconnected, and indeed incompatible with the main body of his thought."[3] And Lewis White Beck opened his 1963 editor's introduction to *On History* by noting that Kant was "a philosopher, with a philosophy that seems singularly unlikely to encourage a philosopher to take history seriously."[4]

In recent years the situation has improved immensely, but it remains the case that even close students of Kant's philosophy of history cannot seem to shake off the underlying suspicion that there is something fundamentally flawed about this particular aspect of his work. Thus Yirmiahu Yovel, in *Kant and the Philosophy of History* (1980), in pursuing—and, even in the eyes of most critics, achieving—his announced goal of shedding much philosophical light "on a crucial, if long neglected, dimension of Kant's thought," nevertheless concludes his book with the claim that Kant's philosophy of history is ultimately "untenable in terms of his system."[5] And William A. Galston, in *Kant and the Problem of History* (1975), concludes (as have many other critics) that Kant's philosophy of history is inconsistent with his ethics. In "Idea for a Universal History," for instance, Kant does admit that in the human species' march toward its destiny, "earlier generations appear to carry through their toilsome labor only for the sake of the later ones" (8:20), which on Galston's reading means that most human beings are being used as mere means for a few lucky others.[6]

The Assumption of Purpose

> Now what is the plan of providence in world history? Has the
> time come to comprehend it?
>
> Hegel, *Die Vernunft in der Geschichte*

Surprisingly, the best entrée into Kant's philosophy of history is not the short essays on history themselves but rather part 2 of the *Critique of Judgment*, the *Critique of Teleological Judgment*. In this work we find not only all of the leading themes of Kant's philosophy of history, but also a more focused presentation and defense of his particular methodology. As Ludwig Siep writes, the "most detailed and for the mature Kant the decisive grounding of his philosophy of history is to be found in the *Critique of Judgment*."[7] The erroneous but still popular assumption that Kant's philosophy of history is a sideline anomaly that does not fit with his more systematic concerns can also be countered in part by approaching the topic in this manner. As Pauline Kleingeld notes in *Vernunft und Geschichte*: "In the *Critique of Judgment* one finds the only text of some size in which Kant touches on the theme of history within a Critique."[8]

Briefly, how does Kant propose to ground his philosophy of history in the *Critique of Judgment*? The crucial claim concerns the necessity for human beings of assuming a concept of purpose in their study of nature: "[I]f we want to investigate nature through continual observation, if we want merely to investigate its organized products in this manner, it is indispensably necessary [*unentbehrlich nöthig*] to assume [*unterlegen*] a concept of purpose" (*KU* 5:398). Kant underscores the point that it is only "*according to the peculiar constitution of my cognitive faculties*" that I (or any other human being) am "unable to judge nature in any other manner [*nicht anders urtheilen*]" (5:397–98). The assumption of purpose on our part in judging nature is a merely reflective rather than determinant judgment, and as such it "should serve as a mere subjective principle for the purposeful use of the cognitive faculties [*als bloß subjectives Princip zum zweckmäßigen Gebrauche der Erkenntnißvermögen*], namely, for reflecting on a type of object" (5:385). In other words, it is a heuristic device, albeit a humanly necessary one. We cannot prove from experience that nature in fact does exhibit purpose, but we human beings supposedly cannot make sense out of nature unless we assume that it does. In the language of the first *Critique*, this assumption of purpose is a *regulative* as opposed to *constitutive* principle. But while "one may not be entitled to exactly grant objective reality (existence) to these ideals, they are not therefore to be regarded as figments of the brain; rather they deliver to reason an indispensable standard of judgment [*unentbehrliches Richtmaß*]" (*KrV* A 569/B 597; cf. *KU* 5:379).

The assumption of purpose is thus a humanly necessary heuristic assumption or regulative idea for the interpretation of nature. And since we human beings are ourselves (at least in part) natural beings, we need also to look at ourselves teleologically. In order for us to make sense of human nature and its history, we must also approach it teleologically. This strong teleological assumption behind Kant's philosophy of history is what he calls the "guiding thread [*Leitfaden*] of reason" in the First Thesis of "Idea for a Universal History from a Cosmopolitan Point of View" (8:18, cf. 29); a thread which allows "a philosophical mind (which must in addition be very well-informed in history)" to discover a purpose "in this absurd course of human affairs [*widersinniger Gang menschlicher Dinge*]" (8:30, 18). But in the *Critique of Judgment* Kant also invokes twice the same term, *Leitfaden*, in arguing that the assumption of purpose is a necessity in the human study of nature (*KU* 5:376, 379).

As is well known, once we begin looking at organized systems teleologically, we soon run into an infinite regress problem. Aristotle, for instance, in his opening inquiry into the good life for human beings in his *Nicomachean Ethics*, reminds us that "we do not choose everything for the sake of something else, since if we do, it will go on into infinity [*eis apeiron*]" (I.2 1094a19–20). Kant addresses this infinite regress problem within the context of nature construed as a teleological system by arguing that there must be a final end [*letzter Zweck*] of nature as a whole. We are "to make out the human being not merely as a natural end [*Naturzweck*] like all organized beings, but also as the being here on earth [*hier auf Erden*][9] who is the *final end* of nature, in relation to whom all remaining natural things form a system of ends" (*KU* 5:429). But what, specifically, is it about the human being that entitles him to be the final end of nature here on earth? In order to qualify, the candidate must be something that is both part human as well as part nature, that is, something that involves the ways in which human beings make use of nature and natural objects. This is what Kant calls 'culture', and he defines it extremely broadly:[10] "The producing of the aptitude in a rational being for any ends generally (therefore in his freedom) is culture [*Kultur*]. Therefore only culture can be the final end that one has cause to confer to nature in respect to the human species (*Menschengattung*)" (*KU* 5:431).

'Culture' in this broad sense includes both the capacity to make use of products of nature for one's ends as well as the ability to free one's will from the dominance of natural needs or desires. The former is what Kant calls 'skill'—human beings' capacity to use the natural and social environments to achieve their ends (whatever they may be) (5:431–32); the latter 'discipline'—"the freeing of the will from the despotism of desires;" desires which, if they are not constrained, would render human beings "incapable even of choosing" (5:432).

History teleologically conceived is thus the story of human cultural progress, or rather of our "steps from rawness to culture" (*Idee* 8:21). Although the long-term emphasis is on progress, it is not for the most part a particularly happy or pretty story; all art and culture "are fruits of unsociability, which is forced by itself to discipline itself" (8:22). Humanity thus progresses despite itself—that is, as an unintended consequence of the actions of selfish individuals. The aim of the "great artist" nature "is to produce a harmony among human beings, against their will and indeed through their discord" (*Frieden* 8:360). Even the improvement of skill "can hardly be developed in the human species other than by means of inequality among human beings" (*KU* 5:432). The cultural elite, who work on "the less necessary parts [*die minder nothwendigen Stücke*] of culture, science, and art," keep the rest of the population "in a state of oppression, hard labor, and little enjoyment" (5:432). However, miseries (*Plagen*) increase equally for both the lower and upper classes, "for the one through domination from the outside, for the other through insatiability from within [*innere Ungenügsamkeit*]" (5:432). To make matters worse, in the present level of culture at which the human race still stands, "war is an indispensable means [*unentbehrliches Mittel*] for bringing it still further" (*Anfang* 8:121).

Nature the great artist thus uses some of the most abhorrent and painful means imaginable (war, class domination, gross inequality) to get what it wants. And it still has a very long way to go. Indeed, if we view culture as a force founded "according to true principles *for the education* both of the human being and citizen, it has perhaps not even properly begun, much less been completed" (*Anfang* 8:116). And finally, when it comes to human history there are no guarantees: at any moment the whole project of progress may backfire.

> Even if the human race, considered in its entirety [*im Ganzen betrachtet*], were to be conceived as progressing and proceeding forward for however long a time, still no one can guarantee that now, at this very moment, with regard to the physical disposition of our species, the epoch of its decline would not be able to take place. . . . For we are dealing with freely acting beings of whom, to be sure, what they *ought* to do may be *dictated* in advance; but of whom it may not be *predicted* what they *will* do. (*Streit* 7:83)

Another leading theme in Kant's philosophy of history that also makes a brief but crucial appearance in the *Critique of Judgment* is civil society. In this work "civil society" is defined as follows:

> The formal condition under which nature can alone reach [*allein erreichen kann*] this, its final aim [*Endabsicht*], is that constitution in the relations of human beings among one another where the abuse of freedom by individuals

striving against one another is opposed by a lawful authority within a whole, which is called *civil society* [*bürgerliche Gesellschaft*]. (*KU* 5:432)

Because "the highest aim of nature, namely the development of all of her capacities which can be achieved by humanity" is attainable "only in society" (*Idee* 8: 22), human beings have a duty to enter civil society (cf. *MdS* 6:306)—"regardless of whether it is just or unjust, as long as it provides an alternative to the lawless state of nature."[11] Without a properly constituted civil society to back them up, both the darker means of cultural development (inequality, domination, war) as well as the brighter ones (education, art, science) will prove ineffective.

An additional favorite theme of Kant's philosophy of history essays makes an even briefer appearance in the *Critique of Judgment* discussion, namely, the idea of "a *cosmopolitan whole* [*weltbürgerliches Ganze*]." "In its absence," we are warned, "*war* is inevitable [*unvermeidlich*]" (*KU* 5:432–33). As Patrick Riley notes, "here he encapsulates in a single paragraph much of *Eternal Peace*, published five years after *Judgment*, and a kind of working up of Section 83 [of *KU*] into a full treatise."[12] This "universal *cosmopolitan condition* [*allgemeiner weltbürgerlicher Zustand*]," Kant announces in the earlier "Idea for a Universal History," "which nature has as its highest aim," is "the womb wherein all of the original predispositions of the human species will be developed" (*Idee* 8:28).

However, there remains a final key element in Kant's discussion of teleology within the *Critique of Judgment*, one that is qualitatively different from all of the preceding ones. While the development of human capacities in interaction with nature is the final end of nature, such development itself is not the "final end of the existence of a world, that is, of creation itself" (*KU* 5:434). To find a final end of creation itself, we need to go outside of nature—to the human being "as a moral being," that is, "the human being considered as noumenon" (5:435).

> Now, of the human being as a moral being (and so for each rational being in the world),[13] it cannot be asked further: For what end does [*quem in finem*] he exist? His existence has the highest end in itself; one to which, as far as he is able, he can subject the whole of nature, or contrary to which at least he must not hold himself subject to any influence of nature. (5:435)

Again though, it is "only as moral subject" that the human being qualifies for the role as *Endzweck* of creation (5:435). And morality itself "is absolutely impossible [*schlechterdings unmöglich*] through natural causes, for the principle of its determination to action is supersensible" (5:436. n). The idea of a "moral course of things in the world" can be ascribed "only to the supersensible (which is understandable [*verständlich*] only in relation to the moral)" (*Ende* 8:328).

External Progress and Internal Progress

Kant's claim that a "moral course of things in the world" can be ascribed "only to the supersensible" suggests strongly that morality itself is off the chart of history. Kantian morality is about "inner" dispositions (and *übersinnliche* ones at that), while history concerns visible or "outer" events. The necessary conclusion seems to be that historical progress is not moral progress. Otfried Höffe endorses this interpretation when he remarks that

> Kant limits progress to political justice, including both national and international law. And law, as such, involves the authority to use force. Since history has to do with outward events, it is not at all possible that its ultimate meaning [*letzter Sinn*] lies in an "inner" progress, in a development of the moral disposition (*Gesinnung*).[14]

Similarly, Wolfgang Kersting holds that history interpreted from a Kantian perspective is solely about legal progress and not moral progress—a legal progress that is brought about by nature rather than the free actions of moral agents:

> History is not understood by Kant as a system of human actions and effects of freedom and its subsidiary results, but rather as a system of immediate and mediate effects of nature, which are organized teleologically in the establishment of the ideas of republicanism and perpetual peace. . . . Legal progress is brought about by nature; the human being is not the protagonist of human history, rather an intentional nature [*eine absichtsvolle Natur*] is. She is the guarantee of perpetual peace.[15]

And Siep concludes his analysis of the Kantian idea of a state of justice (*Rechtzustand*) as the final end of history by commenting that the

> final end of the progress of the human species is the overcoming of war by the state of justice, both internally and externally [that is, domestically and internationally]; the final end of the individual is complete morality, which is not reachable at all in the sensible world [*in der Sinnenwelt gar nicht zu erreichen ist*].[16]

Surprisingly, even Yovel, who on the one hand argues that history on Kant's view "is the process in which the highest good should be realized, and in which the free, formative activity of practical reason remolds the given world into a new, moral world," also claims—paradoxically—that Kant's writings on history "tend to reduce history at large to *political* history."[17]

At the same time, many other commentators have interpreted Kant's philosophy of history as constituting a part—indeed, the single most important part—of his applied ethics. At the turn of the century, Fritz Medicus concluded his article "Zu Kants Philosophie der Geschichte" by asserting: "Kant's philosophy of history is the material half of his ethics."[18] Similarly, Manfred Riedel, in explicating Kant's important claim in the Canon of the first *Critique* that the highest good, as the idea of a "moral world," implies that pure reason contains "in a certain practical use, namely the moral, principles of the *possibility of experience*, namely of such actions as, in accordance with moral precepts, *could* be met with in the *history* of the human being" (*KrV* A 807/B 835), also concludes that it "seems no less than obvious" that Kant's philosophy of history "is a part of practical philosophy." An important part of what Kant is getting at with his idea of a "moral world" (cf. *KrV* A 808/B 836), he continues, is that "moral concepts demand that the human world agree with them; they demand a "moral world." The moral problem is *also* a realization problem, and in this connection, in the field of tension of ought and is, goes the question of the relation of morals and history."[19] W. H. Walsh, in his *Introduction to the Philosophy of History*, also strongly stresses the moral message behind Kant's philosophy of history, noting that with Kant "philosophy of history was a pendant to moral philosophy; indeed, there is little to suggest that he would have treated history at all if it were not for the moral questions it seemed to raise."[20] And Howard Williams, in *Kant's Political Philosophy*, echoes Walsh in concluding: "Fundamentally, then, Kant's concept of history is a moral one. . . . [I]t depicts how men *ought* to see their seemingly naturally determined mutual relations as leading to progress."[21] More recently, Pauline Kleingeld, in *Fortschritt und Vernunft*, argues strongly that political and legal progress are themselves properly understood only as means to *moral* progress within Kant's philosophy of history:

> [N]either of these two kinds of legal progress [*Rechtfortschritt*] [namely, a perfect constitution or a cosmopolitan state] can be called the '*Endzweck*' of history, rather both are themselves means to a further end. The true *Endzweck* is the complete development of the "predispositions of humanity," which culminates in moralization, that is to say, in the transformation of human living-together into a "moral whole."[22]

Similarly, Sharon Anderson-Gold, in "A Common Vocation: Humanity as a Moral Species," maintains that Kant's philosophy of history, unlike certain others, "does not eliminate the moral qualities and moral potentialities of historical activity," and is "critically connected to his moral philosophy."[23]

I believe that these wildly different readings of Kant's philosophy of history stem in large part from an underlying ambiguity within his own presentation. As I will show hereafter, in some places he himself asserts that the philosophy of history is about moral progress, while in other places he denies this. In examining these passages, we need to try and reconcile them by asking whether there are different but nevertheless compatible senses in which Kantian philosophy of history both is and is not about moral progress.

Some of the strongest passages in support of the "external progress only" interpretation occur in the second essay in the *Streit der Fakultäten*. In outlining some of the visible signs of "progress toward the better" that he thinks humanity can eventually expect to witness, Kant begins by noting that such progress will yield not "an ever-growing quantity of *morality* in the disposition [*Gesinnung*], but rather an increase in the products of its *legality* in actions which accord with duty (*pflichtmäßige Handlungen*), through whatever incentives they may be prompted" (*Streit* 7:91). It is only "the good *deeds* of human beings" that we can literally see; and these do form part of "the external phenomena of the moral state of the human race [*die Phänomenen der sittlichen Beschaffenheit des Menschengeschlechts*]." But all of these phenomena are still merely visible, exterior signs—"only *empirical* data (experiences)." They are not "the moral cause [*moralische Ursache*], which contains the concept of duty with respect to what ought to happen, and which alone can be laid down purely a priori" (7:91). Similarly, we can expect to see not only visible signs of improvement such as an overall decrease in violence and a correlative increase in law abidingness, charity, and honesty; but even the realization of the *weltbürgerliche Gesellschaft* itself—all "without the moral foundation in the human race having to be enlarged in the least; for that a kind of new creation [*eine Art von neuer Schöpfung*] (supernatural influence) would be necessary" (7:91–92). Particularly in this last quotation, it is hard not to construe Kant's special sense of *Moralisierung* as implying a totally new beginning—something that constitutes (with a great deal of divine help) a radical transformation of all that has preceded it, a transformation that literally takes us out of this world.[24]

Summing up, we can say that Kant's philosophy of history is about external rather than internal progress in the following senses: (1) History concerns empirical events. It is about phenomena; not noumena. (2) History is about the carrying out of nature's intentions—not the free actions of human individuals. (3) His primary emphasis in the history essays proper is on progress that is achieved largely through political and legal means. Nature herself forces human beings to make progress in these areas whether they want to or not. The invisible hand of our "unsociable sociability" does most of the work here, not the specific intentions of individual agents. (4) Finally, it must be admitted that Kant sometimes does construe moral progress in a qualitatively spiritual sense—one that involves a "*revolution* in the *Gesinnung*" which "penetrates to the intelligible ground of the heart" (*Rel* 6:47, 48) and occurs on a separate plane from historical events in space and time.

On the other hand, there do exist other important passages where Kant asserts that history, while concerned with visible events that we can see and touch, is nevertheless ultimately and most fundamentally about moral progress. In "Theory and Practice," for instance, he writes: "since in respect to its natural end the human race is to be conceived as making steady improvement in culture, it is also in respect to the moral end [*moralischer Zweck*] of its existence to be conceived as making progress toward the better. And while this to be sure may occasionally be *interrupted*, it will never be *broken off*" (8:308–9). Here, as Kleingeld observes, Kant is not representing the moralization of humanity as something that will take place in a far distant and very different future (as he admittedly does elsewhere). Rather, he envisions "a constant moral development that occurs *simultaneously* [*gleichzeitig*] with the development of culture."[25]

Kant also maintains confidently in the same essay that there exists strong empirical evidence for asserting that humanity is progressing morally: "[O]ne can give much evidence [*manche Beweise*] that the human race in its entirety [*das menschliche Geschlecht im Ganzen*] has in our age, in comparison with all earlier ones, actually moved itself forward morally toward the better [*moralisch zum selbst Besseren fortgerückt*]" (8:310). Similarly, in "The End of All Things," he also refers to "the experiential evidence [*Erfahrungsbeweise*] of the superiority of morality in our age in comparison with all previous ones" (8:332). And finally in *Streit*, in a remark that seems to contradict directly the passage cited earlier from the same essay concerning the need for a "new creation" initiated by "supernatural influence," he proclaims that "some sort of experience [*irgend eine Erfahrung*] in the human race must appear which, as an event [*Begebenheit*], points to a quality and a capacity of the human race to be the *cause* of its own advance toward the better, and (since this should be the act of a being endowed with freedom) to be the *author* of this advance" (7:84). That "better" definitely means "morally better" here becomes clear a page later when he refers to this event as a "moral cause flowing into [*moralische einfließende Ursache*]" the course of human events (7:85). This moral cause, as Friedrich Kaulbach notes, points to "*an inner*, moral way of thinking [*Denkungsart*]," [26] or, as Kant himself puts it, "a *Denkungsart* that (due to its unselfishness) demonstrates a moral character [*ein moralischer Charakter . . . beweiset*] of the human race, at least in the predisposition [*Anlage*]" (7:85).

But how can *any* event in experience be said to be a "moral cause," since all moral causes, according to official Kantian doctrine, stem from our intelligible character, a character which "remains completely hidden [*gänzlich verborgen*] from us" and which we therefore "do not know" (*KrV* A 551/B 579 n, A 551/B579)? Isn't Kant himself overstepping the constraints of his own critical philosophy here in a moment of moral enthusiasm? Or, as Allison charges, isn't he handing readers the pipe dream of "an inference route from the empirical to the intelligible, a consequence that the 'critical' Kant could hardly accept"? [27]

"Inference route" is clearly too strong, for when Kant is careful he insists that we "cannot see through [*nicht durchschauen können*] to our *Gesinnung*" (*Rel* 6: 71). We cannot know, in the strict sense of the term, our own (or anyone else's) moral character. However, this does not at all mean that we are to rest content in a state of moral *aporia*. Rather, we must seek "a conclusion regarding the *Gesinnung* solely from its consequences in the way of life, a conclusion which, because it is drawn merely from perceptions as appearances of the good or evil *Gesinnung*, above all can never pronounce with certainty the *strength* of the *Gesinnung*" (6:71). We must, in other words, try to "extract" (*abnehmen*) the *Gesinnung* from actions that we can see (6:77). However, in attempting to read off our *Gesinnung* from our actions, we must not fool ourselves into thinking that we are "directly assessing our *Gesinnung*," for in fact we are "merely assessing it according to our deeds [*nur nach unsern Thaten ermessen*]" (6:75–76). This process of reading moral character from conduct (*if* we find evidence of a good as opposed to evil disposition) can lead to "comfort and hope, but not certainty" (6:76).

In the language of the first *Critique* (and here we can also address the issue of whether or not Kant's enthusiastic remarks about reading moral progress from historical events are consistent with his critical philosophy), we are asked to judge ourselves by undertaking an empirical employment of the transcendental idea of freedom; an employment that serves as a merely regulative rather than constitutive principle of reason (cf. *KrV* A 554/B 582). Because the employment of this idea is merely regulative rather than constitutive, it does not provide us with knowledge. Intelligible character

> could never, in fact, be known directly [*niemals unmittelbar gekannt werden*], because we can perceive nothing except insofar as it appears; but it would still have to be *thought* in accordance with the empirical character, just as we are constrained to think a transcendental object as underlying appearances, even though we know nothing of what it is in itself (*KrV* A 540/B 568).

We do not know intelligible character, but we can nevertheless think about it. And the only way possible for us to think about it is to represent it in accordance with empirical character. As Kant puts it, "we do not know intelligible character, but we describe it through appearances, which really only allow us to cognize directly the way of sensing [*Sinnesart*] (empirical character)" (*KrV* A 551/B 579).

In addition to this infamous Kantian theme of intelligible and empirical character, there is a second, more mundane way in which human history is correctly construed as a story of moral progress. History on Kant's account, as van der Linden, Riley, and others have noted, "sets the stage" for morality;[28] it presents us with "quasi-moral 'veneers' that are not themselves wholly moral"[29] but are necessary preconditions for morality. In an important footnote in the first appendix to *Perpetual Peace*, Kant writes:

> Within each state the evil that human beings do to each other is veiled [*verschleiert*] through the compulsion of civil laws, because the inclination to reciprocal violence among the citizens is strongly counteracted by a stronger power, namely that of the government, and so it gives to the whole not only a moral veneer [*moralischer Anstrich*] [*causae non causae*] but also, due to the fact that it puts a stop to the outbreak of unlawful inclinations, the development of the moral predisposition [*die Entwickelung der moralischen Anlage*] to direct respect for justice is made much easier. For each person now believes of himself that he would hold the concept of justice holy and faithfully follow it, if he could only expect the same of everyone else, and the government does in part assure him of this; thereby a great step toward morality (although not yet a moral step) [*ein großer Schritt zur Moralität (obgleich noch nicht moralischer Schritt)*] is made, which is willing this concept of duty for its own sake, without regard for reciprocity. (8:375–76 n)

This quasi-moral step involves the emergence, identification, and conscious employment of a physical, tangible, political structure in human life that helps prepare the way for (invisible, non-tangible) morality. The structure helps prepare the way for morality by instilling correct habits of behavior, disciplining our emotions, and by making us less partial toward our own interests. Government is certainly not the only institutional structure that prepares the way for morality in this manner (e.g., in a *Reflexion* Kant states that "education, a political constitution, and religion . . . will eventually force moralization," (*Refl* 1460, 15:641), but it is does receive pride of place in Kant's essays on history. However, even in the history essays occasional recognition is given to wider cultural means of moralization. For instance, in a famous passage in *Idee*, Kant asserts that "the idea of morality belongs to culture, but using this idea only in reference to semblances of morality [*Sittenähnliche*] in the love of honor and outward propriety [*äußere Anständigkeit*] constitutes mere civilization" (8:26). Love of honor and outward propriety are obviously still "not quite there," morally speaking. But these civilizing tendencies do head people in the right direction, albeit without a guarantee that the underlying motives will be properly moralized. This is precisely Kant's point in the passage from *Streit* cited earlier, where he notes that some of the external signs of progress to be witnessed include "more charity, less strife in lawsuits, more reliability in keeping one's word, and so on, partly out of love of honor, partly out of well-understood self-interest"—all of which can occur "without the moral foundation in the human race having to be enlarged in the least" (7:91). Love of honor "is the constant companion of virtue" (*Anth* 7:257); but this is not to say that the two are identical. Sometimes the motive of love of honor corresponds with dutiful action; sometimes it does not (cf. *Gr* 4:398). But both motives do involve acting for the sake of an ideal that is larger than oneself; an ideal that often involves significant personal sacrifice and forfeit of pleasure. These are major rather than minor similarities.

Similarly, Kant's emphasis in *KU* and elsewhere on the "negative culture" of discipline as involving a "liberation of the will from the despotism of desires" (5:432; cf. *Päd* 9:451, 453) is another indication of how on his view historical progress also involves moral progress. Liberation or detachment from desire is not, in and of itself, a sufficient guarantee that an agent is moralized; but it is a necessary preparatory step. Without this detachment there is no guarantee that the agent will do the right thing for the right reason. And again, all of the arts and sciences, though they do not necessarily make human beings "morally better [*sittlich besser*]," do

> through a pleasure that can be communicated universally, and by bringing polish and refinement into society, still make human beings civilized [*gesittet*], and do much to overcome the tyranny of the senses and thereby prepare [*bereiten . . . vor*] human beings for a sovereignty in which reason alone shall have power (*KU* 5:433; cf. 267).

As we have seen (see chap. 4), aesthetic experience and scientific activity both promote disinterested pleasure and a sense of universality. These are strongly analogous (though not identical) psychological states to those found in moral judgment. And they have the distinct advantage of being more tangible and graspable for human beings.

It is worth comparing briefly Kant's more skeptical position on the possible connections between external and internal progress to several other well-known views. Aristotle, for instance, subscribes to a much more optimistic position: People become morally good via obedience to just laws. Through repeated acts of obedience to just laws of the polis, we acquire a new internalized habit, one that in time simply becomes moral virtue. "It is difficult for someone to be trained correctly for virtue from his youth if he has not been brought up under correct laws, for to live temperately and hardily is not pleasant to most people, especially when they are young" (*EN* 10.9 1179b31–34). The "it is difficult [*khalepon*]" suggests that Aristotle is not quite assuming a simple causal connection here (i.e., he is not asserting that being brought up under right laws is a necessary and sufficient condition for the acquisition of moral virtue). Absent exposure to good laws, it is difficult (but not impossible) to get a correct training for virtue. Still, the assumed linkage between obedience to law and virtue is very strong. "[S]urely he who wants to make men, whether many or few, better by his care, must try to become capable of legislating, if it is through laws that we can become good" (10.9 1180b23–25). The traditional interpretation of this passage is that we do indeed become morally good through obedience to just laws, and that educators interested in inculcating the former therefore need to learn about the latter. The science of politics, Aristotle announces at the beginning of the *Ethics*, "legislates as to what we are to do and what we are to abstain from"; its end is "the good for man" (1.1 1094b5–7).

But for Kant of course there is no guarantee that behavioral conformity to external standards will produce moral virtue. The agent who habitually obeys just laws acts *pflichtmäßig* but not necessarily *aus Pflicht*. This behavioral conformity is a necessary step in the right direction, but we cannot assert that habitual conformity to external standards necessarily produces virtue. For the latter a "revolution in the *Gesinnung*" is necessary, and being a citizen in a just society is no guarantee that such a revolution is forthcoming.

A third position on this topic, one in between Aristotle and Kant but ultimately closer to Kant, is found in Fichte's series of public lectures entitled *The Fundamental Characteristics of the Present Age* (1806):

> [V]irtue cannot be an end of the state. Virtue is the good will that endures and prevails without exception to promote from all its powers the ends of the human species.... But the state, in its essential characteristic as absolute power, reckons on the lack of good will, and therefore on the lack of virtue, and on the existence of evil. It wants to replace the former, and suppress the outbreak of the latter, by fear of punishment. To keep itself strong in this sphere it does not need to reckon on virtue, and the same is true for calculating the achievement of its goals. If all of the state's members were virtuous, it would lose completely its character as absolute power, and would be merely the director, leader, and trustworthy counsel of the willing.
>
> Nevertheless, the state promotes ... through its bare existence the possibility of the general development of virtue throughout the human race, due to the fact that it brings forth [*hervorbringt*] externally good mores [*äußere gute Sitte*] and morality [*Sittlichkeit*]—which admittedly is not nearly virtue [*freilich noch lange nicht Tugend*].[30]

Like Kant, Fichte identifies virtue with a specified inner disposition; the requisite motivational structure of which cannot be guaranteed by mere external behavioral conformity. Both Kant and Fichte see much more conceptual space between the political institution of the state and moral virtue than does Aristotle. But like Kant as well as Aristotle, Fichte also sees the state as setting the stage for morality. The state plays a necessary preparatory role in the development of morality through the inculcation of correct behavior patterns and customs. However, it must be admitted that for Kant morality is ultimately something much more radically inner than it is for either Fichte or Aristotle: "the moral formation [*moralische Bildung*] of the human being must begin not with the improvement of mores [*Sitten*] but rather with the transformation of the way of thinking and the grounding of a character" (*Rel* 6:48). This radical innerness is in part a reflection of the religious orientation of Kant's conception of ethics. "A new kind of creation (supernatural influence)" is necessary in order to enlarge the moral foundation in the human race (*Streit* 7:92). If and when this new kind of creation comes about, it will usher in a genuine ethical commonwealth rather than merely the continuation of civil society under external law. And such a commonwealth "can be thought of only as a people under divine commands, i.e., as a *people of God*, and indeed *in accordance with laws of virtue*" (*Rel* 6:99).

History, even Kant's rarified philosophical version of history, is about external events in time and space, the most significant of which concern the actions of human beings. Moral character, at least on Kant's view, is not about external events in time and space: indeed, it is not even about an internal process taking place in time and space. The latter is still only empirical character; and morality in the deep sense is fundamentally about intelligible character. If morality is about intelligible character and history is about empirical events, then it does follow that outer progress is not necessarily inner progress. But we can never know the moral *Gesinnung*, "which is supersensible [*übersinnlich*]"; instead, "we must look at the good as it appears in us, i.e., according to the *deed*" (*Rel* 6:67). Human beings are cognitively limited creatures. Given these cognitive limitations, we must make do with what we have; we must try as we best we can to decipher the inner from the outer. And since certain manifestations of the latter (e.g., law, art, culture, religious community) are themselves necessary preparatory steps for the former, it is correct to say that, from a human perspective, clear signs of outer progress also afford us clues regarding inner progress. In this broader sense, Kant's account of historical progress is of a piece with the larger tapestry of impure ethics; it is yet another way of making morality graspable (*faßlich*) to human beings.

Summing up, we can say that Kantian philosophy of history *is* about internal, moral progress in the following ways: (1) the external, empirically visible forms of progress with which history properly concerns itself (cultural, political, legal, etc.) are themselves necessary preparatory steps for moral progress. The former exist for the sake of the latter—external modes of progress are justified by their connection to moral progress. Signs of external progress are correctly taken to also be signs of moral progress. (2) History from a Kantian perspective provides moral agents with a long-term moral goal that they have a duty to promote. As Kaulbach observes (see n 21), one of the primary uses which Kant assigns to the philosophy of history is that of moral orientation. Just as travelers turn to maps in order to identify and find the way toward their destinations, so moral agents need an end-point for their moral efforts and directions concerning how to reach this end-point. Kant's philosophy of history provides human beings with this moral map, the end-point of which (namely, the moral perfection of the human species) infuses all of human history with moral meaning. (3) Human beings have no choice but to try and read inner moral character from its outer, empirical manifestations. This particular art of reading can never produce certain knowledge, but our own epistemic position leaves us with no satisfactory alternative. History, in this sense, is in the same boat as the rest of human experience. Within human experience there is no road that leads to certain knowledge of the moral *Gesinnung*.

These various senses in which philosophy of history from a Kantian perspective both is and is not about inner, moral progress do not contradict one another. However, in approaching Kant's philosophy of history we need to exercise more care than has normally been shown in the past if we are to specify accurately the precise sense and type of progress being referred to at any given point in his texts.

The Means of Progress

Like many western European intellectuals of his era, Kant believed that human civilization had improved and would continue to improve not so much because of intentional efforts on the part of human beings but rather in spite of them. Kant would, in other words, endorse strongly Adam Smith's famous maxim that each individual "is led by an invisible hand to promote an end which was not part of his intention. . . . By pursuing his own interest he frequently promotes that of the society more effectually than when he really intends to promote it."[31] As Kersting notes, "with Kant nature as interpreted by philosophy of history [*die geschichtsphilophischische Natur*] is the sister of Smith's invisible hand and the forerunner of the Hegelian cunning of reason."[32] The precise nature and aim of Kant's "invisible hand" differs in certain respects from Smith's, but both theorists definitely agree that human individuals often unintentionally help each other when they in fact try to help only themselves. As Kant remarks in his essay on "Theory and Practice":

> If we now ask, through what means [*Mittel*] this constant progress toward a better state can be maintained and perhaps even accelerated, one soon sees that this immeasurably distant result depends not so much on what *we* do (for instance, on the education that we give the world's children), nor on what method *we* should act on so as to bring it about; rather it depends on what human *nature* will do in and with us, in order to *compel* us onto a track to which we ourselves would not easily submit. (8:310)

Or, as he puts it in "Perpetual Peace," nature's purposiveness visibly shines forth in "permitting harmony among human beings to emerge through discord, even against their wills" (8:360). Nature "has planted the seed of *discord* in the human species and has willed that the human species through its own reason bring *concord* out of this discord" (*Anth* 7:322; cf. *Frieden* 8:365, 367).

Briefly, what are the chief means of human progress, on Kant's view? The most fundamental one is "unsocial sociability" (*ungesellige Geselligkeit*), an "antagonism" implanted by nature within the human heart through which individuals desire both: (1) to enter into social relations with one another (the "sociability" side), and (2) to constantly fight and compete against one another once they are living in society (the "unsocial" side) (cf. *Idee* 8:20–21). Once within society, the human being discovers within himself "the unsociable characteristic of wanting everything to go according to his own opinions, and he therefore anticipates resistance [*Widerstand*] everywhere" (8:21). At the same time, it is this very resistance which

> awakens all the powers of the human being, brings him to overcome his tendency toward laziness, and, driven through addiction to honor, power, or greed, to gain for himself a rank among his companions, whom he cannot *put up with* but also cannot *let go of*. Now the first true steps from rawness to culture take place, in which the real social worth of the human being consists; all talents are gradually developed, taste is formed [*gebildet*], and through progressive enlightenment the beginning of the grounding of a way of thinking

[*Denkungsart*] is made, which can in time transform the coarse natural disposition for moral discrimination into definite practical principles, and thus transform an agreement determined by *feeling* [*eine pathologisch-abgedrungene Zusammenstimmung*] into a society and, finally, into a *moral* whole. Without those characteristics of unsociability that everyone must necessarily encounter in his own self-seeking arrogance, characteristics which in themselves are not worthy of being loved, and out of which resistance springs . . . all talents would remain eternally hidden in their seeds. . . . Nature should thus be thanked for incompatibility, for distrustful, competitive vanity, for the insatiable desire to possess and also to rule! Without these desires all of the excellent natural predispositions in humanity would lie dormant forever, undeveloped. (*Idee* 8:21)

Kant is making extremely large claims on behalf of our unsociable side in this passage. It is held to be the primary driving force behind *all* branches of human culture, science, politics, and art; indeed, even behind the hoped-for transformation of humanity into a moral whole. "All culture and art which adorn humanity and the most beautiful social order are fruits of unsociability [*Früchte der Ungeselligkeit*] that is forced to discipline itself and so through an imposed art to develop completely the seeds of nature" (8:22). For the development of the arts and sciences themselves, as I showed earlier (see "Art as Preparation for Morality" in chap. 4), help prepare us for this moral whole:

Even if they do not make the human being morally better [*sittlich besser*], yet, through a pleasure that allows itself to be universally shared, and through polish and refinement for society, they still make him civilized [*gesittet*], and do much to overcome the tyranny of the senses and prepare the human being for a sovereignty in which reason alone shall have power. (*KU* 5:433)

However, in Kant's essays on history it becomes clear that the efficient cause of all this art and science is not love of beauty or truth but rather our own selfishness—albeit a selfishness that eventually overcomes itself in order to further moral ends.

At the same time, human *Ungeselligkeit* does not only employ art and culture to further nature's aims. As I have shown, less pretty means also play a central role: "Skill can hardly be developed in the human species except by means of inequality among human beings" (*KU* 5:432). The vast majority of people are kept in "a state of oppression, hard labor, and little enjoyment"; while the elite minority are able to work in "the less necessary branches of culture, science and art" (5:432). Torments increase on both sides—for the poor, through the bitter reality of external oppression; for the rich, through feelings of "insatiablity within." But this widespread misery too is "connected with the development of the natural predispositions in the human species, and the end of nature itself, even though it is not our end, is thereby still reached" (5:432).

Even the destructive power of war is claimed by Kant to be just another means employed by crafty nature to further the development of human beings' capacities and talents against their own wishes. War itself is but "one more incentive for developing in the highest degree all talents that serve culture" (*KU* 5:433). Paradoxically, in the space of a single page in his essay "*Mutmaßlicher Anfang*" Kant somehow manages to describe war as being both the source of "the greatest evils which oppress civilized peoples," and "for the stage of culture at which the human race still stands . . . an indispensable means [*unentbehrliches Mittel*] for bringing culture still further" (8:121).

Why is war an indispensable means for human development? As Kant sees it, for three reasons. First, he claims that the fear of war acts as a spur to internal cultural and economic development, and even encourages heads of state to show respect for humanity:

> [W]ould there even be this culture, the close connection among status groups of the commonwealth for the mutual promotion of their well-being, would there be the large populations; indeed, would there even be the degree of freedom that still remains, in spite of highly restrictive laws . . . if the constant fear of war itself did not necessitate this level of *respect for humanity* even from heads of states (8:121)?

Second, war drives people "even into the most inhospitable regions [of the world] in order to populate them" (*Frieden* 8:363; cf. 364). As I showed earlier in my discussion of race (chap. 3), "the human being was destined for all climates and for every soil condition" (*Racen* 2:436; cf. *Menschenrace* 8:93; *Gebrauch* 8:166). But some of these climates and soil conditions are more desirable than others. To the victors belong the spoils—they can live where they want to, while the losers may need to move to less hospitable regions. Nature thus uses war "as a means to populate the entire earth" (*Frieden* 8:365). And third, war has "compelled people to enter into more or less lawful relations" with one another (8:363)—a process that is to intensify until the point where people are exhausted by fighting and finally agree to abolish war.

War thus differs fundamentally from other means of progress such as art and science insofar as it is programmed to eventually die out. As Yovel notes, war "is the power that drives historical progress forward, leading eventually to its self-cancellation."[33]

Just as universal violence and its resultant misery ultimately must bring a people to the point of

> deciding to submit to the coercion of public laws . . . and to enter a *civil* constitution, so also must the misery of continual wars, in which nations in their turn seek to reduce or subjugate one another, at last bring them to the point of entering into a *cosmopolitan* constitution, even against their wills. (*Gemeinspruch* 8:310; cf. *Idee* 8:24)

Another central vehicle of progress, one that itself is assigned a major role in ending war, is what Kant calls *Handelsgeist* or the spirit of trade. Here his Prussian invisible hand definitely takes on Smithian overtones:

> the *Handelsgeist*, which cannot coexist [*nicht zusammen bestehen kann*] with war, sooner or later takes hold of every people. For of all the powers (or means) subordinate to the power of the state, the *power of money* may well be the most reliable in seeing that states themselves are forced (to be sure, not exactly through incentives of morality) to promote honorable peace. And wherever in the world war threatens to break out, they will try to ward it off through mediation, just as if they stood in permanent leagues. . . . In this way nature

guarantees perpetual peace through the mechanism of human inclinations themselves. (*Frieden* 8:368)

Kant pins extremely high hopes on increased foreign trade as an unintentional means of abolishing war. Unfortunately, events since his time (if not before) show that war and commerce can and often do co-exist with each other; indeed, that they sometimes mutually support and benefit one another. Still, he shows prescience in predicting that the *Handelsgeist* will grow and eventually take hold everywhere; nations today *are* increasingly "linked closely together through trade" (*Idee* 8:28). And his conviction that increased foreign trade between nations can and will lead to greater individual freedom and a more tolerant moral climate (even when politicians don't want it to) is not to be dismissed as mere wishful thinking. He expands on this latter theme a bit in *Idee*:

> If one hinders the citizen from pursuing his well-being in whatever way he holds most dear, so long as it can co-exist with the freedom of others, one hampers the vitality of business enterprise generally and, along with it, the powers of the whole. Accordingly, limitations on personal activities are gradually abolished, and general freedom of religion is granted. And thus *enlightenment* gradually arises, with intermittent folly and caprice. . . . This enlightenment . . . must gradually go up to the thrones and even influence their principles of government. (8:28)

In this manner, "reason outwits princes and allows them to achieve her own end blindly."[34] But of course it is not only politicians who are being outwitted. Businesspeople and consumers alike are also unintentionally furthering the moral ends of nature in pursuing their own private interests. And one may also infer here that Kant was confident that reason would also be able to muster the resources necessary to correct the ethical deficiencies of "the subversive challenge of the market-driven globalism currently being promoted by transnational corporations and banks"[35] in our own time, though unfortunately he offers no specifics.

As the foregoing remarks on trade indicate, government itself is also a fundamental means of progress. However, the story here is essentially two-tiered. At the first level, human beings are forced to leave the state of nature and enter civil society. Here Kant is more Hobbesian than Rousseauian, in the sense that it is primarily our unsociable rather than sociable side that brings us together; "general violence and its resultant misery must ultimately bring a people to the point of deciding to submit to public laws" (*Gemeinspruch* 8:310). The formation of civil society, via the institution of legal authority, brings the problem of "the demolition of freedom by individuals in mutual conflict" (*KU* 5:432) under control. But the problem of the demolition of freedom by nation-states in mutual conflict still remains. Wars between nations comprise in effect an international parallel to the domestic violence between private individuals that the legal authority of the various nation-states has supposedly brought under control. Indeed, until the latter problem is solved domestic life is not secure either (cf. *Idee* 8:24). And so a second tier of government becomes necessary; violence between nations must be brought under control by means of an international federation of nation-states: "[T]he misery of continual wars, in which nations in their turn seek to reduce or subjugate one another, must at last bring them to the point of entering into a *cosmopolitan* constitution, even against their wills" (*Gemeinspruch* 8:310; cf. *MdS* 6:350; *Idee* 8:24). I examine the precise configuration of this cosmopolitan constitution in more detail in the next section. But three basic points need first to be stressed: (1) The invisible hand is at work here too. Humanity will reach this political stage not because it wants to but precisely because it doesn't want to. (2) With the establishment of this confederation war will be abolished. The "*cosmopolitan* whole [*weltbürgerliches Ganze*]" is "a system of all states that are in danger of acting detrimentally to one another. In its absence . . . war is inevitable" (*KU* 5:432–33). (3) The task of establishing this confederation is the most difficult problem facing the human species. "*The greatest problem for the human species, whose solution nature forces it to seek, is the attainment of a universal civil society administered in accordance with justice*" (*Idee* 8:22; cf. 23).

These are the major vehicles of progress stressed by Kant in the essays on history. To them should be added at least two further means stressed elsewhere: education and religion. "What are the means to the improvement of civil society and government? 1. Education. 2. Legislation. 3. Religion" (*Mrongovius* 25: 1427). "But now how is this perfection of humanity to be sought, and from whence is it to be hoped for? From nowhere else except through education (*Collins Moralphilosophie* 27:470–71; cf. *Päd* 9:444; "The Education of Humanity" in chap. 2). Both of these passages stand in tension with Kant's claim in "Theory and Practice," cited earlier in this section, that progress depends "not so much on what *we* do (for instance, on the education that we give the world's children)" (8:310). And in the *Religion* of course the way to moral perfection is held to lie exclusively in the establishment and spreading of a commonwealth of virtue as represented by historical churches—"as far as we can see," the goal "is not otherwise reachable" except via this means (*Rel* 6:94—cf. "The Church as Moral Community" in chap. 4). Kant tends both to ignore some of the means of progress when he is focusing on others and to make exclusivist claims on behalf of some to the detriment of others. If we are to make to his remarks consistent with one another we need to read him more charitably at this point. On this more charitable reading, his considered view is simply that all of these factors are necessary means of human progress, while none is sufficient.

Citizens of the World?

> Asked where he came from, he said, "I am a citizen of the world."
>
> Diogenes Laertius, *Lives of Eminent Philosophers*

Everyone knows that universality is a core concept in Kant's ethics. But what would it actually be like to live in a world where everyone was consistently disposed to treat all people "*both in . . . [their] own person and in the person of every other, always at the same time as an end, never merely as a means*" (*Gr* 4: 429)? A central part of the task of impure ethics is to sketch out what, given

certain basic empirical facts about human nature, we need to do in order effectively to bring ourselves closer to this ideal. As noted earlier (see "'The Whole
Human Race'" in chap. 3), Kantian universality correctly understood is much
more than a head-game of scrutinizing one's maxims. Rather, its most fundamental implication refers to the hard work of figuring out how to change the
world (including above all the attitudes of its human inhabitants) so that each
member of the human species really is "a law-making member in the universal
kingdom of ends" (*Gr* 4:438). What changes in human institutions and practices
need to be made in order to bring all members of the human species into the
moral community on an equal footing? How can relevant, tangible symbols be
better employed in human life so that more people can feel the moral message
of universality? In the essays on history proper it is the external or political side
of this ideal that receives primary emphasis; whereas in the *Religion* (cf. "The
Church as Moral Community" in chap. 4), the internal or moral side receives
pride of place. However, both sides complement and mutually reinforce one another. The external, political side is "secondary to the moral system, from which
its value derives,"[36] and serves also as a necessary preliminary step to the latter.
But improvements in the moral character of citizens will also make the achievement of the political and legal goals of world peace easier to achieve and less
precarious to maintain. Indeed, since "the depravity of human nature" is the
chief impediment to lasting world peace (*Frieden* 8:355), the thin veil placed
over this depravity by legal systems is in perpetual danger of falling off until
people have learned to control the evil within themselves (8:357, 375–76 n, *Rel*
6:124).

What changes are needed on the political side? Just as individuals are forced
eventually to leave the state of nature and join the security of civil society, so
each nation-state too "can and should demand for the sake of its own security
that the others enter with it into a constitution similar to the civil constitution,
where each can be secure in his right" (*Frieden* 8:354). The basic goal, as Howard Williams notes, is "the gradual coming together of independent nations into
one international organization without sovereign powers as the best approximation of what nations ought, but cannot, achieve: an international state"[37]—that
is, a *Völkerbund* (league of nations) as opposed to a *Völkerstaat* (state consisting
of nations, international state). The latter

> would be a contradiction, because each state is comprised of the relation of a
> *ruler* (legislator) to a *subject* (those who obey, namely the people); but many
> nations in one state would constitute only one nation. This contradicts our
> initial assumption, for here we have to weigh the right of *nations* against one
> another, insofar as they constitute many different states, and we should not
> melt them together into a single state [*nicht in einem Staat zusammenschmelzen
> sollen*]. (*Frieden* 8:354)

The goal is not one mega-state into which all political and cultural differences
are dissolved into one another, but a gradually expanding, voluntary "federation
of free states" (*Frieden* 8:354; cf. *MdS* 6:354). Kant repeats his opposition to a
"melting together" (*Zusammenschmelzung*) of states at *Frieden* 8:367; and part of

the justification for the opposition is resistance to the idea of world wide political and cultural homogeneity. But in *MdS* a more pragmatic reason emerges; a world state would be too large to govern effectively. A *Völkerstaat* "would extend over vast regions . . . and consequently the protection of each of its members would, in the end, be impossible" (*MdS* 6:350). A world state is thus not practicable or feasible; leaving us with the *Völkerbund* as a second-best option; "in place of the positive idea of a *world republic* (*Weltrepublik*), there can be only the *negative* surrogate of a *league* that averts wars, endures, spreads, and holds back the stream of hostile inclination that shuns the law, though there is a constant danger of its breaking out again" (*Frieden* 8:357).[38]

However, as is also the case with our own United Nations, such a federation would lack coercive powers of enforcement and thus have little real power over its constituent states (which is one reason why it is only a "negative surrogate"). This second-best federation would be

a league of a special kind, which one can call a *league of peace* [*foedus pacificum*]. . . . This league does not seek to acquire any of the power of the state but only the maintenance and security of the *freedom* of a state itself and at the same time of the other states bound with it, without their having thereby to subject themselves to public laws and coercion under them (as human beings in the state of nature must do). (8:356)

Still, the aim is gradually to incorporate *all* nation-states within this league, for only thus can world peace be secured, albeit precariously; the federation "should extend gradually to all states [*über alle Staaten erstrecken soll*] and thus lead to perpetual peace" (8:356). Perpetual peace is "the highest political good" (*MdS* 6:354), and it is the primary aim of the *Völkerbund* to achieve it. But even an alliance consisting of all nation-states remains in "constant danger" of breaking apart (cf. *Frieden* 8:357; *Anth* 7:331), absent a fundamental change of moral character.

Nevertheless, this precarious peace can (and, according to Kant, *will*) be attained without a fundamental change in moral character occurring. We can expect to see improvement in the external relations of nations toward one another "extending up to the cosmopolitan society [*weltbürgerliche Gesellschaft*], without the moral foundation in the human race having to be enlarged in the least" (*Streit* 7:92). In other words, people can stop fighting each other without necessarily having to treat everyone as ends in themselves. We can put an end to war without necessarily changing the way we ultimately view one another.

However, human beings are destined by their reason not only to cultivate and civilize themselves but to moralize themselves as well (cf. *Anth* 7:324; *Idee* 8:26). And at this deeper, moral level a change not merely in external behavior but a radical change in disposition is called for as well. What is demanded here, as Yovel notes, is "an intersubjective system of *attitudes* that embraces, ideally, the whole human race. Each member in this 'invisible' system recognizes the equal status of all members as free subjects or ends in themselves and is constantly disposed to act from this recognition."[39] But even this description underestimates the extent of the radical change that is supposedly in store for humanity; since what is called for is a system of attitudes that *will* eventually embrace the whole human race. Again, the continual progress of the human race will culminate in "a spreading over all peoples of the earth [*alle Völker der Erde*] who will gradually come to participate" in this process (*Streit* 7:89; cf. "'The Whole Human Race'" in chap. 3).

As I showed earlier (see "The Education of Humanity" in chap. 2; "The Church as Moral Community" in chap. 4) educational and religious institutions are also assigned major roles in promoting this ideal of a universal moral community among human beings. On the last page of his *Lectures on Pedagogy* Kant exhorts teachers to stress "human love [*Menschenliebe*] toward others and then also cosmopolitan dispositions [*weltbürgerliche Gesinnungen*]" in their instruction. In striving to inculcate these cosmopolitan dispositions,

> an interest in the highest good in the world [*das Weltbeste*][40] must come to pass. One must make children familiar with this interest so that they may warm their souls with it. They must rejoice at the highest good in the world even if it is not to the advantage of their fatherland or to their own gain. (*Päd* 9:499; cf. *Streit* 7:92–93; *Idee* 8:26)

On the religious front, the corresponding goal is "the establishment and spreading of a society in accordance with, and for the sake of, laws of virtue," a society that eventually encompasses "the entire human race in its scope [*die ganze Menschengeschlecht in ihrem Umfang*]" (*Rel* 6:94). The ideal of such a moral community immediately takes us beyond national boundaries, for since laws of virtue

> concern the entire human race [*das ganze menschliche Geschlecht angehen*], the concept of an ethical community always refers to the ideal of a whole of all human beings [*ein Ganzes aller Menschen*], and in this respect distinguishes itself from the concept of a political community. Hence a multitude of human beings united in that purpose cannot yet be called the ethical community itself, but only a particular society that strives toward concord [*Einhelligkeit*] with all human beings (indeed, eventually with all finite rational beings [*ja aller endlichen vernünftigen Wesen*]), in order to establish an absolute ethical whole, of which each partial society is only a representation or schema. (*Rel* 6:96)

Political and legal progress are both necessary presuppositions for this deeper moral progress, as are cultural and scientific advances, growth in foreign trade; indeed, as we have seen, even war itself. And again, human wisdom alone is not enough to achieve the moral goal. Our own "negative wisdom" will lead us eventually to renounce war; but the qualitative leap from external to internal progress is to be expected "only on the condition of a wisdom from above" (*Streit* 7:93). Still, we are not to sit around doing nothing, waiting for a wisdom from above; "nature itself has called on everyone to contribute as much to this progress [from worse to better] as may be within his power" (*Anfang* 8:123; cf. *Frieden* 8:368). Each person must act "as if everything depended on him" (*Rel* 6:101).

This ideal of a truly universal moral community is the most important single legacy of Kant's ethics; indeed, of Enlightenment thought generally.[41] Events since Kant's time have shown us that it is much further away than Kant and his contemporaries imagined, but its legitimacy as a regulative ideal on which to focus our efforts has not diminished.

Making the World Moral:
The Highest Good

> Ah, but a man's reach should exceed his
>   grasp,
>   Or what's a heaven for?
>
>   Robert Browning,
>   *Andrea del Sarto*

Kant discusses the concept of the highest good not only in his essays on history but in all three *Critiques* (*KrV* A 806/B 834-A 819/B 847); *KpV* 5:107–32; *KU* 5:442–59, 469–79) as well as in the *Religion* (6:3–8). As many commentators have noted over the years, these various accounts of the highest good often seem difficult to reconcile with each other. In the Dialectic of *KpV*, which is probably Kant's best-known discussion, we are presented with a theological or otherworldly conception of the highest good consisting of happiness in proportion to virtue, to be brought about by God in another world. On the other hand, in the history essays and elsewhere we find a more secular, this-worldly conception, in which the highest good is a moral world to be brought about by human efforts.[42]

Other critics charge that the doctrine of the highest good is incompatible in various ways with the pure part of Kant's ethics. How can the concern for happiness find a legitimate place in Kant's ethics, given his insistent claim that the moral law, which "is merely formal . . . [and] as a determining ground abstracts from all material" is also "the sole determining ground of the pure will" (*KpV* 5: 109)? What exactly is the relation of the highest good to the categorical imperative, from which all moral duties are supposedly derivable (cf. *Gr* 4:421)? How can it literally be our duty to "*bring forth [hervorbringen] the highest good through the freedom of the will*" (*KpV* 5:113), given that this alleged duty is not mentioned in any of the formulations of the categorical imperative (not to mention that such a gargantuan task would clearly seem to be beyond human capacities)?[43]

When interpreted as the *Endzweck* of history, that is, as an ideal moral world that "really can and ought to have its influence upon the sensible world, in order to bring it as much as possible into conformity with this idea" (*KrV* A 808/B 836), the central role of the concept of the highest good within Kant's philosophy of history is obvious and beyond dispute. The highest good functions as the *telos* of history; it is the linchpin of Kant's philosophy of history. In recent years a great deal has been written about Kant's highest good; attempts both to legitimate its role in his moral theory and, more broadly, to demonstrate the importance of Kant's philosophy of history for his ethics, are legion. My aim here is more modest: What roles do the concerns of impure ethics play in the doctrine of the highest good? How do empirical assumptions about human nature influence Kant's particular understanding of the classical concept of the *summum bonum*?

At first glance, Kant's concept of the highest good appears to be totally divorced from any anthropological assumptions. In the first *Critique*, he defines the highest good as an ideal moral world in which all agents always obey the moral law from the motive of duty. We construct this concept, he states, by abstracting "from all conditions (ends) and even all hindrances to morality [weakness or impurity (*Unlauterkeit*) of human nature]" (A 808/B 836). Importantly, his language here of subjective conditions in human nature that are hindrances to morality is virtually identical to that which we find in his later well-known remark in *MdS* that the task of moral anthropology is to investigate those "subjective conditions in human nature that hinder people or help them in *carrying out* the laws of a metaphysics of morals" (6:217; cf. "Aids and Obstacles to Morality" in chap. 1). The highest good is thus the direct opposite of impure ethics, in the sense that the former involves the complete abstraction from all empirical features of human nature that are hindrances to fulfilling the principles of pure ethics, while the latter is defined as that discipline which studies precisely these some empirical features (along with others which could serve as aids to the achievement of moral purposes).

As an ideal of reason, the concept of the highest good is constructed by abstracting from all empirical conditions. Even Kant's more concrete-sounding, this-worldly descriptions of this ideal (the "best world" achievable through our own free actions—cf. n. 40) are portraits of an ideal that lacks objective reality. Yet while lacking in objective reality, such ideals "are not therefore to be regarded as figments of the brain"; for they have "*practical* power (as regulative principles), and lay the ground for the possibility of the perfection of certain *actions*" (A 569/B 597). It is this "practical power" of the ideal of the highest good that allows it to have its influence on the sensible world. We are to use it to help regulate our efforts at transforming the natural world into a moral world.

Nevertheless, its non-empirical nature notwithstanding, there are four interrelated features of Kant's highest good that bear strong traces of anthropological concerns. Consider first a feature often referred to as totalization. The highest good in Kant's sense "totalizes" or brings together all moral actions and endeavors of individuals, so that they can be grasped together from the perspective of one final end toward which they all contribute. In "Theory and Practice," for instance, Kant asserts that there is "a need [*Bedürfnis*] for a final end set by pure reason and comprehending the totality of all ends [*das Ganze aller Zwecke*] under one principle (a world as the highest possible good through our cooperation)" (8:280 n). This need, he implies, is an ineradicably human one necessitated by our cognitive limitations. If it remains unfulfilled, we become frustrated over the seeming discontinuity of our practical endeavors; they lose meaning for us. As Yovel writes: "To the activity of human reason it is essential to aim at growing systematization and the creation of totalities; therefore, even when the absolute condition of the will is fulfilled, reason still demands the integration of all discrete acts in one ultimate object."[44] We are driven then to satisfy "our natural need, which would otherwise be a hindrance to moral resolve, to think for all our actions and omissions taken as a whole [*im Ganzen genommen*] some sort of ultimate end which can be justified by reason" (*Rel* 6:5).

Related to this particular human need for totalization in the practical sphere is what Kant calls an "inescapable limitation" of human practical reason; we are by nature outcome-oriented creatures who are inevitably driven to ask *"What then is to result from this right conduct of ours"* (*Rel* 6:5)? As he writes in a footnote in the preface to the first edition of *Religion*:

> [I]t is one of the inescapable limitations of the human being and of his practical faculty of reason (a limitation, perhaps, of all other worldly beings as well) to be concerned in every action with its result, and to seek something in it that might serve him as an end and also prove the purity of his intention—which result would indeed come last in practice [*nexu effectivo*] but first in representation and intention [*nexu finali*]. (6:7 n)

This particular limitation of human beings does make it extremely difficult for them to meet the demands of pure ethics, and Kant is flirting with danger in articulating his conception of the highest good in such a way as to make consequentialist concessions to this limitation. For according to critics from Garve on, his ethics becomes heteronomous once he allows that "in the absence of all reference to an end no determination of the will can take place in human beings at all" (*Rel* 6:4; cf. *Gemeinspruch* 8:278–89). However, Kant's nuanced position is one that does justice to the claims of both autonomous ethics and human nature; the concept of the highest good "emerges from morality and is not its foundation; it is an end which to make one's own already presupposes ethical principles" (6:5). The concept of the highest good is not the determining ground of the autonomous will, but human beings do necessarily envision it once they commit themselves to moral principles.

The human concern for happiness is a third anthropological constraint that influences Kant's doctrine of the highest good. In his reply to Garve in "Theory and Practice," he writes that "the human being is not expected to *renounce* his natural end, happiness, when the issue of obeying his duty arises; for he cannot do that, no more than any finite rational being in general can" (8:278). Here too, he is walking a tightrope between pure and impure concerns. Human beings must abstract from all considerations of happiness when the question of duty arises; they must never make considerations of happiness a condition of their obeying the moral law. And yet because they have a natural and inevitable concern for happiness (cf. *Gr* 4:415), such considerations will feature prominently in their ends or goals.

Finally, Kant's concept of the highest good, since it is an ideal of reason, is also part of the larger story concerning humanity's natural predisposition to metaphysics. Metaphysics, he states in the *Prolegomena*, "perhaps more than any other science, is placed in us by nature itself" (4:353, cf. *KrV* A 850). And in offering a conjecture as to why nature has placed this natural predisposition in us (for "everything that lies in nature must be originally intended for some useful purpose," 4:362), he explicitly states that such hypotheses belong "not to the system of metaphysics but to anthropology" (4:362). As is well known, Kant's main answer to the question "Why are human beings naturally predisposed toward metaphysics?" is framed in terms of his commitment to the primacy of the practical. When we allow this predisposition to take us back along the familiar roads of speculative metaphysics, we "find no ground to stand on." Rather, it is placed in us "in order that practical principles might find some such scope for their necessary expectation and hope and might expand to the universality which reason unavoidably requires from a moral point of view" (4:363). The highest good, we may thus conclude, is a humanly necessary ideal of reason that enables us to envision concretely the true universality involved in the moralization of the human species. It is the capstone of Kant's impure ethics.

III

Conclusion

6

SAVED BY IMPURITY?

In the preceding chapters I have examined in detail the central fields or areas of Kant's impure ethics as presented in his own published writings and related lecture materials. Because this second part of Kant's ethics is not well known and often conflicts with the standard picture of his moral philosophy, and because there is also no single textual source in which it is presented, it was necessary to quote extensively from a wide variety of texts—both to allow him to speak for himself, and to provide readers with sufficient textual data to form a coherent picture of their own as to what this second part of ethics actually looks like.

In this last chapter my aim is different; now I wish very briefly to reassess Kant's ethics by considering the added content of the second part in conjunction with the first part—that is, to reconsider Kant's ethics by viewing the pure and impure parts together. What are the chief strengths and weaknesses of Kant's ethics, once "the other member of the division of practical philosophy as a whole" (*MdS* 6:217) is re-admitted into its rightful place in his own conception of ethics? To view his project in ethics from this perspective is to evaluate it in the way in which he himself wanted readers to assess it, but no one has yet done so. The first six sections assess the strengths, while the last five evaluate the weaknesses.

Let me begin by sketching the major strengths that the addition of impure ethics brings to Kant's ethical theory.

An Empirically Informed Ethical Theory

From Hegel to Max Scheler and extending on to contemporary descendants such as Bernard Williams and many others, the major criticism of Kant's ethics has always been its alleged "empty formalism,"[1] that is, its commitment to analyzing moral judgments in terms of their logical form alone ("universalizability"), and its subsequent lack of concern for what is materially valuable in human life. Formalist moral theories, according to critics, are too isolated from the moral content of human life, and as a result such theories are insufficiently action-guiding and are severely lacking in substantive moral implications.

However, all versions of the formalist criticism of Kant's ethics have been articulated in ignorance of the second part of his ethics. Hegel, Scheler, Williams, & Co. have not studied the morally relevant aspects of Kant's work on education, anthropology, aesthetics, religion, and history. Had they done so, they would surely have found much with which to disagree. But several key components of the formalism charge no longer stand once the second half of Kant's ethics is taken into consideration.

I am not concerned here with Kantian replies to the formalism charge that are made from within the perspective of the first or pure part of ethics—for example, the familiar rejoinder that the formalism charge typically looks only at the first formulation of the categorical imperative, the so-called formula of universal law, and that later formulas such as the end in itself and the kingdom of ends *do* provide for "the determination of particular duties"[2] in ways in which the first formula (which is normally read as being merely a permissibility test for individual maxims) was never intended to do. Nor am I concerned with replies that, while made from a perspective that does explicitly admit in a certain minimal amount of empirical content, are nevertheless still not made from the perspective of the second or impure part of ethics. An example here would be the attempt to respond to what is sometimes called the "weaker" version of the formalism charge (namely, the claim that Kant's ethics does not give us "an immanent and consistent doctrine of duties"[3]—rather than, as the stronger version has it, no criterion of moral rightness at all) by pointing out that Kant's project in the *Metaphysics of Morals* is precisely that of "the special determination of duties as human duties" (*KpV* 5:8). For this aim of determining moral duties for "human beings as such" (*MdS* 6:468) by means of applying the categorical imperative to a limited amount of empirical knowledge concerning human nature in general is, as I argued earlier, still metaphysics rather than empirical ethics (see "Degrees and Kinds of Impurity" in chap. 1).

Rather, my aim at present is the more limited and manageable one of specifying ways in which the second, impure part of Kant's ethics rebuts certain aspects of Hegel's formalism charge. It should be clear by now that Kant, contrary to what many have assumed for over two hundred years, strongly endorses the claim that moral theory is inapplicable to the human situation (indeed, to any situation) without a massive infusion of relevant empirical knowledge. Indeed, I cannot think of another canonical moral philosopher, with the possible exception of Aristotle, who worked as extensively in as many different areas of empirical research on human nature and who then tried to integrate these different areas into his own ethical theory as did Kant. Given Kant's firm conviction that "[a]ll morals require [*erfordert*] knowledge of the human being" (*Menschenkunde* 25:858), repeated throughout his impure ethics lectures and writings, how does his impure ethics overturn the formalism charge? As I see it, in the following four ways.

1. *Moral education.* As I have shown (chap. 2), Kant clearly acknowledge that human beings must be educated slowly into morality. Human beings on his view are not ready made moral agents who magically pick up abstract moral rules and conscientiously follow them. Kant thus agrees with Hegel's claim that "education [*Pädagogik*] is the art of making human beings ethical [*sittlich*]: it considers the human being as a natural being and shows him the way to be reborn, how to transform his first nature into a second, spiritual nature, so that this spirituality becomes a *habit* [*Gewohnheit*] in him"[4] (cf. "Education as Impure Ethics" in chap. 2).

2. *Institutional supports.* Kant also agrees with Hegel and other defenders of *Sittlichkeit* that human beings throughout their lives need a variety of well-functioning institutional supports in order to achieve moral community. The state plays a necessary preparatory role in the development of morality through the inculcation of correct behavior patterns and customs. Granted, Kant (like Fichte) is less willing to completely identify externally good *Sitten* with moral virtue than is Aristotle or Hegel. As noted earlier (see "External Progress and Internal Progress" in chap. 5), Kant insists that we must always acknowledge a necessary conceptual space between the state, however just its laws, and the moral virtue of its citizens. External conformity to law should not be identified with inner moral disposition. Kant would thus be much more skeptical than Hegel as to whether an individual only becomes morally good "by being the citizen of a good state."[5] Ironically, Kant appears to recognize a wider variety of necessary institutional supports for human morality than does Hegel (e.g., not only the state, but also the arts and sciences, culture generally, as well as the church). At the same time, he also holds that the connection between these supports and a correct moral disposition is weaker. On Kant's view (but not on Hegel's) citizens of good states (like honest grocers) are not necessarily morally virtuous people (see *Gr* 4:397). Still, there is much more agreement here than most defenders as well as critics of Kant have realized.

3. *Judgment.* Like Hegel and other anti-formalists, Kant also recognizes the importance of experientially honed judgment skills in moving from abstract principles to individual cases.[6] As he stresses in the introduction to the *Menschenkunde*, "nothing is more laughable than when one shows no power of discrimination [*judicium discretivum*] and does not see what is fitting for the circumstances" (25:853). And as I stressed in my earlier explorations of the moral dimensions of his work in anthropology and education, the need to inculcate moral judgment skills in human moral agents is a primary aim in both of these areas of impure ethics. In the anthropology lectures, the chief rationale for the fundamental emphasis on *Weltkenntnis* is to provide human beings with the relevant background knowledge of their own empirical situation that is necessary for informed moral judgment (cf. "A Propaedeutic to the Moral Life" in chap. 1; "*Weltkenntnis*" in chap. 3). In the works on moral education, the goal of providing "general instruction (a method) as to how to proceed in judging" (*MdS* 6:411) clearly looms large (cf. "Didactics, Ascetics, Casuistry, Judgment," in chap. 2).

4. *An "ought" that will become an "is."* Finally, Hegel's criticism of what he perceives as the impotence of Kant's moral "ought" ("what *ought* to be, in fact also *is*, and what only *ought* to be without actually *being*, has no truth")[7] is also

rebutted by Kant's impure ethics. As I have shown, a primary aim of the second part of his ethics is to effect an *Übergang* from nature to freedom in order to realize the kingdom of God on earth. The explicit gradualism of this moralization process, which is itself dictated by key changes in the empirical circumstances of human life, indicates not moral impotence but rather ideals that are empirically informed. Kantian moral ideals are not cut off from the world to which they are to be applied. Rather, they obligate human agents to first understand the world around them before seeking to moralize it.

None of this is meant to obscure the obvious fact that a radical particularist who holds that universal principles have no place at all within ethical thinking will not be appeased by Kant's impure ethics. For the aim of impure ethics is not to think ethically without principles but rather to find ways (ways based on objective empirical research into human nature) to make these principles efficacious in human life. Nor is it to suggest that if Hegel had only read the second part of Kant's ethics, he would not have bothered to develop his own competing account of *Sittlichkeit*.[8] But I do hope to have shown that more moderate anti-formalists who seek a better fit between the abstractions of theory and the contingencies of human life will find that Kant's two-tiered approach has much to recommend itself.

For the past two centuries, moral theorists sympathetic to Kant have eschewed empirical research as not being fundamentally relevant to their work. But as we have seen, ethics for Kant was never intended to be exhausted by pure inquiries—pure ethics constitutes only the first step; a second step must follow quickly after it if ethics is to be more than "empty exhortations" (*Menschenkunde* 25:858; cf. *Moralphilosophie Collins* 27:244). Kant is not an enemy but rather a strong supporter of those who hold that theories of ethics must be integrated judiciously with accurate information about human nature if these theories are to be of any use to us.

However, in moving Kant's ethics a bit closer to naturalistic currents, we must also be careful. Kant remains a stern opponent of all vulgar naturalisms in ethics, namely, those holding that moral norms themselves are to be justified by appeal to contingent, empirical facts about human nature. A merely empirical doctrine of morals "may be beautiful but unfortunately it has no brain" (*MdS* 6:230)—that is, it is unable to justify the norms it picks out in a satisfactory manner. The clear appeal to facts about human nature in Kant's impure ethics serves multiple functions, but justifying fundamental moral norms is not one of them. The appeal to human nature is to be made after rather than before basic moral principles are located and established (cf. *Gr* 4:392; "Tracking Kant's Impure Ethics" in chap. 1). An empirically informed theory is not an empirically determined theory.

A More Useful Ethical Theory

An empirically informed ethical theory is a more useful ethical theory, for several reasons. Once theorists acquire relevant knowledge about the kinds of moral subjects to which their theories are to be applied, application problems will sharply diminish. How do the moral subjects in question[9] best learn about moral distinctions and principles, and at what age of emotional and cognitive development should such issues be introduced? What are the requisite judgment skills and virtues needed by such subjects, and how are they best inculcated? What biological and psychological properties do members of this species have that are likely to make adherence to moral principles difficult or easy? What species-specific strategies are best suited to meet these challenges? Which cultural, political, legal, and religious institutions will best foster moral development for the subjects in question, and how do these institutions themselves need to be changed in order to better promote moral growth? As we have seen, these are among the central questions that concern Kant in his impure ethics. And accurate answers to them will greatly facilitate and improve the application of moral theory to human life.

The kind of useful moral theory under discussion at present is substantially different from the clichéd account of an abstract, remote, top-down model of a universal, deductive decision procedure with which Kant's ethics has often been saddled.[10] But such an account, influential though it may be, is a distortion of Kant's intentions. At the same time, unlike many recent rejections of traditional ethical theory, Kant's own attempt to construct a useful moral theory does not cave in to relativism. By holding on to non-empirical principles, it presents us with a theory still powerful enough to critique existing practices and institutional arrangements, but flexible enough to recognize that differently situated moral subjects present different application problems.

However, if what is meant by a "useful" moral theory is one that enables us to definitively identify morally good and morally bad agents, then we had best look elsewhere. For Kant's conviction that "the real morality of actions . . . even that of our own conduct, remains entirely hidden from us" (*KrV* A 551/B 579 n) rules out this sort of "usefulness" for ethical theory. At the same time, Kant's radical skepticism concerning our ability to know inner moral motives comes not from the second but rather from the first part of his ethics. Moral character is not to be equated with empirical character.

Recognition of Human Dependence

The two chief tasks of empirical ethics as conceived by Kant are first, to locate species-specific obstacles and advantages faced by human beings in the carrying out of a priori moral principles; and second, to construct relevant strategies for coping with these obstacles and advantages. Kant is often accused of holding that the human being somehow springs into the world as a free-floating, autonomous moral agent, "free, independent, lonely, powerful, rational, responsible, brave, the hero of so many novels and books of moral philosophy."[11] But this timeworn criticism also has been made without taking into account the second part of his ethics. One of the key messages of Kant's impure ethics is that human beings must be educated slowly into morality, precisely because they are radically dependent creatures:

The human being must first develop his predispositions toward the good. Providence has not placed them already finished in him; they are mere predispositions and without the distinction of morality. . . . That is why education is the greatest and most difficult problem that can be given to the human being. (*Päd* 9:446)

Human beings on Kant's view are creatures who are not only dependent but also interdependent. Even as adults, they need each other in order to develop and realize their moral capacities. Human morality as Kant understands it is a profoundly social phenomenon that necessarily develops in and through culture, society, and well-functioning political institutions.

In short, this third strength can be summarized by saying that the addition of impure ethics to Kant's ethical theory provides the theory with a much more realistic and accurate account of the moral subjects to which the theory is to be applied: human beings.

Recognition of Institutional and Communitarian Aspects of Human Morality

Related to the previous remarks concerning human dependence and interdependence as well as to the opening discussion of formalism is Kant's explicit recognition, within the second part of his ethics, that human beings are creatures who require extensive institutional support and guidance in order for their moral predispositions to develop properly. Additionally, we find a strong emphasis on building moral community; our human vocation morally obligates us to enter into a moral community in which each of us endeavors to the best of our abilities "to further the ends of others" (*Gr* 4:430) and to promote "the highest good as a good common to all [*als ein gemeinschaftliches Gut*]" (*Rel* 6:97).

Kant is often portrayed as an extreme moral individualist, one who holds that each moral agent is an end in itself, a discrete individual owed respect for its autonomy, an autonomy that is safeguarded by inviolable rights. Such an individualism, it is alleged, views persons as atomistic, and cannot readily accommodate larger social units such as the family which transcend mere atomism. Nor can it account for the supposedly social nature of the self.

However, as we have seen, this portrayal of Kant is very wide of the mark once his impure ethics is brought into the picture. Kant does of course proclaim that "the human being and in general every rational being [*jedes vernünftige Wesen*] *exists* as an end in itself" (*Gr* 4:428), but as the language here indicates, this claim is presented in the first or pure part of his ethical theory, where he is concerned with rational beings in general rather than with human beings. When he narrows his focus and turns specifically to human nature and morality in the second part of his ethics, numerous species-specific features of human beings are stressed—features that in turn call into play the multiple roles of educational, civic, legal, artistic, scientific, and religious institutions in forming and shaping human moral character.

Certainly Kant is not a Hegelian "institutionalist" in ethics, if by this is meant the strong claim that moral norms are themselves defined in terms of, or exist only in the presence of, social institutions.[12] But social relations and institutions do play a much stronger role in his ethics than many readers have realized. As concerns the second part of his ethics, we can accurately call Kant an institutionalist in the weaker sense that on his view, human morality can only develop properly within an extensive web of social institutions. Similarly, Kant is clearly not a "communitarian" in the strong sense, insofar as he denies that individual moral agents are themselves constituted and defined by the practices and institutions of the particular communities in which they happen to live, and insofar as he denies that communal and public goods always outweigh individual rights.[13] But contrary to the received account, Kant certainly does not deny that human moral development takes place only within communal relationships. Even the most casual acquaintance with only a single field or part of his impure ethics reveals his recognition of the communal nature of human morality.

An additional positive feature of the institutional side of Kant's ethics bears repeating here. Critics of Kant's impure ethics such as Reinhard Brandt[14] are often dismayed to find that the categorical imperative is seldom treated explicitly in this part of his philosophy, and they conclude that the second part of Kant's ethics is therefore less genuinely Kantian and less philosophically important than the first. But on my view, the proper inference to make is rather that we have been laboring under a false picture of what Kant's overall system of practical philosophy is all about. Kant's ethics is about much, much more than the categorical imperative. Willing universalizable maxims definitely remains at the center of his conception of pure ethics, but in the second part of his ethical theory this theme is explored not as an abstract principle by means of which all rational beings are to scrutinize their maxims, but rather as a fundamental attitude that human beings can only acquire slowly through extensive education and prolonged participation in requisite cultural practices that produce analogous states of mind (e.g., art and science). The institutional dimension of Kant's impure ethics supports this effort to cultivate in human beings the fundamental attitude of willing and acting on universalizable maxims in two ways: first, through its analyses of the various ways in which different institutions are best likely to promote its development; second, through its critique of the same institutions, showing how they themselves need to change if we are truly to bring about a "community of the peoples of the earth" in which "a violation of rights in *one* part of the world is felt *everywhere*" (*Frieden* 8:360).

A More Contiguous History
of Practical Philosophy

Once Kant's impure ethics is restored to its rightful place within his practical philosophy, many of the alleged chasms readers profess to find between Kant and post-Kantian German practical philosophy sharply diminish. Indeed, several cardinal features of the latter are revealed to have odd parallels within Kant's impure ethics. Prominent examples here include Fichte's faith in a moral world order to be created and sustained by human efforts, Hegel's vision of history as the realization of freedom in the world, and Feuerbach's (as well as the early Marx's) understanding of human beings as "species-beings" (*Gattungswesen*)— namely, creatures with the special capacity to think of themselves as members of a species having certain general and perfectible predispositions common to all, predispositions which are to be developed through history and cultural transformation. Even that most extravagant of post-Kantian idealist assumptions, the rejection of things in themselves, is perhaps foreshadowed in Kant's attempt to build a bridge between the realms of nature and freedom (cf. *KU* 5:196 and "Nature and Freedom" in chap. 1). Constructing a bridge between two different domains does not demolish the differences between them, but once a crossing is possible the differences do diminish. The kind of bridge Kant seeks to construct is one that will enable us to conceive of nature (albeit in a way that "does not reach knowledge either theoretically or practically") as being harmonizable with our own moral purposes (cf. *KU* 5:176).

In pointing to parallels between the empirical part of Kant's practical philosophy and developments within post-Kantian German practical philosophy, I do not mean to assert a direct causal relationship between the two. To the best of my knowledge, Fichte, Hegel, Feuerbach, and Marx were not intimately acquainted with Kant's impure ethics—they certainly do not explicitly refer readers to Kantian texts in presenting the doctrines just mentioned. And Kant's own opposition to Fichte's and others' attempts to complete and perfect his own system of philosophy is a matter of public record (see, e.g., Kant's repudiation of Fichte, first published in the *Allgemeine Literatur-Zeitung*, August 29, 1799, reprinted in 12:370–71). Still, it is evident that many of the alleged fundamental differences between Kant's practical philosophy and that of the post-Kantian German idealist tradition diminish once we include the empirical part of ethics within his practical philosophy. Fichte's insistence that "*Kant* has not been understood"[15] contains more than a grain of truth.

Proper inclusion of Kant's impure ethics within his system of practical philosophy also enables us to see more continuity between his work in ethics and that of the major moral philosophers who precede him, nearly all of whom held that moral philosophy correctly construed necessitates close attention to human nature. Kant is often held to have initiated into philosophy an unwelcome "sharp separation" between ethics and the empirical study of human nature,[16] but we know now that this was not in fact his intention. Kant too encourages moral philosophers to undertake "a cautious observation of human life,"[17] though in doing so he of course also admonishes them to let go of the pipe dream of an inductive justification of moral norms pieced together from fragmentary empirical data.

Stressing the inclusion of Kant's impure ethics within his practical philosophy also changes the relationship between his ethics and that of nineteenth and twentieth century English-language moral philosophy. Although Kant's influence on the latter has been and continues to be amazingly strong, it is also true that the most significant English-language moral philosophers who have emphasized the importance of empirical studies of human nature for ethics during the time period in question have not been Kantians. However, this is merely another indication of the large gap between much of what passes for "Kantian" ethics and Kant's own approach to ethics. Given the strong influence that Kant's ethics continues to exert on present-day ethical discussion, one might reasonably hope that correcting the false accounts of his ethics that many friends as well as foes continue to harbor could even change the way people think about the relationship between ethical theory and empirical studies of human beings. Kant cannot be included among those more gung-ho naturalists in ethics who seek to ground moral norms in nature, but he should definitely be included among those philosophers who believe that a wide variety of historical, cultural, anthropological, and psychological forces are clearly relevant to a critical understanding of human morality, and that such factors must therefore be taken into account by any ethical theory that is applied to human beings.

In sum, inclusion of Kant's impure ethics within his own system of practical philosophy enables us to see his efforts in this area as being more contiguous with much of what comes before as well as after him in the history of ethics. The oft-cited conflict between idealism and naturalism in modern and late-modern European philosophy has been overplayed.[18] Once Kant's empirical ethics is restored to its rightful place within his practical philosophy, we find a stronger current of naturalism within his ethical theory than has been previously acknowledged: a current that in turn nurtures the more earth-bound forms of idealism that follow Kant.

Next, the central remaining weaknesses of Kant's ethics, once the pure and impure parts are considered together.

Incompleteness

Even when one casts the net as widely as I have done in this study, it is impossible to come away from Kant's impure ethics without sensing its fragmentary and incomplete nature. The unfinished state of this part of Kant's philosophy makes the job of assessing his ethics much more difficult, but it also constitutes a major weakness in and of itself.

To be sure, Kant himself nowhere claims to have systematically pursued the second part of ethics—indeed, his own rationalist bias against the possibility of systematically classifying empirical data ("any *empirical division* is merely fragmentary," *MdS* 6:284; cf. 6:205) commits him to the view that a complete empirical science of *anything* is impossible. Also, as noted earlier (see "Anthropology and Ethics" in chap. 3), even if one grants Kant his assumption concerning the necessarily fragmentary nature of empirical data, it is evident that he did not place the project of pursuing a detailed empirical ethics at the top of his own research agenda. Although he asserts repeatedly that a second, empirical part of ethics must be developed in order to apply the first, non-empirical part to the human situation, as a philosopher he devotes the bulk of his energies to examining foundational issues in pure rather than impure pursuits. This becomes evident when we remind ourselves of the textual sources for the second part of Kant's ethics. Much of his impure ethics is to be found in lecture materials edited by former students (e.g., the *Physical Geography* and *Pedagogy* lectures of Rink), lecture materials published posthumously by auditors and students of his classes (e.g., the anthropology lectures in volume 25 of the Academy Edition), or works which, while written and published by Kant himself, address themes and issues in empirical ethics only tangentially rather than fundamentally (e.g., the *Critique of Judgment* and *Reason within the Boundaries of Mere Reason*). Although the general contours of the second part of Kant's practical philosophy can be accurately sketched once one re-examines these and other relevant texts, the fragmentary and incomplete nature of the final product is impossible to ignore.

Granted, there is a refreshing humility in Kant's own cautiousness concerning the difficulty of the subject of anthropology and social science generally. We find here little of the methodological arrogance of later social theorists who asserted (and who often succeeded in convincing governments and granting agencies) both that their work deserved to be treated as seriously as natural science, and that (if given sufficient research funds) they would soon be able to permanently solve a host of social ills. Kant has good reasons for avoiding an overly systematic and reductionistic study of human nature.[19] But even when we grant him his arguments here, it remains the case that the second part of his ethics is radically incomplete. He does not provide readers with anything close to a comprehensive statement concerning the specific "subjective conditions in human nature that hinder people or help them in *carrying out* the laws of a metaphysics of morals" (*MdS* 6:217). As a result, his laudable aim of making practical philosophy more than "merely speculative" (*Moralphilosophie Collins* 27:244) by bringing the insights of anthropology to bear on it is not fully achieved.

Lack of Empirical Detail

The primary aim of impure ethics is to make morality efficacious in human life. To achieve this aim, we need to find out what human nature is like, how cultural and institutional practices influence people, and so on. However, in his writings on impure ethics Kant's most energetic and prevalent remarks concern the moral destiny of the human species *as a whole*. Because these remarks themselves are driven by a strong teleological assumption[20] (or what Kant calls a "guiding thread of reason," (*Idee* 8:18, cf. 17), they in fact contain much that is a priori and non-empirical—pure rather than impure. For an author who has a declared interest in developing the discipline of "*philosophia moralis applicata*, moral anthropology, to which the empirical principles belong" (*Moral Mrongovius II* 29:599), Kant's impure ethics is often surprisingly non-empirical. His dual commitment both to approaching human morality at the species level and to understanding this species in terms of an a priori assumption means that much of his applied ethics lacks the requisite empirical detail.

As we have seen, Kant is more than willing to issue occasional normative moral judgments about different subgroups within the human species (e.g., women, blacks). However, when he does so, the aim of making morality efficacious in human life seems to retreat into the background (if not disappear entirely). We find, that is, no sustained analyses of the different obstacles to morality that various subgroups within the species face, and hence no strategies for dealing with them. So here a different lack of empirical detail problem emerges: Kant's applied ethics unfortunately has almost nothing to say concerning the specific obstacles and aids to morality that different subgroups within the human species encounter.

At the more radically contingent level of individual moral deliberation and choice, the situation is somewhat better. Here Kant's impure ethics does offer much more by way of both analysis and prescriptive advice (see "Didactics, Ascetics, Casuistry, Judgment" in chap. 2). Although his work on this topic is scattered among several different texts and not systematically developed, it is clear that the project of developing strategies of moral education for the development of practical judgment skills within individual human moral agents was quite important to Kant. And again, once we examine these texts, it becomes evident that his considered view is not in fact that "judgment is a particular talent that cannot be taught at all, but only practiced" (*KrV* A 133/B 172). Successful moral educators can do much to inculcate practical judgment skills in their students.

Universality and Prejudice

There is a genuine tension in Kant's writings between the strong universalist, inclusivist message found at the core of his ethics and claims made in a variety of works that certain groups of human beings are "incapable of culture" (Native Americans, blacks) and that others are "naturally" inferior (women). I have argued (see "'The Whole Human Race': Kant and Moral Universality" in chap. 3) that the former pole of this tension connects directly to the defining features of his ethics and that the latter is the result of prejudices—prejudices which are not unique to Kant but are literally part of the fabric of his time and place. Kant's explicit and repeated assertions concerning the unity of the human family, the spreading of moral progress over all peoples of the earth, and the perfection of the species rather than of individuals or subgroups within the species logically commit him to the view that the ultimate litmus test for moral progress is whether or not human beings have succeeded in constructing a global ethical order in which *all* individuals are treated as ends in themselves. He is logically committed to this position even though many of his personal remarks do contradict it.

As for the numerous prejudicial statements in his practical philosophy, certainly they should not be hidden or rationalized away. Their presence constitutes a central weakness of Kant's ethics. But neither should they be inflated into something they are not. The prejudices are not centrally connected to the defining features of his theory of human moral development; and it is the theory on which we should focus.

However, a further aspect of the "lack of empirical detail" weakness also resurfaces here. How exactly is the "spreading" of progress "over all peoples of the earth" (*Streit* 7:89) supposed to occur? For example, how should people in rich countries act toward people in poor countries, in order (hopefully) to expedite this spreading? As noted earlier (see "'The Spreading over All Peoples of the Earth'" in chap. 3), Kant's language here clearly commits him to a brand of western-Eurocentric gradualism. His view is that progress always begins in the Occident, and works its way outward from there. And as I showed in my examination of Kant's views concerning how this progress is to be achieved (see "The Means of Progress" in chap. 5), he is also extremely fond of Smithian invisible hand explanations. The quality of life for human beings will improve not so much because of any intentional efforts of individuals or groups to make things better for all but rather as an unintended result of the acts of selfish individuals who are only trying to better their own situations. Similarly, Kant's faith in the *Handelsgeist* (spirit of trade) marks him as a proto-proponent of trickle-down economics; the growth of the free market and of international trade, though stimulated largely by wealthy corporations, will eventually benefit everyone.

But this is definitely not the whole story. Again each person also "must act as if everything depended on him" (*Rel* 6:101)—we are not to sit by passively while the invisible hand stimulates economic growth, a growth which itself is a necessary prerequisite for the spreading of moral progress. And in order to agree positively rather than merely negatively with the formula of the end in itself, "each person [*jedermann*] must also strive, as far as he can, to promote the ends of others" (*Gr* 4:430). But which others? As is well known, no "detailed set of instructions for the allocation of beneficence by Kantians"[21] is possible. Still, when we read the qualification "as far as he can" (cf. *Anfang* 8:123) in light of both Kant's analysis of the historical development of peoples and his explicit commitment to moral "spreading," it is clear that the general duty of beneficence implies a substantial obligation on the part of rich countries to promote the development of poor countries. For the former have progressed through the necessary preparatory stages toward moralization while the latter have not, and the requisite spreading can only occur when all groups have achieved a sufficient quality of life. So while we are given no explicit policy imperatives concerning amounts of foreign aid[22] and no ranking procedures telling us which undeveloped nations we are obligated to help, a definite duty of aid on the part of developed countries toward undeveloped can be gleaned from Kant's impure ethics.

Universality and Cultural Location

> That every practice and sentiment is barbarous which is not according to the usages of modern Europe, seems to be a fundamental maxim with many of our critics and philosophers.
> James Beattie, *An Enquiry on the Nature and Immutability of Truth, in Opposition to Sophistry and Skepticism* (1770)

Any human being who espouses a universalist moral vision is necessarily faced with the dilemma of articulating this vision from within his or her own particular cultural location. It appears that there is no way to articulate this vision in a detailed manner in such a way that the less-than-universal attitudes, conventions, and traditions of one's own culture are totally absent from what is being described. The mere fact that the vision is articulated in, say, late eighteenth century German rather than late twentieth century American English will necessarily affect the content of what is articulated. The style of language used by a theorist also emits innumerable clues to observant readers concerning the theorist's cultural location. Similarly, the specific illustrations employed to help explain abstract principles will often contain further cultural clues. Strictly speaking, the tools that we use to articulate our thoughts are not up to the job when we try to defend universal moral ideals.[23] Any detailed human formulation of such ideals seems to necessarily involve cultural conventions and traditions that are themselves less than universal.[24]

Often, of course, we are not even aware of all of the different ways in which our own attempted articulation of a universal ideal fails to escape its local cultural encodings. Kant is perhaps an extreme case in point. Other critics have pointed to ways in which local cultural assumptions manage to work their way into the first part of his ethics,[25] but when we turn to the second part of his ethics the situation goes from bad to worse. The "*one* (true) *religion*" whose true goal is simply "good life conduct" (*Rel* 6:107, 175) somehow winds up looking very much like an Enlightenment philosopher's version of Protestant Christianity (cf. "The Church as Moral Community" in chap. 4). Similarly, Kant appears constitutionally unable to detect the presence of culture among non-western European peoples when he does not find social practices and institutions that explicitly match those with which he is already familiar (cf. "Culture" in chap. 3).

A related issue concerns the homogenization of culture (and the consequent destruction of traditional cultures) that many critics feel is entailed by Kant's vision of a progress whose end-point is the moralization of the species. Kant's remark that "the world would not lose anything" if Tahiti "died out [*unterging*]" (*Refl* 1500, 15:785; cf. *Gr* 4:423) does not exactly encourage readers to think that he valued traditional cultures. At the same time, his objections to a "melting together [*Zusammenschmelzung*] of states" (*Frieden* 8:367) do imply reservations toward the global mega-culture model of a faceless McWorld.

Kant's failure to speak more directly and clearly about these issues constitutes a further weakness in his practical anthropology. However, in principle there is no necessary conflict between the dual commitments to universal moral values and particular, local cultural traditions. Indeed, a Kantian argument (albeit one that Kant himself did not explicitly make) can be made for the necessity of precisely this dual commitment. Just as human beings are the particular kind of rational creatures who stand in need of visible, tangible symbols of abstract moral concepts in order to effectively grasp them, so too do human beings in different times and places require distinct cultural practices in order to effectively articulate their own thoughts and ideals. We do not need a complete causal story (indeed, we need not accept any causal story) of cultural production in order to grant the obvious fact that different human experiences (or more specifically, the imaginative reflections on these experiences that lead to the creation of cultural artifacts) will give rise to distinct cultural manifestations. It is not realistic or desirable (indeed, not possible) for everyone everywhere to share a single culture, for the simple reason that human experiences and reflections about these experiences are never completely uniform. Certain local cultural practices may conflict with universal moral standards (e.g., female circumcision and genital mutilation); and in cases where there is a genuine conflict between local culture and universal morality the cultural practice should be rejected on moral grounds. But most local customs, manners, and conventions do not conflict with universal moral standards; and in these cases there are no overriding moral grounds on which to criticize them. In sum, moral universalists can embrace cultural diversity, and there is good reason to think that they must embrace it.

Granted, many traditional cultures have disappeared, and more definitely will disappear in the future.[26] But those concerned with causal explanations here would be advised to examine forces stronger than Kant's philosophy. At the same time, new customs, conventions, and manners will also arise among different social groups in the future. The total *Zusammenschmelzung* of human cultures is not going to happen.

Internal Coherence

Finally, there are three different internal coherence problems in Kant's practical philosophy that become more noticeable once one focuses in on his practical anthropology:

Coherence of the Concept of "Empirical Ethics"

Given Kant's commitment to transcendental freedom, and given the centrality of this commitment to his own conception of morality, how can he also embrace the discipline of "empirical ethics?" Many critics (e.g., Paton and Gregor—for references and discussion, see "Nature and Freedom" in chap. 1) charge him with incoherence here, and it is odd that Kant himself does not explicitly address the issue in detail. While I believe that I have demonstrated the coherence of Kant's concept of empirical ethics in this study, it remains strange that he did not undertake a sustained articulation and defense of the "counterpart of a metaphysics of morals" (*MdS* 6:217).[27]

The Role of the Second Part

The task of pure ethics is to locate and justify the fundamental a priori principles of morality. The task of impure ethics is to determine, based on relevant empirical information, how, when, and where to apply these principles to human beings in order to make morality more efficacious in human life. This, in a nutshell, is the job of each of the two parts of Kant's system of practical philosophy. However, in some places Kant tends to overestimate the role of impure ethics, while in other texts he underestimates its role.

For an example of overestimation, consider his famous statement in the *Moralphilosophie Collins* lecture that the pure part of "ethics cannot exist without anthropology, for one must first know the subject in order to know whether he is also capable of doing what is demanded of him" (27:244). The claim that "one must first [erst] know the subject in order to know whether he is also capable of doing what is demanded of him" suggests that the pure part of ethics might stand in need of revision—or even outright rejection—if it turns out the human subject is for whatever reason *not* capable of doing what is demanded of him. But this is not Kant's considered view. Neither the prospect of revised moral principles for human beings nor that of no principles at all is something that can be legitimately expected from the second part of his ethics. A different kind of over-estimation is present in his claim that "the sources of all sciences" can be disclosed through anthropology (letter to Herz, late 1773, 10:38). This remark suggests falsely that all pure as well as impure studies are somehow grounded in empirical studies of human nature.

For an example of underestimation, consider his claim in the preface of the *Groundwork* that "the empirical part [of ethics (*Ethik*)] might be given the special name *practical anthropology*, while the rational [i.e., pure] part might properly be called *morals* [*eigentlich Moral heißen könnte*]" (4:388). Here he seems to be excluding practical anthropology from the field of moral philosophy entirely, in a manner that is not consistent with the more inclusive "counterpart" language of *MdS*. By demoting the status of impure ethics in this manner, he appears now also to be denying *any* moral role for practical anthropology. Similarly, in the introduction to the *Critique of Judgment*, he wishes to include within moral philosophy only principles "founded entirely [*gänzlich*] on the concept of freedom, to the complete exclusion of grounds taken from nature for the determination of the will" (5:173). According to this narrower conception of moral philosophy, practical anthropology is to be construed merely as a "technically practical" subfield of *theoretical* philosophy (for related discussion, see "Nature and Freedom" in chap. 1). Kant's occasional waffling on this fundamental issue of the exact role and place of the second part of practical philosophy is yet another indication that he has not thought things through sufficiently.

This World or the Next?

An unresolved tension that reverberates in many portions of Kant's impure ethics concerns the issue of whether moralization is to be hoped for only in another world and another life and only with the help of "a wisdom from above" (*Streit* 7:93), or whether it is a project that human beings need to bring about on their own in the only world and life that we know anything about (cf. "Making the World Moral: The Highest Good" in chap. 5). Just as Hegel's system generated competing left- and right-wing schools that interpreted his work in either a more secular or religious manner, so Kant's practical philosophy has also given rise to both left and right readings. The German socialist tradition (parts of which have much deeper Kantian roots than many Americans realize)[28] obviously fixated on the former pole of this tension, and most recent analytic appropriations of Kant's ethics also tend to downplay its religious side. My own view is that the otherworldly dimension of Kant's ethics is much more prominent than many of his defenders concede, and that its strong presence is a key reason for the frustration and eventual rejection of Kant's practical philosophy that we find in nineteenth century German idealist thought. At the same time, as I argued in chapter 5, we clearly do find both this-worldly and otherworldly strands in the second part of Kant's practical philosophy, and their co-presence constitutes an unresolved tension in his thought.

Conclusion

"Saved by impurity?" As far as Kant's own moral theory goes, no. The ways in which he tried to incorporate impurity into his ethics are too fraught with tension, ambiguity, and unclarity to save it. The result does not hang together well enough. Additionally, the mass of racial, ethnic, religious, and sexist prejudices that infect it are unworthy of an author who asserts that "the language of true reason is humble. All human beings are equal to one another" (*Moralphilosophie Collins* 27:462). But for those of us who are looking for models of inspiration (if not always precise emulation or imitation) in ethical theory, yes. The broader, two-tiered conception of ethics I have explicated in this study has much to recommend itself, and if philosophers after Kant had not turned their backs on his applied moral philosophy, it is probable that moral theory today would be in much better shape than is unfortunately the case. A purely a priori ethics, as Kant's critics never tire of reminding us, does not take us very far into the practical problems human beings face. On the other hand, a wholly naturalistic ethics cannot make sense of our conviction that we are free subjects who have the power of spontaneity, nor can it give us moral norms that are strong enough to enable us to critique existing conventions and practices.[29] Philosophers who are concerned to construct humanly useful ethical theories ought to take seriously Kant's insistence that the "metaphysics of morals, or *metaphysica pura*, is only the first part of morality; the second part is *philosophia moralis applicata*, moral anthropology, to which the empirical principles belong" (*Moral Mrongovius II* 29:599). This is not at all to say that the particular *philosophia moralis applicata* that we find sketched in Kant's works is a satisfactory one. It clearly is not. Rather, it remains for us today and in the future to develop a viable practical anthropology from the exploratory beginnings that he has left us.

NOTES

1. What Is Impure Ethics?

1. In his earlier work in ethics Kant is not yet committed to pursuing the project of pure ethics (committed, that is, to the view that fundamental moral principles are non-empirical). As is well known, there is a marked empiricist tone to much of his work on ethics throughout the 1760s. In his "Prize Essay" of 1763, for instance, Kant asserts at one point that "the faculty of experiencing the *good* is feeling" (2:299). And in the section on ethics in the *Nachricht* for his lectures for the winter semester 1765–66, he states: "In the doctrine of virtue I shall always [*jederzeit*] begin by considering historically and philosophically what *happens* before specifying what *ought to happen* [*was geschehen soll*]" (2:311). Although Kant mentions plans for a work on the "Metaphysical Foundations of Practical Philosophy" in a letter to Lambert on December 31, 1765 (10:57) and for a "Metaphysics of Morals" in a letter to Herder on May 9, 1768 (10:74), a clear commitment to excising all empirical factors from a pure foundation is not yet present in either of these remarks. However, such a commitment is certainly detectable by 1770, after the *Inaugural Dissertation* is complete. In the *Dissertation* Kant claims that moral concepts "are cognized not by experiencing" but "by pure understanding itself" (2:395). And in a letter to Lambert of September 2, 1770 (along with which Kant sent a copy of the *Dissertation* as well as an extremely tardy reply to some issues raised in Lambert's earlier letter of February 3, 1766, quoted in the epigraph to this chapter), he writes: "I have resolved this winter to put in order and complete my investigations of pure moral philosophy [reine moralische Weltweisheit], in which no empirical principles are to be found, the 'Metaphysics of Morals'" (10:97).

2. Kant's remarks on applied logic are inconsistent. At *Gr* 387 he argues that logic "can have no empirical part," yet at *Gr* 410 n he says that "one can, if one likes, distinguish pure moral philosophy (metaphysics) from applied (namely to human nature)—just as pure mathematics is distinguished from applied mathematics and pure logic from applied logic." In *KrV* he writes:

> Now general logic is either pure or applied logic. In the former we abstract from all conditions under which our understanding is exercised. . . . But *gen-*

eral logic is called *applied*, when it is directed to the rules of the employment of the understanding under subjective empirical conditions dealt with by psychology. Applied logic therefore has empirical principles. (A 53)

Later in the same section, Kant suggests that pure logic is to applied logic as "pure ethics, which contains only the necessary moral laws of a free will in general, stands to the doctrine of the virtues (*Tugendlehre*) proper—the doctrine which considers those laws under the hindrances of the feelings, inclinations, and passions to which human beings are more or less subject" (A 55). The sense of *Tugendlehre* invoked here is what Kant usually refers to as "applied ethics" or "moral anthropology." It is more empirical than the *Tugendlehre* that forms the second half of the later *Metaphysics of Morals* (1797). Although a minimal amount of empirical information concerning human nature in general is employed in this later work, the type of *Tugendlehre* developed in it is intended to be part of "a system of a priori knowledge from [pure] concepts alone [*aus bloßen Begriffen*] (6:216; cf. *KrV* A 850/B 878). One should therefore not expect to find Kant's applied ethics in *MdS*. Finally, in the *Lectures on Logic* edited by his student Gottlob Benjamin Jäsche in 1800, Kant is also critical of applied logic: "Applied logic actually should not be called logic. It is a psychology in which we consider how things customarily go in our thinking, not how they ought to go [*zugehen soll*]" (9:18).

3. See Richard Rorty, who begins his essay "Keeping Philosophy Pure: An Essay on Wittgenstein" by noting:

> Ever since philosophy became a self-conscious and professionalized discipline, around the time of Kant, philosophers have enjoyed explaining how different their subject is from such merely "first-intentional" matters such as science, art, and religion. Philosophers are forever claiming to have discovered methods which are presuppositionless, or perfectly rigorous, or transcendental, or at any rate *purer* than those of nonphilosophers. (Or indeed, of any philosophers save themselves and their friends and disciples.) Philosophers who betray this gnostic ideal (Kierkegaard and Dewey, for example) are often discovered not to have been "real philosophers." (In *Consequences of Pragmatism* [Minneapolis: University of Minnesota Press, 1982], p. 19)

The conviction that pure philosophies are intellectually superior to impure ones certainly does not begin with Kant. On the contrary, it goes back at least as far as Plato. But Rorty is right to single out Kant for playing a defining role in modern professional philosophy's attempt to set itself off "as a special kind of science, as knowledge *a priori*, over against all the other sciences"; Friedrich Paulsen, *The German Universities and University Study*, translated by Frank Thilly and William W. Elwang (New York: Scribner's, 1906), p. 408.

4. Johann Georg Hamann, "Metakritik über den Purismus der Vernunft" (1784), in *Vom Magus im Norden und der Verwegenheit des Geistes: Ein Hamann-Brevier*, edited by Stefan Majetschak (Munich: Deutscher Taschenbuch, 1988), p. 201.

5. This list is taken from Emil Arnoldt, *Kritische Excurse im Gebiete der Kant-Forschung* (Königsberg: Verlag von Ferd, 1894), pp. 641–50. In addition to these public lecture courses, Kant also gave occasional private lectures (e.g, during the Russian administration of the university, he lectured on military fortification and pyrotechnics to Russian officers—cf. J. W. H. Stuckenberg, *The Life of Immanuel Kant* [London: Macmillan, 1882], pp. 68–69), regular *disputoria* (supplementary seminars designed to accompany the lectures), and *repetitoria* (review sessions on points raised in the lectures). For a more recent discussion, see Werner Stark, "Kant als akademischer Lehrer," *Wolfenbüttler Studien zur Aufklärung* 16 (1988): 45–59.

6. According to Karl Vorländer, Kant was one of the very first professors to treat geography as an independent subject of instruction. Because no geography text ex-

isted at the time, Minister of Education Karl Abraham von Zedlitz expressly excused Kant from the Prussian regulation which required all university lecturers to teach from an authorized text, explaining "as is known there is not a completely suitable teaching text"; *Immanuel Kants Leben* (Leipzig: Felix Meiner, 1911), pp. 41, 43. Kant later dedicated the *Critique of Pure Reason* to Zedlitz. Parts of Kant's geography lectures (published, with Kant's approval, by his student Friedrich Theodor Rink in 1802) are relevant to his applied ethics. The first section of part 2 is entitled "Concerning Human Beings" (9:311–20), and toward the end of the introduction Kant contrasts briefly physical geography with other possible geographies including "moral geography," "political geography," "commercial geography," and "theological geography" (9:164–65, cf. 2:312, 2:9).

7. See J. A. May, *Kant's Concept of Geography and its Relation to Recent Geographical Thought* (Toronto: University of Toronto Press, 1970), p. 4.

8. *Contra* Hegel, *Phänomenologie des Geistes*, in *Theorie-Werkausgabe*, edited by Eva Moldenhauer and Karl Markus Michel (Frankfurt: Suhrkamp, 1970), 3:461; and "Über die wissenschaftlichen Behandlungsarten des Naturrechts, seine Stelle in der praktischen Philosophie und sein Verhältnis zu den positiven Rechtswissenschaften," 2:460.

9. Barbara Herman, *The Practice of Moral Judgment* (Cambridge: Harvard University Press, 1993), p. 217. See also Allen D. Rosen's discussion of formal versus material principles in *Kant's Theory of Justice* (Ithaca: Cornell University Press, 1993). "A moral principle," he notes, "is not made 'formal' by eliminating all contents or ends. It is formal if it ignores all merely 'subjective ends'" (p. 8 n. 8).

10. William A. Galston, "What is Living and Dead in Kant's Practical Philosophy?" in *Kant and Political Philosophy: The Contemporary Legacy*, edited by Ronald Beiner and William James Booth (New Haven: Yale University Press, 1992), pp. 211–12.

11. Stuckenberg, *The Life of Immanuel Kant*, p. 68. "First English-language biographer of Kant" is Stuckenberg's self-description (p. ix). He apparently overlooked Thomas De Quincy, *The Last Days of Immanuel Kant*, vol. 9 in *The Works of Thomas De Quincy* (New York: Hurd and Houghton, 1877), pp. 491–552. De Quincy's off-beat account professes to be "a short sketch of Kant's life and domestic habits, drawn from authentic records of his friends and pupils" (p. 491). Included in the author's list of intriguing domestic habits is the claim that Kant "would often ejaculate to himself, (as he used to tell us at dinner,) 'Is it possible to conceive a human being with more perfect health than myself?'" (p. 504). Compare Kant's discussion of masturbation in the *Collins* lectures (27:391). It is included in a long list of crimes against nature that are "contrary to the duty to oneself, because they go against the ends of humanity" (27:390).

12. J. N. Findlay, *Plato: The Written and Unwritten Dialogues* (New York: Humanities Press, 1974). For a critique, see M. F. Burnyeat, "The Virtues of Plato," *New York Review of Books*, September 7, 1979, pp. 56–60. For a while I harbored the hope that one might find Kant's impure ethics somewhere in his bewildering and never completed *Opus postumum*. The general aim of this work is to provide a "transition [*Übergang*] from the metaphysical foundations of natural science to physics"; letter to Garve, September 21, 1798 (12:257); letter to Kiesewetter, October 19, 1798 (12:258–59); 22:282. Toward the end of *MdS*, Kant writes: "just as a passage [*ein Überschritt*] from the metaphysics of nature is needed—one requiring its own special rules—something similar is rightly required from the metaphysics of morals" (6:468). However, to the best of my knowledge, Kant unfortunately does not discuss the question of an analogous transition from the metaphysics of morals to empirical ethics in the *Opus postumum* at all.

13. Arendt writes: "Since Kant did not write his political philosophy, the best way to find out what he thought about this matter is to turn to his 'Critique of Aesthetic Judgment' [in the *Critique of Judgment*]"; *Lectures on Kant's Political Philosophy*, edited by Ronald Beiner (Chicago: University of Chicago Press, 1982), p. 61. For an insightful critique, see Patrick Riley, "Hannah Arendt on Kant, Truth and Politics" in *Essays on Kant's Political Philosophy*, edited by Howard Lloyd Williams (Chicago: University of Chicago Press, 1992), pp. 305–23.

14. Kant stresses empirical ethics more in his lectures on ethics than he does in his published writings on ethics. Part of the explanation for this, I believe, is that philosophers tend to stress the application of theory to real-life situations more in classroom presentations than they do in formal treatises. Also, as J. B. Schneewind reminds readers in his introduction to the Cambridge Edition of Kant's *Lectures on Ethics*, edited by Peter Heath and Schneewind (New York: Cambridge University Press, 1997), "Kant's [classroom] audience consisted largely of unsophisticated boys, younger than present-day college students, usually away from their rural homes for the first time, and for the most part ill-educated" (p. xvii).

15. Søren Kierkegaard, *Concluding Unscientific Postscript*, translated by David F. Swenson and Walter Lowrie (Princeton: Princeton University Press, 1941), p. 99.

16. For a sympathetic account, which also surveys some of the critical literature, see chapter 4 of Patrick Riley, *Kant's Political Philosophy* (Totowa, NJ: Rowman and Allanheld, 1983). Also helpful is chapter 3 of Leonard Krieger, *The German Idea of Freedom* (Boston: Beacon Press, 1957).

17. See G. J. Warnock's counter-claim that "this empirical part of Ethics, whatever it is and whatever it should be called, is in any case quite secondary, nonfundamental"; "Kant and Anthropology," in *Nature and Conduct*, edited by R. S. Peters, Royal Institute of Philosophy Lectures, vol. 8 (1973–74) (London: Macmillan, 1975), p. 36. Empirical ethics is "quite secondary" in the sense that the (a priori) principles of ethics cannot be derived from it; but it is nevertheless fundamental in the sense that these same principles cannot be applied to human beings without it. Empirical ethics is "non-fundamental" only in the specific sense that it is not the source of a priori principles. On the other hand, Allen W. Wood, in "Unsociable Sociability: The Anthropological Basis of Kantian Ethics," *Philosophical Topics* 19 (1991) in my view tends to overestimate the importance of empirical ethics when he claims that Kant's ethics is "*based* [my emphasis] on a knowledge of human nature, on human psychology in a broad sense (Kant's name for it is 'anthropology')" (p. 326). Wood explores the place of anthropological considerations in Kant's ethics at greater length in *Kant's Ethical Thought* (New York: Cambridge University Press, 1999).

18. See John R. Silber, "Kant's Conception of the Highest Good as Immanent and Transcendent," *Philosophical Review* 68 (1959): 476, 480. Similarly, Allen D. Rosen notes that Kantian morality must take account of human nature, "at least to the extent of not requiring the impossible of human beings. Morality must therefore acknowledge the limits of human nature" (*Kant's Theory of Justice*, p. 66). For related discussion to which I am indebted, see Patricia Kitcher's discussion of "weak psychologism" in *Kant's Transcendental Psychology* (New York: Oxford University Press, 1990), pp. 9–10.

19. See Owen Flanagan's discussion of his "Principle of Minimal Psychological Realism" in *Varieties of Moral Personality: Ethics and Psychological Realism* (Cambridge: Harvard University Press, 1992), especially p. 340 n. 1. Flanagan too at one point observes that "Kant's moral theory is less distant in spirit than is usually thought from the great naturalistic theories" (p. 28). However, since he also holds that "the search for a general-purpose moral theory is a waste of time," his own debt to Kant is minimal at best; "Ethics Naturalized: Ethics as Human Ecology," in *Mind*

and Morals: Essays on Cognitive Science and Ethics, edited by Larry May, Marilyn Friedman, and Andy Clark (Cambridge: MIT Press, 1996), p. 36 n. 1.

20. *Contra* Bernard Williams, *Making Sense of Humanity* (New York: Cambridge University Press, 1995), p. 101. See also Samuel Scheffler, who is "convinced that the discussion of some of the central questions of moral philosophy could only benefit from a more serious attention to psychological reality"; *Human Morality* (New York: Oxford University Press, 1992), p. 8.

21. John Dewey, *Human Nature and Conduct* (New York: Henry Holt, 1922), pp. 295–96. See also Mark L. Johnson, "How Moral Psychology Changes Moral Theory," in *Mind and Morals*, pp. 49–50; and Flanagan, "Ethics Naturalized," p. 35.

22. "Impure," in the sense here intended, should not be confused with what Kant, in the *Religion*, calls "the impurity [*Unlauterkeit*] of the human heart." The latter kind of impurity refers to a lack of single-mindedness or integrity in action. An agent knows that x is morally required, but seeks out reasons other than the fact that x is morally required to be the "all-sufficient incentive" of his or her action. As Kant defines it,

> the impurity [*Unlauterkeit, impuritas, improbitas*] of the human heart consists in this, that although the maxim is indeed good in respect of its object (the intended observance of the law) and perhaps even strong enough for practice, it is not yet purely moral [*nicht rein moralisch*]; that is, it has not, as it should have, adopted the law *alone* as its *all-sufficient* incentive [*hinreichender Triebfeder*]: instead, it usually (perhaps every time) stands in need of other incentives beyond this, in determining the power of choice [*Willkür*] to do what duty demands; in other words, actions in accord with duty are not done purely from duty [*nicht rein aus Pflicht*]. (6:29–30; cf. Gr 4:397)

For discussion of this particular sense of impurity in Kant's ethics, see Stephen Engstrom, "Conditioned Autonomy," *Philosophy and Phenomenological Research* 48 (1988): 441–42, 451; and Marcia Baron, "Freedom, Frailty, and Impurity," *Inquiry* 36 (1993): 434.

23. 'Beginning' and 'later' are meant here in a logical or conceptual sense. An ethical theory that aims at universal and necessary foundational principles cannot be built from particular and contingent aspects of experience. However, temporally speaking (say, in terms of human cognitive development), the second part of ethics will actually come first. Children are not able to understand the a priori principles of the metaphysics of morals. Relevant parts of moral anthropology must serve as a propaedeutic to pure ethics in their own moral education.

24. Margaret Urban Walker, "Moral Luck and the Virtues of Impure Agency," *Metaphilosophy* 22 (1991): 17. Walker is elaborating on Bernard Williams's contention, in his essay "Moral Luck," that agency is a concept that "cannot ultimately be purified"; in *Moral Luck: Philosophical Papers 1973–80* (Cambridge: Cambridge University Press, 1981), p. 29.

25. Bernard Williams, "Evolution, Ethics, and the Representation Problem," in *Making Sense of Humanity*, p. 104. See also his earlier discussion of Kant and "the purity of morality" in *Ethics and the Limits of Philosophy* (Cambridge: Harvard University Press, 1985), pp. 195–96.

26. *Contra* Philippa Foot's assertion in "Does Moral Subjectivism Rest on a Mistake?" *Oxford Journal of Legal Studies* 15 (1995): 7.

27. Hegel, *Phänomenologie des Geistes*, 3:460.

28. "Morality's Foundation and Moral Anthropology," in *Making a Necessity of Virtue: Aristotle and Kant on Virtue* (New York: Cambridge University Press, 1997), p. 130. However, it does not follow from this that the categorical imperative "is itself

an anthropological construct" (p. 130). On Kant's view, human beings are not the only kind of finite rational being.

29. See in particular Mary Gregor, *Laws of Freedom: A Study of Kant's Method of Applying the Categorical Imperative in the "Metaphysik der Sitten"* (Oxford: Basil Blackwell, 1963). For more recent work on Kant's *Metaphysics of Morals* see *Southern Journal of Philosophy* 36, supplement 1997, edited by Nelson Potter and Mark Timmons. (Spindel Conference, 1997 Kant's *Metaphysics of Morals*.)

30. In *KrV*, for instance, Kant writes: "I should be ready to stake my all on the contention . . . that at least one of the planets which we see is inhabited" (A 825/B 853). And in *KrV* he also regards "the law of the *ladder of continuity* among creatures" as "certainly a legitimate and excellent regulative principle of reason" for the natural sciences (A 668/B 696). In his *Anthropology* lectures he imagines rational beings who "can have no thoughts they do not *utter*" (7:332), suggesting that they would necessarily have much more stringent duties of truthfulness than is the case with us. (For discussion of this latter passage, see Onora O'Neill, *Constructions of Reason: Explorations of Kant's Practical Philosophy* [New York: Cambridge University Press, 1989], p. 74.) And in a footnote to "The Idea for a Universal History" (1784), he speculates that for some of our "neighbors in the cosmos" it might be possible for each individual "to reach fully his perfection in his own life. With us it is different. Only the species can hope for this" (8:23 n.). However, in his first published book, *Universal Natural History and Theory of the Heavens* (1755), Kant proclaims confidently that "most planets are certainly inhabited [*gewiß bewohnt*], and those that are not, will be one day" (1:354). In the *Universal Natural History* he also asserts that human nature "occupies exactly the middle rung" on the ladder of being between "the most sublime classes of rational creatures," who inhabit Jupiter and Saturn, and the less intelligent ones, who live on Venus and Mercury (1:359). Indeed, the epigraph to the third part of the *Natural History* (1:349) is a passage from Alexander Pope's *Essay on Man*, which reads, in part: "He who through vast immensity can pierce . . . What varied Being peoples every star / May tell us why Heaven has made us as we are" (*Epistle* 1.23–28). Kant's conviction that there are other forms of rational life in the universe was very much an accepted part of the climate of opinion of his time. As Arthur Lovejoy notes, in his classic study *The Great Chain of Being: A Study of the History of an Idea* (Cambridge: Harvard University Press, 1936):

> through the Middle Ages and down to the late eighteenth century, many philosophers, most men of science, and, indeed, most educated men, were to accept without question—the conception of the universe as a "Great Chain of Being," composed of an immense . . . number of links ranging in hierarchical order from the meagerest kind of existents up to . . . [the] highest possible kind of creature. (p. 59)

For further discussion, see Lewis White Beck, "Extraterrestrial Intelligent Life," in *Extraterrestrials: Science and Alien Intelligence*, edited by Edward Regis Jr. (New York: Cambridge University Press, 1985), pp. 3–18; and Michael J. Crowe, *The Extraterrestrial Life Debate, 1750–1900: The Idea of a Plurality of Worlds from Kant to Lowell* (New York: Cambridge University Press, 1986), especially pp. 47–55.

31. Obviously, care needs to be exercised in citing from student or auditor transcriptions of Kant's lectures, since these texts were not written by Kant himself. Several grounds for caution are cited by Kant in his letter to Marcus Herz of October 20, 1778: "Those of my students who are most capable of grasping everything are just the ones who bother least to take explicit and verbatim notes; rather, they write down only the main points, which they can think over afterward. Those who are most thorough in note-taking are seldom capable of distinguishing the important from the unimportant" (10:242; cf. Kant's letter to Herz of August 28, 1778 at

10:240–42). But because the contours of Kant's applied ethics are often more visible in his classroom lectures than in his published writings, extensive use is made of them in this study. Still, they should be used conservatively; namely, as added support for claims made explicitly or implicitly in Kant's published works—not as independent justifications for interpretations.

32. Georg Samuel Albert Mellin, in the important entry "Anthropology" in his *Enzyklopädisches Wörterbuch der kritischen Philosophie* (1797), writes that "in practical anthropology either the human being in general [*überhaupt*] or in special circumstances and under subjective conditions is considered"; reprint ed. (Aalen: Scientia, 1970), 1:280. He describes this second part of practical anthropology further as being "practical anthropology for human beings according to their contingent characteristics and relationships. It can be called particular (special) practical anthropology or special applied morals" (p. 281). Mellin's "special applied morals," which is analogous to what I call the "subgroups within a species" project, does not fit properly within the constraints of Kant's "metaphysics of morals." However, Kant does touch on it in other writings.

33. The table of contents of Baumgarten's text is reprinted in Schneewind, introduction to Heath and Schneewind, *Lectures on Ethics*, pp. xxiv–v.

34. For discussion, see particularly "Sex/Gender," "Peoples," "Races," and "'The Whole Human Race': Kant and Moral Universality" in chapter 3.

35. For discussion, see David James, "Twenty Questions: Kant's Applied Ethics," *Southern Journal of Philosophy* 30 (1992): 67–87. For discussion of the historical and religious background, see H.-D. Kittsteiner, "Kant and Casuistry," in *Conscience and Casuistry in Early Modern Europe*, edited by Edmund Leites (New York: Cambridge University Press, 1988), pp. 185–213. See also "Didactics, Ascetics, Casuistry, Judgment" in chapter 2.

36. Paton, *The Categorical Imperative: A Study in Kant's Moral Philosophy* (London: Hutchinson, 1947; reprint, Philadelphia: University of Pennsylvania Press, 1971), p. 32. Paton also accuses Kant of using the term 'applied ethics' ambiguously: in sense 1, it allegedly refers to the derivation of duties for humans project of the *Metaphysics of Morals*; in sense 2, to the moral anthropology project of ascertaining what subjective conditions in human nature "hinder human beings or help them in carrying out the laws" of a metaphysics of morals (*MdS* 6:217). On my view (see "Aids and Obstacles to Morality" earlier in this chapter), this charge does not hold up. Sense 2 corresponds to Kant's own self-description of his project; he gives this description consistently and unambiguously in many different texts.

37. Mary J. Gregor, *Laws of Freedom*, p. 8.

38. Rosen, *Kant's Theory of Justice*, p. 6 n2.

39. Johann Friedrich Herbart, review of *Immanuel Kant über Pädagogik*, edited by Friedrich Theodor Rink, in *Göttingische gelehrte Anzeigen* 27 (February 18, 1804): 261. Herbart moved to Königsberg in 1809 to occupy the philosophy chair formerly held by Kant, but he clearly rejected his predecessor's transcendentalist assumptions.

40. Pierre Hassner, "Immanuel Kant," in *History of Political Philosophy*, edited by Leo Strauss and Joseph Cropsey, 3rd ed. (Chicago: University of Chicago Press, 1987), p. 618.

41. Kant's conception of the scientific status of chemistry perhaps changed in his final years. According to Michael Friedman, in the *Opus postumum* "Kant wrestles with the central theoretical construct of Lavoisier's new chemistry—the imponderable caloric fluid or aether—and ultimately attempts to show that it has an a priori, not merely hypothetical, status"; *Kant and the Exact Sciences* (Cambridge: Harvard University Press, 1992), p. xv; cf. pp. 264–90. Kant's attitude toward psychology is

also complex. For discussion, see Kitcher, *Kant's Transcendental Psychology*, pp. 11–14.

42. Barbara Herman, *The Practice of Moral Judgment*, pp. 77–78.

43. Samuel Scheffler, *Human Morality*, p. 25. See also my "Pervasiveness," in *Morality and Moral Theory: A Reappraisal and Reaffirmation* (New York: Oxford University Press, 1992), pp. 63–68.

44. Herman, *The Practice of Moral Judgment*, p. 77.

45. For further discussion of the issue of unity in Kant, see Susan Neiman, *The Unity of Reason: Rereading Kant* (New York: Oxford University Press, 1994).

46. This remark of Kant occurs in his introduction to the Doctrine of Virtue, where a sharp distinction is made between the two halves of *MdS* (Doctrine of Right, Doctrine of Virtue) on the ground that the first "has to do only with narrow duties" (6:411); while the second concerns both narrow and wide duties. Wide or imperfect duties are obligations to adopt certain broad ends or maxims of action (e.g., beneficence); narrow or perfect duties are obligations to perform specific actions (e.g., pay one's taxes on time). Kant then states that casuistry and methods of judging are needed only in ethics, "because of the play-room [*Spielraum*] it allows in its imperfect duties" (6:411). His thought seems to be that since there are many different ways in which could promote the general end of beneficence, informed judgment will be needed in order to determine how best to promote this end. The same supposedly cannot be said with respect to the obligation to pay one's taxes on time. However, I think something analogous to both judgment of particular cases and casuistry is needed in the *Rechtslehre* as well. As Otfried Höffe writes: "Even perfect duties are imperfect to the extent that they do not also define the way in which they are fulfilled"; "Universalistische Ethik und Urteilskraft: ein aristotelischer Blick auf Kant," *Zeitschrift für philosophische Forschung* 44 (1990): 555. Similarly, Mary Gregor notes: "If we consider judgment as the work of a court applying juridical laws in particular cases, then, since the judge must determine right according to the laws of a given country, we shall have the positive study of Law following upon *Rechtslehre*" (*Laws of Freedom*, pp. 16–17—cf. *MdS* 6:205–6, 229).

47. It is normally assumed that Kant's idea of constructing a bridge between nature and freedom is a relatively late one, which he first articulated in the *Critique of Judgment* (1790). However, as my discussion indicates, I believe that many earlier hints of it are present in (e.g.) the essays on history from the mid-eighties, the essay "Of the Different Races of Human Beings," from the mid-seventies, and in some of the anthropology and education lectures, which, while difficult to date precisely, certainly precede the third *Critique*. While I would not push claims about the unity of Kant's work as far as Susan Shell does in *The Embodiment of Reason: Kant on Spirit, Generation, and Community* (Chicago: University of Chicago Press, 1996), I do agree with her that certain discussions within Kant's later writings are at least sometimes "best understood not as a radical rejection of all that comes before, but as a solution to problems that often reveal themselves most clearly in earlier works" (p. 2).

48. Lewis White Beck, "Kant on Education," in *Essays on Kant and Hume* (New Haven: Yale University Press, 1978), pp. 197–204.

49. Kant's *Anthropologie* consists of the handbook he used for the course the last time he taught it in the winter semester of 1795–96 (7:354). A few student and auditor versions from earlier courses (e.g., Starke II and Dohna) have also been published previously. The double volume (25.1, 25.2) of the Academy Edition edited by Reinhard Brandt and Werner Stark (first published in 1997) contains seven different sets of earlier anthropology lecture notes. A forthcoming volume in the Cambridge edition of the works of Immanuel Kant, edited and translated by Allen Wood and me, with additional translations by Brian Jacobs and G. Felicitas Munzel, will contain complete English translations of the *Friedländer* and *Mrongovius* lectures, along with

selections from *Collins, Parow, Pillau,* and *Menschenkunde*; Immanuel Kant, *Lectures on Anthropology* (New York: Cambridge University Press, forthcoming).

50. A. F. M. Willich, *Elements of the Critical Philosophy* (London: T. N. Longman, 1798), pp. iii, 140. Willich's description of the second branch of anthropology, "*practical,* applied, and empirical Philosophy of Morals," — is quite in line with the perspective on the second part of Kant's ethics adopted in this study.

51. Political themes also loom large in the essays on history, and here they are treated more pragmatically and less formally than in the *Rechtslehre*. This raises the question of whether politics itself constitutes an additional field of impurity. Although I do discuss a variety of political themes in part 2 of this study (see esp. chapter 5), I approach them from within Kant's philosophy of history rather than as freestanding issues.

2. Education

1. See Otfried Höffe, who, after citing this passage, adds: "[W]e describe the job [of the counterpart of the metaphysics of morals] more appropriately as 'moral pedagogy'"; *Kategorische Rechtsprinzipien* (Frankfurt: Suhrkamp, 1995), p. 104. However, Höffe's own interest lies rather in a "moral anthropology" that "belongs to the essential existence of the metaphysics of morals itself. Not as a counterpart [*Gegenstück*] but as a section [*Teilstück*] of it; even for fundamental ethics [*Fundamentalethik*] it forms an integral element" (p. 104). In pursuing a moral anthropology that allegedly "belongs to the essential existence of the metaphysics of morals itself," Höffe is parting ways with Kant's own strictures against mixing the two parts of ethics together.

2. Emil Arnoldt, *Kritische Excurse im Gebiete der Kant-Forschung* (Konigsberg: von Ferd, 1894), p. 646.

3. Traugott Weisskopf offers a helpful summary of previous scholarly opinions of the text and Rink's editing work on pp. 212–13 of his *Immanuel Kant und die Pädagogik: Beiträge zu einer Monographie* (Zürich: Editio Academica, 1970).

4. Weisskopf, *Immanuel Kant und die Pädagogik*, p. 331. See pp. 239–313 for a detailed discussion of these three hypotheses. For the first (the ethics hypothesis), Weisskopf attempts to lay out numerous parallel passages between the later parts of *Über Pädagogik* and *Eine Vorlesung Kants über Ethik*, edited by Paul Menzer (Berlin: Pan Verlag Rolf Heise, 1924). The latter is itself a reconstruction of Kant's ethics lectures based on three different surviving student notebooks (two of which unfortunately have been missing since World War II). Menzer's book was translated into English by Louis Infield as *Lectures on Ethics* (London: Methuen, 1930). For the second (the anthropology hypothesis), Weisskopf attempts to establish parallel passages between various parts of the *Pädagogik* and the *Reflexionen zur Anthropologie*, which are contained in volume 15 of the Academy Edition. Some use is also made here of other versions of Kant's anthropology lectures, for example, Starke II and the *Menschenkunde*. For the third (the Rousseau hypothesis), Weisskopf attempts to establish parallel passages between early sections in the *Pädagogik* and a German translation of Rousseau's *Emile*. The argument for this third hypothesis is particularly strained. Since no physical record of Kant's allegedly detailed notes on Rousseau's *Emile* have been found, Weisskopf can only assert their existence. Nevertheless, there has long been widespread agreement that the early parts of the *Pädagogik* do show a strong Rousseauian influence. Kant himself refers explicitly to Rousseau four times in the text (9:442, 456, 461, 469).

5. Weisskopf, *Immanuel Kant und die Pädagogik*, p. 330. See pp. 315–30 for detailed discussion.

6. Weisskopf, *Immanuel Kant und die Pädagogik*, p. 331.

7. Arnoldt, *Kritische Excurse im Gebiete der Kant-Forschung*, p. 644.

8. It is also important to note that Kant nearly always lectured on some area of ethics and anthropology during the same semesters in which he lectured on pedagogy. Some overlap in these three sets of lectures is thus almost certainly to be expected. In winter 1776–77, the first time Kant taught pedagogy, he also taught anthropology, as well as "Allgemeine praktische Philosophie nebst Ethik." In summer 1780 he lectured on *Naturrecht* and physical geography. (Geography was normally taught in the summer semesters; anthropology in the winter. But again, these two courses form part of a whole: *Weltkenntnis*.) In winter 1783–84, moral philosophy was originally scheduled but did materialize. Kant lectured instead on natural theology. He also taught anthropology this term. And in winter 1786–87, Kant lectured on both moral philosophy and anthropology. See Weisskopf's summary of Arnoldt, *Immanuel Kant und die Pädagogik*, pp. 98–99.

9. For instance, volume 27 of the Academy Edition, which is itself confusingly subdivided into three separate books (27.1, 27.2.1, 27.2.2), contains various versions of Kant's lectures on moral philosophy. These three books appeared in 1974, 1975, and 1979. (Still more ethics lectures appear in vol. 29.) Perhaps the most significant of the recently published ethics lectures is the *Moralphilosophie Collins*, which dates from 1785, right before Kant's *Groundwork* was published (27:237–473). And again, the Academy double volume 25, edited by Reinhard Brandt and Werner Stark and first published in 1997, contains edited versions of seven different student and auditor transcriptions of Kant's anthropology lectures.

10. Beck, in *Essays on Kant and Hume* (New Haven: Yale University of Press, 1978), p. 196. For more recent assessments of both Weisskopf and Rink, see Werner Stark, "Kants Lehre von der Erziehung: Anthropologie, Pädagogik und Ethik. Bemerkungen aus Anlaß des Erscheinens des Bandes 25 von Kants gesammelten Schriften: *Vorlesungen über Anthropologie*" (typescript); and Heiner F. Klemme, ed., *Die Schule Immanuel Kants: Mit dem Text von Christian Schiffert über das Königsberger Collegium Fridericianum* (Hamburg: Felix Meiner, 1994), esp. pp. 59–60.

11. An even better wish: that Kant himself had published the *Pädagogik* earlier under his own hand—prior to, say, 1798, when he published his *Anthropologie*. Benno Erdmann, for instance, criticizes the latter as being the "laborious compilation of a seventy-four-year-old man, as he stood on the threshold of decrepitude"; *Reflexionen Kants zur Anthropologie* (Leipzig: Fues's Verlag, 1882), p. 37 (this is one reason why the student and auditor transcriptions of Kant's lectures on anthropology are so important). Clearly, by 1803 (the year Rink published *Immanuel Kant über Pädagogik*), failing health had prevented Kant from taking an active role in its publication.

12. The most influential of these creative editing jobs is Theodor Vogt's; *Über Pädagogik. Mit Kant's Biographie* (Langensalza: Hermann Beyer and Söhne, 1878). Vogt's edition of the text is followed by, among others, the two previous English translators of Kant's *Pedagogy*, Annette Churton, trans. and ed., *Kant on Education* (London: Kegan Paul, Trench, Trübner, 1899; reprint, Ann Arbor: University of Michigan Press, 1960), and Edward Franklin Buchner, trans. and ed., *The Educational Theory of Immanuel Kant* (Philadelphia: Lippincott, 1904; reprint, New York: AMS Press, 1971). Buchner's version, which I prefer, also contains extensive editorial notes, an introduction that runs to nearly one hundred pages, and a wide-ranging selection from other writings of Kant that bear on education.

13. See Hermann Holstein's remarks in the introduction to his edition; *Über Pädagogik*, 5th ed. (Bochum, Germany: Ferdinand Kamp, 1984), p. 6. Hans-Hermann Groothoff, in his edition, also states that he finds the efforts of later editors to make Kant's text more readable "unconvincing"; *Ausgewählte Schriften zur Pädagogik und ihrer Begründung*, 2nd ed. (Paderborn, Germany: Ferdinand Schöningh, 1982), p. 158. P. J. Crittenden, on the other hand, in "Kant as Educationist," *Philosophical*

Studies (Ireland) 31 (1986–87): 11–32, pronounces (without assessing) Weisskopf's criticisms of Rink's text "entirely convincing" (p. 13).

14. Paul Natorp, editor of the version of *Über Pädagogik* that appears in volume 9 of the Academy Edition of Kant's works, bases his edition on Rink's. After discussing various conjectures about Rink's text, he concludes: "In the absence of a secure basis of possible correction it seems necessary, as concerns the arrangement of the material, to print Rink's text without alterations" (9:570). I also follow Rink's 1803 text (and the later Academy version of Rink) in my own translation of Kant's *Lectures on Pedagogy*, in Immanuel Kant, *Anthropology, History, and Education*, edited by Guenter Zoeller (New York: Cambridge University Press, 2001).

15. Groothoff's edition, *Ausgewählte Schriften zur Pädagogik und ihrer Begründung*, contains all of these texts, along with short selections from Kant's *Anthropology, Critique of Judgment*, and *Religion within the Boundaries of Mere Reason*. This multi-textual approach is the best strategy to take with Kant's work on education.

16. Here we find one basic difference between Kant's pedagogics and that of the neo-Kantian Leonard Nelson (see the epigraph of this chapter). Both theorists agree in treating pedagogy as a branch of applied ethics. But for Nelson, pedagogy "is the systematic guidance of the individual toward virtue; that is, its aim is to make him capable of the fulfillment of his ethical tasks" (*Vorlesungen über die Grundlagen der Ethik*, vol. 2, *System der philosophischen Ethik und Pädagogik*, edited by Grete Hermann and Minna Specht [Göttingen: "Öffentliches Leben," 1932], p. 31). The applied side of social as opposed to individual ethics is called "politics" by Nelson, and aims at "the systematic guidance of society toward a just condition" (p. 31). In Kant's scheme, on the other hand, pedagogy does not focus primarily on the individual, but rather on the human *species* as a whole. Nelson's individual/social dichotomy is not present in Kant's own conception of applied practical philosophy. Paul Natorp, in "Philosophische Grundlegung der Pädagogik" (1905), reprinted in *Neukantianismus*, edited by Hans-Ludwig Ollig (Stuttgart: Reclam, 1982), also argues against this dichotomy: "all education is on the one hand social, on the other hand individual; but simply to consider individual education is a bare abstraction—the complete view of education is social" (p. 125).

17. In Kant's own view, reform is not enough: a revolution in education is needed. In his second public fundraising appeal on behalf of the Philanthropinum Institute in Dessau, he proclaims:

> [I]t is futile to expect this salvation [*Heil*] of the human species from a gradual improvement of the schools. They must be transformed [*umgeschaffen*] if something good is to come out of them because they are defective in their original organization, and even the teachers must acquire a new culture [*Bildung*]. Not a slow *reform* but a quick *revolution* [*eine schnelle Revolution*] can bring this about (2:449).

The Philanthropinum Institute was an experimental school founded by Johann Bernhard Basedow in 1774, a Rousseau-inspired educational theorist who turned out to be a very poor administrator. In one of the *Zusätze* to the anthropology *Nachschriften*, we are informed that "Basedow's mistake was that he drank too much Malaga"—a sweet, fortified wine originally from Málaga, Spain (25:1538, cf. 1561). Perhaps as a result, his educational experiment was short-lived, albeit highly influential. Kant used Basedow's book, *Das Methodenbüch für Väter und Mütter der Familien und Völker*, The Methodbook for fathers and mothers of families and nations (1770), as a text for his first pedagogy course in 1776, reprint ed. (Paderborn: Schöningh, 1914) and this passage is taken from a magazine article originally published on March 27, 1777. For further discussion, see "Experimentation and Revolution" later in this chapter.

18. Jean-Jacques Rousseau, *Emile or On Education*, trans. Allan Bloom (New York: Basic Books, 1979), p. 37. In summarizing *Emile* I have benefited from R. S. Peters's critical discussion, "The Paradoxes in Rousseau's *Emile*," in his *Essays on Educators* (London: Allen and Unwin, 1981). Much has been made of Kant's debt to Rousseau. Richard L. Velkley, for instance, following Dieter Henrich and others, argues that "of all external influences on Kant, Rousseau is the one having the largest effect on the mature account of the end of reason and of the internal articulation of reason into practical and theoretical employments"; *Freedom and the End of Reason: On the Moral Foundation of Kant's Critical Philosophy* (Chicago: University of Chicago Press, 1989), p. 6; see also pp. 6–8. It is unfortunate that Velkley, in pointing "to a Rousseauian core in the critical architectonic of reason" (p. 8), makes no reference at all to *Über Pädagogik*—clearly one of the most Rousseauian of all of Kant's works.

19. Rousseau, *Emile*, pp. 33–34. See also pp. 79, 107.

20. Rousseau, *Emile*, pp. 107, 79.

21. Rousseau, *Emile*, pp. 42–43. The last sentence echoes Rousseau's famous opening sentence in *The Social Contract*: "Man was born free, and he is everywhere in chains"; trans. Maurice Cranston (New York: Penguin Books, 1968), p. 49. *Emile* and *The Social Contract* were both published in 1762.

22. Rousseau's educational advice is strongly gendered. What sorts of study are appropriate to women?

> The quest for abstract and speculative truths, principles, and axioms in the sciences, for everything that tends to generalize ideas, is not within the competence of women. All their studies ought to be related to practice. . . . [A]ll the reflections of women ought to be directed to the study of men or to the pleasing kinds of knowledge that have only taste as their aim. . . . Nor do women have sufficient precision and attention to succeed at the exact sciences. (*Emile*, pp. 386–87)

As I show later (see "Sex/Gender" in chap. 3), Kant follows Rousseau on this particular point as well.

23. Rousseau, *Emile*, pp. 93–94.

24. Rousseau's "negative" plan of education is referred to frequently in various versions of the *Anthropology* lectures. See, for example, *Collins* 25:26, *Parow* 25:254, *Friedländer* 25:724, *Menschenkunde* 25:891, and Dohna, 86. This particular Rousseauian debt of Kant has long been recognized. For example, J. Lewis McIntyre, in "Kant's Theory of Education," writes: "Kant, like Rousseau, would have the first education a purely negative one, nature being allowed full play in the development of the young body; if art is to enter at all, it must be the art of 'hardening' "; *Educational Review* 16 (1898): 313–27, p. 314.

25. According to Weisskopf, Basedow's *Methodenbuch*, which Kant used as a text for his first pedagogy course in 1776, contains "page-long citations from Rousseau's *Emile*, arbitrarily trimmed and supplemented with commentary" (*Immanuel Kant und die Pädagogik*, p. 120). Some scholars believe that the strong Rousseauian flavor of the early parts of Kant's *Pädagogik* is in fact due to Kant's use of Basedow's text. For discussion, see Weisskopf, *Immanuel Kant und die Pädagogik*, pp. 168–69, 295.

26. As the name 'Philanthropinist' suggests, Basedow's group also had a more internationalist or "cosmopolitan" orientation. This goes a long way toward explaining Kant's atypically fervent endorsement of the Philanthropinist program. In his first fundraising appeal for the Dessau Philanthropinium of March 28, 1776, Kant praises Basedow for his solemn devotion "to the welfare and betterment of human beings" and the institute itself for its readiness "to spread its seeds over other countries and to immortalize its [that is, the human] species" (2:447; cf. *Friedländer* 25:722–23). Basedow himself wrote in 1775 that the goal of the institute was to

educate youths to be "citizens of our world"; "Rede für das pädagogische Philanthropinum in Dessau" (Dessau) 1775, p. 5, quoted by Michael Niedermeier in "Campe als Direktor des Dessauer Philanthropins," in *Visionäre Lebensklugheit: Joachim Heinrich Campe in seiner Zeit*, edited by Hanno Schmidt (Wiesbaden: Harrassowitz, 1996), p. 46. According to Michael Nidermeier, "the founding of the Philanthropinum marked a turning point in the history of education, culture, and literature in Germany. Here for the first time the attempt was made to develop and practice an enlightened, interdenominational, cosmopolitan, and tolerant education and culture which was tuned to the nature of children" (p. 46). But some critics also see a darker, more manipulative side here. See Katharina Rutschky's edited source book, *Schwarze Pädagogik: Quellen zur Naturgeschichte der bürgerlichen Erziehung*, 6th ed. (Berlin: Ullstein, 1993), which contains multiple selections by Basedow, Campe, Wolke, and (alas) Kant.

27. This contrast between the speciesist (or, as Kant himself would put it, "cosmopolitan," 9:447, 499) orientation of his philosophy of education and the individualist slant of other important educational theorists of his era is well stressed by Kingsley Price in his entry "History of Philosophy of Education" in *The Encyclopedia of Philosophy*, 1967 ed. Kant's strong cosmopolitanism also contrasts sharply with the nationalist bent of later German philosophers who wrote on education, such as Johann Gottlieb Fichte (1762–1814). In his *Addresses to the German Nation* (1808), edited by George Armstrong Kelly (New York: Harper and Row, 1968), Fichte elaborates at length on his vision for a "new national education of the Germans" that "will include love of the German fatherland as one of its essential elements" (pp. 130, 134).

28. See the selections in *The Portable Enlightenment Reader*, edited by Isaac Kramnick (New York: Penguin Books, 1995).

29. Gotthold Ephraim Lessing, *Die Erziehung des Menschengeschlechts*, sec. 85, in *Gesammelte Werke*, edited by Wolfgang Stammler, vol. 1 (Munich: Carl Hanser, 1959), p. 1030. Henry E. Allison, in *Lessing and the Enlightenment* (Ann Arbor: University of Michigan Press, 1966), glosses this passage as follows: "Thus, in anticipation of the Kantian ethic, Lessing finds the goal of human development in the achievement of moral autonomy" (p. 160). "Anticipating Kant" is a favorite scholarly pastime, and the list of candidates (e.g., Crusius, Rousseau, the British moralists) seems to grow longer each year. Kant was influenced by all sorts of people, but he was definitely committed to the view that the moral perfection of humanity was attainable only through education before Lessing's text was published in 1780. While it is difficult to assign a precise date to the *Pädagogik* (I believe Rink's version is a compendium that Kant wrote over a period of years), we do know that Kant's second fundraising appeal for the Philanthropinum Institute was published on March 27, 1777. At the beginning of this essay, he writes that the "salvation of the human species" can be achieved "only by education" (2:449).

30. See Groothoff, *Ausgewählte Schriften zur Pädagogik und ihrer Begründung*, p. 159. Beck, in "Kant on Education," argues that education on Kant's view is simply "a recapitulation of history; the ages of individual life correspond to the stages in the history of the world" as outlined in Kant's essays on history (p. 197). While Beck is certainly correct to emphasize interconnections between Kant's writings on history and education, his approach to Kant's theory of education seems to me to be overly reductionistic. Among other things, he overlooks the double meaning of key terms like "culture" in the education writings. Education on Kant's view does not simply "recapitulate" history. Rather, the two processes interact with one another.

31. Kant sometimes distinguishes between *Weltklugheit* and *Privatklugheit*. For instance, in the *Groundwork* the former is defined as "the skill of a human being in influencing others in order to use them for his own intentions"; the latter as "the

understanding in uniting all these intentions to his own lasting advantage" (4:416 n). However, in the more informal educational and anthropological lectures he normally speaks simply of *Klugheit* in a generic sense.

32. For instance, in his definition of moral virtue Aristotle stresses both that it is a "state of character concerned with choice" and that this choice consists in a mean that "is determined by reason [*logos*]" (*EN* 2.6 1106b36–07a1). For discussion, see my "Kant's Virtue Ethics," *Philosophy* 61 (1986): 473–89; reprinted in *Kant: Critical Assessments*, edited by Ruth F. Chadwick, vol. 3, *Kant's Moral and Political Philosophy* (London: Routledge, 1992). See also Henry E. Allison, "Kant's Concept of *Gesinnung*," in *Kant's Theory of Freedom* (New York: Cambridge University Press, 1990), pp. 136–45.

33. Here the habit side (*Gewohnheit, Angewohnheit*) of the Kantian moral Gesinnung is revealed, though it admittedly stands in tension with other anti-habit passages cited earlier.

34. Ultimately, what Kant means by the moralization of the human species is an ideal condition in which *all* human beings have acquired the disposition to choose only good ends. Thus understood, it represents a condition we can continually approach but never completely instantiate.

35. Hans Ebeling, "Die Ethik in Kants Anthropologie," epilogue to Immanuel Kant, *Anthropologie in pragmatischer Hinsicht*, edited by Wolfgang Becker (Stuttgart: Reclam, 1983), p. 378. This strong normative dimension of Kant's pedagogy and anthropology—indeed, of *all* aspects of his empirical studies of human nature— marks one obvious difference between his own conception of social science and later positivist ones.

36. The exception would be proposed educational programs whose acceptance would clearly impede rather than promote the end to be pursued. In such cases, it would not be necessary to experiment with them; they could be ruled out on a priori grounds.

37. In drawing attention to Kant's views concerning the need for revolution in education, I do not wish to deny the presence of a competing reformist strand. Both strands are present. In the *Pädagogik* lectures, for instance, he writes:

> [N]ow for the first time we are beginning to judge rightly and understand clearly what actually belongs to a good education. It is delightful to imagine that human nature might be developed better and better by means of education, and that the latter can be brought into a form appropriate for humanity. This opens to us the prospect of a future happier human species. (9:444)

This gradualist, "better and better" approach to a "future happier human species" also helps makes sense of the widespread assertion of "the inner connection between education and politics" that one finds stressed in related practical writings of the time by, for example, the Philanthropinist Campe. For discussion, see Ulrich Herrmann, "Campes Pädagogik—oder: die Erziehung und Bildung des Menschen zum Menschen *und* Bürger," in Schmidt, *Visionäre Lebensklugheit*, especially pp. 153–54. Similarly, in the conclusion of the *Menschenkunde* lectures Kant himself hints that educational and political reform are necessarily interconnected:

> "[W]hether with time a more perfect civil constitution will come about cannot be hoped for until human beings and their education have become better; this improvement appears not to be possible until government in turn becomes better. Which one will come first cannot be guessed; perhaps both will accompany each other." (25:1202)

38. Lewis White Beck, *A Commentary on Kant's Critique of Pure Reason* (Chicago: University of Chicago Press, 1960), p. 235. (See *Rel* 6:47–48, 41.) The odd combina-

tion of the phrases "strictly speaking" and "perhaps impossible" makes Beck's sentence a bit slippery. He seems to have not quite made up his mind.

39. Hans-Hermann Groothoff, *Ausgewählte Schriften zur Pädagogik und ihrer Begründung*, p. 170 n. 99.

40. As noted earlier (chap. 1 n. 46), Kant claims that the *Rechtslehre* (unlike the *Tugendlehre*) has no need of "general directions (a method) as to how one should proceed in judging" because it concerns only "narrow duties" which "must be determined strictly (precisely)" (*MdS* 6:411). The *Tugendlehre*, on the other hand, "because of the play-room [*Spielraum*] it allows in its imperfect duties, inevitably leads to questions that call upon judgment to decide how a maxim is to be applied in particular cases." (6:411). But narrow or perfect duties are also "imperfect" in the sense that they are not totally self-deploying: judgment is also needed to know how and when to apply them. To this extent, a *Methodenlehre* would seem to be appropriate for the *Rechtslehre* as well.

41. Volker Gerhardt, "Die Selbstdisziplin der Vernunft," in *Kant: Kritik der reinen Vernunft*, edited by Georg Mohr and Marcus Willaschek (Berlin: Akademie, 1998), p. 572.

42. For further discussion, see my "Go-carts of Judgment: Exemplars in Kantian Moral Education," *Archiv für Geschichte der Philosophie* 74 (1992): 303–22; and my entry "Examples in Ethics" in the *Routledge Encyclopedia of Philosophy*, 1998 ed.

43. From the Greek *akroaomai*, "to listen to," and *eromai*, "to ask, inquire."

44. Kant states at *MdS* 6:478 that with the catechestic manner of teaching "only the memory" rather than the reason of the pupil is queried. But at the beginning of his "Fragment of a Moral Catechism" a few pages later he also claims that the teacher here "queries the reason of his pupil" and tries to guide "his reason" (6:480). Kant does not faithfully adhere to the memory/reason dichotomy in his discussions of the methods of moral catechism and dialogue. Perhaps his point is simply that at the level of catechistic teaching the pupil's answers are to be written down and then committed to memory (cf. *MdS* 6:479).

45. As Mary Gregor points out in her translator's notes to *The Metaphysics of Morals, Practical Philosophy* (New York: Cambridge University Press, 1996), p. 591 n.g, Kant is somewhat inconsistent on this point too. At 6:413, only catechistics is mentioned in the "second division of ethics" under the first part of the *Methodenlehre*, whereas at 6:411 and 478 catechistics is described as being but one of several methods of teaching ethics. I take the remark at 6:413 to be a slip.

46. Kant explicitly mentions *moralische Asketik* once in the *Religion*, stating that it "must begin with the assumption of a wickedness of the will (*Willkür*) in adopting its maxims contrary to the original moral predisposition" (6:51). This is the only specific reference to moral ascetics that I have been able to find other than the discussion at the end of *MdS*.

47. See the relevant entries in Liddell and Scott's *Greek-English Lexicon*. I am not suggesting here that Kant was intentionally invoking these ancient Greek definitions in his discussion of moral ascetics. Though he did receive extensive training in Latin as a student at the Collegium Fridericianum, a training by means of which he also acquired "a respect for and an exact acquaintance with the Latin classics, which he retained into his old age . . . [he] seems to have been affected hardly at all by the spirit of Greek, which was taught exclusively by use of the New Testament"; Ernst Cassirer, *Kant's Life and Thought*, trans. James Haden (New Haven: Yale University Press, 1981), p. 15.

48. Yirmiahu Yovel, *Kant and the Philosophy of History* (Princeton: Princeton University Press, 1980), p. 144. Kant himself would presumably deny that the ancient sage had leaped to "rational perfection" by himself. Perfection was not attainable in

ancient societies, though this certainly does not rule out examples of outstanding individual achievement.

49. William K. Frankena, *Three Historical Philosophies of Education: Aristotle, Kant, Dewey* (Chicago: Scott, Foresman, 1965), p. 102. Frankena's account is the most philosophically informed discussion of Kant's philosophy of education in English with which I am familiar. See also pp. 53–54 for a brief comparison with Aristotle on this point.

50. Hannah Arendt, *Lectures on Kant's Political Philosophy* edited by Ronald Beiner (Chicago: University of Chicago Press, 1982), p. 77. See also William A. Galston, *Kant and the Problem of History* (Chicago: University of Chicago Press, 1975), pp. 231–33; Paul Stern, "The Problem of History and Temporality in Kantian Ethics," *Review of Metaphysics* 39 (1986): 535–39.

51. Emil Fackenheim, "Kant's Concept of History," *Kant-Studien* 48 (1957): 397.

52. Susan Meld Shell, *The Embodiment of Reason: Kant on Spirit, Education, and Community* (Chicago: University of Chicago Press, 1996), p. 161.

53. Beck and Frankena are both worried by this alleged contradiction. See Beck, "Kant on Education," pp. 200–201; Frankena, *Three Historical Philosophies of Education*, pp. 109–10.

54. Johann Friedrich Herbart, review of *Immanuel Kant über Pädagogik*, in *Göttingische gelehrte Anzeigen* 27 (February 18, 1804): 261. Herbart's philosophy of education was extraordinarily influential throughout the nineteenth century.

55. Beck, "Kant on Education," p. 203.

56. Galston, *Kant and the Problem of History*, p. 233. See also Harry van der Linden, *Kantian Ethics and Socialism* (Indianapolis: Hackett, 1988), p. 103.

57. I thank Allen Wood for discussion on this topic. For a related discussion to which I am indebted, see van der Linden, *Kantian Ethics and Socialism*, pp. 103–4, 122–28. For further discussion of the concept of dignity in Kant's ethics, see Thomas E. Hill Jr., *Dignity and Practical Reason in Kant's Moral Theory* (Ithaca: Cornell University Press, 1992), especially pp. 47–55.

58. To assert that a species is "immortal" (*unsterblich*) means, I take it, that the species will never become extinct. This assumption is rejected by most scientists today.

59. Kant's examples of "laws" here are merely the setting of times "for sleep, for work, for amusement." See also *Friedländer* 25:725, where he mentions "observances and customs of school and of the household." The idea is to familiarize young students to a schedule and order in life that they must follow.

60. See Daniel Statman, ed., *Moral Luck* (Albany: State University of New York Press, 1993), p. 26 n. 3. Because Kant holds both that "the inequality of the wealth of human beings comes only from accidental circumstances [*gelegentliche Umstände*]" (9:491; cf. *MdS* 6:454), and that private (though hopefully philanthropic- and cosmopolitan-motivated) experiments in education are preferable to state-regulated ones, the role of luck in education is on his view extremely large. For related discussion, see my "Response" to Bernard Williams, in *The Greeks and Us: Essays in Honor of Arthur W. H. Adkins*, edited by Robert B. Louden and Paul Schollmeier (Chicago: University of Chicago Press, 1996), pp. 55–56.

61. Nicholas Rescher, *Ethical Idealism: An Inquiry into the Nature and Function of Ideals* (Berkeley: University of California Press, 1987), p. 1.

62. Niccolò Machiavelli, *The Prince*, trans. Peter Bondanella and Mark Musa (New York: Oxford University Press, 1984), p. 20. See Aristotle, *EN* 1.2 1094a24, 6.1 1138b22, 2.7 1106b19. I thank Steve Tigner for drawing my attention to the passage from Machiavelli.

3. Anthropology

1. Emil Arnoldt, *Kritische Excurse im Gebiete der Kant-Forschung* (Königsberg: Verlag von Ferd, 1894), pp. 278–81.

2. That is, different from Ernst Platner's *Anthropologie für Ärzte und Weltweise* (Leipzig, 1772), which Herz had reviewed in the *Allgemeine deutsche Bibliothek* 20 (1773): 25–51, and to which Kant refers to earlier in the letter. In the opening section of the *Menschenkunde*, Kant states that what he means by anthropology "is not lectured on at any other academy," adding that "Platner has written a scholastic anthropology" (25:856; cf. *Mrongovius* 25:1210–11, *Friedländer* 25:472).

3. This announced aim of disclosing "the sources of all sciences, of ethics [etc.]" might seem to foreshadow Kant's famous claim that the fundamental questions of metaphysics, ethics, and religion "could all be reckoned to be anthropology" since they all "relate to" (*beziehen auf*) the question "What is the human being?" (*Jäsche Logik* 10:25; cf. letter to C. F. Stäudlin of May 4, 1793, 11:414; *KrV* B 833; *Metaphysik-Pölitz* 28:534). However, I argue later that for the most part in his anthropology lectures Kant is trying to develop a fairly straightforward empirical (rather than transcendental) anthropology.

4. Kant's use of the term *Weisheit* here is definitely intended in a moral sense, and this usage is one early hint of the moral dimension of his *Anthropology* lectures. In a related *Reflexion* he writes: "Three kinds of teaching. 1) That which makes one skilled. 2) That which makes one prudent. 3) That which makes one wise [*weise*]: scholastic, pragmatic, and moral knowledge. (Some knowledge cultivates, some civilizes, and some moralizes.) Pragmatic anthropology" (*Refl* 1482, 15:689; cf. *Menschenkunde* 25:855; *Busolt* 25:1436; *Pillau* 25:735, *Mrongovius* 25:1211). "Pragmatic" is at least sometimes used by Kant in a wide sense to refer to the entire field of the practical (skill, prudence, and morality). See Reinhard Brandt, "Einleitung," 25: xvi n. 2.

5. Benno Erdmann, *Reflexionen Kants zur Anthropologie* (Leipzig: Fues's Verlag, 1882), p. 48. Erdmann also argued that Kant first taught his anthropology course in the winter semester of 1773–74 (p. 53) rather than (as Arnoldt was to argue more convincingly in his later work) of 1772–73.

6. Arnoldt, *Kritische Excurse im Gebiete der Kant-Forschung*, p. 293; cf. pp. 292–316. Brandt is also quite critical of Erdmann's claim that the *Anthropology* lectures derive from the *Physical Geography* lectures ("Einleitung," 25:xxiii–iv).

7. Paul Schilpp, in *Kant's Pre-critical Ethics* (Evanston: Northwestern University Press, 1938), also argues that here we see early evidence of Kant's anthropological interests (p. 20).

8. Norbert Hinske, "Kants Idee der Anthropologie," in *Die Frage nach dem Menschen*, edited by Heinrich Rombach (Freiburg: Karl Alber, 1966), p. 413. Actually, Erdmann himself, in 1882, also wrote that "Baumgarten's chapter on empirical psychology in . . . [his] compendium of metaphysics was the guide" for Kant's early anthropology lectures (*Reflexionen Kants zur Anthropologie*, p. 3). For more recent analyses of the empirical psychology roots of Kant's anthropology lectures, see Reinhard Brandt, "Ausgewählte Probleme der Kantischen Anthropologie," in *Der ganze Mensch: Anthropologie und Literatur im 18. Jahrhundert*, edited by Hans-Jürgen Schings (Stuttgart: J. B. Metzler, 1994), pp. 14–21; "Beobachtungen zur Anthropologie bei Kant (und Hegel)," in *Psychologie und Anthropologie oder Philosophie des Geistes*, edited by Franz Hespie and Burkhard Tuschling (Stuttgart-Bad Cannstatt: Frommann-Holzboog, 1991), pp. 79–87; "Einleitung," 25:vi–ix.

9. Frederick P. van de Pitte, *Kant as Philosophical Anthropologist* (The Hague: Nijhoff, 1971), p. 15. A third important source is Kant's *Observations on the Feeling of the Beautiful and the Sublime* (1764). Though usually read as a pre-critical work in aesthetics, the *Observations* in fact contains a great deal of the same sort of infor-

mally-presented, empirical data concerning character types, the sexes, peoples, and human nature in general that one finds later in the various anthropology lectures. Ironically, it is precisely this anthropological character of the *Observations* that has led some readers to judge it negatively. Schiller, for instance, in a letter to Goethe on February 19, 1795, writes: "The execution [in the *Observations*] is merely anthropological, and one learns nothing in there of the final grounds of the beautiful. But as physics and natural history of the sublime and beautiful it contains much fruitful material"; quoted by Arnold Kowalewski in his introduction Dohna (60).

10. Odo Marquard, "Zur Geschichte des philosophischen Begriffs 'Anthropologie' seit dem Ende des achtzehnten Jahrhunderts" in *Collegium philosophicum* (Basel: Schwabe, 1965), pp. 212, 211. See also his entry "Anthropologie" in *Historisches Wörterbuch der Philosophie*, edited by Joachim Ritter (Basel: Schwabe, 1971), vol. 1, pp. 362–74.

11. See Werner Stark's contribution to the "Einleitung" of this volume (25:liv–cxiv) for a detailed discussion of the origin and dating of these *Anthropology* lectures.

12. See the opening section of *Mrongovius*, where he remarks that "a solid knowledge of the human being interests everyone and gives food for conversation, even [*selbst*] for women" (25:1213). Although Kant makes a point of stating that his anthropology and physical geography lectures were "attended by people of other status groups [*andere Stände*]" (*Anth* 7:122 n), it should be kept in mind that women were not allowed to study at German universities during his lifetime. At the same time, women could of course purchase copies of his lectures to read on their own. Brandt speculates that the remark about women "must stem from an editor of the lecture" rather than from Kant himself ("Einleitung," 25:xlix–l n. 2), but it would seem to me to be a very odd editorial addition.

13. Reinhold Bernhard Jachmann, *Immanuel Kant geschildert in Briefen an einen Freund* (1804), in *Immanuel Kant: Sein Leben in Darstellungen von Zeitgenossen. Die Biographien von L. E. Borowski, R. B. Jachmann, und E. A. Wasianski*, edited by Felix Groß, reprint (Darmstadt: Wissenschaftliche Buchgesellschaft, 1993), p. 118. For additional testimonials, see the section on "Documents for the Lecture on Anthropology," in Rudolf Malter "Anhang II" to *Anthropologie in pragmatischer Hinsicht*, edited by Karl Vorländer 7th ed. (Hamburg: Felix Meiner, 1980), pp. 329–33.

14. Wolfgang Becker, "Einleitung: Kants pragmatische Anthropologie," in *Anthropologie in pragmatischer Hinsicht*, edited by Becker (Stuttgart: Philipp Reclam, 1983), p. 15. In preparing this section I have also benefited from Norbert Hinske's informative discussion in "Kants Idee der Anthropologie," especially pp. 423–27.

15. Kant uses the term "*Stand*" fairly frequently in his anthropology lectures. Following Talcott Parsons's suggestion, I have rendered it as "status group," though I am not entirely happy with this choice. Parsons, in a footnote to his translation of parts of Max Weber's *Wirtschaft und Gesellschaft*, writes that the German term "*Stand*" "refers to a social group the members of which share a relatively well-defined common status. . . . [T]here is the further criterion that the members of a *Stand* have a common mode of life and usually more or less well-defined code of behavior. There is no English term which even approaches adequacy in rendering this concept"; in Max Weber, *The Theory of Economic and Social Organizations*, translated by Talcott Parsons and A. M. Henderson (New York: Oxford University Press, 1947), pp. 347–48 n. 27.

16. *Vorlesungsnachschrift Reichel*, p. 3, cited by Brandt, "Einleitung," 25:xi n. 1.

17. Schleiermacher, in his 1799 review of Kant's *Anthropology from a Pragmatic Point of View*, also complained that Kant "has wanted to present something impossible: namely that anthropology should be at once systematic and also popular"; [*Athenaeum* 2 (1799): 300–306; reprinted in Karl Vorländer, *Anthropologie in pragmatischer Hinsicht*, p. 342.

18. The dissertations in question are Volker Simmermacher, "Kants Kritik der reinen Vernunft als Grundlegung einer Anthropologia transcendentalis" (University of Heidelberg, 1951) and Monika Firla, *Untersuchungen zum Verhältnis von Anthropologie und Moralphilosophie bei Kant* (Frankfurt: Peter Lang, 1981), especially p. 45 n 113. See also Hinske, "Kants Idee der Anthropologie," p. 427, and Brandt, "Ausgewählte Probleme der Kantischen Anthropologie," pp. 16–17.

19. Volker Gerhardt, "Was ist ein vernünftiges Wesen?" *South African Journal of Philosophy* 8 (1989): 156. See also his "Vernunft und Leben: Eine Annäherung," *Deutsche Zeitschrift der Philosophie* 43 (1995): 591–609, especially p. 597. See n. 3 earlier, for one possible early hint of similar transcendental concerns in the *Anthropology* lectures.

20. Brandt, "Beobachtungen," p. 89, cf. p. 80. See also his "Ausgewählte Probleme," p. 17; "Einleitung," 25:xxii; and Marquard, "Anthropologie," pp. 365–66.

21. Kant is often quite critical of novels, although it looks as though he probably enjoyed reading them himself. For example, at one point in *Mrongovius* he even asserts that "novels and comedies are necessary for anthropology" (25:1212; cf. *Collins* 25:8). But later in the 1798 *Anthropology* he complains that "reading novels, in addition to causing many other mental discords, also has the consequence that it makes distraction [*Zerstreung*] habitual" (*Anth* 7:208). And in the *Pedagogy* lectures he advises that "all novels should be taken out of the hands of children" on the ground that they "weaken the memory" (9:473). Novels seem almost to be candidates of last resort for anthropological source material (there are few other satisfactory alternatives). Still, his own use of them for anthropological purposes seems to be genuine. Rink writes, in his 1805 biography of Kant, that in his anthropology lectures Kant's observations were sometimes "borrowed from the best English novel writers"; *Ansichten aus Immanuel Kants Leben* (Königsberg: Göbbels und Unzer, 1805), p. 46.

22. Kant's own pride in his hometown of Königsberg comes out in a revealing footnote to this sentence. Because of its geographic location as well as its political, cultural, and business activities, "a city like Königsberg on the river Pregel can well be taken as an appropriate place for broadening one's *Menschenkenntnis* as well as *Weltkenntnis*" (7:120 n).

23. Rudolf Eisler, *Wörterbuch der philosophischen Begriffe*, 4th ed. (Berlin: E. S. Mittler, 1929), 2:484, s.v. "*Pragmatisch*." See also Brandt, "Ausgewählte Probleme," p. 21; "Einleitung" 25:xiv–xv. Although it is not known whether Kant read this particular passage in Wolff, it is highly likely that he was aware of the older, well-established usage of the term "pragmatic" among German intellectuals.

24. See Brandt's discussions in "Ausgewählte Probleme," pp. 25–26; "Beobachtungen," p. 91; and "Einleitung," 25:xxiv–xxxi. He draws a skeptical conclusion regarding Kant's different ways of dividing up anthropology: "Kant is not successful in finding a satisfactory conceptual solution for the relation of the two parts of anthropology" ("Ausgewählte Probleme," p. 26). "The putting together of the two parts of the Anthropology . . . is an historical accident" ("Einleitung" 25:xxx). I believe that the general theory/application thread which links together the various attempts basically mirrors the *Elementarlehre/Methodenlehre* "conceptual solution" that we find in many of Kant's best-known works (e.g., *KrV, KpV, KU, MdS, Jäsche Logik*). See my earlier discussion of the *Elementarlehre/Methodenlehre* distinction in "Didactics, Ascetics, Casuistry, Judgment" in chapter 2.

25. Arnoldt, *Kritische Excurse im Gebiete der Kant-Forschung*, p. 351. Arnoldt then proceeds (on pp. 352–54) to lay out a complicated schema which is intended to integrate what he believes are the multiple relations between practical philosophy and empirical anthropology. Hinske in turn complains that "the violence and inadequacy" of Arnoldt's effort "is not to be overlooked" and is "suitable for making the

incoherence of the Kantian executions visible" ("Kants Idee der Anthropologie," p. 426 n. 30).

26. Annemarie Pieper, "Ethik als Verhältnis von Moralphilosophie und Anthropologie: Kants Entwurf einer Transzendentalpragmatik und ihre Transformation durch Apel," *Kant-Studien* 69 (1978): 318. Pieper's further assertion that Kant's pragmatic anthropology serves a "mediating function" that is "analogous to the function of the 'schema' in the *Critique of Pure Reason* on the one hand and analogous to the function that Kant assigns to the 'typic of the moral law' in the *Critique of Practical Reason* on the other hand" (p. 318), though intriguing, lacks textual support. In his *Anthropology* Kant nowhere refers either to the schematism (cf. *KrV* A 137/B 176–B 187) or to the "typic of pure practical judgment" (cf. *KpV* 5:67–71).

27. "True in a qualified sense" for three reasons: 1) These writing are not simply or solely about the carried-out application of moral theory. The *Anthropology* as well as the history and politics essays are intended to serve multiple goals; applying a priori ethical theory to the human situation is just one of these goals. 2) Lectures and essays alone cannot be a "carried-out application" of morality. At most, they can provide readers with suggestions and advice as to how *they themselves* can carry out the application of morality. Whether the application is carried out depends on what moral agents do. 3) Finally, as we have already seen (cf. "The Education of Humanity" in chap. 2), there is a fundamental sense in which Kant believes that the real application of morality is a long, arduous process that the human species is still preparing for. "We live in a time of disciplinary training, culture, and civilization, but not by any means in a time of moralization [*Moralisierung*]" (*Päd* 9:451; cf. 8:26; *Refl* 1460, 15:641; Starke II, 124–25). What we are intended to gain from the *Anthropology* and related writings is the *Weltkenntnis* needed to begin the carrying out of this *Moralisierung*.

28. However, many other relevant terms such as "moralize" (*moralisieren*) (7:324), "moralization" (*Moralisierung*) (7:326), and "morality" (*Moralität, Moral*) (7:192–93, 200, 244, 328) do occur. Also, whether a given term does or does not occur in a text does not resolve the more difficult question of whether or not a given theme is addressed in a text. (Brandt, in many places, adopts a narrowly lexicographic perspective that leads him astray.) Obviously, any given theme can be addressed by means of many different terms. At the same time, when an author declines to employ the most obvious term(s) for addressing a theme, readers have good reason to be suspicious that the theme is (at best) being approached obliquely rather than directly.

29. Brandt, "Beobachtungen," p. 77. See also "Ausgewählte Probleme," p. 29. He begins the "Anthropology and Ethics" section of the Academy Edition "Einleitung" on an even more skeptical note: "Pragmatic anthropology is not identical in any of its phases of development with the anthropology that Kant repeatedly earmarks as the complementary part (*Komplementärstück*) of his moral theory after 1770" (25:xlvi).

30. Wolfgang Becker, "Einleitung: Kants pragmatische Anthropologie," p. 14.

31. Brandt, "Beobachtungen," pp. 77–78; cf. pp. 92–93.

32. *Mrongovious* has unfortunately reversed Kant's intended analogy in the last sentence. It should read: "Anthropology is to morality as geodesy is to spatial geometry." Geodesy (*geō*, earth + *daiein*, to divide) is an obsolete term for "land measurement" or "that branch of applied mathematics which determines the figures and areas of large portions of the earth's surface, and the figure of the earth as a whole" (*OED*). Kant's position is that anthropology is to moral philosophy as applied geometry is to pure geometry.

33. Georg Samuel Albert Mellin, *Enzyclopädisches Wörterbuch der kritischen Philosophie*, reprint ed., 6 vols. (Aalen: Scientia Verlag, 1970), 1:v. In his letter to Kant

of September 6, 1797, Mellin writes: "I permit myself to send you the enclosed copy of [the first volume of] my *Encyclopedic Dictionary of the Critical Philosophy*. . . . I flatter myself that I have seized the spirit of this philosophy through a continuous, twelve-year study of it and that I have understood your writings, deeply esteemed professor, at least for the most part" (12:195–96; cf. 12:234, 303–4).

34. Mellin, *Encyclopädisches Wörterbuch*, 1:277, 279. See also my discussion in "Anthropology" in chapter 1. The citation there from Willich (n. 50) adds additional support to the claim that many of Kant's contemporaries definitely construed his anthropology as including a strong moral component.

35. Mellin, *Enzyclopädisches Wörterbuch*, 1:280.

36. Carl Christian Erhard Schmid, *Wörterbuch zum leichtern Gebrauch der kantischen Schriften* (Jena: Crökerschen Buchhandlung, 1798; reprint ed., Darmstadt: Wissenschaftliche Buchgesellschaft, 1976), pp. 62–63. The first edition of this work appeared in 1788.

37. The contents page of *Pillau* (25:731) does not include section titles of any of these topics. But they do receive attention (along with sub-section titles) in the body of the text (25:821–47). The final section of *Busolt* is entitled "On the Character of the Person," but the manuscript breaks off in mid-sentence (25:1531).

38. Is Kant implying here that only men can acquire moral character? This is Brandt's position. "It is not accidental that in the last sentence of the discussion of character as a manner of thinking in the *Anthropology* of 1798 the word *Mensch* [human being] is replaced by *Mann* [man]. The highest value is 'to be a man of principles' [*Mann von Grundsätzen*]" (7:295; "Ausgewählte Probleme," pp. 29–30). But Brandt is wrong to imply that the word *Mensch* is replaced by *Mann* only at *Anth* 7:295. As we have just seen, Kant also uses the same exact phrase (*Mann von Grundsätzen*) at the beginning of his discussion entitled "The Character of the Person" (7:285)! Also, in the same sentence to which Brandt refers, Kant explicitly states that it "is possible for the most common human reason [*die gemeinste Menschenvernunft möglich*]" to be "a man of principle" (7:295). Kant's position is that *every* human being is capable of being a "man of principle." For further discussion, see "Sex/Gender" and "'The Whole Human Race'" later in this chapter.

39. Brandt is misleading when he claims that the categorical imperative "is neither mentioned in the *Anthropology* of 1798 nor in the *Vorlesungsnachschriften*" ("Ausgewählte Probleme," p. 29); "neither in the *Nachschriften* nor in the book version do the words 'categorical' or 'imperative' or 'autonomy' occur" ("Einleitung" 25:xlvi–vii). Again, this narrowly lexicographic approach misses the forest for the trees. An idea can be referred to by many different words. Kant clearly is referring to the idea of a categorical imperative by means of phrases such as "principles which are valid for everyone."

40. For discussion, see H. J. Paton, *The Categorical Imperative: A Study in Kant's Moral Philosophy* (London: Hutchinson, 1947; reprint, Philadelphia: University of Pennsylvania Press, 1971), pp. 48–50; and Henry E. Allison, *Kant's Theory of Freedom* (New York: Cambridge University Press, 1990), pp. 110–20.

41. In the first edition as well as in the Rostock manuscript, the word "doctrine" (*Lehre*) is used rather than "art" (*Kunst*). In *Mrongovius* the language is looser: "Physiognomy should be a *Kunst* to distinguish and to divine the interior from the exterior. It is a *Wissenschaft* of the exterior characteristics of the temperaments, talents, and character of the human being" (25:1376). *Pillau* is more skeptical: "*Physiognomy*. It is a skill (*Kunst* one cannot say, even less *Wissenschaft*) of knowing the soul from the facial features" (25:826).

42. It is unfortunate that Kant himself, who spent his entire life in Königsberg, does not heed this warning when he discusses other races and peoples.

43. "Physiognomy," in *The Oxford Companion to the Mind*, edited by Richard L. Gregory (New York: Oxford University Press, 1987). I have borrowed several points from this informative article in the following discussion.

44. This is the kind of physiognomy that Darwin went in for in *The Expression of the Emotions in Man and Animals*. He was building on the earlier work of Sir Charles Bell, whose *Essays on the Anatomy of Expression in Painting* (1806) related specific muscles to facial expressions. This type of physiognomy is also explicitly mentioned and endorsed by Kant at *Anth* 7:301. But none of these are *moral* physiognomies.

45. "Insanity: Early Theories," in Gregory, *The Oxford Companion to the Mind*. In preparing this section I have also benefited from the entries on "Galen" and "Hippocrates" in *The Cambridge Dictionary of Philosophy*, 1995 ed.

46. One key difference between the 1764 *Observations* and 1798 *Anthropology* accounts of the four temperaments is that in the former Kant is much more willing to make inferences from temperament to moral character (cf. 2:218–19) than he is in the latter. This accords with the more empiricist tone of his ethical theory from the mid-sixties.

47. Shell, in *The Embodiment of Reason: Kant on Spirit, Generation, and Community* (Chicago: University of Chicago Press, 1996), argues that such remarks are part of an "early encomium to melancholy" which are to be sharply distinguished from "more negative later treatments" (pp. 288–89; cf. Brandt, "Einleitung," 25:xxvi n. 2. The contrast is a bit overdrawn: in the *Observations* as well in the various versions of the *Anthropology* lectures, the person of melancholic temperament is basically presented as someone who thinks for himself but tends to dwell on the dark side a bit too much. At the same time, I think Brandt errs too much in the opposite direction in asserting that Kant "simply falls back on his *Observations on the Feeling of the Beautiful and Sublime* of 1764" when he discusses temperament in the second part of the *Anthropology* lectures ("Ausgewählte Probleme," p. 25). There are some important differences between the discussions of temperament in these two texts.

48. However, in *Mrongovius* we read the following odd assertion: "To the moral character of the human being himself where I consider him as a free being belong.—
   a) the character of the sexes
   b) the character of the nations
   c) the character of the human species" (25:1368).

49. Mellin, *Enzyklopädisches Wörterbuch der kritischen Philosophie*, 1:280.

50. Brandt writes: "From its beginning in 1772–73 the *Anthropology* is determined by a thoroughgoing finalism" ("Einleitung," 25:xlv). The main message of this teleology concerns the liberation and moral perfection of the species, and here we find yet another indication of the progressive, moral intent of Kantian anthropology. But in discussing sex and gender differences his teleology often has a conservative effect. ("This is the way nature designed things. It is not our place to question or alter the arrangement.") For a different analysis of the role of teleology in Kant's anthropology and ethics, see Holly L. Wilson, "Kant's Integration of Morality and Anthropology," *Kant-Studien* 88 (1997): 87–104. *Note*: at present most writers use the term "gender" to refer to socio-cultural differences between men and women; reserving "sex" for biological differences. Kant's discussion incorporates aspects of both kinds of difference, though he does not always distinguish between the two. In cases where he clearly is referring to differences between men and women that he regards as socio-cultural, I use the term "gender." Otherwise, I use the more traditional term "sex."

51. Compare Rousseau: "[W]omen are the natural judges of men's merit. . . . Woe to the age in which women lose their ascendancy and in which their judgments no longer have an effect on men! This is the last degree of depravity. All peoples who have had morals have respected women"; *Emile*, p. 390.

52. The most intriguing example in Germany is that of Theodor Gottlieb von Hippel, one-time mayor of Königsberg and longstanding personal friend of Kant, who in 1792 published anonymously a book entitled *Über die bürgerliche Verbesserung der Weiber* (On the civil improvement of women). Reprinted. (Frankfurt: Syndikat, 1977.) Soon thereafter rumors began to circulate that Kant in fact wrote this particular text of Hippel. Even though Kant protested in his "Public Explanation," first published in the *Allgemeine literarische Anzeiger* on January 5, 1797, that "I am not the author of this text, neither alone, nor jointly with him [Hippel]" (12: 386; cf. 13:586), some people remained unconvinced. For discussion, see Ursula Pia Jauch, *Immanuel Kant zur Geschlechterdifferenz: Aufklärerische Vorurteilskritik und bürgerliche Geschlechtsvormundschaft*, 2nd ed. (Vienna: Passagen, 1989), pp. 203–36; and Hannelore Schröder, "Kant's Patriarchal Order," in *Feminist Interpretations of Immanuel Kant*, edited by Robin May Schott (University Park: Pennsylvania State University Press, 1997), pp. 275–96. Jauch, while not asserting categorically that Kant was indeed the author, holds that "the astounding quantity of references, connections, and questions to and for Kant could absolutely lead to the interpretation that Kant was led by Hippel from a friendly to a literary collaboration on 'The Civil Improvement of Women'" (p. 219).

53. "The only quality necessary for being a citizen, other than the *natural* one (that he is neither a child nor a woman), is that he be *his own master*" (*Gemeinspruch* 8:295). However, in a related discussion in *MdS* he takes a more ameliorative stance, claiming that "anyone can work his way up from this passive condition [of being dependent on others] to an active one" (*MdS* 6:315). For discussion, see Susan Mendus, "Kant: 'An Honest but Narrow-Minded Bourgeois'?" reprinted in *Immanuel Kant: Critical Assessments*, edited by Ruth F. Chadwick (London: Routledge, 1992), 3: 370–88.

54. Robin May Schott, "The Gender of Enlightenment," in *What is Enlightenment? Eighteenth-Century Answers and Twentieth-Century Questions*, edited by James Schmidt (Berkeley: University of California Press, 1996), p. 474. See also her earlier book, *Cognition and Eros: A Critique of the Kantian Paradigm* (Boston: Beacon Press, 1988), especially part 2; and the contributions to her edited anthology, *Feminist Interpretations of Kant*.

55. Susan Mendus, "Kant: 'An Honest but Narrow-Minded Bourgeois'?" p. 382. Similarly, in her more recent essay, "How Androcentric Is Western Philosophy? A Reply," *Philosophical Quarterly* 46 (1996), she states that Kant denies "that women are rational beings" in his political philosophy (p. 62). Brandt makes similar claims in "Ausgewählte Probleme," pp. 29–30; "Beobachtungen," p. 99; "Einleitung," 25: xlix.

56. Pauline Kleingeld, *Fortschritt und Vernunft: Zur Geschichtsphilosophie Kants* (Würzburg: Königshausen and Neumann, 1995), pp. 32, 35. See also Kleingeld's essay, "The Problematic Status of Gender-Neutral Language in the History of Philosophy: The Case of Kant," *Philosophical Forum* 25 (1993), where she writes: "To assume that women are included since Kant uses the word 'Mensch' is to beg the question" (p. 142). Kleingeld's point that the German word *Mensch* was often used in a more restrictive sense in Kant's time to refer exclusively to men is well taken. However, the more important terms here are *Gattung* (species) and *Menschengeschlecht* (human race), both of which clearly include women as members. For discussion, see "'The Whole Human Race': Kant and Moral Universality" later in this chapter.

57. Jauch claims that Kant is "directly raising the question of political reform" for women with "hidden clarity" at this point (*Immanuel Kant zur Geschlechterdifferenz*, p. 123); while Schott, in her comment on the same passage, bemoans Kant's "general indifference to differentiating the possibilities of enlightenment for men and women" (p. 476, "The Gender of Enlightenment").

58. Immediately before this sentence in Starke II we read: "The male understanding has an entirely different measure [*einen ganz anderen Maßstab*] than the female understanding, and differs from the latter in that it judges things only according to their true worth [*nur nach ihrem wahren Werthe beurtheilt*]" (67). Here Kant is asserting in yet another way that women do not think sufficiently for themselves—instead of coming to their own conclusions about something based on an objective assessment of its true worth, they form their judgements on the basis of what others say about the matter. Kleingeld, in "The Problematic Status of Gender-Neutral Language," writes: "Nowhere in his critical work does Kant draw a distinction between two different kinds of reason (which he could hardly be expected to do)" (p. 141). Starke II is not a "critical work," but Kant is nevertheless here drawing "a distinction between two types of reason." Heidemarie Bennent, in her analysis, tries to link this passage from Starke (though in citing it she leaves out the important adjective *wahr!*) with several claims made by Kant in the first *Critique* concerning the criteria of truth in order to support her claim that on Kant's view "only an object that also appeals to her feeling awakens the interest of woman," and that because her knowledge is "controlled by feeling" she "remains unfree"; *Galanterie und Verachtung: Eine philosophiegeschichtliche Untersuchung zur Stellung der Frau in Gesellschaft und Kultur* (Frankfurt: Campus, 1985), p. 98; cf. *KrV* B 83–84, A 820/B 848, A 822/B 850.

59. Aristotle's basic position on women's practical reasoning capabilities is also similar to Kant's; "deliberating well is above all the function of the man of practical wisdom [*phronimos*]" (*EN* 6.7 1141b8–10); "the slave has no deliberative faculty at all; the woman has, but it is without authority [*akuron*]" (*Politics* 1.13 1260a12–13). Both philosophers include women within the set of human beings who are also rational beings, but both of them intimate (without offering much in the way of detail or support) that the exercise of women's reason is faulty.

60. J. W. H. Stuckenberg, *The Life of Immanuel Kant* (London: MacMillan, 1892), p. 186. See also Kleingeld, "The Problematic Status of Gender-Neutral Language," pp. 143–44.

61. Schleiermacher, review of *Anthropology from a Pragmatic Point of View*, in Vorländer, *Anthropologie in pragmatischer Hinsicht* (the three passages cited occur on pp. 339, 340, and 343 of Vorländer's edition).

62. Hume does begin his essay "Of National Characters" by asserting: "The vulgar are apt to carry all *national characters* to extremes." But he then continues: "Men of sense condemn these undistinguishing judgments: Though at the same time, they allow, that each nation has a peculiar set of manners, and that some particular qualities are more frequently to be met with among one people than among their neighbours"; in *Essays: Moral, Political, and Literary*, edited by T. H. Green and T. H. Grose (London: Longmans, Green, 1907), 1:244. Hume and Kant are not far apart here.

63. But not necessarily all; "we understand under national character not that each one of the *Volk* must have exactly the same character, but only that with a *Volk* a principal character that stands out will be found" (*Parow* 25:450; cf. Dohna, 347).

64. Compare Hume: "[N]or do I think, that men owe any thing of their temper or genius to the air, food, or climate" ("Of National Characters," p. 246). The influence of Hume's essay is detectable at several points in Kant's discussion of *Volkscharakter*.

65. Given Kant's infamous pronouncement that music "has the lowest place among the fine arts" (*KU* 5:329), one might be tempted to ignore his remarks concerning Asian musical taste. At the same time, his low estimate of Asian ethics stands in sharp contrast to the earlier praise of China found in texts of Leibniz and Wolff. Wolff, for instance, in his *Oratorio de Sinarum philosophia practica* (1721), pro-

claims: "In fact I do not know anyone who has paid better attention to the development of human morality than the Chinese"; in *Oratorio de Sinarum philosophia practica. Rede über die praktische Philosophie der Chinesen*, edited by Michael Albrecht (Hamburg: Felix Meiner Verlag, 1985), p. 37. As a result of his public praise of the morality of the Chinese, Wolff was dismissed from his university position at Halle. For discussion, see my "'What does Heaven Say?' Christian Wolff and Western Interpretations of Confucian Ethics," in *Essays on the Analects of Confucius*, edited by Bryan William van Norden (New York: Oxford University Press, 2000). See also Julia Ching, "Chinese Ethics and Kant," *Philosophy East and West* 28 (1978): 161–72.

66. Kant does not generally follow this "focus on the negatives" strategy in his discussions of sexes and races. Certain sub-groups within the latter categories are routinely cast in a positive light; others are described much more negatively. Why the change of strategy? Does criticism somehow not lead to improvement in these two areas?

67. For discussion, see Howard Williams, "Kant and the French Revolution," in *Kant's Political Philosophy* (New York: St. Martin's Press, 1983), pp. 208–14. For a more positive judgment on Kant's part, see *Streit* 7:85–86.

68. The German word here is actually "*Buchhandlungen,* bookstores." But I think it is a mistake. In other versions of the lectures (e.g., Starke II, 114) as well as in the second sentence of the above quotation from Dohna, the word is "*Buchhaltung,* bookkeeping."

69. "On the Different Races of Human Beings" (first published in 1775 as an announcement for his physical geography lectures of summer semester of that year) (2:427–443), "Determination of the Concept of a Human Race" (1785—8:89–106), and "On the Use of Teleological Principles in Philosophy" (1788—8:159–84). Holly L. Wilson and Guenter Zoeller have prepared English translations of the first two essays; Zoeller, of the third—all are in *Anthropology, History, and Education,* edited by Zoeller, in the Cambridge Edition of the works of Immanuel Kant. (New York: Cambridge University Press, 2001). I thank Holly Wilson and Guenter Zoeller for sharing copies of their translations with me.

70. "Concerning Human Beings" (9:311–19). An English translation of the entire *Physische Geographie* has been prepared recently by David Oldroyd and Olaf Reinhardt, in *Natural Science,* edited by H. B. Nisbet, in the Cambridge Edition of the works of Immanuel Kant (New York: Cambridge University Press, forthcoming). I thank H. B. Nisbet for sending me a copy of their translation.

71. The *Menschenkunde* manuscript regards the discussion of race as properly belonging to the *Physical Geography* lectures: "In spite of the unity of the human species [*die Einheit der menschlichen Gattung*], there is nevertheless a difference of the races assumed, whose special character belongs to physical geography" (25:1195). But the more interesting question is whether Kant himself may have had doubts about including the material. Again, the section on race in the official 1798 *Anthropology* is only a page long, and rather tame looking. Within his anthropology materials, the most detailed remarks about race are to be found in the *Reflexionen zur Anthropologie,* notes which, while written by Kant, were not published during his lifetime. A shortened and rearranged version of this same material occurs in *Menschenkunde* 25:1186–88 (cf. 15:793 n. 9). With the sole exception of *Menschenkunde,* none of the other anthropology *Nachschriften* in volume 25 of the Academy Edition contains a specific section devoted to race. As noted earlier (n. 70), the *Physical Geography* lectures do contain a fairly detailed discussion of race, but these notes were also edited by someone else (Rink) and did not appear until 1802, when Kant was too ill to proofread the manuscript. Did Kant perhaps come to believe that his views in this area were wrong (or at least not appropriate material for publication)? Unfortunately, the published statements on race that we find in his three earlier

essays on this topic (cf. n. 69) do not differ substantially in tone from claims made in these other edited and unpublished works.

72. Erich Adickes, *Untersuchungen zu Kants physischer Geographie* (Tübingen: J. C. B. Mohr, 1911), pp. 278, 30. (There is a distressing parallel here with scholarly opinion of Rink's editing of the *Pädagogik* lectures—cf. "Education as Impure Ethics" in chap. 2.) Adickes discusses aspects of the race theory presented in these lectures on pp. 75–79, 194–99. See also Paul Gedan's remarks in Academy Edition 9: 509–11 concerning additional problems with the text as a whole. Emil Arnoldt describes Kant's task in the *Physical Geography* as the attempt to understand

> the human being as a piece, product, and member of nature; his relation to it and to other human beings as products and members of nature. More precisely: physical geography, as far as the human being is concerned, has to come to know the human race [*das Menschengeschlecht*] according to the original determinations through which nature places differences in him, and according to the gradual changes which he undergoes under the influence of nature and his own measures, so far as the latter are caused by natural influences. (*Kritische Excurse im Gebiete der Kant-Forschung*, p. 342)

73. If one reads this passage not with races but with sexes in mind, it does appear to contradict the remark of Kant in the *Observations*, quoted earlier, that men and women constitute "two species of human beings [*zwei Menschengattungen*]" (2:228). In the latter passage, he appears to be using *Gattung* in a looser, less technical sense. However, as I show later many of Kant's statements about race also strain his commitment to the unity of the species.

74. For example, Lothar G. Tirala, described by Ashley Montagu as "a leading exponent of Nazi 'race science,'" asserts that it is "highly probable that different human races originated independently of one another and that they evolved out of different species of ape-men. The so-called main races of mankind are not races, but species"; *Rasse, Geist und Seele* (Munich: Lehmans, 1935), quoted by Montagu, *Man's Most Dangerous Myth: The Fallacy of Race*, 2nd ed. (New York: Columbia University Press, 1945), p. 6. For discussion of the monogeneticism versus polygeneticism debate in the eighteenth and nineteenth centuries, see Marvin Harris, *The Rise of Anthropological Theory: A History of Theories of Culture* (New York: Thomas Y. Crowell, 1968), chapter 4.

75. Needless to say, polygeneticism was not the only issue on which Kant and Forster disagreed. In Kant's view, the most important issue of disagreement concerned "the entitlement of being allowed to use the teleological principle where sources of theoretical cognition are not sufficient" (8:160—hence the essay's title). Kant believes teleological principles play a necessary role in all cases where "theory leaves us" (8:159). But Forster, Kant writes, "finds it dangerous to establish a *principle* at the very beginning, which is supposed to guide the naturalist even in *searching* and observing, and specifically a principle that is said to orient observation toward a *natural history*" (8:161). Or, as Forster himself puts it, "the order of nature does not follow our divisions, and as soon as one wants to intrude on it, one falls into contradictions. A system should only be a guide [*Leitfaden*] for the memory"; "Noch etwas über die Menschenraßen," in *Georg Forsters Werke: Sämtliche Schriften, Tagebücher, Briefe*, edited by the Akademie der Wissenschaften der DDR (Berlin: Akademie, 1974), 8:146. Also, although Forster's account of race is polygenetic, his commitment to this position (as befits his open-ended empiricism) appears to be tentative and undogmatic. For instance, at one point he asserts: "Nevertheless I do not at all allow myself to answer decisively the question: Whether there are several original human phyla? [*mehrere ursprüngliche Menschenstämme*]" (8:153, cf. 157). Finally, Forster tries to cut off racist applications of his polygenetic hypothesis by answering

the following question in the negative: "But when we separate the Negro from the white man as an originally different phylum, do we not slice the last thread through which this mishandled people was connected to us, and in the presence of European cruelty still found some protection and mercy?" (8:154). Still, Kant's own opposition to polygeneticism is an important part of his own theory of race, and his opposition to this view is based partly on moral grounds. Partly but not solely. Conceptual economy appears to be his major consideration; "reason will not without need start from two principles, if it can make do with one" (8:165). For discussion, see Michael Neumann, "Philosophische Nachrichten aus der Südsee: Georg Forsters *Reise um die Welt*," in *Der ganze Mensch: Anthropologie und Literatur im 18. Jahrhundert*, edited by Hans-Jürgen Schings (Stuttgart: J. B. Metzler, 1994), especially pp. 533–37; J. D. McFarland, *Kant's Concept of Teleology* (Edinburgh: University of Edinburgh Press, 1970), pp. 56–68; John H. Zammito, *The Genesis of Kant's Critique of Judgment* (Chicago: University of Chicago Press, 1992), pp. 207–15; and Shell, *The Embodiment of Reason*, pp. 196–201.

76. Arthur O. Lovejoy, "Kant and Evolution," in *Forerunners of Darwin: 1745–1859*, edited by Bentley Glass, Owsei Temkin, and William L. Straus Jr. (Baltimore: Johns Hopkins University Press, 1959), p. 188. Kant was certainly not the first to argue that racial differences were originally caused by climatic conditions. Indeed, it the was the dominant position among Enlightenment intellectuals (Harris, *The Rise of Anthropological Theory*, p. 83; cf. 43). Leibniz, for instance, wrote in 1718 that there is "no reason why all men who inhabit the earth should not be of the same race [*race*], which has been altered by different climates"; *Otium Hanoveranum sive Miscellanea [etc.]* (Leipzig: Joann. Christiani Martini, 1718), p. 17. See also Montesquieu, *The Spirit of the Laws* (1748), translated by Thomas Nugent (New York: Hafner, 1949), books 14–16. At the same time, Kant himself clearly does want to hold on to the category of race and to use it to mark what he believes are real subdivisions within the species. One of Kant's many criticisms of his former student Johann Gottfried Herder, in his review of the latter's *Ideen zur Philosophie der Geschichte der Menschheit*, is that Herder too cavalierly dispenses with race. In his *Ideen* Herder (in what appears to be a veiled criticism of Kant) writes:

> Some, for example, have ventured to designate the term *races* for four or five divisions, made originally according to regions or colors; I see no reason for this nomenclature. . . . [T]here are neither four or five races, nor exclusive varieties, on this earth. Colors fade away into each other [*verlieren sich in einander*], forms follow the genetic character, and on the whole all are but shades of one and the same great portrait which extends through all space and time on the earth. (in *Herders Sämmtliche Werke*, edited by Bernhard Suphan [Berlin: Weidmann, 1887], 13:257–58)

Kant replies in his review: "Our author [Herder] is not disposed toward the division of the human species into *races*; first and foremost to one which is grounded on hereditary colors [*anerbende Farben*], presumably because the concept of a race is not yet clearly precise to him" (8:62).

77. Lovejoy, in his essay "Kant and Evolution," reads Kant similarly on this particular point: "it is worth noting that he [Kant] believes that the only character which is 'invariably inherited' from both parents—and therefore the only mark of a true or 'natural' race—is skin-color" (p. 182). Unfortunately, as I show later, Kant is not always consistent on this point.

78. In addition to Buffon, the writings of the German anthropologist and physician Johann Friedrich Blumenbach were a second major influence on Kant's race theory. Blumenbach's book, *De generis humani variatione nativa* (*On the natural variety of human beings*) was first published in 1775, when the author was only twenty-

three years old. According to Lovejoy, the beginnings of the science of physical anthropology "in its systematic form, are usually credited to the treatise of Blumenbach" ("Kant and Evolution," p. 178). Kant refers to Blumenbach in a number of different works (e.g., *Anth* 7:299; *Streit* 7:89; *KU* 5:424), and they were in personal contact with one another (see Karl Vorländer, *Immanuel Kants Leben* (Leipzig: Felix Meiner, 1911), pp. 151, 153). In his letter to Blumenbach of August 5, 1790, Kant writes: "Your writings have taught me in a variety of ways" (11:185). For discussion, see Stephen Jay Gould, "The Geometer of Race," *Discover* 15 (November 1994): 65–69.

79. Alex Sutter, "Kant und die 'Wilden': Zum impliziten Rassismus in der Kantischen Geschichtsphilosophie," *Prima Philosophie* 2 (1989): 253. See also Joachim Moebus, "Bemerkungen zu Kants Anthropologie und physicher Geographie," in Klaus Holzkamp and Karl-Heinz Brann, eds., *Kritische Psychologie: Bericht über den 1. Internationalen Kongreß kritische Psychologie vom 13.–15. Mai in Marburg* (Cologne: Paul-Rugenstein Verlag, 1977), 2:365–80, who argues that Kant's anthropology reflects the background of a "mercantile slave-holding society over against the raw product of labor power" (p. 379). See also Annette Barkhaus, "Kants Konstruktion des Begriffs der Rasse und seine Hierarchisierung der Rassen," *Biologisches Zentralblatt* 113 (1994): 197–203, who argues that Kant defines race as an "unchanging genetic community" and that with this definition he is able to offer a "naturalistic justification of the hierarchical relationship of Europeans to non-white peoples" (pp. 197–98).

80. Emmanuel Chukwudi Eze, "The Color of Reason: The Idea of 'Race' in Kant's Anthropology," in *Anthropology and the German Enlightenment*, edited by Katherine Faull (Lewisburg: Bucknell University Press, 1994), p. 218. In the editor's introduction to his anthology *Race and the Enlightenment* (Cambridge: Blackwell, 1997), Eze also states that "the Enlightenment's declaration of itself as 'the Age of Reason' was predicated upon precisely the assumption that reason could historically only come to maturity in modern Europe" (p. 4). Similarly, Tsenay Serequeberhan, in "Eurocentrism in Philosophy: The Case of Immanuel Kant," *Philosophical Forum* 27 (1996): 333–56, argues that "for Kant non-white or non-European humanity, properly speaking, lies beyond the realm of reason and thus beyond the possibility of rational redemption" (p. 337).

81. Reinhard Brandt, *D'Artagnan und die Urteilstafel: Über ein Ordungsprinzip der europäischen Kulturgeschichte* (Stuttgart: Franz Steiner, 1991), p. 135. See also "Ausgewählte Probleme," pp. 29–30; "Einleitung," 25:xlix.

82. Hume begins a long footnote in his essay "Of National Characters" with the following:

> I am apt to suspect the Negroes, and in general all the other species of men (for there are four or five different kinds) to be naturally inferior to the whites. There never was a civilized nation of any other complexion than white, nor even any individual eminent either in action or speculation. No ingenious manufactures amongst them, no arts, no sciences. On the other hand, the most rude and barbarous of the whites, such as the ancient GERMANS [!], the present TARTARS, have still something eminent about them. (*Essays: Moral, Political, and Literary*, 1:252 n)

See also James Beattie's 1770 response to Hume, in which the Eurocentric prejudices of Hume and "many of our critics and philosophers" are strongly criticized; *An Essay on the Nature and Immutability of Truth, in Opposition to Sophistry and Skepticism*, reprinted in Eze, *Race and the Enlightenment*, p. 36. Eze conjectures that Hume "responded to some of Beattie's criticisms by making some alterations" in a 1776 revision of his essay. The above citation is from the 1754 version. The 1776 revision reads: "I am apt to suspect the Negroes to be naturally inferior to the whites. There scarcely ever was a civilized nation of that complexion"; Eze, *Race and the Enlightenment*, p. 37.

83. Eze, "The Color of Reason," p. 217; cf. Sutter, "Kant und die 'Wilden'," p. 244; Shell, *The Embodiment of Reason*, p. 193.

84. It is significant that Kant points out the dark hair coloring of these people, adding that they are not to be confused with Germans, who are "light blonde [*hochblonde*] with tender white skin, reddish hair, [and] pale blue eyes" (2:441). But by 1785 the *Stammgattung* hypothesis is dropped. In "Determination of the Concept of a Human Race," he states that it is "impossible to guess the shape of the first human phylum (as far as the character of the skin is concerned); even the character of the whites is only the development of one of the original predispositions" (8:106). Nathan Rotenstreich refers to this passage to support his claim that on Kant's view "we cannot conjecture about what the first human tribe may have been like"; "Races and Peoples," in *Practice and Realization: Studies in Kant's Moral Philosophy* (The Hague: Martinus Nijhoff, 1979), p. 102.

85. At the same time, Kant is at least sometimes deeply skeptical about any normative implications to be drawn from skin color. For instance, in a section on "Opinions as to the Cause" of black skin color in human beings in the *Physical Geography* lectures, he begins by writing: "Some believe Ham to have been the father of the Moors and to have been punished by God with the color black, that was then handed down to his descendants. But no reason [*kein Grund*] can be advanced as to why the color black should be more suited to be a sign of a curse than the color white" (9:313).

86. Montagu, *Man's Most Dangerous Myth: The Fallacy of Race*, p. 11.

87. Ernst Cassirer, *The Myth of the State* (New Haven: Yale University Press, 1946), p. 235. Comte Arthur de Gobineau's work, *Essai sur l'inégalité des races humaines* (1853), is described by Hannah Arendt as a book "which, only some fifty years later, at the turn of the century, was to become a kind of standard work for race theories"; "Race-Thinking before Racism," *Review of Politics* 6 (1944): 54. The first principle of Gobineau's race theory is that "[h]istory springs only from contact of the white races" (as quoted by Cassirer, *The Myth of the State*, p. 226. Chap. 16 of Cassirer's book is a critique of Gobineau.) In pitting Kant against Gobineau, Cassirer quotes from *Gr* 4:434–35, where Kant distinguishes between price and dignity, claiming that "morality, and humanity so far as it is capable of morality, is that which alone has dignity" (4:435). But as I have shown, Kant also seems to think that history "springs only from contact of the white races": "Many people do not progress further by themselves. Greenlanders. Asians. It must come from Europe" (*Refl* 1499, 15:781). "We must look for the continual progress of the human race toward perfection in the Occident and from there the spreading around the world" (*Refl* 1501, 15:789; cf. Sutter, "Kant und die 'Wilden'," p. 248). Cassirer, one of the outstanding representatives of the Marburg school of Neo-Kantianism, was also Jewish, and left Germany in 1933, immediately after Hitler became *Reichskanzler*. Dimitry Gawronsky reports that upon first hearing the notorious Nazi slogan *Recht ist, was unserem Führer dient* ("Justice is what serves our Führer"), Cassirer replied, "This is the end of Germany"; "Ernst Cassirer: Leben und Werk," in *Ernst Cassirer*, edited by Paul Arthur Schilpp (Stuttgart: W. Kohlhammer, 1966), p. 20. After working first in England and then in Sweden, Cassirer came to the United States, where he taught at both Yale and Columbia. *The Myth of the State* was his last book, finished only a few days before his death in 1945.

88. *Collins* and *Parow* both end with an examination of the character of the sexes. The last section of *Friedländer* is on education. *Busolt*, again, breaks off in its discussion of the character of the person.

89. By 1798 Kant's extraterrestrial enthusiasms have cooled somewhat. No longer does he assert confidently that "most planets are certainly inhabited [*gewiß bewohnt*], and those that are not, will be one day" (*Naturgeschichte* 1:354); or that human nature "occupies exactly the middle rung" in the great chain of being (1: 359). See chapter 1 note 30 earlier. In *Pillau* he advocates a more comparative historical strategy, arguing that we are most likely to ascertain the true character of the species if we "compare one generation with the other" (25:838).

90. Brandt, "Ausgewählte Probleme," p. 30. See also "Einleitung," 25:xlix; *D'Artagnan und die Urteilstafel*, pp. 135–36; "Beobachtungen," p. 99.

91. Brandt, "Ausgewählte Probleme," p. 29.

92. For example, *Reflexion* 1500: "The human being has such a drive to perfect himself that he even regards as superfluous [*überflussig*] a *Volk* which has completed [*vollendet*] its development and simply enjoys [life]; and believes the world would not lose anything at all, if Tahiti also died out [*untergingt*]" (15:785). Adickes, in an editorial note on this remark, says that the island of Tahiti "was described by its [western] discovers as a paradisiacal island, which through the richest gifts of nature enabled its inhabitants to enjoy an effortless life" (15:785 n). However, Kant is not by any means defending the genocide or mistreatment of non-Europeans by Europeans. Rather, his position is that certain populations lack sufficient energy to develop culturally and that they will eventually kill themselves off. As he argues in *Pillau*:

> We find peoples who do not appear to progress in the perfection of human nature but have reached a standstill, while others, such as the Europeans, always progress. . . . [I]t appears that all of the Americans will be wiped out [*alle ausgerottet werden*], not through the act of murder—that would be cruel— but they will die out [*aussterben*]. . . . A private conflict [*Selbst-Streit*] will emerge among them, and they will destroy each other [*sie werden sich einander aufreiben*]. (25:840)

For a more favorable Enlightenment portrait of Tahiti, see Diderot's "Conversation Between the Chaplain and Orou," in his *Supplement to the Voyage of Bougainville* (1772), reprinted in *The Portable Enlightenment Reader*, edited by Isaac Kramnick (New York: Penguin Books, 1995). Orou, a Tahitian, judges European mores to be "opposed to nature and contrary to reason" (p. 270).

93. For discussion, see Kurt Röttgers, "Kants Zigeuner," *Kant-Studien* 88 (1997): 60–86. Röttgers holds that Kant's relative silence on this topic represents not "an accidental gap of knowledge" but rather "a conspicuous displacement of knowledge [*Wissensverdrängung*]" (p. 63).

94. "Ausgewählte Probleme," p. 29; "Einleitung," 25:xlix.

95. Rotenstreich, "Races and Peoples," p. 103.

96. In fact, Kant held that in 1795 the peoples of the earth had *already entered* into this kind of community! But here, alas, his Enlightenment optimism has distorted his perception.

97. Max Horkheimer and Theodor W. Adorno, *Dialectic of Enlightenment*, translated by John Cumming (New York: Continuum, 1972), p. xv.

4. Art and Religion

1. See, for example, Predrag Cicovacki, "Kant's Aesthetics between 1980 and 1990: A Bibliography," which runs fourteen pages long and lists seventy-one books and 162 articles; in *Kant's Aesthetics*, edited by Ralf Meerbote (Atascadero, CA: Ridgeview, 1991), pp. 129–43. For an earlier survey of literature on Kant's aesthetics,

see Paul Guyer's bibliography in *Essays in Kant's Aesthetics*, edited by Ted Cohen and Paul Guyer (Chicago: University of Chicago Press, 1982), pp. 307–23, particularly part 4. For secondary literature on Kant's *Religion*, see the notes to "Religion" in this chapter.)

2. Judgments of taste are defined as "aesthetic" by Kant in so far as they are essentially connected with a feeling of disinterested pleasure on the part of the judging subject. As he asserts in section 1 of *The Critique of Aesthetic Judgment*:

> In order to discern whether something is beautiful or not, we refer the representation not by means of the understanding to the object for cognition, but by means of the imagination (perhaps in connection with the understanding) to the subject and the feeling of pleasure or pain. The judgment of taste is therefore not a cognitive judgment, and so is not logical but aesthetic, by which is meant a judgment whose determining ground *cannot be other* than *subjective.* (5:203)

3. Although Kant quickly praises the virtues of subjects such as foreign languages (cf. *Friedländer* 25:724), geography, and mathematics in this section, no mention at all is made of any of the fine arts. Edward Franklin Buchner, in his 1904 translation and commentary of the *Lectures on Education*, roundly criticizes Kant's omission, noting that the "feelings of the individual are practically banished from any share in education, and the claims of aesthetics as making positive contribution to the realization of pedagogy's ideal are neglected"; *The Educational Theory of Immanuel Kant*, p. 89.

4. Near the end of the preface of *KU* Kant leads the reader to think that there will be no discussion of this topic at all: "The investigation of the faculty of taste, as an aesthetic power of judgment, is not being taken on here with regard to the formation and culture [*Bildung und Kultur*] of taste (for this will take its course in the future, as it has in the past, without any such researches), but merely in regard to a transcendental aim [*bloß in transzendentaler Absicht*]" (5:170). Fortunately, Kant does not always adhere to this transcendental stricture.

5. For a detailed discussion that is sensitive both to the various historical roots of disinterestedness in aesthetic theory and its important connection to Kant's ethics, see Paul Guyer, "The Dialectic of Disinterestedness," in *Kant and the Experience of Freedom: Essays on Aesthetics and Morality* (New York: Cambridge University Press, 1993), pp. 48–130.

6. Guyer, "The Dialectic of Disinterestedness," p. 96.

7. Guyer, *Kant and the Experience of Freedom*, p. 18. Several reviewers of Guyer's book have also commented on the frequent presence of the term 'palpable'. Karl Ameriks, for instance, notes that it is "a favorite and crucial phrase"; "On Paul Guyer's *Kant and the Experience of Freedom*," *Philosophy and Phenomenological Research* 55 (1995): 362. Nancy Sherman also states that "'palpable' comes to be an important term in this project [of showing how we embody moral agency]"; "Reasons and Feelings in Kantian Morality," *Philosophy and Phenomenological Research* 55 (1995): 369. See Guyer, *Kant and the Experience of Freedom*, pp. 21, 37, 41, 98, 100, 111, 177, 254, 358–59. 'Palpable' seems to be Guyer's preferred translation for *fühlbar*, 'sensible' or literally 'feelable'—cf. *KU* 5:262; Guyer, *Kant and the Experience of Freedom*, p. 37.

8. 'Might' but in fact does not. Kant is certainly not holding up this extreme character type as a moral exemplar. His point is simply that actions performed from inclination lack moral worth—only actions performed *aus Pflicht* possess moral worth. If we look at cases of action where inclinations are absent, we are more likely to find examples where duty is the motive. See H. J. Paton, "The Method of Isolation," in *The Categorical Imperative: A Study in Kant's Moral Philosophy* (London:

Hutchinson, 1947; reprint, Philadelphia: University of Pennsylvania Press, 1971), pp. 47–48.

9. Stuart Hampshire, "The Social Spirit of Mankind," in *Kant's Transcendental Deductions*, edited by Eckart Förster (Stanford: Stanford University Press, 1989), p. 154. Hampshire's title comes from an important passage at *KU* 5:355, cited later.

10. In the second (1793) and third (1799) editions of *KU* the word *Glückseligkeit* ("happiness") appears here instead of *Geselligkeit* (5:538). Hampshire writes: "Surely *Geselligkeit* is the preferred reading, rather than *Glückseligkeit* as in some editions" (p. 154). But it is not clear (nor does Hampshire provide an argument for convincing us) that *Glückseligkeit* is "surely" an error. In the *Religion*, for instance, Kant defines *Glückseligkeit* as a harmonizing of all natural inclinations into a whole, adding that "the reason that accomplishes this is called *prudence*" (6:58). In other words, Kant's own conception of *Glückseligkeit* (at least in some places) involves the choice of ends as well as means. Hampshire's understanding of happiness as "a naturally occurring phenomenon" (p. 151) is not synonymous with Kant's conception. For discussion, see Paton, "The Pursuit of Happiness," in *The Categorical Imperative*, pp. 85–87.

11. "Feeling and Freedom: Kant on Aesthetics and Morality," in *Kant and the Experience of Freedom*, p. 35. However, Guyer himself seems to have trouble making up his mind on this point. Later he cites again this same passage from *KU* 5:356, putting a different spin on it: "his [Kant's] real conviction seems to be that sound moral principles are necessary for the development of taste, rather than vice versa . . . Thus a primary concern of Kant's discussion of the arts seems to be precisely to reject a justification of our interest in them by an easy appeal to their beneficial impact on allegedly moral inclinations"; *Kant and the Experience of Freedom*, p. 255.

12. See Iris Murdoch, "Art and Eros: A Dialogue about Art," in *Acastos: Two Platonic Dialogues* (New York: Viking, 1987), p. 63.

13. Kant's title for section 59 is *Von der Schönheit als Symbol der Sittlichkeit* (5: 351). James Creed Meredith translates this as "Beauty as the symbol of morality"; *The Critique of Judgement* (Oxford: Clarendon Press, 1928), p. 221; J. H. Bernard renders it as "Of beauty as the symbol of morality"; *Critique of Judgement* (London: Collier Macmillan, 1892; reprint ed., New York: Hafner Press, 1951), p. 196; and Werner S. Pluhar opts for "On Beauty as the Symbol of Morality"; *Critique of Judgment* (Indianapolis: Hackett, 1987), p. 225. However, Kant's *als* ("as") leaves open the question of whether beauty is *the only* symbol of morality or simply *a* symbol of morality. Contrary to the assumptions of many translators and commentators, it is not at all clear that Kant wishes to assert that beauty is the only symbol of morality. The basic issue here is the need for human beings to find a tangible representation of abstract moral concepts, and Kant does discuss this general problem in other texts as well. For instance, in the *Religion* he asserts that we human beings "always need to make a certain analogy [*gewisse Analogie*] with natural beings in order to make supersensible qualities graspable to ourselves [*uns . . . faßlich zu machen*]," and he also notes that the Scriptures "accommodate themselves to this mode of representation" (*Rel* 6: 65 n). Similarly, as noted earlier in my discussion of the *Methodenlehre* of the second *Critique*, Kant recommends that one way of making "objectively-practical reason subjectively-practical" is to search through "biographies of ancient and modern times with the purpose of having examples at hand of the duties they lay down" (*KpV* 5: 151, 154—cf. "Didactics, Ascetics, Casuistry, Judgment" in chap. 2). See also my "Go-Carts of Judgment: Exemplars in Kantian Moral Education," *Archiv für Geschichte der Philosophie* 74 (1992): 303–22, pp. 312–313.) Finally, as I argue later, even within the *KU* alone Kant presents a competing (and superior) symbol of morality: the sublime. On my reading of Kant, his view is that beauty is *one* way of concretely symbolizing morality, but not the only way.

14. 'The' or 'a'? (See n. 13.) Ted Cohen, in "Why Beauty Is a Symbol of Morality," seems to want to have it both ways when he argues that we must suppose Kant "to hold that *only* the experience of beauty has the kind of richness needed to stand for moral experience" and that "there might be many different symbols all of which indirectly present the same concept"; in Cohen and Guyer, *Essays in Kant's Aesthetics*, p. 235, 235 n. 8).

15. For discussion, see my "*Gemeine Menschenvernunft* and *Ta Endoxa*," in *Morality and Moral Theory: A Reappraisal and Reaffirmation* (New York: Oxford University Press, 1992), pp. 116–20.

16. See Guyer: "[T]he aesthetic is indispensable to the sensible representation of morality"; *Kant and the Experience of Freedom*, p. 317. Elsewhere in this book he makes the even stronger claim that beauty "must indeed be the only available symbol of morality" (p. 110; cf. pp. 115, 178). These two claims are not synonymous: X could be an indispensable symbol for indirectly presenting morality to human beings without necessarily being the only such symbol. I accept a weak version of the "indispensability" claim, but reject the stronger "only" claim. For discussion, see Karl Ameriks's critical remarks (as well as Guyer's response to them) concerning "the Requirement Claim" in "On Paul Guyer's *Kant and the Experience of Freedom*," pp. 363–67; Guyer, "Moral Anthropology in Kant's Aesthetics and Ethics: A Reply to Ameriks and Sherman," *Philosophy and Phenomenological Research* 55 (1995): 384–85.

17. Guyer, "Moral Anthropology in Kant's Aesthetics and Ethics," p. 387. See also p. 385.

18. Francis X. J. Coleman, for instance, writes: "A twentieth-century reader might ask, with a certain smile, whether the sublime really needs an analysis . . . as an aesthetic category with its roots in our culture, the sublime seems largely irrelevant"; *The Harmony of Reason: A Study of Kant's Aesthetics* (Pittsburgh: University of Pittsburgh Press, 1974), p. 85. And Paul Guyer, in an oft-cited footnote from his first book, *Kant and the Claims of Taste* (Cambridge: Harvard University Press, 1979) claims that Kant's analysis of the sublime "will not be of much interest to modern sensibilities, and thus . . . most of what we can or will learn from Kant must come from his discussion of judgments of beauty" (p. 400 n. 2). At the beginning of his 1982 essay "The Beautiful and the Sublime," he writes: "No statement in . . . [*Kant and the Claims of Taste*] has come in for more criticism than this remark, and justifiably so" (*Kant and the Experience of Freedom*, p. 187). The statement is deleted from the second edition of *Kant and the Claims of Taste* (New York: Cambridge University Press, 1997).

19. This is Guyer's strategy. See *Kant and the Experience of Freedom*, pp. 258, 253–54. As he sees it, the beautiful represents our experience of freedom, while the sublime represents the submission of our inclinations to pure practical reason. But at both *KU* 5:353 and 271 it is the concept of the morally good that the beautiful and sublime respectively are said to represent. Kant himself does not differentiate their representative functions, but rather argues for the superiority of one (namely, the sublime) over the other as moral symbol. This particular tension between Kant's accounts of the beautiful and the sublime may itself be part of a larger problem. Commentators have often remarked on the difficulties of seeing how exactly the Analytics of the Beautiful and the Sublime are supposed to fit with one another. See, for example, Mary A. McCloskey, *Kant's Aesthetic* (London: Macmillan, 1987), pp. 94, 104, as well as her references to Bousanquet and Lindsay, pp. 101–2.

20. John H. Zammito, *The Genesis of Kant's Critique of Judgment*, (Chicago: University of Chicago Press, 1992), p. 280. See also Jean-François Lyotard's discussion of subreption in *Lessons on the Analytic of the Sublime*, translated by Elizabeth Rottenberg (Stanford: Stanford University Press, 1994), pp. 69–70, 182, 195.

21. Donald W. Crawford, "The Place of the Sublime in Kant's Aesthetic Theory," in *The Philosophy of Immanuel Kant*, edited by Richard Kennington (Washington, D.C.: Catholic University of America Press, 1985), p. 171. See also McCloskey, *Kant's Aesthetic*, p. 98.

22. Crawford, "The Place of the Sublime in Kant's Aesthetic Theory," p. 172; cf. McCloskey, *Kant's Aesthetic*, p. 98.

23. Here as elsewhere there is a strong Burkean flavor in Kant's analysis of the sublime. See, for example, Burke's discussion, "How Pain Can Be a Cause of Delight," in *A Philosophical Inquiry into the Origin of Our Ideas of the Sublime and Beautiful*, reprinted in *The Works of the Right Honourable Edmund Burke*, edited by Henry Frowde (London: Oxford University Press, 1906), 1:179–80.

24. Beck points out that Kant often represents the heavens and the moral law together in earlier writings as well (e.g., *Naturgeschichte* 1:367–68; *Beob* 2:208–9, *Träume* 2:332; *Beweisgrund* 2:141), suggesting also that his connecting of the two experiences is due to the fact of their "having first been joined by Kant's mother . . . [as] attested by the early biographers who knew him personally" (*A Commentary on Kant's Critique of Practical Reason* (Chicago: University of Chicago Press, 1960), pp. 282, 281). Beck refers the reader to Kant's statement concerning his reverence for his mother, as recorded in R. B. Jachmann, *Immanuel Kant geschildert in Briefen an einen Freund*. In the ninth letter, Kant writes: "I will never forget my mother, because she planted and nourished the seed of good in me, [and] opened my heart to the impressions of nature"; in *Immanuel Kant: Sein Leben in Darstellungen von Zeitgenossen: Die Biographien von L. E. Borowski, R. B. Jachmann und E. A. Wasianski*, edited by Felix Groß (reprint, Darmstadt: Wissenschaftliche Buchgesellschaft, 1993), p. 143). Paul Menzer, in the opening chapter of *Kants Aesthetik in ihrer Entwicklung* (Berlin: Akademie, 1952), tries to track the origin and development of Kant's aesthetics back to his early work in natural philosophy. Menzer cites the same passage from Jachmann, and then adds: "No more with the eyes of a child, but with the eyes of the thinker who knew the laws of the heavenly events, the author of the '*Naturgeschichte*' looked up to the starry heavens, and then thoughts of God, death, and immortality came to him. Kant's experience of nature is thus at the same time a religious experience" (p. 6).

25. For discussion see Paul Crowther, "Kant's Critical Ethics and the Sublime," in *The Kantian Sublime: From Morality to Art* (Oxford: Clarendon Press, 1989), pp. 19–37; and Milton C. Nahm, " 'Sublimity' and the 'Moral Law' in Kant's Philosophy," *Kant-Studien* 48 (1956–57): 502–24. Ronald Beiner, in "Kant, the Sublime, and Nature," follows Heidegger, Arendt, Hans Jonas, and others in claiming that Kant's analysis of the sublime "marks an apotheosis of western subjectivism" in its assertion of the superiority of moral personality over nature; in *Kant and Political Philosophy: The Contemporary Legacy*, edited by Beiner and William James Booth (New Haven: Yale University Press, 1993), p. 281. Beiner also complains that "the notion of an extrahuman standard that limits the uses to which we may put nature in submission to our ends is simply unintelligible" (p. 284). Beiner overlooks the fact that moral personality itself is an "extrahuman standard" on Kant's view and thus not an example of "western subjectivism." The feeling of the sublime is a way for human beings to gain a glimpse of noumenal moral character, but it is by no means an attempt to exert mere human standards over nature.

26. Beck, *A Commentary on Kant's Critique of Practical Reason*, p. 220.

27. This particular labeling of respect as a *negative* pleasure (cf. 5:269) seems to contradict his remark in *KpV* that respect is "the ground of a positive feeling which is not of empirical origin" (5:73; cf. 75). His double dualisms (pain/pleasure; negative/positive) do not leave him with enough options. Still, perhaps we are entitled to say both that the more serious feeling of the sublime appears negative when compared

to the bright charms of the beautiful, and that on its own it produces a positive feeling of admiration.

28. Zammito, *The Genesis of Kant's Critique of Judgment*, p. 300.

29. See Barbara Herman, *The Practice of Moral Judgment* (Cambridge: Harvard University Press, 1993), pp. 122, 55–56, 86, 127, 235.

30. Zammito, *The Genesis of Kant's Critique of Judgment*, p. 300.

31. Beck, *A Commentary on Kant's Critique of Practical Reason*, pp. 220–21. See also Zammito, *The Genesis of Kant's Critique of Judgment*, pp. 300–301.

32. See chapter 5 "History" for discussion of the Critique of Teleological Judgment. On imagination, see Rudolf A. Makkreel, *Imagination and Interpretation in Kant* (Chicago: University of Chicago Press, 1990), and Jane Kneller, "Imaginative Freedom and the German Enlightenment," *Journal of the History of Ideas* 51 (1990): 217–32, and "Imagination and the Possibility of Moral Reform in the *Critique of Aesthetic Judgment*," in *Akten des Siebenten Internationalen Kant-Kongresses*, edited by G. Funke (Bonn: Bouvier, 1991), pp. 665–75. Kneller argues in the second article that Kant's position on the role of imagination in ethics is unsteady. In the first *Critique* imagination "is granted only dependent status"; in the second it seems to become "irrelevant" (p. 668). And in the third *Critique*, the strong role advocated for the imagination in ethics at the end of section 17—where Kant argues that human imagination can express, in a direct, non-symbolic form, the effects of morality: "make visible, as it were, in bodily expression (as an effect of the inner)" (5:235)—is undercut by the merely symbolic role assigned to the imagination in section 59 (pp. 672–73).

33. "Moral Anthropology in Kant's Aesthetics and Ethics," pp. 391, 387. If Guyer means to imply here that Kant's aesthetic theory is *simply* a subdivision of his moral anthropology, the claim is clearly false. Again (cf. n. 4), Kant asserts in the preface to *KU* that his investigation of taste is not being undertaken "with regard to the formation and culture of taste . . . but merely in regard to a transcendental aim [*transcendentale Absicht*]" (5:170). Although Kant does not always adhere to this self-imposed restriction, it is clear that much of *KU* is concerned with transcendental aspects of aesthetic judgment. On the other hand, as I have argued at length (see chap. 3), Kant's moral anthropology is primarily an empirical, non-transcendental inquiry. The fact that Kant officially presents his anthropology in "a handbook . . . for undergraduate lectures" is itself a hint that we are dealing with a popular, applied, empirical doctrine rather than a tome of transcendental philosophy.

34. "The Deductions in the *Critique of Judgment*: Comments on Hampshire and Horstmann," in Förster, *Kant's Transcendental Deductions*, p. 188.

35. Michel Despland, *Kant on History and Religion* (Montreal: McGill-Queens University Press, 1973), p. 205. Despland does not specify which "observed facts of history" he has in mind in this discussion.

36. Hans Michael Baumgartner, "Das 'Ethische Gemeine Wesen' und die Kirche in Kants 'Religionsschrift'," in *Kant über Religion*, edited by Friedo Ricken and Francois Marty (Stuttgart: W. Kohlhammer, 1992), p. 163.

37. James Collins, *The Emergence of Philosophy of Religion* (New Haven: Yale University Press, 1967), p. 185. Similarly, Gordon E. Michalson Jr., in *The Historical Dimensions of a Rational Faith: The Role of History in Kant's Religious Thought* (Washington, D.C.: University Press of America, 1979), repeatedly stresses the point that "as limited and sensuous beings, we are unable consistently to appreciate the truth and mandates of a pure moral faith and need heuristic aids suited to our sensuous condition. . . . For epistemological reasons, then, Kant's theory of historical religion is a necessary concession to man's conditioned situation as finite rational creature" (p. 60, cf. pp. 5–6, 12, 96, 120, 122, 124, 126). Kant's frequent references to (human) conditions of experience, or *Erfahrungsbedingungen* (cf. 6:105), in his account of the church also cast doubt on the strength of his alleged commitment to deism.

Unlike the deists, Kant does not reject revealed religion, but rather views it as (humanly) necessary. For discussion, see Allen Wood, "Kant's Deism," in *Kant's Philosophy of Religion Reconsidered*, edited by Philip J. Rossi and Michael Wreen (Bloomington: Indiana University Press, 1991), pp. 1–21.

38. See Howard Williams, *Kant's Political Philosophy* (New York: St. Martin's Press, 1983), p. 261.

39. See Philip J. Rossi, "The Ethical Commonwealth: Moral Progress and the Human Place in the Cosmos," (typescript), p. 6; cf. p. 1. Similarly, in "The Social Authority of Reason: The 'True Church' as the Locus for Moral Progress," Rossi argues that "Kant's account . . . does not adequately specify the means by which" the social authority of the church is to accomplish its task of building moral community; in *Proceedings of the Eighth International Kant Congress*, edited by Hoke Robinson (Milwaukee: Marquette University Press, 1995), vol. 2, pt. 2, p. 679; cf. p. 684.

40. See Despland, *Kant on History and Religion*, p. 205.

41. Hans Michael Baumgartner, "Das 'Ethische Gemeine Wesen' und die Kirche in Kants 'Religionsschrift'," p. 162.

42. Allen W. Wood, *Kant's Moral Religion* (Ithaca: Cornell University Press, 1970), p. 196. Similarly, in his more recent essay "Rational Theology, Moral Faith, and Religion," Wood suggests that Kant is arguing not for "the abolition of ecclesiastical faith, but only the appreciation of which aspects of it are superfluous" in *The Cambridge Companion to Kant*, edited by Paul Guyer (New York: Cambridge University Press, 1992, p. 409.

43. Michalson, *The Historical Dimensions of a Rational Faith*, pp. 124–25.

44. See Despland, *Kant on History and Religion*, p. 227; Wood, *Kant's Moral Religion*, p. 200.

45. Kant and the Jews: another sad story. On the one hand (as the saying goes), some of his best friends were Jews. In a letter to Moses Mendelssohn of February 7, 1766, he writes: "I accept your offer of future continuation of correspondence with pleasure" (10:67–68). (Mendelssohn beat out Kant in the 1763 essay competition sponsored by the Berlin Royal Academy of Science; Kant's second-place effort was published the following year as *Inquiry Concerning the Clarity of the Principles of Natural Theology and Morality*. Their subsequent correspondence with one another is extensive.) And in a letter of August 20, 1777, to his former student Marcus Herz, Kant writes: "both in talent and in feeling you are that rare student who makes all the effort that goes into my often thankless job seem amply rewarded" (10:211–12). Herz returns the compliment in his letter to Kant of November 24, 1778: "[N]ot a day passes where I do not reflect on how impossible it is that I could ever repay you, through all of my actions in the world, the tenth part of happiness that I enjoy in a single hour, which I owe to you and to you alone" (10:244).

But Kant was also prone to stereotypical anti-Semitic remarks in both his private correspondence and published writings. In a notorious letter to Karl Leonhard Reinhold of May 12, 1789, he complains about an unflattering portrait of him painted by Moses Samuel Löwe with the quip: "a Jew always paints people to look like Jews, and the proof of this is in the nose" (11:33). (The evidence of Kant's *Totenmaske* shows that Löwe rendered Kant's nose very accurately.) And in a later letter to Reinhold of March 28, 1794, he speaks disparagingly of Salomon Maimon: "as to what Maimon with his *touching up* [*Nachbesserung*] of the critical philosophy actually wants (Jews always like to do that sort of thing, to give themselves an air of importance at the expense of a stranger), I have never really been able to grasp what he is after" (11:495). Finally, in a lengthy footnote in *Anthropology from a Pragmatic Point of View* he refers to Jews as "a whole nation of merchants" who are "nonproductive members of society," "the great majority of whom have received the not ungrounded reputation of deceivers" (7:205–6 n; cf. *Prak. Phil. Herder* 27:61, 75).

46. In this passage we see what might be called Kant's immortality assumption at work. The assumption is made explicit a few lines later: "Now since no religion at all can be conceived without belief in a future life, Judaism, which, when taken in its purity is seen to lack this belief, therefore contains no religious faith at all" (6: 126).

47. Compare Paul Laurence Rose's discussion, "Kant and the 'Euthanasia of Judaism,'" in *German Question/Jewish Question: Revolutionary Antisemitism from Kant to Wagner* (Princeton: Princeton University Press, 1990), pp. 93–97. I agree with Rose's claim that we unfortunately find "a collection of potent anti-Jewish concepts" in Kant (p. 96). However, I think Rose also fails to appreciate the basic rationalistic thrust of Kant's philosophy of religion. Most of what Kant says about Judaism applies to *all* historical faiths. All of them eventually must be "euthanized"; all of them need to work at "throwing off the garments of the ancient cult." Admittedly though, some faiths will have to shed more garments than others. But the metaphor Kant employs in this discussion also confuses matters. By "euthanasia" he does not mean (as Rose seems to think) total extinction, but rather (as the garment metaphor implies) a shedding of the exterior, phenomenal trappings of the ancient cult so that the unadorned moral core can shine through. Rose is able to exploit effective rhetorical capital from the fact that the Nazis also later used the term "euthanasia" to promote the mass killings of thousands of handicapped and mentally retarded people for the sake of "racial purity," but Kant is not the guilty party here. For a less inflammatory portrait, see Fritz Gause, "Kant und die Juden," reprinted in Fritz Gause and Jürgen Lebuhn, *Kant und Königsberg bis Heute* (Leer, Germany: Gerhard Rautenberg, 1989), pp. 147–49.

48. Helmuth von Glasenapp, *Kant und die Religionen des Ostens* (Kitzingen-Main: Holzner, 1954), p. 105. Glasenapp is citing here from a *Diktattext* which comes from an early version (according to Adickes, circa 1760) of Kant's *Physical Geography* lectures. See pp. 4–5. Glasenapp's study includes detailed citations and evaluations of Kant's occasional remarks (often located in unpublished lectures) on the religions of India, Tibet, China, and Japan.

49. Nietzsche, "'Reason' in Philosophy," section 6 in *Twilight of the Idols*, in *The Portable Nietzsche*, edited by Walter Kaufmann (New York: Viking Press, 1954), p. 484.

50. This lack of specificity perhaps allows us to ask: Why (only?) the church? Might there not be other (institutional as well as non-institutional) ways to promote moral community, "to find yet other, and more successful, ways to unite well-being and virtue in our public practices" (Thomas Auxter, *Kant's Moral Teleology* [Macon: Mercer University Press, 1982], p. 181)? While I don't think Kant is opposed to the inclusion of other means of promoting moral culture (Auxter mentions "dramatic presentations, readings, festivals"; and, as we have seen, *all* of the arts and sciences deserve mention here), certainly a major motive behind his discussion of the church concerns his desire to demonstrate the religious significance of ethics. As Michalson argues, Kant in effect *must* turn to the church in explicating the idea of a moral community, for "given his theory of what genuinely obeying the moral law implies (i.e., viewing *moral* duties as *divine commands*), the concept of an authentic ethical commonwealth can be meaningful only when understood in reference to God"; *The Historical Dimensions of a Rational Faith*, p. 122. As Kant writes: "[A] moral community is conceivable only as a people under divine commands, that is, as a *people of God*, and indeed *in accordance with laws of virtue*" (6:99).

51. Michalson, for instance, remarks that Kant holds that human beings are pervaded by radical evil for reasons that "somewhat surprisingly—stem as much from a survey of empirical data as from a priori reasoning about human nature"; "The Inscrutability of Moral Evil in Kant," *Thomist* 51 (1987): 256. Similarly, Otfried

Höffe notes in "Ein Thema wiedergewinnen: Kant über das Böse" that Kant's thesis that evil belongs to human beings by nature "has an anthropological status, although this point is absent in the corresponding debates" in the secondary literature; Otfried Höffe and Annemarie Pieper, eds., *F. W. J. Schelling: Über das Wesen der menschlichen Freiheit* (Berlin: Akademie, 1995), p. 29. Marcus Willaschek, in his discussion "How One Obtains an Intelligible Character," also notes that Kant's argument concerning radical evil in the *Religion* rests on an "empirical-anthropological insight;" in *Praktische Vernunft: Handlungstheorie und Moralbegründung bei Kant* (J. B. Metzler: Stuttgart, 1992), p. 152.

52. "Part One. Concerning the Indwelling of the Evil Principle next to the Good: or, On the Radical Evil in Human Nature" (6:18). "I. Concerning the Original Predisposition to Good in Human Nature" (6:26). "II. Concerning the Propensity to Evil in Human Nature" (6:28). "III. The Human Being is by Nature Evil" (6:32). "IV. Concerning the Origin of Evil in Human Nature" (6:39). See also 6:11.

53. However, the argument is not solely empirical. Moral evil (like moral good) is a matter of maxims rather than of external behavior,

> but one cannot observe maxims, not even those within oneself with certainty; hence the judgment that the agent is an evil human being cannot be grounded with certainty on experience. In order, then, to call a human being evil one must be able to infer a priori from several consciously evil acts, or even from one, an evil maxim lying at the ground, and, from this, the presence in the subject of a common underlying ground of all particular morally-evil maxims, which is itself again a maxim. (6:20)

All attributions of moral evil in human beings involve inferences from visible behavior to invisible motives. But the arguments at the behavioral level are inductive.

54. Pierre Laberge, "Das radikale Böse und der Völkerstand," in *Kant über Religion* edited by Friedo Ricken and Francois Marty (Stuttgart: W. Wohlhammer, 1992), p. 112.

55. Kant's litany of examples under this first heading includes "scenes of unprovoked cruelty in the ritual murders of Tofoa, New Zealand, and the Navigator Islands, and the never-ending cruelty in the wide wastes of northwestern America (which Captain Hearne cites), cruelty from which no human being reaps the smallest benefit" (6:33). Samuel Hearne (1745–92) accompanied Cook on his third voyage. Georg Wobbermin, editor of the Academy Edition of Kant's *Religion*, notes that "one finds a short report of the results of Hearne's voyage in *The Third Voyage of Discovery of Captain J. Cook*, translated by [Georg] Forster, 1798, I, Introduction, p. 51A ff. The explanation that Kant alludes to is on p. 54 ff" (6:501). But *Religion* was published in 1793, and part 1 (from which the above quotation is taken) appeared even earlier, in the April 1792 issue of Biester's *Berlinische Monatsschrift*. How did Kant manage to cite from a 1798 publication in his own text of 1792? Answer: Forster's translation was published in 1789, not 1798. The Academy date is incorrect. George di Giovanni, in a note to his recent English translation of Kant's *Religion*, lists a publication date of 1792 for Forster's translation, but also manages to misspell "Forster" as "Förster"; *Religion and Rational Theology* (New York: Cambridge University Press, 1996), p. 458 n. 22. Theodore M. Greene and Hoyt H. Hudson, in their earlier translation, surmise that "Kant evidently had read the brief account of Hearne's travels in Douglas's Introduction to *Cook's Third Voyage*, London, 1784"; *Religion within the Limits of Reason Alone* (Chicago: Open Court, 1934; reprint, New York: Harper and Row, 1960), p. 28 n. 2]. But Kant supposedly could not read English! At any rate, this mysterious passage not only indicates Kant's opposition to more romantic, Rousseauian accounts of the state of nature (that is to say his alignment with Hobbes on this point—cf. *Frieden* 8:348–49), but also echoes his conviction

that non-western European peoples stand entirely outside of culture and civilization. (See "Races" and "Peoples" in chap. 3.) Finally, Kant's position as to whether moral evil can be ascribed accurately to *die Wilden* also changed over the years. In one of his *Reflexionen zur Anthropologie*, he writes that "evil can not be ascribed to *die Wilden*, but only to the civilized human being" (*Refl* 1498, 15:781).

56. Kant also elaborates twice on "the wickedness in human nature, which reveals itself openly in the free relations among *Völker*" in *Perpetual Peace* (8:355, cf. 375 n). Laberge examines these parallels in "Das radikale Böse und der Völkerzustand."

57. An additional appeal to experience can be found in the following passage from *Anthropology from a Pragmatic Point of View*:

> [E]xperience shows [*die Erfahrung zeigt*], that in the human being there is a propensity toward the active desire of what is not allowed, although he knows at the same time that it is not allowed; that is to say, toward *evil*, [and it] arises as unavoidably and as soon as the human being rises up to make use of his freedom, and that is why the propensity can be regarded as innate [*angeboren*]. (7:324)

This passage summarizes several key points from Kant's longer argument in part 1 of the *Religion*.

58. This second, "heroic [*heroische*] opinion," Kant notes, "has gained standing only among philosophers, and in our time chiefly among educators [*Pädagogen*]" (6: 19–20). Here he indicates that his earlier enthusiasm for Basedow and the Philanthropinist movement has cooled somewhat. See my earlier discussion in chapter 2, "Experimentation and Revolution."

59. Michalson, *Fallen Freedom: Kant on Radical Evil and Moral Regeneration* (New York: Cambridge University Press, 1990), p. 46. Michalson also notes "the peculiarity of this appeal to experience, one which cannot possibly support the argumentative weight Kant seems to be placing on it" (p. 46). As is well known, in *KrV* Kant is adamant that empirical universality is "only an arbitrary extension of a validity holding in most cases to one which holds in all" (B 4)—experience "gives us no true universality" (A 1). It is odd that in the *Religion* he tries to support the claim that "[a]ll human beings are evil" by appealing to experience.

60. Edith Nahler and Horst Nahler, eds., *Schillers Werke* (Weimar: Hermann Böhlaus Nachfolger, 1992), 26:219.

61. Karl Robert Mandelkow, ed., *Goethes Briefe* (Hamburg: Christian Wegner, 1964), 2:166. See Despland, *Kant on History and Religion*, p. 169; Emil L. Fackenheim, "Kant and Radical Evil," *University of Toronto Quarterly* 33 (1954): 340; and Karl Barth, *Protestant Thought: From Rousseau to Ritschl*, trans. Brian Cozens (New York: Simon and Schuster, 1969), p. 178.

62. Barth, *Protestant Thought: From Rousseau to Ritschl*, p. 176.

63. Despland, *Kant on History and Religion*, p. 170. Despland sees two texts as crucial here: *An Attempt at some Reflections on Optimism* (1759), and *On the Failure of All Philosophical Attempts in Theodicy* (1791). In the former piece, which is a short essay that Kant used as a vehicle to announce his lecture courses on numerous subjects for the coming semester (2:35), he defends a Leibnizian view of evil as the mere absence of good, proclaiming cavalierly at the beginning that evil is an idea "which is so easy, so natural, that one eventually says that it is common and disgusts [*verekelt*] people of more refined taste, [and] cannot maintain itself as an object of respect for long" (2:29). Despland then cites Borowski, one of Kant's earliest biographers, who once asked Kant for a copy of the essay. Kant, Borowski relates, "with a genuinely solemn seriousness, asked me not to think any more about this writing on optimism, urging me, if I ever came across it anywhere, to give it to no one, but to put it away quickly" (*Darstellung des Lebens und Charakters Immanuel Kants* (1804),

reprinted in Groß, *Immanuel Kant. Sein Leben in Darstellungen von Zeitgenossen*, p. 29 n. 19. Despland regards *Optimism's* "treatment of evil and its acceptance of Leibnizian optimism" as the cause of Kant's repudiation (p. 170). In the second essay, which Despland calls "the decisive turning point," evil appears as something "that must be suffered and borne by man, Job-like in patience and faith" (p. 171). God shows Job "the horrible side" of creation, where "harmful and fearsome things are named" (8: 266).

64. Fackenheim, in "Kant and Radical Evil," refers to part of this passage to support his claim that "Kant had spoken of evil before, but never radical evil" (p. 340). Allen Wood refers to the same passage to support his counterclaim that "Kant had even addressed himself to the question of radical evil, though his early discussion exhibits nothing of the sophistication found in the *Religion's* treatment of this question"; *Kant's Moral Religion* (Ithaca: Cornell University Press: 1970), p. 209; cf. Kant, *Lectures on Philosophical Theology*, translated by Allen W. Wood and Gertrude M. Clark (Ithaca: Cornell University Press, 1978), p. 117 n. 6]. In my view, it is stretching things a bit to claim that this passage from Pölitz constitutes a discussion of "radical" evil. At the same time, as I demonstrate later, there are numerous other passages from Kant's pre-*Religion* writings that clearly do fit this description. See also my citations from *An Attempt at Some Reflections on Optimism* in note 63 for further evidence of Kant's early Leibnizian views of evil.

65. Henry Allison, "Reflections on the Banality of (Radical) Evil: A Kantian Analysis," in *Idealism and Freedom: Essays on Kant's Theoretical and Practical Philosophy* (New York: Cambridge University Press, 1996), p. 174; Fackenheim, "Kant and Radical Evil," p. 340.

66. See Sidgwick's discussion, "The Kantian Conception of Free Will," included as an appendix in the seventh edition of *The Methods of Ethics* (London: Macmillan, 1907; reprint, Indianapolis: Hackett, 1981), especially p. 516. For discussion, see Christine Korsgaard, "Morality as Freedom," reprinted in *Creating the Kingdom of Ends* (New York: Cambridge University Press, 1996), especially pp. 171–72 and Heiner F. Klemme, "Die Freiheit der Willkür und die Herrschaft des Bösen: Kants Lehre vom radikalen Bösen zwischen Moral, Religion und Recht," in Heiner F. Klemme, Bernd Ludwig, Miachel Pauen, and Werner Stark, eds., *Aufklarung und Interpretation: Studien zu Kants Philosophie und ihrem Umkreis* (Würzbug: Königshausen & Neumann, 1999).

67. Paton, translator's notes to *Groundwork of the Metaphysic of Morals*, 3rd ed. (London: Hutchinson, 1956; reprint, New York: Harper and Row, 1964), p. 142 (see 98 n. 2). See also his discussion "Is Only a Good Will Free?" in *The Categorical Imperative*, pp. 213–14.

68. Hannah Arendt, *The Origins of Totalitarianism* (New York: Harcourt, Brace and World, 1951), p. 459, as quoted by Allison, "Reflections on the Banality of (Radical) Evil: A Kantian Analysis," p. 169. In her later work *Eichmann in Jerusalem: A Report on the Banality of Evil*, rev. and enl. ed. (New York: Viking Press, 1964), Arendt argues that evil is merely banal rather than diabolical. Allison argues convincingly that what Arendt means by "banal" evil (e.g., the thoughtlessness and self-deception revealed in Eichmann's character) is in fact part of what Kant means by "radical" evil, and that her own later view of evil (particularly in its denial of the existence of radical evil) "reflects a deep misunderstanding of what Kant intended by this conception" (p. xxi).

69. Michalson, *Fallen Freedom*, p. 54.

70. As Bernard Carnois notes, we find here "an astonishing reversal of Kant's terminology," in which "the term 'nature' receives a meaning altogether different from that which ordinarily is attached to it and comes to designate freedom" rather than determinism; *The Coherence of Kant's Doctrine of Freedom*, translated by David Booth (Chicago: University of Chicago Press, 1987), pp. 95–96. This odd and un-

expected usage adds to the difficulty of deciphering Kant's position in part 1 of *Religion*.

71. In the *Groundwork*, for instance, Kant at one point expresses undisguised hostility toward the inclinations: "[I]t must be the universal wish of every rational being to be entirely free" from inclinations (4:428). Schiller may have this passage in mind when he notes that Kantian radical evil is not to be confused with "the provocations of sensibility" (cf. n. 60).

72. Michalson complains that "it is not at all clear what the point of the . . . [first] two degrees of evil is, or whether they are in fact examples of 'moral' evil" (*Fallen Freedom*, p. 45). Admittedly, it would sound odd to refer to weakness of will itself (level 1) as a form of evil. But again, Kant refers to them only as degrees of the *propensity to* (*Hang zum*) evil, rather than as degrees of evil per se. Acting from weakness of will is not an example of radical evil, but insofar as it involves acting from a non-moral motive it "heads one down the same track," where wickedness (level 3) is the last stop. For further discussion, see Carnois, *The Coherence of Kant's Doctrine of Freedom*, pp. 104–6.

73. John Silber objects vehemently to this particular aspect of Kant's position: "[I]n dismissing the devilish rejection of the law as an illusion, Kant called attention to the limitations of his conception of freedom rather than to the limits of human freedom itself. . . . Kant's insistence to the contrary, man's free power to reject the law in defiance is an ineradicable fact of human experience"; "The Ethical Significance of Kant's *Religion*," in *Religion within the Limits of Reason Alone*, translated by Theodor M. Greene and Hoyt H. Hudson (New York: Harper and Row, 1960), p. cxxix. For discussion to which I am indebted, see Wood, *Kant's Moral Religion*, pp. 212–14.

74. Allison, "Reflections on the Banality of (Radical) Evil," p. 174.

75. Despland, *Kant on History and Religion*, p. 192.

5. History

1. The publication story here is a bit more complicated. This essay was actually first published by Kant in 1798 as the second part of *The Conflict of the Faculties*. But in a letter to J. H. Tieftrunk of October 13, 1797, Kant writes that "Herr Professor Genischen" (one of his regular dinner companions) "has come across two essays in my bureau . . . [that] have been there for more than two years" (12:208; cf. 12:312). Most scholars today believe that the manuscripts in question were what eventually became parts 1 and 2 of *Conflict*. It is also not certain just what Kant is alluding to he when he speaks in his title of "an old question raised again [*Erneuerte Frage*]." For two conflicting hypotheses, see Klaus Reich's introduction to his edition of the *Streit der Fakultäten* (Hamburg: Felix Meiner, 1959), p. xv–xvii; and Reinhard Brandt, "Zum 'Streit der Fakultäten'," in *Neue Autographen und Dokumente zu Kant's Leben, Schriften und Vorlesungen*, edited by Brandt and Werner Stark (Hamburg: Felix Meiner, 1987), pp. 46–48. But these minor mysteries notwithstanding, the second part of *Streit* is definitely one of Kant's most important efforts in the philosophy of history.

2. Ludwig Landgrebe, "Die Geschichte im Denken Kants," *Studium Generale* 7 (1954): 533.

3. Emil L. Fackenheim, "Kant's Concept of History," *Kant-Studien* 48 (1957): 381.

4. Immanuel Kant, *On History*, edited by Lewis White Beck (Indianapolis: Bobbs-Merrill, 1963), p. vii.

5. Yirmiahu Yovel, *Kant and the Philosophy of History* (Princeton University Press, 1980), p. x; cf. pp. 21, 271–72. Yovel presents his untenability claim as part of a "historical antinomy." Thesis: Kant's philosophy of history is "both genuine and cen-

tral in Kant's system" (271). Antithesis: his philosophy of history is untenable in terms of his system. However, unlike Kant's own analysis of antinomies in *KrV*, Yovel denies that the incongruity between this particular thesis and antithesis "can be resolved" (300).

6. William A. Galston, *Kant and the Problem of History* (Chicago: University of Chicago Press, 1975), p. 232. For a reply, see van der Linden, *Kantian Ethics and Socialism* (Indianapolis: Hackett, 1988), pp. 103–4, 116–22. See also my earlier discussions "Born Too Early" and "The Lucky Ones" in chapter 2.

7. Ludwig Siep, "Das Recht als Ziel der Geschichte: Überlegungen im Anschluß an Kant und Hegel," in *Das Recht der Vernunft: Kant und Hegel über Denken, Erkennen und Handeln*, edited by Christel Fricke, Peter König, and Thomas Petersen (Stuttgart: Frommann-Holzboog, 1995), p. 356. I am indebted to Siep's analysis on several points in the following discussion.

8. Pauline Kleingeld, *Fortschritt und Vernunft: Zur Geschichtsphilosophie Kants* (Würzburg: Könighausen und Neumann, 1995), p. 36.

9. That is, there may be other rational beings in other systems of nature elsewhere who constitute the final end of nature within their own particular system. Kant's philosophy of history texts, like his aesthetics and religion writings generally, assume for the most part a "humans only" scope. This narrower scope connects them all directly to the concerns of impure ethics. At the same time, in each of these three areas of his work we find occasional allusions to other kinds of rational beings elsewhere.

10. That is, it is not the case, as Alex Sutter and other critics of the Enlightenment have asserted, that Kant is merely "stylizing the recent European culture of domination of nature into a universally valid concept of culture"; "Kant und die 'Wilden'": Zum impliziten Rassismus in der Kantischen Geschichtphilosophie," *Prima Philosophie* 2 (1989): 258. Cultivation (namely, the forming of human talents and capacities through participation in cultural activities) is a necessary preparatory step to moralization (cf. *Anth* 7:324, *KU* 5:433). Kant is committed to the claim that participation in *some sort of* culture is a necessary presupposition to active participation in the human moral community. But he is not logically committed to the claim that only one specific kind of culture can satisfy this requirement—his occasional racist remarks about the incapacity of certain peoples to produce culture notwithstanding. For discussion, see "Culture" and "The Whole Human Race" in chapter 3.

11. Allen D. Rosen, *Kant's Theory of Justice* (Ithaca: Cornell University Press, 1993), p. 119. In his discussion entitled "Justifying Political Society" (pp. 118–28), Rosen fails to mention Kant's position that civil society itself is a necessary precondition for the development of culture. This claim itself strengthens the Kantian argument concerning the duty to enter civil society.

12. Patrick Riley, *Kant's Political Philosophy* (Totowa, NJ: Rowman and Allenheld, 1983), p. 78.

13. Kant normally asserts that human beings in fact are the only rational beings "in the world"—that is, on planet Earth (cf. *Anth* 7:321). Does 'world' (*Welt*) here perhaps not mean "planet Earth?" At any rate, it is clear that his considered view is that *every type* of rational being considered as a moral being constitutes the highest end of natural creation (cf. *Gr* 4:428). Human beings are not the only creatures who meet this criterion, and they meet it only in so far as they are rational beings.

14. Otfried Höffe, *Immanuel Kant*, translated by Marshall Farrier (Albany: State University of New York Press, 1994), p. 198 (translation modified slightly).

15. Wolfgang Kersting, "Exkurs: Geschichte als Rechtsfortschritt gelesen," in *Wohlgeordnete Freiheit: Immanuel Kants Rechts- und Staatsphilosophie* (Frankfurt: Suhrkamp, 1993), pp. 84–85. The Suhrkamp paperback edition of this work contains an extensive introduction—from which the preceding passage is taken—"Kant und die

politische Philosophie der Gegenwart," pp. 9–87. The original edition was published by Walter de Gruyter in 1984.

16. Siep, "Das Recht als Ziel der Geschichte," p. 363. Compare Klaus Weyand, who, in his discussion entitled "The Place of Philosophy of History in Kant's System"—a much-debated question— asserts: "Kant's philosophy of history is no part of the ethics and therefore its entire structure cannot be made into a subordinate group of that discipline"; in *Kants Geschichtsphilosophie: Ihre Entwicklung und ihr Verhältnis zur Aufklärung* (Cologne: Kölner Universitäts-Verlag, 1964), p. 37.

17. Yovel, *Kant and the Philosophy of History*, pp. 31, 127.

18. Fritz Medicus, "Zu Kants Philosophie der Geschichte mit besonderer Beziehung auf K. Lamprecht," *Kant-Studien* 4 (1900): 66. See also R. G. Collingwood, who holds that "the Kantian theory of history is an application of the Kantian ethics. . . . This doctrine is not unworthy of its great author"; *The Idea of History* (Oxford: Clarendon Press, 1946), p. 102. Similarly, Yovel argues that Kant's practical system should "be divided into two parts or stages, the formal and the material"; *Kant and the Philosophy of History*, p. 32. To the "old" imperative of the first part (namely, the categorical imperative) Yovel adds "a new imperative with a definite content—'act to promote the highest good in the world'"; what he calls the "*historical* imperative" (pp. 33, 7). One drawback of the Hegelian terminology of both Medicus and Yovel is that it implies that first part of Kant's ethics is "merely" formal, that is, totally lacking in content. But as I have argued previously (see chap. 1, n. 9), this is not Kant's position. Formal principles on his view have necessary and universal (that is to say non-contingent and non-empirical) content; which is to say that they are far from empty. However, the content at this first level is admittedly abstract and general, since it is intentionally not tailored to the needs and situation of any particular type of finite rational being. My distinction between pure (non-empirical) and impure (empirical) parts of ethics does not make this mistake of placing content only in the second part, and also allows us to more readily understand why the study of human history belongs in the second part of ethics. See also Manfred Riedel, who also argues that Kant's philosophy of history properly belongs "to the empirical part of moral philosophy"; "Einleitung," in Kant, *Schriften zur Geschichtsphilosophie* (Stuttgart: Reclam, 1974), p. 11. A second drawback of the formal/material dichotomy (particularly as Yovel formulates it) is that it becomes virtually impossible to understand Kant's conviction that the categorical imperative itself *grounds* the duty to promote the highest good, that is, that it is "*a priori* (morally) necessary, *to bring forth the highest good through the freedom of the will*" (*KpV* 5:113). For discussion, see van der Linden, *Kantian Ethics and Socialism*, especially pp. 18–38.

19. Manfred Riedel, "Einleitung," p. 10. See also Yovel's characterization of Kant's "philosophy of practice" as "the *realization* of morality in the realm of nature . . . the reshaping of given empirical orders to fit moral demands"; *Kant and the Philosophy of History*, p. 29. Riedel understandably goes a bit over the top in proclaiming that moral concepts demand that the human world "agree with them," as does Yovel when he suggests that morality can be completely realized in nature. What Kant actually says is only that the idea of a "moral world" is "a practical idea that really can and ought to have its influence on the sensible world, in order to bring it as much as possible into conformity [*so viel als möglich gemäß*] with this idea" (*KrV* A 808/B 836). Total agreement between the two is impossible; indeed if such agreement were reached, the idea of a moral world would lose its status as a regulative rather than constitutive principle (cf. *KrV* B 223).

20. W. H. Walsh, *An Introduction to Philosophy of History* (London: Hutchinson's University Library, 1951), p. 123.

21. Howard Williams, *Kant's Political Philosophy* (New York: St. Martin's Press, 1983), p. 19. Williams refers specifically to my previous citation from Walsh in a

footnote at this point, but his overall interpretation of Kant's philosophy of history as applied moral philosophy ("applied" in the sense that it provides human beings specific directions and aims for their moral efforts) perhaps owes even more to Friedrich Kaulbach's work. On Kaulbach's interpretation, Kant's philosophy of history is "itself an orientation for praxis." The human being as a free-acting subject needs to make use of a context of orientation, "just as a traveler helps himself to a map, in order to identify the way and the destination"; "Welchen Nutzen gibt Kant der Geschichtsphilosophie?" in *Kant-Studien* 66 (1975): 70, 78–79. Similarly, in his earlier essay "Weltorientierung, Weltkenntnis und pragmatische Vernunft bei Kant," Kaulbach tried to show how materials from Kant's *Physical Geography* and *Anthropology* lectures also build on the idea of a global orientation task that seeks to provide one with "a plan, a map of the whole, within which one is able to determine one's own position and can trace out for oneself the path by which one can reach one's chosen goals"; *Kritik und Metaphysik. Studien. Heinz Heimsoeth zum achtzigsten Geburtstag*, edited by Friedrich Kaulbach and Joachim Ritter (Berlin: Walter de Gruyter, 1966), p. 61.

22. Kleingeld, *Fortschritt und Vernunft*, p. 14.

23. Sharon Anderson-Gold, "A Common Vocation: Humanity as a Moral Species," in *Proceedings of the Eighth International Kant Congress*, edited by Hoke Robinson, vol. 2, pt. 2 (Milwaukee: Marquette University Press, 1995), p. 693.

24. See Lewis White Beck's gloss on *Streit* 7:91–92 in his editor's introduction to *On History* (Indianapolis: Bobbs-Merrill, 1963), p. xxvi.

25. Kleingeld, *Fortschritt und Vernunft*, p. 52.

26. Friedrich Kaulbach, "Welchen Nutzen gibt Kant der Geschichtsphilosophie?" p. 83.

27. Allison, *Kant's Theory of Freedom* (New York: Cambridge University Press, 1990), p. 32. For a reply, see Kleingeld, *Fortschritt und Vernunft*, pp. 74–75.

28. Van der Linden, *Kantian Ethics and Socialism*, p. 137.

29. Riley, *Kant's Political Philosophy*, p. 80.

30. Johann Gottlieb Fichte, *Die Grundzüge des gegenwärtigen Zeitalters*, with an introduction by Alwin Diemer (Hamburg: Felix Meiner, 1978), 11th lecture, pp. 174–75. These lectures were originally presented in Berlin in 1804–5.

31. Adam Smith, *An Inquiry into the Nature and Causes of the Wealth of Nations* (1776), edited by Edwin Cannan (New York: Modern Library, 1937), p. 423. See also Galston, *Kant and the Problem of History*, p. 212. For similar "invisible hand" accounts of human progress in Joseph Butler and others, see my essay "Butler's Divine Utilitarianism," *History of Philosophy Quarterly* 12 (1995): 265–80.

32. Kersting, *Wohlgeordnete Freiheit*, p. 85. See Hegel: "It is not the universal idea that involves itself in opposition and combat and exposes itself to danger; it remains in the background, unaffected and uninjured. One can call this the *cunning of reason* [*List der Vernunft*]—that it sets the passions to work for itself, while that through which it develops itself pays the penalty and suffers the loss"; *Vorlesungen über die Philosophie der Geschichte*, vol. 1, *Die Vernunft in der Geschichte*, edited by Johannes Hoffmeister (Hamburg: Felix Meiner, 1955), p. 105.

33. Yovel, "The Role of War," in *Kant and the Philosophy of History*, p. 152. Compare p. 187:

> Of all the forms of human conflict serving the cunning of nature, war is the most formidable, the most enduring, and the most effective in spurring societies and individuals to the utmost exertion of their talents and natural faculties. But at a certain point it is likely to turn dialectically against itself, when the particular nations, driven by fear, suffering, greed, and intelligent self-interest, will unite to create a world confederation and abolish war.

However, as noted earlier (see "Art as Preparation for Morality" in chap. 4), Kant sometimes seems to suggest that the arts and sciences themselves are also programmed to eventually die out. They prepare us for "a sovereignty in which reason alone shall have power," and in which "the tyranny of the senses" has been overcome (*KU* 5:433). Once reason alone has authority, it is doubtful that human beings would still be in a position to make aesthetic judgments.

34. Reinhard Brandt, "Vom Weltbürgerrecht," in *Immanuel Kant: Zum ewigen Frieden*, edited by Otfried Höffe (Berlin: Akademie, 1995), p. 147. See also Höffe, "Ausblick: Die Vereinten Nationen im Lichte Kants," pp. 248–49 in the same volume. Recent U.S. efforts to improve the human rights situation in China by holding out the economic carrot of increased trade with the West are a case in point.

35. Richard Falk, "Revisioning Cosmopolitanism," in Martha C. Nussbaum with respondents, *For Love of Country: Debating the Limits of Patriotism*, edited by Joshua Cohen (Boston: Beacon Press, 1996), p. 57. Compare Benjamin R. Barber's lament against "'McWorld' . . . my name for the toxic cosmopolitanism of global markets" in the same collection (p. 36).

36. Yovel, *Kant and the Philosophy of History*, p. 139.

37. Williams, *Kant's Political Philosophy*, p. 255.

38. Höffe, in his essay "Völkerbund oder Weltrepublik?" argues that "without a doubt there is a contradiction" between Kant's argument at 8:354 in defense of a *Völkerbund* and his later praise of the "positive idea" of a *Weltrepublik* at 8:357, the latter of which (as Höffe notes) is indeed described as a *Völkerstaat* a few lines earlier; in Höffe, *Immanuel Kant: Zum ewigen Frieden*, p. 124; cf. p. 110). This seems to me to overstate matters. When the passage cited earlier from *MdS* 6:350 is brought into the equation, we can see that Kant's considered view is that a world state would be ineffective and thus not realizable in practice. Höffe's assertion that "the establishing of the *Völkerstaat* is categorically necessary [*kategorisch geboten*]" (p. 124) is not a thesis to which Kant subscribes.

39. Yovel, *Kant and the Philosophy of History*, p. 139. See also p. 194.

40. Literally "the best world." The same term is used at *KU* 5:453. Here we are told that the *Weltbeste* "consists in the combination of the greatest welfare [*Wohl*] of the rational beings in the world [*Weltwesen*] with the supreme condition of their being good, that is, universal happiness in combination with the most law-conforming morality [*gesetzmäßigste Sittlichkeit*]" (cf. *Gemeinspruch* 8:279, 279 n). Related passages in *KU* include 5:435 ("the highest good in the world"), 5:450 ("the *highest good in the world* possible through freedom"), and 5:469 ("the *highest good* in the world to be achieved through freedom").

41. But of course it does not originate with Kant (cf. the epigraph from Diogenes Laertius, attributed to Diogenes the Cynic). For discussion of the Stoic roots of Kant's moral cosmopolitanism, see Martha C. Nussbaum, "Kant and Stoic Cosmopolitanism," *Journal of Political Philosophy* 5 (1997): 1–25. For discussion of the larger cultural setting of German enlightenment cosmopolitanism, see Sabine Roehr, *A Primer on German Enlightenment: With a Translation of Karl Leonhard Reinhold's "The Fundamental Concepts and Principles of Ethics"* (Columbia: University of Missouri Press, 1995), especially pp. 90–91, 114, 117–18.

42. See John R. Silber, "Kant's Conception of the Highest Good as Immanent and Transcendent," *Philosophical Review* 68 (1959): 469–92; and Andrews Reath, "Two Conceptions of the Highest Good in Kant," *Journal of the History of Philosophy* 26 (1988): 593–619. Reath argues that "the theological version is more predominant in the earlier works, such as the first and second *Critiques*, while the secular version is predominant in the third *Critique* and later works" (p. 601). This seems to me to be wishful thinking on Reath's part. As we have seen, even in *Streit*—which was not published until 1798 and is, with the exception of his lectures on *Anthropology*,

the last book Kant published—he asserts that "a new kind of creation (supernatural influence) would be necessary in order for the moral foundation in the human race to be enlarged" (7:92). Also, in *KU* he is very clear in arguing that "*the sole conditions conceivable by us under which* [the] *possibility*" of achieving the highest good is possible are "the existence of God and the immortality of the soul" (5:469). For an attempt to draw some interconnections between this-worldly and other worldly conceptions of the highest good, see Pauline Kleingeld, "What Do the Virtuous Hope For? Rereading Kant's Doctrine of the Highest Good," in Robinson, *Proceedings of the Eighth International Kant Congress*. vol. 1, pt. 1, pp. 91–112.

43. See Beck, "The Concept of the Highest Good," in *A Commentary on Kant's Critique of Practical Reason*, pp. 242–45. For more on the "beyond human capacities" charge, see Thomas Auxter, "The Unimportance of Kant's Highest Good," *Journal of the History of Philosophy* 17 (1979): 121–34. Beck's criticisms of the highest good (he concludes that the assumption of possibility of the highest good is neither "directly necessary to morality" nor something "that we have a moral duty to promote"; p. 245) are to a certain extent foreshadowed by earlier critics such as Hermann Cohen and Arthur Schopenhauer. Cohen, for instance, in *Kants Begründung der Ethik*, 2nd ed. (Berlin: Bruno Cassirer, 1910), asserts that the highest good with its included concept of happiness is inconsistent with the pure foundations of Kant's ethics, concluding that "we can safely do without" any spur or ideal other than the moral law itself (p. 352). And Schopenhauer, in *The World as Will and Representation* (1819), translated by E. F. J. Payne (New York: Dover Publications, 1966), argues that Kant's doctrine of the highest good is incompatible with the thesis of the autonomy of the will; "supreme happiness in the highest good should not really be the motive for virtue; yet there it is like a secret article, the presence of which makes all the rest a mere sham contract. It is not really the reward of virtue, but yet is a voluntary gift for which virtue, after work has been done, stealthily holds its hand open" (1:524). For further discussion, see Wood, *Kant's Moral Religion*, pp. 38–39; Klaus Düsing, "Das Problem des höchsten Gutes in Kants praktischer Philosophie," *Kant-Studien* 62 (1971): 5–42, especially pp. 6, 29; and Stephen Engstrom, "The Concept of the Highest Good in Kant's Moral Theory," *Philosophy and Phenomenological Research* 52 (1992): 747–80.

44. Yovel, *Kant and the Philosophy of History*, pp. 39–40. See also Kleingeld, "What Do the Virtuous Hope For?" pp. 94–95.

6. Saved by Impurity?

1. See Hegel, *Grundlinien der Philosophie des Rechts*, in *Theorie-Werkausgabe*, edited by Eva Moldenhauer and Karl Markus Michel (Frankfurt: Suhrkamp, 1970), vol. 7, section 135, Remark, for the *locus classicus* of this criticism. For discussion of Hegel's formalism charge, see Allen W. Wood, *Hegel's Ethical Thought* (New York: Cambridge University Press, 1990), especially chapter 9. Scheler's critique is presented in *Formalism in Ethics and Non-Formal Ethics of Values*, translated by Manfred S. Frings and Roger L. Funk, 5th rev. ed. (Evanston: Northwestern University Press, 1973). For discussion of Scheler, see Philip Blosser, *Scheler's Critique of Kant's Ethics* (Athens: Ohio University Press, 1995). A number of different "formalism" charges have been made against Kant's ethics; the term is unfortunately used in different ways by different authors. In what follows I am primarily concerned with some of Hegel's criticisms in this area.

2. Hegel, *Grundlinien der Philosophie des Rechts*, section 135, Remark. (Later in the same paragraph Hegel refers to "the further *Kantian* form, the capacity of an action to be represented as a *universal* maxim"; denying that it provides agents with any criterion of moral rightness.) See also Wood, *Hegel's Ethical Thought*, p. 156.

3. Hegel, *Grundlinien der Philosophie des Rechts*, section 148, Remark. Wood distinguishes between weaker and stronger forms of Hegel's empty formalism charge in *Hegel's Ethical Thought*, p. 154. Needless to say, Hegel would not accept Kant's position that an adequate doctrine of moral duties can be generated simply by applying the a priori moral law to a minimal amount of empirical information concerning human nature in general. On Hegel's view, we can reach such a doctrine only via the specific content of *Sittlichkeit* or ethical life.

4. Hegel, *Grundlinien der Philosophie des Rechts*, section 151, Addition.

5. Hegel, *Grundlinien der Philosophie des Rechts*, section 153, Addition.

6. Hegel does not explicitly discuss the need for this kind of moral judgment in his *Philosophy of Right*, but I believe it is implicit in his criticisms of the "abstract universality" of Kant's ethics (section 135). Arguments in defense of moral judgment skills that go beyond reliance on rules are also legion in contemporary anti-formalist discussions, many of which trace their ancestry to Hegel. For discussion, see Onora O'neill's entry on "Formalism" in the *Encyclopedia of Ethics*, 1992 ed.; and my entry "Examples in Ethics," in the *Routledge Encyclopedia of Philosophy*, 1998 ed.

7. Hegel, *Phänomenologie des Geistes* in *Theorie-Werkausgabe*, edited by Eva Moldenhauer and Karl Markus Michel (Frankfurt: Suhrkamp, 1970), 3:192. Strictly speaking, this is a separate criticism from the "empty formalism" charge that Hegel makes later in the *Philosophy of Right*. But it seems to me to be connected, insofar as here also Hegel is claiming that Kant's ethics is impotent; insufficiently action-guiding. For discussion, see Wood, *Hegel's Ethical Thought*, pp. 12, 130, 154.

8. Hegel was in fact more familiar with Kant's practical philosophy than his overly casual remarks about it in the *Philosophy of Right* might lead one to think. For example, he knew well not only the *Critique of Practical Reason* but also Kant's writings in religion and in the philosophy of history. I thank Ludwig Siep for discussion on this topic.

9. Throughout this discussion I assume (as Kant does in his own discussions concerning the second part of ethics) that human beings are our paradigm case of moral subjects. However, if and when human beings establish contact with other forms of rational life, the prospect of our own need to acquire empirical knowledge about other kinds of moral subjects opens up. (See "Species-specific Applications" in chap. 1.) J. B. Schneewind, in the epilogue to his comprehensive study *The Invention of Autonomy: A History of Modern Moral Philosophy* (New York: Cambridge University Press, 1998), suggests that secularists who are otherwise sympathetic to the aims and assumptions of Kant's moral philosophy can settle for a restricted scope: "Principles for humans may be enough" for those of us who "do not think that a prime task for moral philosophy is to show that God and we belong to a single moral community" (p. 554). But there are other reasons for thinking that principles for humans might not be enough even if God is not part of the picture.

10. For related discussion, see part 2 of my *Morality and Moral Theory: A Reappraisal and Reaffirmation* (New York: Oxford University Press, 1992). For more recent discussions focusing on specific tensions between applied ethics and grand-scale normative theory efforts, see the entries by Tim Dare ("Applied Ethics, Challenges to") and Earl R. Winkler ("Applied Ethics, Overview") in the *Encyclopedia of Applied Ethics*, 1998 ed.

11. Iris Murdoch, "The Sovereignty of Good over Other Concepts," reprinted in *Virtue Ethics*, edited by Roger Crisp and Michael Slote, Oxford Readings in Philosophy (New York: Oxford University Press, 1997), p. 101.

12. See Wood's discussion of "Hegel's institutionalism" in *Hegel's Ethical Thought*, pp. 73–74. "An existent right for Hegel," Wood writes, "seems always to involve (explicitly or implicitly) a social institution" (p. 73).

13. In one of his discussions Wood does state that "Kantian morality is communitarian, not individualistic" ("Rational Theology, Moral Faith, and Religion," in *The Cambridge Companion to Kant*, edited by Paul Guyer (New York: Cambridge University Press, 1992), pp. 407–8). The claim needs qualification: Kant's ethics is communitarian in the sense that he explicitly asserts that our moral vocation must be pursued through membership in a community, and also insofar as he holds that human moral character is not given but is rather contingent upon certain social relations and human practices. But there is a standard sense in which Kant's ethics is not communitarian—again, on his view, communal and public goods do not always win out over individual rights.

14. In his essay "Ausgewählte Probleme der Kantischen Anthropologie," Brandt claims that the categorical imperative "is mentioned neither in the *Anthropology* of 1798 nor in [related] lectures"; in *Der ganze Mensch: Anthropologie und Literatur im 18. Jahrhundert*, edited by Hans-Jürgen Schings (Stuttgart: J. B. Metzler, 1994), p. 29; cf. "Einleitung," 25:xlvi–vii. As noted earlier (chap. 3, n. 39), this narrowly lexicographic perspective distorts Kant's position. Phrases such as "principles which are valid for everyone" (*Anth* 7:293) clearly do refer to the idea of a categorical imperative. However, it is definitely the case that issues relating to the categorical imperative are mentioned only occasionally in Kant's impure ethics.

15. Fichte, "First Introduction to the *Science of Knowledge*," in *Fichte: Science of Knowledge (Wissenschaftslehre) with the First and Second Introductions*, edited and translated by Peter Heath and John Lachs (New York: Appleton-Century-Crofts, 1970), p. 5.

16. See, for example, Owen Flanagan's attack on what he calls "Kant's dogma" in his entry "Moral Psychology" in *The Encyclopedia of Philosophy Supplement*, 1996 ed.

17. Hume, *A Treatise of Human Nature* (1739–40), edited by L. A. Selby-Bigge, 2nd ed. with text revised and variant readings by P. H. Nidditch (Oxford: Clarendon Press, 1978), p. xix.

18. See, for example, John Skorupski, *English-Language Philosophy 1750–1945* (New York: Oxford University Press, 1993), who makes the alleged conflict between idealism and naturalism the "main theme" in his account (p. vii; cf. p. 218). Like others, I prefer to soften this conflict by pointing to naturalistic currents within idealism. However, in doing so one needs to underscore the fact the "naturalism" in (e.g.) Hegel's ethics is nevertheless different from what American philosophers often mean by "ethical naturalism." For helpful discussion, see Wood's defense of what he calls *historicized* naturalism in *Hegel's Ethical Thought*, pp. 33–35; cf. pp. 12–14.

19. The focus in this last chapter is on the strengths and weakness of Kant's *ethics*, once the second, empirical part of it is re-admitted into its rightful place. But perhaps a few words concerning the strengths of Kantian social science are also in order. In addition to his appropriate skepticism concerning the viability of the project of an objective, observation-based social science (see "Empirical Science" in chap. 3), Kant also rejects the Weberian "requirement of 'value-freedom' in discussion of empirical matters"; Max Weber, "Value-judgments in Social Science," in *Max Weber: Selections in Translation*, edited by W. G. Runciman (New York: Cambridge University Press, 1978), p. 81. This alleged requirement of value-freedom has been one of the primary ideologies invoked by social scientists in the scientific legitimization of their enterprise. Kantian social science, in contrast, is not value-free but morally guided. We seek *Weltkenntnis* in order to further the goal of moralization. Knowing the world stands under the moral imperative of making the world better.

20. The related core assumption of progress (particularly *moral* progress) would of course strike many readers as an additional weakness. I agree that the over-assumption of progress is a flaw, but do not include it in my list of weaknesses in Kant's ethics; it is not so much a specific defect arising from within his practical

philosophy as it is an overly confident attitude that infects all Enlightenment philosophy. For further discussion, see "The Education of Humanity" in chap. 2.

21. Onora O'Neill, "Kantian Approaches to Some Famine Problems," in *Matters of Life and Death*, edited by Tom Regan (New York: Random House, 1980); reprinted in *Introduction to Philosophy*, edited by John Perry and Michael Bratman, 2nd ed. (New York: Oxford University Press, 1993), p. 597. For a more extensive discussion, see her *Faces of Hunger: An Essay on Poverty, Development and Justice* (London: Allen and Unwin, 1986). For an overview of relevant issues, see Nigel Dower's entry "Development Ethics" in the *Encyclopedia of Applied Ethics*, 1998 ed.

22. Given Kant's views concerning, for example, art and culture as necessary preparatory stages for moralization, it is also clear that the *kinds* of aid his development ethics must advocate would consist of much more than mere financial aid. On his view, economic growth is a necessary but not sufficient condition for true human development.

23. Mathematics and the artificial languages used in logic and computer programming are sometimes thought to be exceptions. However, it is significant that no one has ever employed such tools in the detailed articulation of moral ideals. They do not seem well suited for the task. Similarly, it is often said that one can rise above the limits of natural languages by expressing moral ideals via the arts, for example, music. But artistic media themselves are certainly not free of cultural conventions. Furthermore, it is doubtful that any moral message embedded in a musical work could contain the degree of articulation and detail that one finds in highly developed moral theories, or that sufficient numbers of listeners would interpret the message in the same way.

24. For discussion, see Judith Butler, "Universality in Culture," in Nussbaum, *For Love of Country*, pp. 45–52.

25. See, for example, Rüdiger Bittner, "Das Unternehmen einer Grundlegung zur Metaphysik der Sitten," and Ludwig Siep, "Wozu Metaphysik der Sitten?" in *Grundlegung zur Metaphysik der Sitten: Ein kooperativer Kommentar*, edited by Otfried Höffe (Frankfurt: Vittorio Klostermann, 1989), pp. 13–30, 31–44.

26. For discussion, see James Brooke, "Indians Striving to Save Their Languages," *New York Times*, April 9, 1998, pp. A1, A22. Brooke writes: "With the rise of a global economy and increased communications, about half of the world's 6,000 languages are expected to disappear over the next century" (A1).

27. Brandt, for instance, notes with puzzlement that "pragmatic anthropology is in none of its development phases identical with that anthropology which Kant after 1770 repeatedly earmarks as a counterpart of the first part of his ethics" ("Einleitung," 25:xlvi).

28. For discussion, see Harry van der Linden, *Kantian Ethics and Socialism* (Indianapolis: Hackett, 1988). Hans Vaihinger, particularly in his discussion of Friedrich C. Forberg's role in the famous *Atheismusstreit* which led to Fichte's dismissal at Jena, also indicates left and right readings of Kant's moral argument for the existence of God; *The Philosophy of "As If"* (1911), translated by C. K. Ogden (London: Routledge and Kegan Paul, 1924), appendixes A and B.

29. For discussion, see Karl Ameriks, "From Kant to Frank: The Ineliminable Subject," in *The Modern Subject: Conceptions of the Self in Classical German Philosophy*, edited by Karl Ameriks and Dieter Sturma (Albany: State University of New York Press, 1995): 217–30. Ameriks concludes that Kant is rightfully regarded "as an ally in the rescue of the subject today" (p. 227). See also Laurence Bonjour's attempt to show that "the vast preponderance of what we think of as empirical knowledge must involve an indispensable *a priori* component" in his *In Defense of Pure Reason: A Rationalist Account of A Priori Justification* (New York: Cambridge University Press, 1998), p. 3.

BIBLIOGRAPHY

Adickes, Erich. *Untersuchungen zu Kants physischer Geographie.* Tübingen: J. C. B. Mohr, 1911.

Allison, Henry E. *Lessing and the Enlightenment.* Ann Arbor: University of Michigan Press, 1966.

———. *Kant's Theory of Freedom.* New York: Cambridge University Press, 1990.

———. *Idealism and Freedom: Essays on Kant's Theoretical and Practical Philosophy.* New York: Cambridge University Press, 1996.

Ameriks, Karl. "From Kant to Frank: The Ineliminable Subject." In *The Modern Subject: Conceptions of the Self in Classical German Philosophy,* edited by Karl Ameriks and Dieter Sturma, 217–30. Albany: State University of New York Press, 1995.

———. "On Paul Guyer's *Kant and the Experience of Freedom.*" *Philosophy and Phenomenological Research* 55 (1995): 361–67.

Anderson-Gold, Sharon. "A Common Vocation: Humanity as a Moral Species." In *Proceedings of the Eighth International Kant Congress,* edited by Hoke Robinson, vol. 2, pt. 2, 599–696. Milwaukee: Marquette University Press, 1995.

Arendt, Hannah. "Race-Thinking before Racism." *Review of Politics* 6 (1944): 36–73.

———. *The Origins of Totalitarianism.* New York: Harcourt, Brace and World, 1951.

———. *Eichmann in Jerusalem: A Report on the Banality of Evil.* Rev. ed. New York: Viking Press, 1964.

———. *Lectures on Kant's Political Philosophy.* Edited by Ronald Beiner. Chicago: University of Chicago Press, 1982.

Arnoldt, Emil. *Kritische Excurse im Gebiete der Kant-Forschung.* Königsberg: von Ferd, 1894.

Auxter, Thomas. "The Unimportance of Kant's Highest Good." *Journal of the History of Philosophy* 17 (1979): 121–34.

———. *Kant's Moral Teleology.* Macon: Mercer University Press, 1982.

Barkhaus, Annette. "Kants Konstruktion des Begriffs der Rasse und seine Hierarchisierung der Rassen." *Biologisches Zentralblatt* 113 (1994): 197–203.

Baron, Marcia. "Freedom, Frailty, and Impurity." *Inquiry* 36 (1993): 431–41.

Barth, Karl. *Protestant Thought: From Rousseau to Ritschl.* Translated by Brian Cozens. New York: Simon and Schuster, 1969.

Basedow, Johann Bernhard. *Das Methodenbüch für Väter und Mütter der Familien und Volker* (1770). Reprinted. Paderborn: Schöningh, 1914.

Baumgartner, Hans Michael. "Das 'Ethische Gemeine Wesen' und die Kirche in Kants 'Religionsschrift'." In *Kant über Religion,* edited by Friedo Ricken and Francois Marty, 156–67. Stuttgart: W. Kohlhammer, 1992.

Beattie, James. "A Response to Hume." [Excerpt from *An Essay on the Nature and Immutability of Truth, in Opposition to Sophistry and Skepticism* (1770).] Reprinted in *Race and the Enlightenment,* edited by Emmanuel Chukwudi Eze, 34–37. Cambridge: Blackwell, 1997.

Beck, Lewis White. *A Commentary on Kant's Critique of Practical Reason.* Chicago: University of Chicago Press, 1960.

———. Editor's introduction to *On History,* by Immanuel Kant, vii–xxvi. Indianapolis: Bobbs-Merrill, 1963.

———. "Kant on Education." In *Essays on Kant and Hume,* 188–204. New Haven: Yale University Press, 1978.

———. "Extraterrestrial Intelligent Life." In *Extraterrestrials: Science and Alien Intelligence,* edited by Edward Regis Jr., 3–18. New York: Cambridge University Press, 1985.

Becker, Wolfgang. "Einleitung: Kants pragmatischer Anthropologie." In *Anthropologie in pragmatischer Hinsicht,* by Immanuel Kant, edited by Wolfgang Becker, 9–26. Stuttgart: Reclam, 1983.

Beiner, Ronald. "Kant, the Sublime, and Nature." In *Kant and Political Philosophy: The Contemporary Legacy,* edited by Ronald Beiner and William James Booth, 276–88. New Haven: Yale University Press, 1993.

Bell, Charles. *Essays on the Anatomy of Expression in Painting.* London: Longman, Hurst, Rees, and Orme, 1806.

Bennent, Heidemarie. *Galanterie und Verachtung: Eine philosophiegeschichtliche Untersuchung zur Stellung der Frau in Gesellschaft und Kultur.* Frankfurt: Campus, 1985.

Bittner, Rüdiger. "Das Unternehmen einer Grundlegung zur Metaphysik der Sitten." In *Grundlegung zur Metaphysik der Sitten: Ein kooperativer Kommentar,* edited by Otfried Höffe, 13–30. Frankfurt: Vittorio Klostermann, 1989.

Blosser, Philip. *Scheler's Critique of Kant's Ethics.* Athens: Ohio University Press, 1995.

Blumenbach, Johann Friedrich. *De generis humani variatione nativa* (1775). English translation in *The Anthropological Treatises of Johann Friedrich Blumenbach,* translated by Thomas Bendyshe. London: Longman, 1869; reprint, Boston: Longwood Press, 1978.

Bonjour, Laurence. *In Defense of Pure Reason: A Rationalist Account of A Priori Justification.* New York: Cambridge University Press, 1998.

Borowski, Ludwig Ernst. *Darstellung des Lebens und Charakters Immanuel Kant* (1804). In *Immanuel Kant: Sein Leben in Darstellungen von Zeitgenossen. Die Biographien von L. E. Borowski, R. B. Jachmann, und E. A. Wasianski,* edited by Felix Groß. Reprint. Darmstadt: Wisssenschaftliche Buchgesellschaft, 1993.

Brandt, Reinhard. "Zum 'Streit der Fakultäten.'" In *Neue Autographen und Dokumente zu Kant's Leben, Schriften und Vorlesungen,* edited by Reinhard Brandt and Werner Stark, 31–78. Hamburg: Felix Meiner, 1987.

———. "The Deductions in the *Critique of Judgment*: Comments on Hampshire and Horstmann." In *Kant's Transcendental Deductions,* edited by Eckart Förster, 177–90. Stanford: Stanford University Press, 1989.

———. "Beobachtungen zur Anthropologie bei Kant (und Hegel)." In *Psychologie und Anthropologie oder Philosophie des Geistes,* edited by Franz Hespe and Burkhard Tuschling, 75–106. Stuttgart–Bad Cannstatt: Frommann-Holzboog, 1991.

————. *D'Artagnan und die Urteilstafel: Über ein Ordungsprinzip der europäischen Kultur-geschichte*. Stuttgart: Franz Steiner, 1991.

————. "Ausgewählte Probleme der Kantischen Anthropologie." In *Der ganze Mensch: Anthropologie und Literatur im 18. Jahrhundert*, edited by Hans-Jürgen Schings, 14–32. Stuttgart: J. B. Metzler, 1994.

————. "Vom Weltbürgerrecht." In *Immanuel Kant: Zum ewigen Frieden*, edited by Otfried Höffe, 133–48. Berlin: Akademie, 1995.

————. "Einleitung." In *Vorlesungen über Anthropologie*, by Immanuel Kant. Vol. 25 in *Kant's gesammelte Schriften*, edited by Reinhard Brandt and Werner Stark, vii–liv. Berlin: Walter de Gruyter, 1997.

Brooke, James. "Indians Striving to Save Their Languages." *New York Times*, 9 April 1998, pp. A1, A22.

Buffon, Georges Louis Leclerc. *Histoire naturelle, générale et particulière*. Paris: De l'Imprimerie royale. 1749.

Burke, Edmund. *A Philosophical Inquiry into the Origin of our Ideas of the Sublime and Beautiful* (1757). In *The Works of the Right Honourable Edmund Burke*, vol. 1, edited by Henry Frowde. London: Oxford University Press, 1906.

Burnyeat, M. F. "The Virtues of Plato." *New York Review of Books*, September 7, 1979, 56–60.

Butler, Judith. "Universality in Culture." In *For Love of Country: Debating the Limits of Patriotism*, by Martha C. Nussbaum with Respondents, edited by Joshua Cohen, 45–52. Boston: Beacon Press, 1996.

The Cambridge Dictionary of Philosophy, 1995 ed. S.v. "Galen" and "Hippocrates."

Carnois, Bernard. *The Coherence of Kant's Doctrine of Freedom*. Translated by David Booth. Chicago: University of Chicago Press, 1987.

Cassirer, Ernst. *The Myth of the State*. New Haven: Yale University Press, 1946.

————. *Kant's Life and Thought*. Translated by James Haden. New Haven: Yale University Press, 1981.

Ching, Julia. "Chinese Ethics and Kant." *Philosophy East and West* 28 (1978): 161–72.

Cicovacki, Predrag. "Kant's Aesthetics between 1980 and 1990: A Bibliography." In *Kant's Aesthetics*, edited by Ralf Meerbote, 130–43. Atascadero, CA: Ridgeview, 1991.

Cohen, Hermann. *Kants Begründung der Ethik*. 2nd ed. Berlin: Bruno Cassirer, 1910.

Cohen, Ted. "Why Beauty Is a Symbol of Morality." In *Essays in Kant's Aesthetics*, edited by Ted Cohen and Paul Guyer, 221–36. Chicago: University of Chicago Press, 1982.

Coleman, Francis X. J. *The Harmony of Reason: A Study of Kant's Aesthetics*. Pittsburgh: University of Pittsburgh Press, 1974.

Collingwood, R. G. *The Idea of History*. Oxford: Clarendon Press, 1946.

Collins, James. *The Emergence of the Philosophy of Religion*. New Haven: Yale University Press, 1967.

Cook, James. *Cook's Third Voyage*. London: Alex. Hogg, 1784. German translation: *Des Captain J. Cook dritte Entdeckungsreise* [etc.]. 4 vols. Translated by Georg Forster. Berlin: Haude and Spener, 1789.

Crawford, Donald W. "The Place of the Sublime in Kant's Aesthetic Theory." In *The Philosophy of Immanuel Kant*, edited by Richard Kennington, 161–83. Washington, D.C.: Catholic University of America Press, 1985.

Crittenden, P. J. "Kant as Educationist." *Philosophical Studies* (Ireland) 31 (1986–87): 11–32.

Crowe, Michael J. *The Extraterrestrial Life Debate: The Idea of a Plurality of Worlds from Kant to Lowell*. New York: Cambridge University Press, 1986.

Crowther, Paul. *The Kantian Sublime: From Morality to Art*. Oxford: Clarendon Press, 1989.

Darwin, Charles. *The Expression of the Emotions in Man and Animals*. London: J. Murray, 1872.

De Quincy, Thomas. *The Works of Thomas De Quincy*. Vol. 9, *The Last Days of Immanuel Kant*. New York: Hurd and Houghton, 1877.

Despland, Michel. *Kant on History and Religion*. Montreal: McGill-Queens University Press, 1973.

Dewey, John. *Human Nature and Conduct*. New York: Henry Holt, 1922.

Diderot, Denis. *Supplement to the Voyage of Bougainville* (1772). Selection reprinted in *The Portable Enlightenment Reader*, edited by Isaac Kramnick, 265–74. New York: Penguin Books, 1995.

di Giovanni, George. Notes to *Religion and Rational Theology*, by Immanuel Kant, translated and edited by Allen W. Wood and George Di Giovanni. New York: Cambridge University Press, 1996.

Düsing, Klaus. "Das Problem des höchsten Gutes in Kants praktischer Philosophie." *Kant-Studien* 62 (1971): 5–42.

Ebeling, Hans. "Die Ethik in Kants Anthropologie." Epilogue to *Anthropologie in pragmatischer Hinsicht*, by Immanuel Kant, edited by Wolfgang Becker, 369–79. Stuttgart: Reclam, 1983.

Eisler, Rudolf. *Wörterbuch der philosophischen Begriffe*. 4th edited by Berlin: E. S. Mittler, 1929. S.v. "Pragmatisch."

Encyclopedia of Applied Ethics, 1998 ed. S.v. "Applied Ethics, Challenges to," by Tim Dare; "Applied Ethics, Overview," by Earl R. Winkler; and "Development Ethics" by Nigel Dower.

Encyclopedia of Ethics, 1992 ed. S.v. "Formalism," by Onora O'Neill.

The Encyclopedia of Philosophy, 1967 ed. S.v. "History of Philosophy of Education," by Kingsley Price.

The Encyclopedia of Philosophy Supplement, 1996 ed. S.v. "Moral Psychology," by Owen Flanagan.

Engstrom, Stephen. "Conditioned Autonomy." *Philosophy and Phenomenological Research* 48 (1988): 435–53.

———. "The Concept of the Highest Good in Kant's Moral Theory." *Philosophy and Phenomenological Research* 522 (1992): 747–80.

Erdmann, Benno. *Reflexionen Kants zur Anthropologie*. Leipzig: Fues's Verlag, 1882.

Eze, Emmanuel Chukwudi. "The Color of Reason: The Idea of 'Race' in Kant's Anthropology." In *Anthropology and the German Enlightenment*, edited by Katherine Faull, 200–241. Lewisburg: Bucknell University Press, 1994.

———, ed. *Race and the Enlightenment*. Cambridge: Blackwell, 1997.

Fackenheim, Emil L. "Kant's Concept of History." *Kant-Studien* 48 (1957): 381–98.

———. "Kant and Radical Evil." *University of Toronto Quarterly* 33 (1954): 339–53.

Falk, Richard. "Revisioning Cosmopolitanism." In *For Love of Country: Debating the Limits of Patriotism*, by Martha C. Nussbaum with Respondents, edited by Joshua Cohen, 53–60. Boston: Beacon Press, 1996.

Fichte, Johann Gottlieb. *Die Grundzüge des gegenwärtigen Zeitalters* (1804–05). Hamburg: Felix Meiner, 1978.

———. *Addresses to the German Nation* (1808). Edited by George Armstrong Kelly. New York: Harper and Row, 1968.

———. *Fichte: Science of Knowledge (Wissenschaftslehre) with the First and Second Introductions*. Edited and translated by Peter Heath and John Lachs. New York: Appleton-Century-Crofts, 1970.

Findlay, J. N. *Plato: The Written and Unwritten Dialogues*. New York: Humanities Press, 1974.

Firla, Monika. *Untersuchungen zum Verhältnis von Anthropologie und Moralphilosophie bei Kant.* Frankfurt: Peter Lang, 1981.

Flanagan, Owen. *Varieties of Moral Personality: Ethics and Psychological Realism.* Cambridge: Harvard University Press, 1992.

————. "Ethics Naturalized: Ethics as Human Ecology." In *Mind and Morals: Essays on Cognitive Science and Ethics,* edited by Larry May, Marilyn Friedman, and Andy Clark, 19–43. Cambridge: MIT Press, 1996.

————. "The Moral Network." In *The Churchlands and their Critics,* edited by Robert N. McCauley, 192–215. Cambridge: Blackwell, 1996.

Foot, Philippa. "Does Moral Subjectivism Rest on a Mistake?" *Oxford Journal of Legal Studies* 15 (1995): 1–14.

Forster, Georg. "Noch etwas über die Menschenraßen." In *Georg Forsters Werke: Sämtliche Schriften, Tagebücher, Briefe.* Vol. 8, edited by the Akademie der Wissenschaften der DDR, 130–56. Berlin: Akademie, 1974.

Frankena, William K. *Three Historical Philosophies of Education: Aristotle, Kant, and Dewey.* Chicago: Scott, Foresman, 1965.

Friedman, Michael. *Kant and the Exact Sciences.* Cambridge: Harvard University Press, 1992.

Galston, William A. *Kant and the Problem of History.* Chicago: University of Chicago Press, 1975.

————. "What is Living and Dead in Kant's Practical Philosophy?" In *Kant and Political Philosophy: The Contemporary Legacy,* edited by Ronald Beiner and William James Booth, 207–23. New Haven: Yale University Press, 1992.

Gause, Fritz. "Kant und die Juden." Reprinted in *Kant und Königsberg bis Heute,* edited by Fritz Gause, and Jürgen Lebuhn, 147–49. Leer: Gerhard Rautenberg, 1989.

Gawronsky, Dimitry. "Ernst Cassirer: Leben und Werk." In *Ernst Cassirer,* edited by Paul Arthur Schilpp, 1–27. Stuttgart: W. Kohlhammer, 1966.

Gerhardt, Volker. "Was ist ein vernunftiges Wesen?" *South African Journal of Philosophy* 8 (1989): 155–65.

————. "Vernunft und Leben: Eine Annäherung." *Deutsche Zeitschrift der Philosophie* 43 (1995): 591–609.

————. "Die Selbstdisziplin der Vernunft." In *Kant: Kritik der reinen Vernunft,* edited by Georg Mohr and Marcus Willaschek. Berlin: Akademie, 571–96.

Glasenapp, Helmuth von. *Kant und die Religionen des Ostens.* Kitzingen-Main: Holzner-Verlag, 1954.

Gobineau, Counte Arthur de. *Essai sur l'inegalité des races humaines* (1853). English translation: *The Inequality of Human Races.* Translated by Adrian Collins. New York: Howard Fertig, 1967. (Reprint of 1915 ed.)

Goethe, Johann Wolfgang von. *Goethes Briefe.* Edited by Karl Robert Mandelkow. Hamburg: Christian Wegner, 1964.

Gould, Steven Jay. "The Geometer of Race." *Discover* 15 (November 1994): 65–69.

Greene, Theodore M., and Hoyt H. Hudson. Translators' notes. *Religion within the Limits of Reason Alone,* by Immanuel Kant. Chicago: Open Court, 1934; reprint, New York: Harper and Row, 1960.

Gregor, Mary J. *Laws of Freedom: A Study of Kant's Method of Applying the Categorical Imperative in the "Metaphysik der Sitten".* Oxford: Basil Blackwell, 1963.

————. Translator's notes to *Practical Philosophy,* by Immanuel Kant, edited and translated by Mary J. Gregor. New York: Cambridge University Press, 1996.

Gregory, Richard L., ed. *The Oxford Companion to the Mind.* New York: Oxford University Press, 1987. S.v. "Insanity: Early Theories," "Physiognomy."

Guyer, Paul. *Kant and the Claims of Taste.* Cambridge: Harvard University Press, 1979; 2nd ed., New York: Cambridge University Press, 1997.

————. Bibliography in *Essays in Kant's Aesthetics*, edited by Ted Cohen and Paul Guyer, 307–23. Chicago: University of Chicago Press, 1982.

————. *Kant and the Experience of Freedom: Essays on Aesthetics and Morality*. New York: Cambridge University Press, 1993.

————. "Moral Anthropology in Kant's Aesthetics and Ethics: A Reply to Ameriks and Sherman." *Philosophy and Phenomenological Research* 55 (1995): 379–91.

Hamann, Johann Georg. *Vom Magus im Norden und der Verwegenheit des Geistes: Ein Hamann-Brevier*. Edited by Stefan Majetschak. Munich: Deutscher Taschenbuch, 1988.

Hampshire, Stuart. "The Social Spirit of Mankind." In *Kant's Transcendental Deductions*, edited by Eckart Förster, 145–56. Stanford: Stanford University Press, 1989.

Harris, Marvin. *The Rise of Anthropological Theory: A History of Theories of Culture*. New York: Thomas Y. Crowell, 1968.

Hassner, Pierre. "Immanuel Kant." In *History of Political Philosophy*, edited by Leo Strauss and Joseph Cropsey, 581–621. 3rd ed. Chicago: University of Chicago Press, 1987.

Hegel, Georg Wilhelm Friedrich. *Theorie-Werkausgabe*. Edited by Eva Moldenhauer and Karl Markus Michel. Frankfurt: Suhrkamp, 1970.

————. *Vorlesungen über die Philosophie der Geschichte*. Vol. 1, *Die Vernunft in der Geschichte*. Edited by Johannes Hofmeister. Hamburg: Felix Meiner, 1955.

Herbart, Johann Friedrich. Review of *Immanuel Kant über Pädagogik*, edited by Friedrich Theodor Rink. *Göttingische gelehrte Anzeigen* 27 (18 February 1804): 257–61.

Herder, Johann Gottfried von. *Ideen zur Philosophie der Geschichte der Menschheit*. In *Herders Sämmtliche Werke*, vol. 13. Edited by Bernhard Suphan. Berlin: Weidmann, 1887.

Herman, Barbara. *The Practice of Moral Judgment*. Cambridge: Harvard University Press, 1993.

Herrmann, Ulrich. "Campes Pädagogik—oder: die Erziehung und Bildung des Menschen zum Menschen und Bürger." In *Visionäre Lebensklugheit: Joachim Heinrich Campe in seiner Zeit*, edited by Hanno Schmidt, 151–58. Wiesbaden: Harrassowitz, 1996.

Hill, Thomas E., Jr. *Dignity and Practical Reason in Kant's Moral Theory*. Ithaca: Cornell University Press, 1992.

Hinske, Norbert. "Kants Idee der Anthropologie." In *Die Frage nach dem Menschen*, edited by Heinrich Rombach, 410–27. Freiburg: Karl Alber, 1966.

Hippel, Theodor Gottlieb von. *Über die bürgerliche Verbesserung der Weiber* (1792). Reprint ed. Frankfurt: Syndikat, 1977.

Horkheimer, Max, and Theodor W. Adorno. *Dialectic of Enlightenment*. Translated by John Cumming. New York: Continuum, 1972.

Höffe, Otfried. "Universalistische Ethik und Urteilskraft: ein aristotelischer Blick auf Kant." *Zeitschrift für philosophische Forschung* 44 (1990): 537–63.

————. *Immanuel Kant*. Translated by Marshall Farrier. Albany. State University of New York Press, 1994.

————. *Kategorische Rechtsprinzipien*. Frankfurt: Suhrkamp, 1995.

————. "Ein Thema wiedergewinnen: Kant über das Bose." In *F. W. J. Schelling: Über das Wesen der menschlichen Freiheit*, edited by Otfried Höffe and Annemarie Pieper, 11–34. Berlin: Akademie, 1995.

————. "Völkerbund oder Weltrepublik?" In *Immanuel Kant: Zum ewigen Frieden*, edited by Otfried Höffe, 109–32. Berlin: Akademie, 1995.

————. "Ausblick: Die Vereinten Nationen im Lichte Kants." In *Immanuel Kant: Zum ewigen Frieden*, edited by Otfried Höffe, 245–72. Berlin: Akademie Verlag, 1995.

Hume, David. "Of National Characters." In *Essays: Moral, Political, and Literary*, edited by T. H. Green and T. H. Grose. London: Longmans, Green, 1907.

————. *A Treatise of Human Nature* (1739–40). Edited by L. A. Selby-Bigge. 2nd ed. with text revised and variant readings by P. H. Nidditch. Oxford: Clarendon Press, 1978.

Jachmann, Reinhold Bernard. *Immanuel Kant geschildert in Briefen an einen Freund* (1804). In *Immanuel Kant: Sein Leben in Darstellungen von Zeitgenossen. Die Biographien von L. E. Borowski, R. B. Jachmann, und E. A. Wasianski*, edited by Felix Groß. Reprint. Darmstadt: Wisssenschaftliche Buchgesellschaft, 1993.

James, David. "Twenty Questions: Kant's Applied Ethics." *Southern Journal of Philosophy* 30 (1992): 67–87.

Jauch, Ursula Pia. *Immanuel Kant zur Geschlechterdifferenz: Aufklärerische Vorurteilskritik und bürgerliche Geschlechtsvormundschaft*. 2nd ed. Vienna: Passagen, 1989.

Kant, Immanuel. *Über Pädagogik. Mit Kant's Biographie*. Edited by Theodor Vogt. Langensalza, Germany: Hermann Beyer, 1878.

Kant, Immanuel. *Eine Vorlesung Kants über Ethik*. Edited by Paul Menzer. Berlin: Pan Verlag Rolf Heise, 1924.

————. *The Critique of Judgement*. Translated by James Creed Meredith. Oxford: Clarendon Press, 1928.

————. *Lectures on Ethics*. Translated by Louis Infield. London: Methuen, 1930.

————. *The Critique of Judgement*. Translated by J. H. Bernard. London: Collier Macmillan, 1892; reprint, New York: Hafner Press, 1951.

————. *Kant on Education*. Translated by Annette Churton. London: Kegan Paul, Trench, Trübner, 1899; reprint *Education*, Ann Arbor: University of Michigan Press, 1960.

————. *The Educational Theory of Immanuel Kant*. Translated and edited by Edward Franklin Buchner. Philadelphia: Lippincott, 1904; reprint, New York: AMS Press, 1971.

————. *Anthropology From a Pragmatic Point of View*. Translated by Victor Lyle Dowdell. Carbondale: Southern Illinois University Press, 1978.

————. *Lectures on Philosophical Theology*. Translated by Allen W. Wood and Gertrude M. Clark. Ithaca: Cornell University Press, 1978.

————. *Ausgewählte Schriften zur Pädagogik und ihrer Begründung*. Edited by Hans-Hermann Groothoff. 2nd ed. Paderborn: Ferdinand Schöningh, 1982.

————. *Über Pädagogik*. Edited by Hermann Holstein. 5th ed. Bochum, Germany: Verlag Ferdinand Kamp, 1984.

————. *Critique of Judgment*. Translated by Werner S. Pluhar. Indianapolis: Hackett, 1987.

————. *Anthropology, History, and Education*. Edited by Guenter Zoeller and translated by Mary Gregor, Robert B. Louden, Holly L. Wilson, and Guenter Zoeller. New York: Cambridge University Press, 2001.

————. *Lectures on Anthropology*. Edited by Allen W. Wood and Robert B. Louden and translated by Brian Jacobs, G. Felicitas Munzel, Robert B. Louden, and Allen W. Wood. New York: Cambridge University Press, forthcoming.

————. *Natural Science*. Edited by H. B. Nisbet and translated by David Oldroyd, Olafheinhardt, and H. B. Nisbet. New York: Cambridge University Press, forthcoming.

Kaulbach, Friedrich. "Weltorientierung, Weltkenntnis und pragmatische Vernunft bei Kant." In *Kritik und Metaphysik. Studien. Heinz Heimsoeth zum achtzigsten Geburtstag*, edited by Friedrich Kaulbach and Joachim Ritter, 60–75. Berlin: Walter de Gruyter, 1966.

————. "Welchen Nutzen gibt Kant der Geschichtsphilosophie?" *Kant-Studien* 66 (1975): 65–84.

Kersting, Wolfgang. *Wohlgeordnete Freiheit: Immanuel Kants Rechts- und Staatsphiloso-phie*. Rev. edited by Frankfurt: Suhrkamp, 1993.

Kierkegaard, Søren. *Concluding Unscientific Postscript* (1846). Translated by David F. Swenson and Walter Lowrie. Princeton: Princeton University Press, 1941.

Kitcher, Patricia. *Kant's Transcendental Psychology*. New York: Oxford University Press, 1990.

Kittsteiner, H.-D. "Kant and Casuistry." In *Conscience and Casuistry in Early Modern Europe*, edited by Edmund Leites, 185–213. New York: Cambridge University Press, 1988.

Kleingeld, Pauline. "The Problematic Status of Gender-Neutral Language in the History of Philosophy: The Case of Kant." *Philosophical Forum* 25 (1993): 134–50.

————. *Fortschritt und Vernunft: Zur Geschichtsphilosophie Kants*. Würzburg: König-hausen und Neumann, 1995.

————. "What Do the Virtuous Hope For? Re-reading Kant's Doctrine of the Highest Good." In *Proceedings of the Eighth International Kant Congress*, edited by Hoke Robinson, vol. 1, pt. 1, 91–112. Milwaukee: Marquette University Press, 1995.

————, ed. *Die Schule Immanuel Kants: Mit dem Text von christian Schiffert übar das Königsberger Collegium Fridericianum*. Hamburg: Felix Meiner Verlag, 1994.

Klemme, Heiner F. "Die Freiheit der Willkür und die Herrschaft des Bösen: Kants Lehre vom radikalen Bösen zwischen Moral, Religion und Recht," in Heiner F. Klemme, Bernd Ludwig, Miachel Pauen and Werner Start, eds., *Aufklärung und Interpretation: Studien zu Kants Philosophie und ihrem Umkreis* (Würzbug: Königs-hausen & Neumann, 1999).

Kneller, Jane. "Imaginative Freedom and the German Enlightenment." *Journal of the History of Ideas* 51 (1990): 217–32.

————. "Imagination and the Possibility of Moral Reform in the *Critique of Aesthetic Judgment*." In *Akten des Siebenten Internationalen Kant-Kongresses*, edited by G. Funke, 665–75. Bonn: Bouvier, 1991.

Korsgaard, Christine. *Creating the Kingdom of Ends*. New York: Cambridge University Press, 1996.

Kramnick, Isaac, ed. *The Portable Enlightenment Reader*. New York: Penguin Books, 1995.

Krieger, Leonard. *The German Idea of Freedom*. Boston: Beacon Press, 1957.

Laberge, Pierre. "Das radikale Böse und der Völkerstand." In *Kant über Religion*, edited by Friedo Ricken and Francois Marty, 112–23. Stuttgart: W. Wohlhammer, 1992.

Landgrebe, Ludwig. "Die Geschichte im Denken Kants." *Studium Generale* 7 (1954): 533–44.

Leibniz, Gottfried Wilhelm. *Otium Hanoveranum sive Miscellanea [etc.]*. Leipzig: Joann. Christiani Martini, 1718.

Lessing, Gotthold Ephraim. *Die Erziehung des Menschengeschlechts*. Vol. 1 of *Gesam-melte Werke*. Edited by Wolfgang Stammler. Munich: Carl Hanser, 1959.

Louden, Robert B. "Go-carts of Judgment: Exemplars in Kantian Moral Education." *Archiv für Geschichte der Philosophie* 74 (1992): 303–22.

————. *Morality and Moral Theory: A Reappraisal and Reaffirmation*. New York: Oxford University Press, 1992.

————. "Kant's Virtue Ethics." *Philosophy* 61 (1986): 473–89. Reprinted in *Kant: Critical Assessments*, vol. 3, edited by Ruth F. Chadwick. London: Routledge, 1992.

————. "Butler's Divine Utilitarianism." *History of Philosophy Quarterly* 12 (1995): 265–80.

————. "Response." In *The Greeks and Us: Essays in Honor of Arthur W. H. Adkins*, edited by Robert B. Louden and Paul Schollmeier, 53–65. Chicago: University of Chicago Press, 1996.

————. "The Education of Humanity: A Kantian Primer." *Journal of Education* 179 (1997): 77–98.

————. "'What does Heaven Say?' Christian Wolff and Western Interpretations of Confucian Ethics." In *Essays on the Analects of Confucius*, edited by Bryan William van Norden. New York: Oxford University Press, 2000.

Lovejoy, Arthur O. *The Great Chain of Being: A Study in the History of an Idea*. Cambridge: Harvard University Press, 1936.

————. "Kant and Evolution." In *Forerunners of Darwin: 1745–1859*, edited by Bentley Glass, Owsei Temkin, and William L. Straus Jr., 173–206. Baltimore: Johns Hopkins University Press, 1959.

Lyotard, Jean-François. *Lessons on the Analytic of the Sublime*. Translated by Elizabeth Rottenberg. Stanford: Stanford University Press, 1994.

Machiavelli, Niccolò. *The Prince*. Translated by Peter Bondanella and Mark Musa. New York: Oxford University Press, 1984.

Makkreel, Rudolf A. *Imagination and Interpretation in Kant: The Hermeneutical Import of the Critique of Judgment*. Chicago: University of Chicago Press, 1990.

Malter, Rudolf. "Anhang II." In *Anthropologie in pragmatischer Hinsicht*, by Immanuel Kant, edited by Karl Vorländer. 7th ed., 315–50. Hamburg: Felix Meiner, 1980.

Marquad, Odo. "Zur Geschichte des philosophischen Begriffs 'Anthropologie' seit dem Ende des achtzehnten Jahrhunderts." In *Collegium philosophicum*, 209–39. Basel: Schwabe, 1965.

————. "Anthropologie." In *Historisches Wörterbuch der Philosophie*, edited by Joachim Ritter, 362–74. Basel: Schwabe, 1971.

May, J. A. *Kant's Concept of Geography and its Relation to Recent Geographical Thought*. Toronto: University of Toronto Press, 1970.

McCloskey, Mary A. *Kant's Aesthetic*. London: Macmillan, 1987.

McFarland, J. D. *Kant's Concept of Teleology*. Edinburgh: University of Edinburgh Press, 1970.

McIntyre, J. Lewis. "Kant's Theory of Education." *Educational Review* 16 (1898): 313–27.

Medicus, Fritz. "Zu Kants Philosophie der Geschichte mit besonderer Beziehung auf K. Lamprecht." *Kant-Studien* 4 (1900): 61–67.

Mellin, Georg Samuel Albert. *Enzyklopädisches Wörterbuch der kritischen Philosophie* (1797); reprint, Aalen: Scientia, 1970.

Mendus, Susan. "Kant: 'An Honest but Narrow-Minded Bourgeois'?" In *Women in Western Political Philosophy*, edited by Susan Mendus and Ellen Kennedy. Brighton: Harvester Wheatsheaf, 1987; reprinted in *Immanuel Kant: Critical Assessments*, edited by Ruth F. Chadwick, vol. 3, 370–88. Routledge, 1992.

————. "How Androcentric Is Western Philosophy? A Reply." *Philosophical Quarterly* 46 (1996): 60–66.

Menzer, Paul. *Kants Aesthetik in ihrer Entwicklung*. Berlin: Akademie-Verlag, 1952.

Michalson, Gordon E., Jr. *The Historical Dimensions of a Rational Faith: The Role of History in Kant's Religious Thought*. Washington, D.C.: University Press of America, 1979.

————. "The Inscrutability of Moral Evil in Kant." *Thomist* 51 (1987): 246–69.

————. *Fallen Freedom: Kant on Radical Evil and Moral Regeneration*. New York: Cambridge University Press, 1990.

Moebus, Joachim. "Bemerkungen zu Kants Anthropologie und physischer Geographie." In *Kritische Psychologie: Bericht über den 1. Internationalen Kongreß kritische*

Psychologie vom 13.–15. Mai in Marburg, edited by Klaus Holzkamp and Karl-Heinz Brann, vol. 2, 365–80. Köln: Paul-Rugenstein, 1977.

Montagu, M. F. Ashley. *Man's Most Dangerous Myth: The Fallacy of Race.* 2nd ed. New York: Columbia University Press, 1945.

Montesquieu, Baron de La Brède et de. *The Spirit of the Laws* (1748). Translated by Thomas Nugent. New York: Hafner, 1949.

Murdoch, Iris. "Art and Eros: A Dialogue about Art." In *Acastos: Two Platonic Dialogues.* New York: Viking, 1987.

————. "The Sovereignty of Good over Other Concepts." In *The Sovereignty of Good.* London: Routledge and Kegan Paul, 1970; reprinted in *Virtue Ethics*, edited by Roger Crisp and Michael Slote. Oxford Readings in Philosophy, 99–117. New York: Oxford University Press, 1997.

Nahm, Milton C. "'Sublimity' and the 'Moral Law' in Kant's Philosophy." *Kant-Studien* 48 (1956–57): 502–24.

Natorp, Paul. "Anmerkungen." In *Kants gesammelte Schriften*, edited by the Königliche Preußische Akademie der Wissenschaften, vol. 9. Berlin: Walter de Gruyter, 1923.

————. "Philosophische Grundlegung der Pädagogik" (1905); reprinted in *Neukantianismus: Texte der Marburger und der Südwestdeutschen Schule, ihrer Vorläufer und Kritiker*, edited by Hans-Ludwig Ollig, 97–126. Stuttgart: Reclam, 1982.

Neiman, Susan. *The Unity of Reason: Rereading Kant.* New York: Oxford University Press, 1994.

Nelson, Leonard. *Vorlesungen über die Grundlagen der Ethik.* Vol. 2, *System der philosophischen Ethik und Pädagogik.* Edited by Grete Hermann and Miuna Specht. Göttiugen: "Öffentliches Leben," 1932.

Neumann, Michael. "Philosophische Nachrichten aus der Südsee: Georg Forsters *Reise um die Welt.*" In *Der ganze Mensch: Anthropologie und Literatur im 18.Jahrhundert*, edited by Hans-Jürgen Schings, 517–44. Stuttgart: J. B. Metzler, 1994.

Niedermeier, Michael. "Campe als Direktor des Dessauer Philanthropins." In *Visionäre Lebensklugheit: Joachim Heinrich Campe in seiner Zeit*, edited by Hanno Schmidt, 45–66. Wiesbaden: Harrassowitz, 1996.

Nietzsche, Friedrich. *Twilight of the Idols.* In *The Portable Nietzsche*, edited by Walter Kaufmann. New York: Viking Press, 1954.

Nussbaum, Martha C. "Kant and Stoic Cosmopolitanism." *Journal of Political Philosophy* 5 (1997): 1–25.

O'Neill, Onora. *Faces of Hunger: An Essay on Poverty, Development and Justice.* London: Allen and Unwin, 1986.

————. "Kantian Approaches to Some Famine Problems." In *Matters of Life and Death*, edited by Tom Regan. New York: Random House, 1980. Reprinted in *Introduction to Philosophy*, edited by John Perry and Michael Bratman, 2nd ed., 592–98. New York: Oxford University Press, 1993.

————. *Constructions of Reason: Explorations of Kant's Practical Philosophy.* New York: Cambridge University Press, 1989.

Paton, H. J. *The Categorical Imperative: A Study in Kant's Moral Philosophy.* London: Hutchinson, 1947; reprint, Philadelphia: University of Pennsylvania Press, 1971.

————. Translator's notes to *Groundwork of the Metaphysic of Morals*, by Immanuel Kant. 3rd ed. London: Hutchinson, 1956; reprint, New York: Harper and Row, 1964.

Paulsen, Friedrich. *The German Universities and University Study.* Translated by Frank Thilly and William W. Elwang. New York: Scribner's, 1906.

Peters, R. S. "The Paradoxes in Rousseau's *Emile.*" In *Essays on Educators*, 15–31. London: Allen and Unwin, 1981.

Pieper, Annemarie. "Ethik als Verhältnis von Moralphilosophie und Anthropologie: Kants Entwurf einer Transzendentalpragmatik und ihre Transformation durch Apel." *Kant-Studien* 69 (1978): 314–29.

Platner, Ernst. *Anthropologie für Ärzte und Weltweise*. Leipzig: Dyck, 1772.

Potter, Nelson, and Mark Timmons, ed. *Kant's Metaphysics of Morals. Southern Journal of Philosophy* 36, Supplement (1997). (Spindel Conference, 1997. Kant's *Metaphysics of Morals*.)

Reath, Andrews. "Two Conceptions of the Highest Good in Kant." *Journal of the History of Philosophy* 26 (1988): 593–619.

Reich, Klaus. "Einleitung des Herausgebers." In *Der Streit der Fakultäten*, by Immanuel Kants, edited by Klaus Reich, ix–xxvi. Hamburg: Felix Meiner, 1959.

Rescher, Nicholas. *Ethical Idealism: An Inquiry into the Nature and Function of Ideals*. Berkeley: University of California Press, 1987.

Riedel, Manfred. "Einleitung." In *Schriften zur Geschichtsphilosophie*, by Immanuel Kant, edited by Manfred Riedel, 3–20. Stuttgart: Reclam, 1974.

Riley, Patrick. *Kant's Political Philosophy*. Totowa: Rowman and Allanheld, 1983.

———. "Hannah Arendt on Kant, Truth and Politics." In *Essays on Kant's Political Philosophy*, edited by Howard Lloyd Williams, 305–23. Chicago: University of Chicago Press, 1992.

Rink, Friedrich Theodor. *Ansichten aus Immanuel Kants Leben*. Königsberg: Göbbels und Unzer, 1805.

Roehr, Sabine. *A Primer on German Enlightenment: with a Translation of Karl Leonhard Reinhold's The Fundamental Concepts and Principles of Ethics*. Columbia: University of Missouri Press, 1995.

Rorty, Richard. "Keeping Philosophy Pure: An Essay on Wittgenstein." In *Consequences of Pragmatism*, 19–36. Minneapolis: University of Minnesota Press, 1982.

Rose, Paul Laurence. *German Question/Jewish Question: Revolutionary Anti-Semitism from Kant to Wagner*. Princeton: Princeton University Press, 1990.

Rosen, Allen D. *Kant's Theory of Justice*. Ithaca: Cornell University Press, 1993.

Rossi, Philip J. "The Social Authority of Reason: The 'True Church' as the Locus of Moral Progress." In *Proceedings of the Eighth International Kant Congress*, edited by Hoke Robinson, vol. 2, pt. 2, 679–88. Milwaukee: Marquette University Press, 1995.

———. "The Ethical Commonwealth: Moral Progress and the Human Place in the Cosmos." (Typescript.)

Rotenstreich, Nathan. *Practice and Realization: Studies in Kant's Moral Philosophy*. The Hague: Martinus Nijhoff, 1979.

Röttgers, Kurt. "Kants Zigeuner." *Kant-Studien* 88 (1997): 60–86.

Rousseau, Jean-Jacques. *Emile or On Education* (1762). Translated by Allan Bloom. New York: Basic Books, 1979.

———. *The Social Contract* (1762). Translated by Maurice Cranston. New York: Penguin Books, 1968.

Routledge Encyclopedia of Philosophy, 1998 ed. S.v. "Examples in Ethics," by Robert B. Louden.

Rutschky, Katharina, ed. *Schwarze Pädagogik: Quellen zur Naturgeschichte der bürgerlichen Erziehung*. 6th ed. Berlin: Ullstein, 1993.

Scheffler, Samuel. *Human Morality*. New York: Oxford University Press, 1992.

Scheler, Max. *Formalism in Ethics and Non-Formal Ethics of Values*. Translated by Manfred S. Frings and Roger L. Funk. 5th rev. ed. Evanston: Northwestern University Press, 1973.

Schiller, Johann Christoph Friedrich. *Schillers Werke*. Vol. 26. Edited by Edith Nahler and Horst Nahler. Weimar: Hermann Böhlaus Nachfolger, 1992.

Schilpp, Paul. *Kant's Pre-critical Ethics*. Evanston: Northwestern University Press, 1938.

Schleiermacher, Friedrich. Review of Kant, Immanuel. *Anthropologie in pragmatischer Hinsicht*, by Immanuel Kant. *Athenaeum* 2 (1799): 300–306; reprinted in *Anthropologie in pragmatischer Hinsicht*, by Immanuel Kant, edited by Karl Vorländer. 7th ed., 338–43. Hamburg: Felix Meiner, 1980.

Schmid, Carl Christian Erhard. *Wörterbuch zum leichtern Gebrauch der kantischen Schriften*. Jena: Crökerschen Buchhandlung, 1798; reprint, Darmstadt: Wissenschaftliche Buchgesellschaft, 1976.

Schneewind, J. B. Introduction to *Lectures on Ethics*, by Immanuel Kant, edited by Peter Heath and J. B. Schneewind. New York: Cambridge University Press, 1997.

———. *The Invention of Autonomy: A History of Modern Moral Philosophy*. New York: Cambridge University Press, 1998.

Schopenhauer, Arthur. *The World as Will and Representation* (1818). Translated by E. F. J. Payne. New York: Dover, 1966.

Schott, Robin May. *Cognition and Eros: A Critique of the Kantian Paradigm*. Boston: Beacon Press, 1988.

———. "The Gender of Enlightenment." In *What is Enlightenment? Eighteenth-Century Answers and Twentieth-Century Questions*, edited by James Schmidt. Berkeley: University of California Press, 1996.

———, ed. *Feminist Interpretations of Immanuel Kant*. University Park: Pennsylvania State University Press, 1997.

Schröder, Hannelore. "Kant's Patriarchal Order." In *Feminist Interpretations of Immanuel Kant*, edited by Robin Schott, 275–96. University Park: Pennsylvania State University Press, 1997.

Serequeberhan, Tsenay. "Eurocentrism in Philosophy: The Case of Immanuel Kant." *Philosophical Forum* 27 (1996): 333–56.

Shell, Susan. *The Embodiment of Reason: Kant on Spirit, Generation, and Community*. Chicago: University of Chicago Press, 1996.

Sherman, Nancy. "Reasons and Feelings in Kantian Morality." *Philosophy and Phenomenological Research* 55 (1995): 369–77.

———. *Making a Necessity of Virtue: Aristotle and Kant on Virtue*. New York: Cambridge University Press, 1997.

Sidgwick, Henry. *The Methods of Ethics*. 7th ed. London: Macmillan, 1907; reprint, Indianapolis: Hackett, 1981.

Siep, Ludwig. "Wozu Metaphysik der Sitten?" In *Grundlegung zur Metaphysik der Sitten: Ein kooperativer Kommentar*, edited by Otfried Höffe, 31–44. Frankfurt: Vittorio Klostermann, 1989.

———. "Das Recht als Ziel der Geschichte: Überlegungen im Anschluß an Kant und Hegel." In *Das Recht der Vernunft: Kant und Hegel über Denken, Erkennen und Handeln*, edited by Christel Fricke, Peter König, and Thomas Peterson, 355–79. Stuttgart: Frommann-Holzboog, 1995.

Silber, John R. "Kant's Conception of the Highest Good as Immanent and Transcendent." *Philosophical Review* 68 (1959): 469–92.

———. "The Ethical Significance of Kant's *Religion*." In *Religion Within the Limits of Reason Alone*, by Immanuel Kant, translated by Theodore M. Greene and Hoyt H. Hudson. New York: Harper and Row, 1960.

Simmermacher, Volker. "Kants Kritik der reinen Vernunft als Grundlegung einer Anthropologia transcendentalis." Ph.D. diss., University of Heidelberg, 1951.

Skorupski, John. *English-Language Philosophy 1750–1945*. New York: Oxford University Press, 1993.

Smith, Adam. *An Inquiry into the Nature and Causes of the Wealth of Nations* (1776). Edited by Edwin Cannan. New York: Modern Library, 1937.

Stark, Werner. "Kant als akademischer Lehrer." *Wolfenbüttler Studien zur Aufklärung* 16 (1988): 45–59.

———. "Einleitung." In *Vorlesungen über Anthropologie*, by Immanuel Kant, edited by Reinhard Brandt and Werner Stark. Vol. 25 in *Kant's gesammelte Schriften*, liv–cxv. Berlin: Walter de Gruyter, 1997.

———. "Kants Lehre von der Erziehung: Anthropologie, Pädagogik und Ethik. Bemerkungen aus Anlaß des Erscheinens des Bandes 25 von Kants gesammelten Schriften: *Vorlesungen über Anthropologie*." (Typescript.)

Statman, Daniel, ed. *Moral Luck*. Albany: State University of New York Press, 1993.

Stern, Paul. "The Problem of History and Temporality in Kantian Ethics." *Review of Metaphysics* 39 (1986): 505–45.

Stuckenberg, J. W. H. *The Life of Immanuel Kant*. London: Macmillan, 1892.

Sutter, Alex. "Kant und die 'Wilden': Zum impliziten Rassismus in der Kantischen Geschichtsphilosophie." *Prima Philosophie* 2 (1989): 241–65.

Tirala, Lothar G. *Rasse, Geist und Seele*. Munich: Lehmans, 1935.

Vaihinger, Hans. *The Philosophy of "As If"* (1911). Translated by C. K. Ogden. London: Routledge and Kegan Paul, 1924.

van de Pitte, Frederick P. *Kant as Philosophical Anthropologist*. The Hague: Martinus Nijhoff, 1971.

van der Linden, Harry. *Kantian Ethics and Socialism*. Indianapolis: Hackett, 1988.

Velkley, Richard L. *Freedom and the End of Reason: On the Moral Foundation of Kant's Critical Philosophy*. Chicago: University of Chicago Press, 1986.

Vorländer, Karl. *Immanuel Kants Leben*. Leipzig: Felix Meiner, 1911.

Walker, Margaret Urban. "Moral Luck and the Virtues of Impure Agency." *Metaphilosophy* 22 (1991): 14–27.

Walsh, W. H. *An Introduction to Philosophy of History*. London: Hutchinson's University Library, 1951.

Warnock, G. J. "Kant and Anthropology." In *Nature and Conduct*, edited by R. S. Peters. Royal Institute of Philosophy Lectures. Vol. 8 (1973–74), 36–45. London: Macmillan, 1975.

Weber, Max. *The Theory of Economic and Social Organizations*. Translated by Talcott Parsons and A. M. Henderson. New York: Oxford University Press, 1947.

———. "Value-judgments in Social Science." In *Max Weber: Selections in Translation*, edited by W. G. Runciman, 69–98. New York: Cambridge University Press, 1978.

Weisskopf, Traugott. *Immanuel Kant und die Pädagogik: Beiträge zu einer Monographie*. Zürich: Editio Academica, 1970.

Weyand, Klaus. *Kants Geschichtsphilosophie: Ihre Entwicklung und ihr Verhältnis zur Aufklärung*. Cologne: Kölner Universitäts-Verlag, 1964.

Willaschek, Marcus. *Praktsiche Vernunft: Handlungstheorie und Moralbegründung bei Kant*. Stuttgart: J. B. Metzler, 1992.

Williams, Bernard. *Moral Luck: Philosophical Papers 1973–80*. New York: Cambridge University Press, 1981.

———. *Ethics and the Limits of Philosophy*. Cambridge: Harvard University Press, 1985.

———. *Making Sense of Humanity*. New York: Cambridge University Press, 1995.

Williams, Howard. *Kant's Political Philosophy*. New York: St. Martin's Press, 1983.

Willich, A. F. M. *Elements of the Critical Philosophy*. London: T. N. Longman, 1798.

Wilson, Holly L. "Kant's Integration of Morality and Anthropology." *Kant-Studien* 88 (1997): 87–104.

Wobbermin, Georg. "Annmerkungen." In *Kants gesammelte Schriften*, edited by the Königliche Preußische Akademie der Wissenschaften. Vol. 6. Berlin: Georg Reimer, 1907.

Wolff, Christian. *Oratio de Sinarum philosophia practica. Rede über die praktische Philosophie der Chinesen* (1721). Edited by Michael Albrecht. Hamburg: Felix Meiner, 1985.

Wood, Allen W. *Kant's Moral Religion.* Ithaca: Cornell University Press, 1970.

———. "Kant's Deism." In *Kant's Philosophy of Religion Reconsidered,* edited by Philip J. Rossi and Michael Wreen. Bloomington: Indiana University Press, 1991.

———. "Unsociable Sociability: The Anthropological Basis of Kantian Ethics." *Philosophical Topics* 19 (1991): 325–51.

———. "Rational Theology, Moral Faith, and Religion." In *The Cambridge Companion to Kant,* edited by Paul Guyer, 394–416. New York: Cambridge University Press, 1992.

———. *Hegel's Ethical Thought.* New York: Cambridge University Press, 1995.

———. *Kant's Ethical Thought.* New York: Cambridge University Press, 1999.

Yovel, Yirmiahu. *Kant and the Philosophy of History.* Princeton: Princeton University Press, 1980.

Zammito, John H. *The Genesis of Kant's Critique of Judgment.* Chicago: University of Chicago Press, 1992.

INDEX

as not empirically determined, 170
and recognition of human dependence, 171–72
and recognition of institutional and communitarian aspects of human morality, 172–73
tension between this-worldly and otherworldly orientations, 181–82
unclarity over role of second part, 180–81
usefulness of, 170–71
Existentialism and philosophical anthropology, 67
Extraterrestrials, 188 n. 30, 212 n. 89, 224 nn. 10, 13, 229 n. 9
Eze, Emmanuel Chukwudi, 210–11 nn. 80, 82–83

Fackenheim, Emil, 55, 140, 222 nn. 64–65
Falk, Richard, 227 n. 35
Feuerbach, Ludwig, 174
Fichte, Johann Gottlieb, 151, 169, 173–74, 195 n. 27, 231 n. 28
Findlay, J. N., 6
Finite rational beings, morality for, 11–12
Firla, Monika, 201 n. 18
Flanagan, Owen, 186–87 n. 19, 230 n. 16
Foot, Philippa, 187 n. 26
Foreign aid policies, 178
Formalism charge, 167–70, 185 n. 9, 225 n. 18, 228 n. 1
  aesthetic formalism, 110
  and impure ethics, 168
  and institutional supports, 169
  and judgment, 169
  and moral education, 169
  "ought" and "is," 169–70
  weaker version of, 168
Frankena, William, 55, 198 nn. 49, 53
Franklin, Benjamin, 37
Forberg, Friedrich, 231 n. 28
Forster, Georg, 96, 208–09 n. 75
French Revolution, 59, 91, 104
Friedman, Michael, 189 n. 41
Froebel, F., 37

Galen, 79
Galston, William F., 5, 57, 141, 198 n. 50
Garve, Christian, 163, 185 n. 12

Gause, Fritz, 219 n. 47
Gawronsky, Dimitry, 211 n. 87
Gedan, Paul, 208 n. 72
Gender, 204 n. 50. See also Women
Gerhardt, Volker, 48, 66
Glasenapp, Helmuth von, 219 n. 48
Gobineau, Comte Arthur de, 100, 211 n. 87
Goethe, Johann Wolfgang von, 134, 136, 139, 200 n. 9
Gould, Stephen Jay, 210 n. 78
Gradualism, moral, 105, 170, 178
Greene, Theodore M., 220 n. 55
Gregor, Mary J., 17–18, 180, 190 n. 46, 197 n. 45
Groothoff, Hans-Hermann, 46–47, 192 n. 13, 193 n. 15
Guyer, Paul, 113, 212–13 nn. 1, 5, 214 n. 11, 215 n. 16
  Kant's aesthetics as part of his anthropology, 125, 217 n. 33
  on Kant and the sublime, 215 nn. 18–19
  and palpable experience of freedom, 110–11, 213 n. 7

Habit (Angewohnheit), 42–43, 196 n. 33
Hamann, Johann Georg, 4
Hampshire, Stuart, 112, 214 nn. 9–10
Harris, Marvin, 208 n. 74
Hassner, Pierre, 19
Hearne, Samuel, 220 n. 55
Hegel, Georg Wilhelm Friedrich, 82, 174, 181
  and cunning of reason, 153, 226 n. 32
  and formalism charge, 92, 167–70, 185 n. 8, 228 nn. 1–2, 229 nn. 3, 5, 8
  and institutionalism, 173
Herbart, Johann Friedrich, 19, 56, 189 n. 39, 198 n. 54. See also Nature and Freedom
Herder, Johann Gottfried, 57, 68, 104, 134, 183 n. 1
  on race, 209 n. 76
Herman, Barbara, 5, 22, 23, 217 n. 29
Herrmann, Ulrich, 196 n. 37
Herz, Marcus, 62, 66, 181, 188–89 n. 31, 199 n. 2
Highest good, 161–64
  empirical assumptions and, 161–64
  as Endzweck of history, 161

Highest good (*Cont.*)
  and happiness, 163
  and human concern with outcomes, 163
  otherworldly conception of, 161
  and predisposition to metaphysics, 163–64
  this-worldly conception of, 161
  and totalization, 162
  in the world (*Weltbeste*), 160, 227 n. 40
Hill, Thomas E., Jr., 198 n. 57
Hinske, Norbert, 63, 200 n. 14
Hippel, Theodor Gottlieb von, 205 n. 52
Hippocrates, 79
History, 29–30, 140–64
  relation of, to Kant's major writings, 140–41
  See also Highest good; Progress, external and internal; Purpose (teleology), assumption of
Hitler, Adolf, 60, 135, 211 n. 87, 219 n. 47
Hobbes, Thomas, 156, 220 n. 55
Höffe, Otfried, 145, 190 n. 46, 191 n. 1, 219–20 n. 51, 227 nn. 34, 38
Holstein, Hermann, 192 n. 13
Honor, motive of 149–50. *See also* Women, and honor
Horkheimer, Max, 212 n. 97
Hudson, Hoyt H. 220 n. 55
"Human beings as such," determination of duties for, 12
Humanity (*Menschheit*) 84, 205 n. 56. *See also* Human race (species), destiny of
Human race (species), destiny of, 101
  membership of, 102–06
  and "the spreading over all peoples of the earth," 105–06, 127
  unity of, 103–04
  and "the whole human race," 104–05
Hume, David, 82, 88, 206 nn. 62, 64, 230 n. 17
  on race, 99, 103, 210–11 n. 82
Humors (temperaments), four, 79–82
  of activity, 80
  choleric, 80–81
  of feeling, 80
  melancholic, 80

phlegmatic, 81–82
sanguine, 80
See also Character, empirical, individual

Immaturity (*Unmündigkeit*), 84–85, 87, 102
Impure (empirical) ethics, 3–30
  as bridging gap between nature and freedom, 25–26
  and completion of the system, 23–24
  difficulty of locating, 6–7, 9
  fields of, 26–30
  and material content, 23
  politics, as additional field of? 191 n. 51
  and progress of the power of judgment, 25
  as propaedeutic to the moral life, 20–22
  as propaedeutic to moral science, 22–23
  as second part of ethical theory, 24
  and tangible symbols of morality 127, 152, 158
  See also Efficaciousness of morality in human life
Impurity, 3–5
  degrees and kinds of, 10–16
  fields of, 26–30
  saved by? 30, 167–82

Jachmann, Reinhold Bernard, 65, 216 n. 24
Jauch, Ursula Pia 205–06 nn. 52, 57
Judgment, 15–16, 25, 49–50, 169, 177
  as bridging gap between nature and freedom, 18, 25–26

Kant and Collegium Fridericianum, 197 n. 47
  and Königsberg, 201 n. 22, 203 n. 42
  lecture courses of, 5, 33–34, 62
  and masturbation, 185 n. 11
  on music, 206–07 n. 65
  on note-takers, 188–89 n. 31
  on novels, 201 n. 21
Kaulbach, Friedrich, 148, 226 n. 21
Kersting, Wolfgang, 145, 153
Kierkegaard, Søren, 7
Kiesewetter, J. G. C. C., 185 n. 12

Peoples (*Cont.*)
  Danish, 90
  Dutch, 90
  English, 92
  French, 91–92 (*see also* French Revolution)
  German, 81, 92–93, 211 n. 84
  of Greenland, 91
  Gypsy, 103, 212, n. 93
  Italian, 92
  Oriental, 90, 91
  Native American, 90, 91
  Non-European, 90
  Nordic, 90
  Polish, 89–90, 91
  Russian, 89–90, 91
  Swedish, 90
  Swiss, 90
  of Tahiti, 103, 179, 212 n. 92
  Turkish, 88–89, 91
Pestalozzi, J. H., 37
Peters, R. S., 194 n. 18
Philanthropinum Institute, 37, 44–47, 193 n. 17, 194–95 n. 26, 221 n. 58
Physiognomy, 77–79. *See also* Character, empirical, individual
Pieper, Annemarie, 202 nn. 26–27
Platner, Ernst, 199 n.2
Pluhar, Werner S., 214 n. 13
"Practical," narrow versus broad conceptions, 18
"Pragmatic," four different senses of term, 68–69
Pragmatic imperatives, 69
Priestley, Joseph, 37
Progress, external and internal, 144–52
  ambiguity in Kant's remarks about, 146
  Aristotle and, 150–51
  external, 144–47
  Fichte and, 151
  internal, 145–48
  as a quasi-moral step, 149
Progress, means of, 153–57
  and arts and sciences, 154
  and class domination, 143, 154
  and cosmopolitanism, 157
  and cunning of reason, 153, 226 n. 32
  and education, legislation, and religion, 157

and globalization, 156
and inequality, 143, 154
and invisible hand, 153, 155, 157, 178
and spirit of trade (*Handelsgeist*), 155–56, 178
and unsocial sociability (*ungesellige Geselligkeit*), 153–54
and war, 143, 154–55, 226–27 n. 33
Prudence (*Klugheit*), 28, 40–41, 195–96 n. 31
Pure ethics, 5, 10–11, 20. *See also* Impure (empirical) ethics
Pure philosophy, 3–5
  as metaphysics, 4
Purist readings of Kant's ethics, 6, 9–10
Purpose (teleology), assumption of, 83, 96, 141–44, 176, 204 n. 50
  as humanly necessary heuristic device, 142
  and naive teleologism, 83
  necessary for study of nature, 141

Race, 15, 93–100
  black, 15, 99–100, 103, 105
  and Buffon's rule, 96
  and character, 95
  and climate, 98
  and culture, 99–100
  and eugenics, 97
  hierarchy and the *Stammgattung*, 100, 211 n. 84
  Indian, 15, 99–100
  and intelligence, 98, 99
  and intermarriage, 97
  Kant versus Forster, 96, 208–09 n. 75
  Kant versus Herder, 209 n. 76
  and monogenism, 96, 103–04
  Native American, 15, 98–99, 100, 103
  and polygenism, 96, 103–04, 208–09 n. 75
  and sensitivity, 98–99
  and skin color, 98, 209 n. 77
  and talents, 99
  and teleology, 96–97, 98
  white, 15, 99–100
Radical evil, presence in human nature of, 132–39

Sublime, the (*Cont.*)
  and respect (*Achtung*), 122–25
  and subreption, 121, 124–25
  as a superior symbol of the morally
    good, 109, 119–20, 122
  as a uniquely human experience,
    118
Sutter, Alex, 210 n. 79, 211 n. 83,
  224 n. 10
Systematicity and the empirical, 7, 24,
  175

Taste, duty to cultivate, 116–18
Temperaments, four. *See* Humors, four
Tieftrunk, J. H., 223 n. 1
Tigner, Steven, 198 n. 62
Tirala, Lothar G., 208 n. 74

Universality (universalizability), 43, 55,
    101–106, 112, 157–58, 173
  and artificial languages, 231 n. 23
  and cultural location, 178–79
  and music, 231 n. 23
  and prejudice, 177–78
University faculties, higher versus
  lower, 4

Vaihinger, Hans, 231 n. 28
Van de Pitte, Frederick, 63
Van der Linden, 149, 198 nn. 56–57,
  231 n. 28
Velkley, Richard L., 194 n. 18
Vogt, Theodor, 192 n. 12

Walker, Margaret Urban, 187 n. 24
Walsh, W. H., 146
War, inevitable in absence of cosmopoli-
    tan whole, 144
  as means of advancing civilization,
    143
  programmed to die out? 155, 157,
    226–27 n. 33
  See also Progress, means of
Warnock, G. J., 186 n. 17
Way of thinking (*Denkungsart*), 42–43,
  77

Weber, Max, 200 n. 15, 230 n. 19
Weisskopf, Traugott, 34–36, 135, 191
  n. 41, 194 n. 25
Weyand, Klaus, 225 n. 16
Willaschek, Marcus, 220 n. 51
Williams, Bernard, 167, 168, 187 nn.
  20, 25, 198 n. 60
Williams, Howard, 146, 158, 207 n.
  67, 218 n. 38, 227 n. 37
Willich, A. F. M., 28
Wilson, Holly L. 204 n. 50, 207 n.
  69
Winkler, Earl R., 229 n. 10
Wisdom (*Weisheit*), 62, 199 n. 3
Wobbermin, Georg, 220 n. 55
Wolff, Christian, 69, 207 n. 65
Wolke, G. H. 37, 195 n. 26
Women, 15, 82–87
  and honor, 86, 103
  and immaturity (*Unmündigkeit*), 84–
    85, 87, 203 n. 38
  and inclination, 84, 86, 200 n. 12
  and moral character, 85–87, 208 n.
    73
  nature's purpose, in creating, 83–84
  and reason, 84, 86, 200 n. 12
  Rousseau on, 194 n. 21
Wood, Allen W., 186 n. 17, 198 n. 57,
  228 n. 43
  on Hegel and formalism charge, 228
    nn. 1–2, 229 nn. 3, 7, 12, 230 n.
    13
  on Kant and religion, 218 nn. 37,
    42, 44

Yovel, Yirmiahu, 159, 162, 197–98 n.
  48, 226–27 n. 36
  and tenability of Kant's philosophy
    of history, 141, 145, 225 nn.
    18–19
  on war and historical progress, 155,
    226–27 n. 33

Zammito, John H., 121, 124
Zedlitz, Karl Abraham von, 185 n. 6
Zoeller, Guenter, 207 n. 69